Becoming a
Graphic
Designer

[SECOND EDITION]

A GUIDE TO CAREERS IN DESIGN

Becoming a Graphic Designer

[SECOND EDITION]

Steven Heller & Teresa Fernandes

JOHN WILEY & SONS, INC.

Dedication

This book is dedicated to the memory of Julian Allen, artist and teacher.

Acknowledgments

WE ARE INDEBTED to Karen Mynatt, Daniel Drennan, and Beth Thompson for their invaluable assistance and expertise. Thanks also to Margaret Cummins, our editor at John Wiley & Sons, Inc. and thanks to Liz Roles at Wiley for shepherding this book through the revision process. Finally, much appreciation goes to all the designers who contributed their words and pictures to this book.

— SH & TF

This book is typeset in Garamond, Officina, Clarendon and Commercial Script and is printed on acid-free paper. ⊗

Art Director/Designer: Teresa Fernandes/TFD Studio
Art Production Associate: Daniel Drennan
Associate Editor: Karen Mynatt
Research Assistant: Kim Orlando

Cover Credits:
"MTV fashionably loud week – show package." Designers: Jonathon Notaro, Jens Gelhaar, Sean Dougherty. Creative Director/Producer: Jonathon Notaro. Producer: Angela de Oliveira. Client: MTV Networks. Year: 2000

"Enemy of the State." Creative Director/Designer: Garson Yu. Designers/Animators: Ying Fan, Steve Kusuma. Producer: Grace Huang. Client: Touchstone Pictures. Year: 1998

"I AM." Designers/Directors: Matthew Mulder, Paul Schneider. Client: CODEX 3. Year: 2001.

"centertheatregroup.com." Designer: Eric Brown. Creative Director: Karen Barranco. Client: Red Ant Media Group. Year: 2000.

"Busted Rhymes: A Bohemian Poetry Reading." Designer: Mark Pagano. Creative Director: David Vogler. Client: Nickelodeon Online. Year: 2001. ©2001 Viacom International Inc. All Rights Reserved.

Library of Congress Cataloging-in-Publication Data:
Heller, Steven.
Becoming a graphic designer, second edition/Steven Heller and Teresa Fernandes.
p. cm.
Includes bibliographical references and index.
ISBN 0-471-17677-X (pbk.)
1. Commercial art—Vocational guidance. 2. Graphic arts—Vocational guidance. I. Fernandes, Teresa. II. Title.

Printed in the United States of America.

10 9 8 7 6 5 4 3 2 1

Table of Contents

Title: Couleur 3 Poster Series
Designer/Art Director:
Matthew Mulder **Agency:** WGR
Lausanne, CH **Client:** Swiss
State Radio **Year:** 1999

The graphic design profession has experienced two seismic shifts since the publication of the first edition of *Becoming a Graphic Designer*. The first is obvious: The World Wide Web has not only given interactivity new prominence, it has forced designers to demonstratively address nonprint media, including motion and sound. The second took us off guard: With the rise and fall of dotcoms, designers who were weaned on interactivity have had to reassess their commitment to new media. Indeed, some have retreated to print as the dominant medium.

The first edition of this book was admittedly print-centric, insofar as print is our first love and the most traditional graphic design medium. While we included sections on motion and the Web, they were subordinate to the focal media because we believed that this emphasis was reasonable and logical. However, over the past few years, the demands of the Web have meant that an increasing number of graphic designers must be expert in its theory and practice.

Print will not be replaced by interactivity, but as the bar is raised on what constitutes "good" Web design, so too, the traditional forms must be reevaluated. Interactivity and motion do not supplant print in this new edition any more than in the general world of graphic design, but we have bolstered their representation by adding many new voices and replacing less current ones. The interviewees in the new "Interactivity" section and expanded "Motion" and "Education" sections are working in a realm that will not disappear in the foreseeable future. They speak as journeymen and iconoclasts within this growing media.

In the "Interactivity" (formerly the "Web") section, we address the new approaches to editorial and commerce and how new programs have made typography more important than ever. In the "Motion" section, we discuss how more design commissions draw upon kinetic methods to convey messages and ideas. In the "Education" section, we introduce the concept of design authorship and with it the need to develop and manufacture original ideas using various design skills.

Graphic design is a more compelling profession because of these multidisciplinary opportunities. Rather than becoming more specialized, the field has opened to generalists who are fluent in old and new design languages and in hybrids of the two. This second edition makes clear that the term *graphic design* is not antiquated but more broadly encompassing than it was. – *Steven Heller, 2002*

So You Want To Become

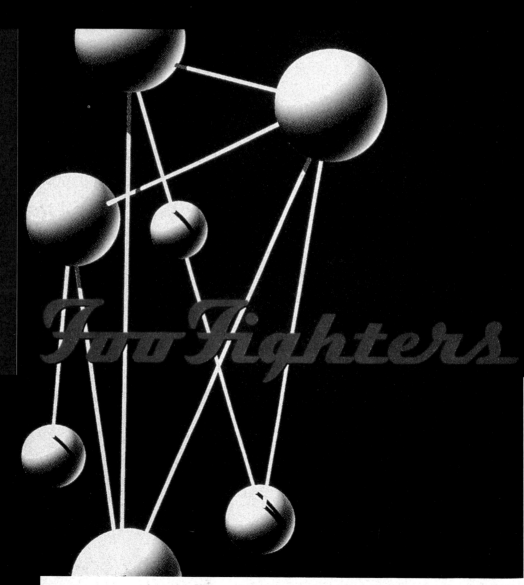

Title: Foo Fighters
Designer: Jeff Fey
Creative Directors:
Tommy Steele, Jeff
Fey, Foo Fighters
Client: Capitol
Records **Illustrator:**
Giacomo Marchesi
Photographer: Josh
Kessler **Year:** 1997

a Graphic Designer?

The 1960s rock band The Byrds recorded a song that underscored the obsession of its generation: "So you wanna be a rock and roll star / well listen now to what I say / go and get an electric guitar / and take the time to learn how to play." Given the current interest in graphic communications, these lyrics might be rewritten in the twenty-first century to read: "So you wanna to be a graphic designer / well listen now to what I say / go and get a Macintosh G4 / and take the time to learn how to play." Okay, it doesn't parse as well, but you get the point. The Mac is to graphic design what the electric guitar was to early rock 'n' roll. The electric guitar changed everything from the sound to the look of music; the Mac has had a profound influence on the look as well as the *sound* of graphic design.

The first lesson for all prospective graphic designers is how to use the computer and its numerous layout, illustration, photo, and type programs. The second lesson is how to make the computer work for the designer, not the other way around. The computer is a tool, just as the ruler, X-Acto, and waxer were tools not long ago. Like the electric guitar, the computer is an expensive machine that without the intervention of human intelligence and talent produces noise — so at the outset it is important to establish as fact the graphic designer's need to know how to work (as well as play) with the tool; this is a necessary step toward proficiency.

However, this does not answer the question, "How do I become a graphic designer?"

Actually, this is not the proper first question. Given the sea changes in graphic design and visual communications (terms that are used interchangeably) in the 1990s, the initial question should be: "What is graphic design?" Once the many graphic design disciplines — and there are many specialties — are identified, "How do I learn more about them?" can be asked. Only afterward is the question about becoming a graphic designer applicable.

Becoming a Graphic Designer is not going to teach the neophyte how to use the computer. Scores of books and thousands of courses offer basic, intermediate, and advanced instruction. Rather, this book is an introduction — a navigational guide, if you like — to what in recent years has become a complex profession comprising many print, film, and electronic genres. In the music business, it is not enough to play a few chords on the guitar; it is useful to be proficient in R&B, folk, reggae, punk, hip-hop, etc. Likewise, graphic design is not simply about the exclusive practice of editorial, book, advertising, or poster design; all these forms can (and even should) be practiced by individuals depending on their relative skill, expertise, and inclination. More important, with the recent development of desktop publishing as well as computer-driven multimedia, the field has expanded to such an extent that entirely new divisions of labor, unprecedented collaborations, and specializations have emerged. This book describes both traditional and new disciplines.

Before becoming a graphic designer, it is imperative to learn as much about the profession as possible. Knowledge is the key to saving time and energy. Nevertheless, many practitioners naively stumbled into the field through their love of art or letterforms while others fiddled with PageMaker or QuarkXPress and were therefore drafted to produce the occasional newsletter or flyer. Becoming a graphic designer does not always require advanced university degrees or years of intense academic training. True, many of the interviewees cited in this book logged considerable time in undergraduate and postgraduate design schools, but others originally held jobs as writers, painters, illustrators, cartoonists, printers, and typesetters, and one was even a graffiti artist. In fact, the impulse to become a graphic designer is not exclusive to those in the applied or fine arts; anyone interested in "visuals" is a prospective candidate. Once engaged in a graphic design practice, however, in-house or staff designers, freelancers, and principals of independent firms, all need a shared fundamental knowledge.

Graphic designers all speak the same basic vocabulary (and use the same jargon), and while some designers are more adept at fine typography than others who may

How Many Graphic Designers Are There? What Do They Earn?

Statistics concerning the graphic design profession are sketchy because the industry encompasses a number of design areas. Studies often lump architects, interior designers, set designers, furniture designers, industrial designers, and even floral designers, together with graphic designers.

According to the U.S. Department of Labor data (provided by Research Division, National Endowment for the Arts), there are 557,000 designers in the United States, which includes architects and interior designers. The Bureau of Labor Statistics weighs in with a staggering 682,000 designers, including architects, and projects that the number grew at a rate of 30 percent through the year 2000. But in a report by Strategies for Management, Inc., in cooperation with Creative Access, of the total number of designers in the United States, 160,000 are *graphic* designers.

According to the American Institute of Graphic Arts (AIGA), annual salaries range from $16,000 for a junior designer to $32,000 – $60,500 for an art director to $124,000 and upwards for a creative director. Each design specialty has its own salary range, which can vary greatly. For example, the magazine publishing industry starts off junior designers with much lower salaries than advertising agencies do.

be better skilled at sequential narratives or information management, graphic design is not an intuitive endeavor. It cannot be done without knowledge of the task, genre, or medium in question. Contrary to the now infamous 1987 television advertisement that introduced the first Macintosh by arrogantly announcing that, with the advent of this revolutionary machine, graphic designers were a thing of the past, graphic design must be studied, learned, and continually practiced to achieve even basic proficiency. To go further, to transcend simple service and craft with inspiring work, graphic design must be totally embraced, body and soul.

This sounds hyperbolic, but it is not. For their designs to rise above the commonplace reams of hack work that flood the market, graphic designers must be devoted to as many aspects of the endeavor as possible. They must know who is doing what and how it is done. They must understand the history of the field to avoid reinventing the wheel. It is not enough to mimic fashions and trends as if they were schematics for success. To practice well means to master the tools and marshal the talent that eschews cliché.

Graphic design is a business (an aspect discussed in detail below), but equally as important, it is a tool of visual expression, a process whereby ideas and products are given concrete forms through the often conceptual manipulation of type and imagery. A graphically designed object — whether a page, package, or screen — can be expressive or neutral, hard sell or soft sell, classical or radical. The level of complexity or simplicity is determined either by the nature of the message or the preference of the designer. Graphic design has its share of recurring procedures and repetitive tasks — ask anyone who works with-

in a strictly prescribed book, magazine, or Web page format — but there is always potential for surprising outcomes that are novel and, indeed, innovative. Within the parameters of a given project, graphic design can be anything short of art for art's sake. It is a mistake to think that graphic design is only about positioning type on a page regardless of content and aesthetics. Graphic design may be utilitarian, but it is not void of the creative essence.

Graphic design is indeed a commercial art. Yet contrary to shortsighted notions, the qualifier *commercial* does not diminish the noun *art*. The commercial arena is where the graphic designer performs a difficult balancing act — to sell, entertain, and inform in a manner that also adds aesthetic value to the receiver's (or audience's) experience. Art is what distinguishes the designer's expertise from the layperson's ignorance. With the widespread availability of template software programs, it is easier today than during the years B.C. (before computers) for anyone to compose a layout in a semiprofessional manner, yet to imbue it with the nuance and uniqueness (as well as imagination) that demands an audience's attention requires the artist's deft touch. The techniques of graphic design can be learned, but the instinct for making art needs to be nurtured over time.

Like painting and sculpture, graphic design is influenced by myriad movements, ideologies, and aesthetic points of view that derive from well over a century of modern practice. This legacy cannot be imparted through even the most sophisticated computer programs. Neither knowledge nor inspiration is an instant fix. Moreover, knowledge is more than simply knowing the names of a few typefaces, or when to use justified columns, or how to specify colors; a graphic designer must understand both the stylistic and aesthetic options that are available and how to use them for optimum advantage. A good graphic designer is able to adapt existing historical or contemporary models and derive unique approaches; this comes from patient study and dedicated practice. A great graphic designer can apply these unique approaches to solving complex problems in a manner that appears effortless. While in theory prolonged schooling is unnecessary to becoming a graphic designer, forging knowledge and instinct into critical thinking is. More often than not, this comes from the marriage of academics and on-the-job training.

Graphic design was never easy, although veterans sometimes pine for the good old days. Prior to the introduction of digital media, the field appeared simpler than it does today. Back then, one could start a design business with a few low-tech tools on a kitchen table. Today, a major financial investment in hardware and software is required just to be in the position to start learning. Yet even in 1900, graphic design was more complex than positioning type on a page. In fact, it was helpful to be adept at the difficult crafts of printing, hot metal type composition, and hand lettering. Back then, as today, specialties existed, various skills were necessary, and many aesthetic options were possible. The only difference between current and past practice is the type of work available. Early in the century, many more graphic design activities were exclusive to trained specialists, whereas those specialties are no longer exclusive.

Where once type design was the sole province of skilled punch cutters and type designers, the computer makes it possible for anyone proficient in certain font programs to design custom typefaces. Not everyone is skilled enough to design a viable, multipurpose typeface, but the potential exists for those outside the traditional discipline, including many graphic designers (as opposed to professional type designers), to contribute quirky faces that are made available through digital foundries and shareware on the Internet. Another example is desktop publishing; the term suggests a wellspring of amateur activity. Anyone sitting at a computer loaded with a page layout program and a newsletter/periodical/flyer template can pretend to be a graphic designer. At the turn of the century, printers alone did the design. In the 1920s and until recently, it was more or less the exclusive province of art directors and layout persons. In the 1960s the availability of transfer type and photocopy machines made it easier for amateurs to try their hands at layout, but today, all the tools of editorial design are at the amateur's disposal, which opens up unfettered access to every possible mistake.

As the boundaries between professional and amateur break down, it is more important than ever for graphic designers to maintain standards that distinguish the two. Becoming a graphic designer means accepting, promoting, and, perhaps, eventually helping to change the existing standards.

The dissolution of certain specialties coincided with the emergence of new ones. Career guides published only a decade ago do not mention the handful of new disciplines that currently fall under the graphic design rubric or are areas where graphic designers are currently finding work as collaborators in broader design activities. Among them, information architecture (the design of data-driven charts, maps, graphs) is a genre of graphic design open to those with a penchant for conceptual thinking. Another is Web page design, which has become an entry point for a wide range of artists and designers. Some Web designers come directly from print media, while others bypass print entirely. In the attempt to redefine graphic design in the year 2000 and beyond, the Web has become a pivotal realm because it involves traditional graphic applications, such as type and page layout, wed to nontraditional graphic design components, such as sound and motion. With these new options, becoming a graphic designer requires neophytes to thoughtfully decide on the media in which they will devote the time and energy to acquiring expertise.

New venues, like the Web and multimedia, do not remain wide open for long. After an initial surge to fill the new jobs, standards tighten, openings constrict, and competition becomes tougher. It is axiomatic that in the early stages, until the dust settles, new media attract the lion's share of students and neophytes because it is cool to be involved. But graphic design is not a fly-by-night endeavor; it's a venerable profession with enough facets to keep a practitioner absorbed for a lifetime. Nonetheless, graphic design is also a springboard to enter other communications industries.

Becoming a Graphic Designer is a survey of many aspects of the profession: traditional print media, including type, book, periodical, advertising, and corporate; new media, including CD-ROM, Web, and motion graphics; and cross-disciplinary practices, including collaborations with architects and environmental designers. In recent years the increased availability of high-end production tools that, in many cases, eliminate production middlemen has allowed graphic designers who were once only cogs in the wheel to become involved in the total conception and manufacture of designed products. Through the aid of the computer, a graphic designer is not relegated to framing content but can now determine, conceive, and produce it as well. A designer is now capable of being an auteur, entrepreneur, or "authorpreneur."

Meant for those who have not been introduced to or have had only a passing understanding of graphic design, this book showcases a multileveled profession that is as accessible as it is intricate. The numerous voices reveal through interviews both the commonalities and the differences among disciplines. And because this is a profession populated by individuals, we have also included iconoclasts whose conflicting viewpoints underscore the healthy diversity that contributes to making graphic design a rich, creative profession are represented in addition to practitioners in the accepted movements, styles, and schools of contemporary design.

Once upon a time, graphic designers grumbled that the world ignored their contributions. "Not even my parents understand what I do," was a common plaint. Today, graphic design is less arcane and more mainstream than in any other period. Thanks, in large part, to the computer, graphic design is not only an integral component of the communication, retail, and entertainment industries but also an entrepreneurial activity that allows for, and contributes to, cultural advancement. These are exciting prospects for those who decide to join the continuum of graphic design at this juncture. Beginners who use *Becoming a Graphic Designer* to identify their first career step (or long-term niche) may not wind up running a successful studio or producing a unique design product, but for those who master the skills, possess the talent, and have the drive, graphic design offers the potential for a creative future.

Glossary

Job Divisions

Graphic designers are employed in virtually all kinds of businesses, industries, and institutions. Here are some of the typical terms used interchangeably for *in-house design department*.

Art Department
Art and Design Department
Art Services Department
Design Department
Design Services Department
Creative Services Department
Creative Group
Graphics Group

Different companies are organized differently depending on their focus and goals. A large corporation may distinguish package design from promotion design, or editorial design from advertising design; a smaller business may keep all design activities under one umbrella design department.

Likewise, proprietary or independent design firms, studios, or offices — design businesses that service large corporations and small businesses — may or may not distinguish among design functions, such as a print design department separate from a multimedia design department, or promotion and collateral separate from editorial departments.

Job Titles

The titles given to specific jobs and tasks throughout the design field vary according to the hierarchy of the specific company, institution, or firm — for example, an art director for one company may be a design director at another; a senior designer at one may have different responsibilities than a senior at another. Starting from the top, here are typical job titles as used by in-house art departments in publishing, advertising, corporations, and proprietary design firms, studios, and offices.

1. The *managerial level*, where jobs may or may not involve hands-on design work in addition to the oversight of other designers:

Creative Director
Design Director
Corporate Art Director
Creative Services Manager
Design Manager

2. The *creative* or *design level*, which involves directly serving clients. These titles embody different responsibilities depending on the organizational hierarchy of a particular business:

Senior Designer
Designer
Senior Art Director
Art Director
Graphics Editor

3. The *support level*, which involves working directly with the seniors in both design and production capacities:

Junior Designer
Assistant Designer
Deputy Art Director
Associate Art Director
Assistant Art Director
Production Artist
Art Associate

4. Entry level:
Assistant designer
Junior designer
Intern (This category is temporary — a stepping stone, perhaps — and often unpaid.)

Freelance

Freelancers, as opposed to principals of proprietary studios or firms, do not manage businesses with additional employees (although they may hire assistants as needed). They often take on individual, finite freelance projects either on the premises of the client or in their own studios. Freelancers usually do not use titles but rather advertise themselves as "Jane Doe, Graphic Designer," or "John Doe, Design Production."

On Being an Influence

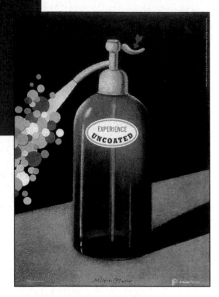

Title: Experience Uncoated
Designer/Illustrator: Milton
Glaser **Company:** Milton Glaser
Inc. **Client:** Fraser Papers
Year: 1998

Title: Brooklyn Brewery
Designer: Milton Glaser
Company: Milton Glaser Inc.
Client: Brooklyn Brewery
Typefaces: Copper Plate Gothic,
hand-lettering

MILTON GLASER
Graphic Designer, Milton Glaser Inc., New York City

**Many of the designers we interviewed for this book mentioned you
and your work as an influence on them. This is a big responsibility.
How do you see your influence on the design community?**
Any practitioner wants to be influential, fundamentally. I've always
seen myself as someone who worked in the realm of ideas and who was
susceptible to influence. My own practice is one where I consciously
try to absorb and be influenced by many of my experiences, so the idea
of influence and being influential is important to me. My entire vocabulary, you might say, could be analyzed as a series of influences. The
idea is being in the stream of artistic ideas, as someone who sees himself not so much as somebody who has a private vision but rather who
is in the stream and who wants to continue that stream, and who
wants to participate in disseminating ideas. I imagine it's the same
impulse that keeps me teaching. The idea of teaching is basically for
students to see themselves as part of the continuity of ideas and visual
history, rather than as a deviation from that. So if, in fact, I have been
influential, it's extremely pleasing to me.

What were your early influences?
One of the big influences was the comic strip. The comics were our
academy, in effect. Drawing from life casts is what we would have been

Title: Art Directors Club
Invitation **Designer:** Milton
Glaser **Company:** Milton
Glaser Inc. **Client:** Art
Directors Club **Year:** 1997

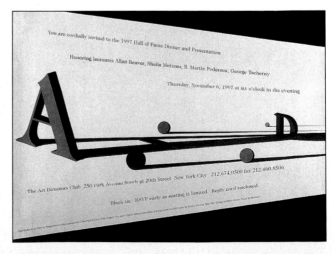

doing if we were growing up as an art student in Europe — but we copied the comic strips. Most of the American artists that I have talked to — of a certain generation, obviously — whether they ended up as painters or illustrators or interior designers, got their start copying the comics. And the comics were in fact, one of the most profound influences, in many ways. One influence, I'm quite sure, is the idea that comics were linked to narration; two, they had a particular sense of form, sort of a bounded form, designed in black and white, and then filled in with color — they were graphic rather than tonal. Particularly things like *Dick Tracy*, *Terry and the Pirates*, and certainly *L'il Abner*, and even, to some extent, *Mickey Mouse* — all those were, I would say, in terms of early influence, very strong elements.

Title: Trattoria Dell 'Arte (restaurant) **Designer:** Milton Glaser **Company:** Milton Glaser Inc. **Client:** Sheldon Fireman **Year:** 1988

Your work encompasses many areas of design. Did you have a plan early in your career to cross all these disciplines?
No. When I started, my greatest objective was to be a comic strip artist. That's all I wanted to be when I was a kid. Then I went to the High School of Music and Art and there I awakened to the idea both of painting and of design. By the time I left Music and Art to go to the Cooper Union, I knew there was this thing called *design* and another called *typography*. By the time I got into Cooper I was already interested in those things. Then at Cooper I got a pretty good foundation in sculpture and architecture and so on.

After all your years in this art and craft, what would you say is the most important concern upon entering the design field?
A real question for many of us, if we have an artistic vision, is how to reconcile our sense of artistry and the pleasure we get from making things with the demands of a business that very often is not interested in that. So the advice I would give somebody is to think in the long run because if you have a long career — it can span thirty, forty, fifty years — you have to think of what will sustain you and keep you interested for that length of time. For one of the great problems of being a designer is that you get parochialized and you find yourself increasingly narrowed, doing more and more specialized things that you've done a hundred times before. For me, the way out was to broaden the canvas, to try to do things that I was not very experienced doing, to try to develop a range of activities so that I couldn't be forced into a corner and left to dry. While that is not the solution for everyone, that is a consideration people must at least examine before they embark on a course, for once they have mastered the professional requirement it may no longer have any interest in it for them.

Title: Picasso **Designer/Illustrator:** Milton Glaser **Company:** Milton Glaser Inc. **Client:** New York Times Book Review **Year:** 1996

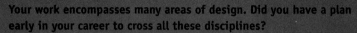

"What motivated you to become a graphic designer?"

I remember being starved for visual stimuli, even before I knew what that meant. I remember looking at every detail of every sign, poster, picture, page, book, newspaper, magazine, comparing the styles and distribution of information. And it wasn't just words and pictures but also the shapes of letters that formed the words, the spaces between the letters, and the messages and feelings — the total combination of things conveyed. I remember being twenty-one and someone telling me I might as well be earning credits for being so visually obsessed and perhaps someday being paid to make the things.
—**Sharoz Makarechi**

It was winning the fire prevention poster contest in the third grade. I got my picture in the paper. It was the taste of winning awards at an early age.
—**Kent Hunter**

I thought art direction was a great way to be a starving artist without the starving part.
—**Abi Aron Spencer**

I was always interested in design — in the old theater posters brought to me by my father from Poland, in the matchbooks and menus I collected as a teenager. I studied art and photography until I took my first typography and design classes, at which point my varied interests suddenly found form together and made sense.
—**Kelly Doe**

I loved photography and I loved film, so I ended up studying filmmaking at Cooper Union. I didn't study design because it was about taste and I wasn't interested in good taste. I was interested in collaboration. That's why I loved studying film. So graphic design sort of crept into my life.
—**Yolanda Cuomo**

I flunked out of architecture school. No formal education in anything. But I have taught at UCLA, Art Center, Cal Arts...what gives with that? I first designed logos in trade for surfboards — they are still being used today. I also painted flames on hotrods and designed the yearbooks and newspaper in school. My first real job was as the art director/reporter/cartoonist/ad designer of *Surfer* magazine.
—**Mike Salisbury**

As far back as I can remember, I was very interested in art, which to me consisted of the graphic illustrations in comic books, along with the ads and the amazing products that they offered. Growing up in a small town in Iowa, I'm not sure I had ever heard the words graphic design until I received a catalog from the Minneapolis College of Art and Design.
—**Charles Spencer Anderson**

I was interested in typography since I was a little kid. My uncle was a calligrapher and he brought me some of those old Speedball lettering books, which always interested me. At the time, I thought those were all the typefaces available in the world — in that book. I practiced drawing them, but then I became a fine art major in college. Back then there was really nothing known as design. Most design, at least as far as a kid would know, was associated with advertising. I didn't want to do advertising mainly because it seemed so commercial and so much of it seemed to be based on cleverness rather than artistic ability. So I went into fine art. I'd often mix type with my drawing in a sort of a juvenile, high-schoolish kind of way. And I was still getting the type from that Speedball book.

—Martin Venezky

Way back when, I had one typography class at Ohio University that really turned me on to type and that guided me in my decision to go into graphic design rather than woodworking or pottery or painting.

—Melissa Tardiff

I never really decided, but I liked Color-Aid; it made everything look good.

—John Martinez

I turned to graphic design from illustration mostly out of boredom. I had been a freelance illustrator for eight years.

—R.O. Blechman

My father is an architect and at an early age I was exposed to a world where your ideas could be built. Nothing was more amazing to me as a child than watching my father drawing a building on his table at home on a Saturday and then, a few months later, being able to walk through that same space. It was magic that you could take a pencil and paper and make something that people could experience. I wanted to do something like that.

—Alexander Isley

When I was in high school I had a phenomenal teacher who ran something called the Art Squad. All of the kids who were in the Art Squad had to present a portfolio in order to get into it. We were responsible for all of the billboards and posters that went up in the school, for designing the yearbook, for designing the literary magazine. And I fell in love with type at that point and I loved graphic design. I wasn't particularly sophisticated. I wasn't aware of any graphic designers in the larger world. I just loved doing this.

—Janet Froelich

To be absolutely honest, I was not motivated to be a graphic designer. I was motivated to make pictures and enjoyed the process of image-making. When I was nineteen, design projects at the Pratt Institute motivated me in that I enjoyed the challenge and was comfortable in processes that relied on formalism. My formal education consists of a BFA in Graphic Design/Advertising at Pratt Institute and an MFA in Printmaking and Painting from NYU, where I am a doctoral candidate in Language and Communication. I never completed my dissertation for my degree. I landed my first job in 1965 — design director of Pratt Publications, a job I was not prepared for but fortunately survived and prospered at.

—Richard Wilde

Although I have been drawing and painting since I was a child, I had little interest in pursuing a career as a fine artist. The application of these artistic skills for commercial purposes, working within certain practical constraints and communicating to a larger general public, were more appealing challenges. It was during college that I discovered that graphic design would allow me to pursue these artistic goals.

—Ken Carbone

The first time I heard the term *graphic designer* was in high school. I was taking a class called Mass Media and we were making a film and somebody had to do the credits, and that was the graphic designer. But I didn't think about becoming a graphic designer when I first went to the Nova Scotia College of Art and Design. I was interested in photography and journalism and just ended up studying graphic design, which was a great way to combine my interest in words and images.

—**Rhonda Rubenstein**

I didn't set out to become a graphic designer. I started out with an undergraduate degree in political science. In the process of doing graduate work in political science I decided I didn't want to do that. And I took a job and one thing led to another, and I discovered design.

—**Nancye Green**

I designed the program for my high school's musical production of *The Unsinkable Molly Brown*. The act of putting art and type together in a format was very intriguing to me. Once I received the printed piece with my name on the masthead, it was all over...I knew what I wanted to do.

—**Patrick Mitchell**

I was going to Boston University and signed up for a course that was called Graphics, which I thought was about printmaking. It turned out to be commercial art. On my first day of the class this man was talking about Baskerville and showing these great big slide shows of one letter at a time, and I thought, "Wow, letters are beautiful, isn't that something! Maybe I could get a job if I took this course." I took a lot of illustration and photography as well, and I ended up getting a very well-rounded education because I also studied history, a lot of art history, and a lot of history of photography, which was my favorite course.

—**Gael Towey**

I always had the idea in my mind that I would go to Pratt Institute. That was a sort of Shangri-la in my mind. That was this golden art school on a hill. Just the name of it used to take my breath away. I grew up in Buffalo and Pratt just seemed like this great, amazing dream. I went to Catholic High School and people would ask if I were going to go to St. Bonaventure or Notre Dame? No one had the faintest idea what Pratt was but for me. Then for some inexplicable reason I actually got in.

—**Tom Bentowski**

I used to collect shopping bags and labels, like hang tags from clothes, and put them up on my wall. But beyond that, I really didn't know that graphic design existed until later on in high school. I always felt that I wanted to go into advertising; when I started thinking about colleges, that's what I wanted to study. And graphic design, I guess, popped up about then.

—**Michael Ian Kaye**

Following a stint in the army — where I ended up being classified as an illustrator assigned to a psychological operations (propaganda) unit — and several years as a freelance designer in San Francisco, I applied to graduate school at Cranbrook. Under the mentorship of Katherine and Michael McCoy, Cranbrook was a watershed experience for me. In addition to my being in a veritable design laboratory, I had the advantages of interacting with the fine art students and attending seminars with visiting artists. For me, this provided a valuable complement to the practical constraints inherent to the design discipline. After Cranbrook, I returned to San Francisco to work at Landor Associates, where I remained, except for a brief hiatus working for an architect, for the next ten years.

—**Michael J. Carabetta**

My father was a graphic designer, a poster designer. Initially, I chose not to follow that path. I went to university and studied English, and while I was there I started to become involved in doing posters for societies and designing their magazines, that sort of thing. And I discovered that I liked it very much and that my English degree was probably not going to give me a living. I had some illusion that I could have a lot of fun and be paid for it by becoming a designer. So at night I went to the London College of Printing and did a design course.

—Richard Eckersley

Being artistic or artsy was the second-easiest way to get out of doing work at school. With athletics and art, you could basically coast through most of junior high school and high school. I remember getting all kinds of special treatment doing bulletin boards, even in fifth and sixth grades. It was a way to feel special. The more you do something like that, the better off you get, the more you can understand the materials, the more it does have a physical manifestation into something that other people like, the more it becomes something fun.

—Joseph Essex

I have never become a graphic designer in the full sense of the term. I live lower in the food chain, providing one of the raw materials of graphic design: type. Graphic designers are my clients; I rely on them to put my work to use.

—Matthew Carter

One day, my painting instructor was ill and a substitute teacher showed up at our critique. He told us everything on the wall was shit, and for me that was it! I had had it with design — I was humiliated and furious. I told him that of course it was shit — all design was shit — and only painting mattered. He then told me that I did not know anything about design. He asked me if I knew who Joseph Muller-Brockmann was; I said no. The next day, I went to the library and found a book on Muller-Brockmann. I opened it up, saw his Beethoven poster, and flipped! That was it for me — I wanted to be a graphic designer.

—Michael Manwaring

I liked the fact that design was disciplined and rigorous, that it was a part of the everyday "real" world; the fact that you could actually make a living at it was reassuring for my parents.

—Jeffery Keedy

My mother, Elaine Lustig Cohen, was a designer in the early 1960s. She was married to Alvin Lustig. So I grew up around her doing these things at her desk and I guess not really totally understanding what it was she did. As I grew up, I learned more about it and learned to appreciate it. My parents also had a rare-art book business called Ex-Libris, so I really grew up around a lot of avant-garde twentieth-century design art books, posters, ephemera. I didn't go to art school. I went to Oberlin College. I studied art history and studio art and got a very well-rounded basic education with an emphasis on art. When I graduated from Oberlin, I guess I always thought in the back of my mind that I wanted to do design.

—Tamar Cohen

I had to make a choice of what to study, and I had taken some art classes in high school that I really liked, but my parents felt that it wasn't very practical. When we went to the university the teachers were proud to tell my parents that now there was this new field of graphic design where you could be creative and still make money. So everybody was happy. That's how I got started.

—Rita Marshall

My father was a writer in the advertising industry, and my mother worked in printing. Between the two of them, print mechanicals, type specimens, color specimens, etc., were all over the house. I was always aware that someone somewhere had the job of drawing the letters but didn't think about it for a long time. When I began to get some training as a writer, which I had planned to be, I understood why anyone bothered with the forms of the letters themselves. When the power of language was introduced to me, I saw the power in the letterforms themselves.

—**Tobias Frere-Jones**

What fascinated me about graphic design was the notion of organizing information in a logical and emotional way through the use of space, size, and color. I haven't changed much; the same things still excite me today. My formal education was basically architecture, not graphic design. My first jobs were in every design area, too many to mention here. The most important notions I was taught as a student was that "an architect should be able to design anything from a spoon to a city" and that "less is more." My life reflects those notions.

—**Massimo Vignelli**

I needed to work on something more practical than painting. In graphic design, the work is done when the problem is solved or the deadline comes. There may be many solutions to one problem but, ultimately, when you move your audience to act as you hope they will, the job is complete. I also wanted a job that would be fun, like the scenes from the *Dick Van Dyke Show* when all the comedy writers go in the back room and make up jokes all day, even when they're not working. That's what I wanted, not to be a suffering autocratic artist.

—**Barbara de Wilde**

I was always good at drawing, but I never had the personal vision that seems to drive fine artists. Instead, even in high school, I was interested in applied art — things like magazine covers, film titles, record jackets. I was always the guy who would volunteer to paint the name of the band on the bass drum. In my junior year of high school I found out, almost by accident, that this kind of activity had a name: graphic design. I was so relieved that I didn't have to devote my life to coming up with ideas for paintings that I've never looked back.

—**Michael Bierut**

I seem to have been born a graphic designer. I was one of those kids who hid in the back of the classroom drawing pictures. One summer in Virginia, when my best friend and I were about six or seven years old, we built a lemonade stand. But the thing I was most interested in was naming our "company" and drawing a trademark for the front of the stand.

—**John Plunkett**

My father is a graphic designer and he often took me to his studio as a child. I started tracing type out of type books at age six, logos at age seven. In addition, I was chosen as an AFS (American Field Service) exchange student for my senior year in high school, and the program sent me to a design school in Belgium where I learned about typography, color, geometric design, and other skills. I was lucky to have been born in a time (1956) and place (New York City) where the great practitioners of graphic design were accessible to young people. I had the great fortune of training at The Cooper Union, studying under practicing designers like Massimo Vignelli, Henry Wolf, Herb Lubalin, Seymour Chwast, Milton Glaser, James McMullan, Cipe Pineles, and Walter Bernard. This was an extraordinary time to be a graphic design student.

—**Michael Aron**

As a high school student being asked to choose a major in college, or, in other words, what I was going to do for the rest of my life, I made the naive decision to go into commercial art. Luckily, as I was exposed to graphic design and educated on what exactly it was, I realized this was the field I wanted to be in.

—Ron Louie

When I was in college (majoring in American history) I had no concept that the field of graphic design existed. I had a strong visual interest and had taken pre-architecture electives and what drawing and painting I could find. But I felt there had to be something that one could call a profession between the poles of architecture and painting, neither of which seemed right for me. It wasn't until I was deep into my senior thesis that I discovered what a graphic designer did for a living.

—Chris Pullman

My high school teacher, Leon Friend, introduced me and decades of other Abraham Lincoln High students to art and graphic design. He may have be the first to use the term in print; in 1936 McGraw-Hill published the book he wrote with Joseph Hefter entitled *Graphic Design*. Ever eager to share his knowledge, his book includes an eclectic choice of the processes and images from the printing arts as well as a short bibliography, a glossary of terms, and samples of a course of study. While I did not know about the book when I was a high school student the attitudes in it were part of my daily experience.

—Sheila Levrant de Bretteville

When I was about seven, (1962), I visited Condé Nast, where my aunt was an editor, and met with Micki Denkoff, the art director. The art department was covered in Avedon and Warhol, white Formica and Eames, Bodoni, and Helvetica. As a teenager in the late sixties, my awareness of design was formalized with the dynamic illustrative images of Push Pin Studios. Their images were everywhere—on buses, on barricade walls, on my favorite albums. So by the time I was fifteen, I was certain I wanted to be designer.

—Jennifer Morla

I was writing some articles for a tiny left-wing magazine in Vorarlberg, Austria, when I realized that I enjoyed working on the layout and coming up with ideas for the cover better than writing articles. Nobody else wanted to do the layout so I was it.

—Stefan Sagmeister

My initial motivation for entering graphic design was money. As a fine arts major, I wasn't earning any, and certainly not by doing anything I had gone to school for. I couldn't see a life of building renovation as a day job and working on my art at night. Thus, at the age of twenty-one, did I land my first job designing elementary school books for McGraw-Hill, Inc., by showing a portfolio of my printmaking.

—Christopher Austopchuk

I went to a school where, if you couldn't paint, you were "graphically oriented." Moreover, from a very early age I was fascinated with letterforms; later, in high school, I sent away for an Osmiroid pen and taught myself calligraphy. I soon discovered that this skill could prove lucrative. A career was born!

—Louise Fili

Like the main character in Chaim Potok's book *My Name Is Asher Lev*, I began to "see" things early on. When I was a kid, I thought things and said things I thought were truly funny. Unfortunately, no one else did. My talents (for lack of a better word) went unnoticed, even by me, until I was run out of town.

—James Victore

Title: Batman Collected
Designer/Creative Director:
Chip Kidd **Publisher:** Bullfinch
Press **Client:** Little, Brown &
Co. **Photographer:** Geoff Spear
Typeface: Bodoni **Year:** 1996

Design

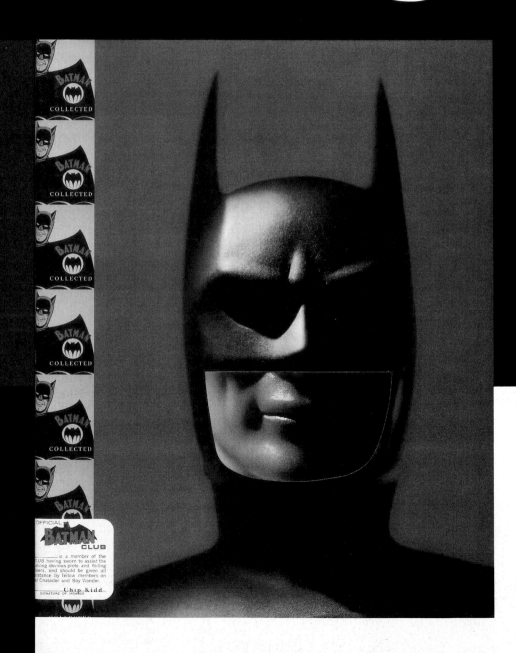

Specialties

Most art schools wisely teach graphic design as a general practice, the theory being that the orchestration of type and image, whether on paper or screen, is always based on the same fundamental formal principles. Different media, however, have different requirements. Editorial design is not the same as advertising; advertising is not the same as book design. Each has a unique focus and target. In most cases, the tools are similar yet the methodologies are not.

Many graphic designers perform a broad range of tasks, switching media as clients and jobs demand. A designer cannot always afford to specialize because the volume of work in a specialty may not warrant it or competition may be too intense. Therefore, it is prudent at the outset of a career to learn about and practice all the disciplines that strike your interest and fancy as well as those that are growth areas for employment. Although it is not necessary to be expert in everything, it is useful to be fluent in as many forms as possible, at least while you are looking for a possible career niche.

How is this accomplished? For those bound for art school, there may not even be a choice. The average design program provides instruction in the basics while spotlighting specialties such as magazine layout, book and record covers, posters, advertising, Web design, etc., in order to provide students with a well-rounded professional portfolio. Once out of school, however, specialization usually calls. If you are hired by a general design firm, exposure to a variety of disciplines is very likely. But if you are hired by an in-house art/design department, specialization is inevitable.

A junior designer at a design firm usually assists on different aspects of various projects, from annual reports to brochures to Web pages. Even if you do not feel entirely confident with a particularly new medium, never refuse an opportunity—in fact, volunteer for as much extra duty as possible within the limits of monetary remuneration (learn as much as you can, but do not allow yourself to become financially exploited in the process).

A junior designer at an in-house corporate or business art/design department is often given a single task. While it is important to build expertise in whatever field this may be, it is also consequential to expand your potential knowledge base. If possible, volunteer for additional jobs that depart from your basic assignment. If the company art department has several divisions, such as print, Web, exhibition, etc., attempt to assist outside your own area; there is a very good chance you will be given the opportunity to do so.

This advice is not aimed exclusively at neophytes. Experienced designers must also continually broaden their range of expertise, if only to thwart impending obsolescence. For example, when digital technology entered the realm of graphic design, many dedicated print designers turned their attention toward CD-ROM and Internet opportunities A few enrolled in graduate schools to get more intensive training; others gave up senior print jobs to apprentice or assist others already working in the digital arena. Moving from print to electronic media is not the only possible career change. Many designers who fall into their specialties without previous exposure elsewhere want new challenges and so switch from, say, advertising to editorial, perhaps accepting a lower position to get on-the-job-training until achieving proficiency in the new discipline.

Ultimately, the majority of designers pick a specialty (or specialties) and stick with it (them) until the learning curve flattens out or the projects become routine. Of course, depending on their comfort level some designers spend their entire lives in one job either moving up the corporate hierarchy or, if content with the status quo, remaining at the same basic level. Everyone's ambition is individual and depends on personal needs, wants, drive, and ability. If one hungers for creative challenges, then general practice is preferred; if one longs for consistency, then specialization is a good option.

Your decision to practice in a specific discipline should be considered thoughtfully. While it is true that many designers stumble into their specialties simply because a particular job is available to them, others carefully reconnoiter the job market for the position that most appeals to their passion or interest. Then there is the hip-factor: Some job seekers simply want to be hired by the hippest firms — MTV and Nickelodeon Networks rate high among that demographic. There is nothing wrong with this goal — except, of course, that you must be aware that these sought-after companies receive hundreds of applications for comparatively few openings.

It is axiomatic that more is much better than less knowledge, which means that it is important to know what disciplines are available, what they require of a prospective candidate, and how to apply for the job. This section examines genres that hire the greatest number of graphic designers and offers basic information concerning the nature of each at the entry and senior levels. Becoming a graphic designer in any of these showcased disciplines is based on skill and accomplishment — graphic design is nothing if not a meritocracy. When your portfolio is professional (no loose or disorganized scraps of paper), well edited (the number of pieces is limited to the few that show how proficient you are), and smartly paced (showing that you know how to make ideas appear dynamic), then you have a greater likelihood of influencing a prospective employer, if not for the job being considered, then for other possibilities and referrals. Even if you don't get the job, it is important to make a positive impression so that you are remembered for future positions.

Knowing the field is one important way to maximize your chances of entering it. Each specialty has unique needs and wants. Job candidates who desire to make a good impression should design a portfolio that indicates interest, and at least a modicum of expertise, in the selected area.

I. Editorial

FACTS AND FIGURES issued by the United States Department of Labor are sketchy regarding exactly which medium is the largest employer of graphic designers. Nonetheless, it is a sound assumption that magazines and newspapers give opportunities to a large percentage of junior and senior designers and art directors.

Within a magazine or newspaper infrastructure, design duties are often divided into two fundamental groups: editorial and promotion. The latter, which administers advertising and publicity, including the conception and design of ads, billboards, and collateral materials, such as advertising rate cards, subscription campaigns, and promotional booklets and brochures, may be large or small, depending on the priorities of the specific company. The former, however, is the creative heart of an institution. Editorial designers are the people who give the publication is aura, image, and format. And yet the editorial art department is configured differently from publication to publication, so it is not always possible for a job candidate to know the makeup of specific departments before interviewing for a job (which may or may not help anyway). The following are typical scenarios that illustrate the variety of editorial opportunities.

MAGAZINES

MAGAZINES COME in various shapes, sizes, and frequencies. In any given year thousands are published on such a wide range of subjects that it is difficult to list them all here. The quality of their design also ranges widely from high to low, with much competence in between. While this book is not a critical guide to design quality, one important part of any professional equation is indeed the publication's design standard. Does the publisher expect the highest and most rigorous quality or merely competent work? The evidence is usually clear from the look of the magazine itself. The job seeker should decide whether working for a particular publication is going to enhance or detract from future prospects—and from compiling good portfolio samples. Of course, this is ultimately a personal decision. Sometimes acquiring experience is more important than any other concern; sometimes working on the best not only encourages the best but results in greater opportunities later.

Design positions at magazines are frequently available for all experiential levels. The intense and constant work flow that goes into periodical design and production demands many participants. A typical hierarchy begins at the top with a *design director* or *art director*, who manages the overall design department and design of the magazine, including the format (which either he or an outside design consultant originally designed); this may include overseeing the work of senior and junior page designers and designing pages and covers himself. It may also involve assigning illustration, photography, and typography (when the budget allows, custom typefaces are also commissioned). In addition, the art director is involved in meetings with editors (and sometimes authors) concerning article presentation. Some of these duties are invariably delegated to a deputy or *associate art director*, who does many of the same design tasks as the art director and also may manage, depending on the workload. The deputy or associate may be on a track to move into the art director's position, should it open, or, after acquiring the requisite experience, move on to an art director position at another magazine.

On the next lower level, *senior* and *junior designers* are responsible for designing separate components of a magazine (features, columns, inserts, etc.). Some design entire spreads or pages and commission the artwork and photography; others design elements of a feature and use the illustrations supplied to them by the art director or the deputy. Some are better typographers than users of art. The difference between senior and junior is usually the degree of experience and talent. The former may have been a junior first or may have been hired directly as a senior from another job; the latter is often right out of school or had an internship while a student. Based on achievement, a senior or junior designer can be promoted to a deputy or associate position. There are no codified rules of acceleration other than merit and need. Therefore it is not impossible for a junior to be so professionally adept that promotion to the next level is fairly swift. Conversely, merely competent

The Case of the Default Art Director

In art departments of small publications, such as a neighborhood newspaper, it is very possible to rise from production artist to art director in a short time. A veteran art director relates his phenomenal accession: "I was hired right out of high school for what I thought would be a summer job as a mechanical artist for a small New York newspaper. Within a month, after the art director taught me the job — at that time, doing pasteups — he was hired to be the art director of a larger, more prestigious magazine. With barely two weeks' notice, I was plunged into the role of art director while the publisher looked for a replacement. I don't know why, but fortuitously, no good applicants emerged and by default I was given the job. It was an incredible experience — a frightening one, too, as I knew absolutely nothing about art direction. But I was forced to learn very quickly. I remained art director for a year until the newspaper folded, by which time I was hooked on publication design. I decided not to continue with my liberal arts studies at college, briefly enrolled in art school, and continued to get increasingly better art directorial jobs at magazines and newspapers."

progress in a job is rarely rewarded.

The junior designer position is often at the entry level. Some magazines have additional entry-level jobs, such as unpaid *interns* or paid *assistants* who do less critical, yet nevertheless necessary, support work. The most common task is production, such as scanning images into the computer or maintaining electronic files; occasionally, a minimal amount of layout or design work on tightly formatted pages may be assigned. In addition, the intern or assistant is invariably required to act as a gofer, attending to all the odd jobs that need to be done. This is actually a critical juncture for the wannabe because an employer can measure the relative competence or excellence of a worker. Even the lowliest job can result in significant advancement.

The art department is only one nerve junction of a magazine. In some environments it is on a par with the editorial department (editors and writers), while in others it is the handmaiden. The relative importance of art and design is often linked to the comparative strength and power of the design or art director. Whatever the hierarchy, it is important that editorial designers (at any level) be aware of the editorial process—not merely the schedule but the editorial philosophy of the magazine. Too many bad relationships between design and editorial departments exist because their missions are not in sync. The two departments must complement each other; achieving this is one of the jobs of the design or art director. But even the lowest-level designer must have an astute understanding of what is being editorially communicated in order for the design to not only carry but enhance the content of the publication.

NEWSPAPERS

ALTHOUGH FINANCIAL analysts report that, due to fierce competition with television and on-line services, newspapers are currently a faltering industry, nonetheless there is an increased demand for art directors, designers, graphics editors, and production personnel at newspapers today. The reasons are fairly simple. Once many newspapers (afternoon, morning, and evening editions) competed in the same locales for the same readership and advertisers. That number has been radically reduced (for example, from their peak in the 1950s, New York City's dailies have been reduced from twelve to three). In most cases, this means that the remaining few papers are larger in size and offer more extensive coverage. In addition, over the past two decades, newspapers have augmented hard news with soft news features, such as lifestyle or home sections. At the same time, printing technology has significantly advanced to allow more innovative visual display (including full-color reproduction). In the past, newspaper composition was carried out by editorial makeup persons, who were not trained as artists or designers; today, art directors and designers are responsible for the basic look and feel of the average newspaper.

Another paradox that makes newspapers a welcoming job market is the precipitous decline in the number of art directors and designers specifically trained for this medium. Despite the newspaper's ubiquity, few art schools and colleges have courses dedicated to its design. If they exist at all, they are folded into a general publication design curriculum. Many who work in newspaper design departments never formally studied the discipline in school classes — they came through school newspapers, internships/apprenticeships, or junior or senior design positions at magazines — hence, the current demand for designers exclusively trained in the newspaper environment. Various journalism schools have started news design courses, but getting a newspaper job and learning from hands-on experience is still a viable option at the entry-level stage.

Over the past decade, newspapers have introduced new job categories unique to this industry. One notable entry is graphics editor, a hybrid of editor and designer, who is responsible for the information graphics (charts, graphs, and maps) that appear regularly in most newspapers. This new sub-genre has become essential to contemporary newspaper content.

The newspaper industry has distinct hierarchies, but each newspaper has different jobs and job descriptions; the following are typical. Beginning at the entry level, the best way to start is as an *intern*. All newspapers employ seasonal (usually paid) interns as junior copypersons, who act as assistants-in-training to the various news desks. Likewise, the art department (which is often under the wing of the news department) employs a design intern to work directly with designers or art directors. The *New York Times*, for example, hires one intern a year for a ten-week stint. Often, art department interns are selected from art schools or universities with publication design programs (the candidates need not have had newspaper experience, although some newspaper work is a definite advantage). The tasks given the intern vary depending on the publication; one newspaper may offer intensive training in design, production, and information graphics, while another may have the intern do gofer work (scanning, making copies, or whatever clerk-like tasks are necessary). Internships sometimes lead to permanent employment; sometimes they do not. An internship is a kind of test for an employer to ascertain how well an individual fits, professionally and personally, into a specific art department.

The next level is usually more permanent. If a newspaper has *junior designer* or *design assistant* positions, these are often full-time jobs with various responsibilities. The experience necessary may be an internship at a newspaper or magazine or a junior position, preferably at a newspaper. Nevertheless, regardless of experience, juniors may be hired on the formal and conceptual strength of the portfolio.

Every newspaper art department is organized differently, so the assistant in one may work closely with the senior designer or art director actually designing some of the pages of a hard or soft news section, or the junior may assist many designers in the daily process, which might include doing routine production chores (such as electronic mechanical, color preparation, and photo processing). The degree of responsibility is based on the volume of work *and* the art director's desire to delegate.

In many newspapers, the junior or assistant is a union job, which means that salary, benefits, etc., are governed and job security is ensured by the union contract. Membership in a guild or union is mandatory at this level and the security offered is both good and bad–good for the obvious reasons and bad because it encourages people to stay in their jobs for a long time, which is not always advantageous to creative pursuits. In fact, in many union shops there is so little movement that the junior may be stuck with the same title for an excessively long time — and this is an important consideration in joining a newspaper art department.

Continuing Education

A certain amount of design know-how can be obtained by osmosis on the job. The ambitious neophyte who lands a production job at a periodical is in an excellent position to learn practical skills as well as the procedures involved in that specific publication. But the likelihood of promotion to a design job is minimal without additional design experience. One way to convince an employer that your ambition should be rewarded is to enroll in continuing education classes specializing in publication design. Most art schools and some colleges offer intermediate and advanced courses. Some are under the desktop publishing umbrella; others are components of broader graphic design programs. Most classes of this kind are at night, but some of the larger art schools offer intensive editorial design workshops during the summer months. Supplementing on-the-job experience with classroom instruction pays off in the long run.

The next job designation is *senior designer* or *art director*. (In some newspapers the title *graphics editor* is also given to those who design hard and soft news sections.) Experience required is almost always a periodical design job, whether as a junior or a senior at a magazine or newspaper. Designers without this experience or training are rarely qualified. Nonetheless, opportunities exist in locales where few newspaper or magazine design specialists are found. The responsibilities vary depending on the size of the newspaper. An art director may design a specific section of a newspaper, assign the illustration and photography, and design the so-called dress or feature pages. (An *assistant designer* or, at many newspapers, a makeup editor, may design the more routine pages.) The senior designer or art director works with text editors, picture editors, and graphics editors (when that designation only applies to information graphics). Usually, a production person or production editor works in concert with the senior designer to translate the design layouts into a final electronic or mechanical form. The senior designer may work on one or more sections of a newspaper; at a small paper the job may involve many subject areas.

Parallel to the senior designer or art director is the *graphics editor* responsible for information graphics. The experience required is a combination of reporting and graphic expertise. In many instances, the prospective candidate must pass a test that determines news judgment and editing skills, as well as the ability to consolidate raw data into accessible visual form. The requirements are no less rigorous than for designers and, in fact, are more complex because of the intersection of news and art disciplines. In some newspapers, this job involves page design; in others it is limited to information design alone. The graphics editor works with the news and feature editors, who decide on the daily news report, to conceive and shape a particular graphic presentation. The graphics editor coordinates work with the senior designer in order to achieve a seamless overall page design. For those who are interested in typography, graphics, and research and reporting, this is a wide-open area in which to seek employment.

The top level at a newspaper is called the *design director, senior art director, senior graphics editor*, or, in some places, the *managing editor for design*, who is supported by a *deputy, assistant*, or *managing design director*. Extensive experience is required for this job, including the administration and management skills needed to oversee a staff of designers and production personnel. The design director is usually responsible for maintaining the overall design quality and is often the original designer of the formats that senior designer and art directors work within. Sometimes the design director has a hands-on role in the design of special features, but often the demands of a newsroom require that such

work be delegated to others under watchful supervision.

Newspaper design is essentially different from magazine design. First, it is expressed on a larger scale — more editorial components must be balanced on the broadsheet pages. Second, it occurs at a different frequency — the luxury of a weekly or monthly magazine deadline allows for more detail work, whereas at a daily newspaper little time is available for the nuances of design. Third, the production values are not as high–working with newsprint on web-offset presses does not allow for the fine printing common to most glossy magazines. And yet the newspaper is every bit as challenging and offers equal creative possibilities for the designer who is interested, indeed passionate, about editorial work. While one can use a newspaper job as a stepping stone to other job opportunities, a majority of newspaper designers find that this medium provides a good place to build a career.

Freelancers Always Wanted

Most magazines and newspapers hire freelance designers and support personnel to meet excess creative and production needs. Over the past 15 years, freelance employees have become prevalent throughout the publishing industries, especially because seasonal shifts in editorial emphasis (special issues and sections) add to the workload. Freelancers are hired to do secondary design and production tasks and skilled freelance designers are

often assigned to work on primary components of a publication. For the junior, this kind of work is experientially important; for the senior it can be creatively (and financially) beneficial. Freelance assignments can be either long- or short-term and are perfect for designers who are not yet, or have no desire to be, committed to any specific discipline. Most freelancers work in the art department of the publication on their equipment.

Entry level

Most entry-level portfolios include a large percentage of school assignments, often one or two redesigns of existing magazines or fantasy magazines. This work exhibits original thinking unfettered by the constraints of a real job, and yet the solutions are realistic. The editorial portfolio should include mostly editorial work, but general samples (posters, brochures, letterheads) are useful to gauge typography and layout skills.

Contents

Ten to twenty samples:

a. Feature pages and spread designs (showing range of stylistic and conceptual thinking)
b. Cover designs (showing two or three logo and illustration approaches)
c. Department pages (to show how routine editorial material is designed)
d. Two to four noneditorial examples

Junior/Senior Designer

By this stage, portfolios should include a large percentage of published work. The junior may continue to include school projects, but the senior should jettison them. The samples should be of high quality. Not everything in print rates showing in a portfolio. Through these samples, the important thing is to show your taste, talent, and expertise.

Contents

Fifteen to twenty-five samples:

a. Feature pages and spreads from published periodicals
b. Cover designs (if available)
c. Examples of illustration and photograph assignments (if available)
d. Department pages (if available)
e. Two noneditorial examples

Format

35mm slides (in slide tray), 4×5 transparencies, dry-mounted proofs (lamination preferable), entire publications. Portfolio presentations on CD-ROM or Zip Disk.

Title: Pictures of the Year
Designers: Don Morris, Josh Klenert, Jennifer Starr **Creative Director:** Don Morris **Company:** Don Morris Design **Client:** Entertainment Weekly **Typeface:** Bureau Grotesque **Year:** 1997

Magazine Envy

Title: Bloomberg Personal
Designers: Don Morris, Josh Klenert, James Reyman, Jennifer Starr **Creative Director:** Don Morris **Company:** Don Morris Design **Client:** Bloomberg **Photographer:** Jana Leon **Typeface:** Thesis **Year:** 1996

DON MORRIS
Principal, Don Morris Design, New York City

How did you get started in editorial design?
After graduating from Parsons School of Design with a major in illustration, I worked the summer at the Ford assembly plant in Edison, New Jersey. I received a call from a friend who was working at *New York* magazine and was about to quit because his illustration career was taking off. I found myself thrust into the middle of an exciting, churning machine: a weekly magazine art department. I ran the stat machine and tried to make myself the most unobtrusive fly that ever scaled a wall so I could hear any and every art-related conversation: post-illustrator interview critiques, new talent finds, actual assignment psychodramas. I never thought I'd be there more than a few weeks, so I wanted to gain priceless insight into the business.

I stayed in editorial design because I was intrigued with magazines as a collaborative exchange of ideas. Weekly magazines like *New York* bring out the best and worst in people. The best comes from the fact that there's no time to waste, so you're cutting to the core. The worst happens if you're working alongside someone who starts to burn out from the monklike devotion of long hours, little pay, and even more minuscule thanks. Still, as a place to gain knowledge of the many facets of putting out a high-quality publication, it's hard to beat.

What motivated you to start your own design studio?
After my job at *New York*, I went to *Metropolitan Home*. Dorothy Kalins, the editor in chief, realized that the magazine could put on an eclectic designer showcase to help DIFFA (Design Industries Foundation for AIDS) with its excellent connections in the design, architecture, and production design fields and its friends in the

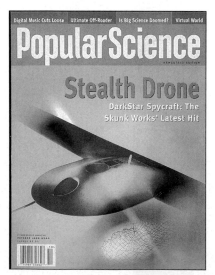

Title: Popular Science Redesign
Designers: Don Morris, James Reyman, Teresa Fernandes **Creative Directors:** Don Morris, Teresa Fernandes **Company:** Don Morris Design **Client:** Times Mirror **Photographer:** Geoff Spear **Typefaces:** Meta, Franklin Gothic **Year:** 1995

Title: Black Wolf **Designers:** Don Morris, Josh Klenert **Creative Director:** Don Morris **Company:** Don Morris Design **Client:** Smithsonian Magazine **Typeface:** Village, Caecilia **Year:** 1997

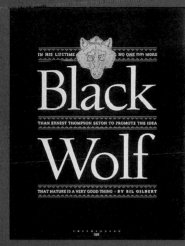

restaurant community. I found myself designing posters, brochures, banners, signage, menus, tickets, and shopping bags as
well as the commemorative magazine. I was never the same again.
Coming up with a central theme that captured the feeling of the
endeavor and applying it to all shapes, sizes, and media was fasci-
nating. I wanted to do that kind of work everyday.

How does your firm run?

I've tried to keep my studio small so that I can handle the chores
of running a staff and a business, represent the studio for potential projects, and actively design as well as art-direct. More staff,
space, and equipment could perhaps complicate my life more than
make things easier. This way, I'm able to stay choosy about what
we get involved with because I'm controlling my overhead. That
feeling of freedom and discretion is something I guard closely.

What is the most fulfilling aspect of your job? The least?

The most fulfilling aspect is realizing the breadth and diversity of
what we're asked to do and how well we do it. The least fulfilling
is dealing with clients who cannot sustain the vision of what's
been delivered to them. In editorial work, design studios are frequently on the outside of part of the process, and it can be incredibly frustrating. One example: We submitted a book cover design
to the art director of a major publishing house. The art director
reported back to us that the author was so taken with our solution
that she was inspired to rewrite the manuscript. Not bad, right?
But the book turned up in the bookstore with a bastardized version of our cover design! Why did the book cover change? I guess
I'll never know.

Title: Sundance Film Festival Poster
Designers: Don Morris, Josh Klenert, Cay
Tolson, Jennifer Starr **Creative Director:**
Don Morris **Company:** Don Morris Design
Client: Sundance Institute **Photo-
grapher:** Sylvia Otte **Typeface:** Bauer
Topic **Year:** 1999

Title: Fifth Anniversary Issue **Designers:**
Don Morris, James Reyman **Creative
Director:** Don Morris **Company:** Don
Morris Design **Client:** Entertainment
Weekly **Photographers:** Various **Type-
face:** Bureau Grotesque **Year:** 1995

Designing the News

Title: The New Jazz Age
Designer: Lisa Naftolin
Creative Director: Janet
Froelich **Publication:** The New
York Times Magazine **Photo-
grapher:** Richard Burbridge
Typefaces: Champion, Chel-
tenham Roman **Year:** 1995

Title: The Eye of the Photojour-
nalist **Designer/Creative
Director:** Janet Froelich
Publication: The New York
Times Magazine **Photographer:**
Sebastiao Salgado **Typeface:**
John Hancock
Year: 1991

JANET FROELICH
Art Director, *The New York Times Magazine*,
New York City

**Did you go straight into editorial design or did you dabble
first?**
I did a lot of freelance work. I tried to get as many jobs as I
could. I did lots of brochures. I did a lot of what now might be
called pro bono work. And then I worked for *Look* magazine for a
very short while as a freelance gig until I answered an ad in the
New York Times for a magazine art director. It turned out to be for
the *Daily News*. I went up there with my portfolio and the man
who ultimately hired me told me that I did not have enough experience — but he needed a young designer and he took a chance. I
started out doing newspaper pages at the *Daily News*. The thing
that I remember most was that I took every bit of it really seriously and I would sit there for hours struggling with pages trying
to make them look as good as I could.

**Was it a conscious decision to go into editorial design, or did
the newspaper job lead you there?**
Well, I fit well with journalism. I just love the news. I love
designing magazine pages because there's an immediacy to them
and it happens very quickly and it turns around constantly; it
repeats. Every week you have another challenge. You don't sit
there for a month or two designing one thing.

Title: Some Enchanted Evening Clothes Designer: Janet Froelich Creative Director: Janet Froelich Publication: The New York Times Magazine Photographer: Lillian Bassman Typeface: Champion Year: 1995

Have you ever had any interest in doing another form of design?

I can't say that I never had an interest. I've toyed with it from time to time. Everybody would sit around and sort of assess their career or their life and think about moving in another direction. But there was never a natural opportunity or reason to move out of the path that I was in.

As the design director of *The New York Times Magazine*, what is the most fulfilling aspect of your job?

The personal relationships. I know that may be funny to say for a designer, but I just love working with the people that I work with. They challenge me, they question things. We develop ideas together. I love to listen to them talk about writing and what makes good writing, and to talk about events and how you turn events into a story. The other part of my job is that I really think of myself as a sort of impresario or team builder. What is really crucial when you're managing a department, when you're art-directing or being a creative director, is your ability to choose good people, to nurture them, to make the atmosphere satisfying for them to do good work in, to create an atmosphere in which they get along well with each other and they feel like they contribute.

What is the single most important skill a designer needs to be successful?

The ability to be self-critical. In order to get anywhere, you need to be able to look at your own work and see how it solves a problem, what works well and what doesn't. To be able to judge your own work and to be able to know how to push it to another place is the most important skill of all.

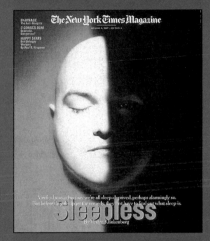

Title: The Next Hundred Years Designers: Joel Cuyler, Lisa Naftolin Creative Director: Janet Froelich Publication: The New York Times Magazine Typefaces: Stymie, Champion Year: 1996

Title: Sleepless Designer: Joel Cuyler Creative Director: Janet Froelich Publication: The New York Times Magazine Photographer: Lisa Spindler Typefaces: Champion, Cheltenham Year: 1997

A Magazine from Scratch

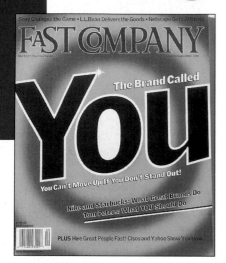

Title: The Brand Called You
Designer/Creative Director:
Patrick Mitchell **Publication:**
Fast Company Magazine **Year:**
1997

Title: You Decide **Designer/
Creative Director:** Patrick
Mitchell **Publication:** Fast
Company Magazine **Typeface:**
Griffith Gothic **Year:** 1998

Title: We Want You
Designer/Creative Director:
Patrick Mitchell **Publication:**
Fast Company Magazine **Illus-
trator:** Paul Davis **Typefaces:**
Interstate, New Century School-
book **Year:** 1998

PATRICK MITCHELL

Art Director, *Fast Company* Magazine, Boston,
Massachusetts

How did you get involved with editorial design?
In college I worked on my school newspaper as an editorial car-
toonist. It was a thrill to see my drawings get printed in mass
media. But after that thrill wore off, I started looking at the page
as a whole: the fonts they were using, the column layouts, etc.
I thought, "These pages should look better." Although they had
never had one, they made me the graphics director. I started
experimenting with the logo, the page headings, the text type,
the cropping of photos, and page layouts. When I figured out that
in the real world people were actually doing the stuff I was doing
and getting paid, I pretty much knew what I wanted to be.

How would you describe a good work environment?
If you wake up in the morning and can't wait to get there, that's
a good work environment.

Is that how you feel about your job?
Creating a magazine from scratch with a small group of people is

one of the most fulfilling things I've ever done. The only downside is how little I see my wife and kids.

Do you have a specific approach to hiring magazine designers?
I get a particular thrill out of hiring people in nontraditional ways. I hate soliciting candidates in the newspaper. Maybe it's my way of testing my powers of judging character, or maybe I'm just too lazy to go through tons of resumes. One of my senior designers was a managing editor at one of my client's magazines. We worked well together and I perceived a real design sense in her. She's thriving now as a designer. Once, another designer was leaving a local design studio. We met for lunch (with my six-year-old), hit it off, and the rest is history. Another example is a production manager I had worked with at a previous job who couldn't get a design job because of title prejudice. I hired her because we knew how to work together and because she was willing to go the extra mile to learn design. She's now an associate art director at a small publishing company.

What would you still like to accomplish in your career?
I'd like to design a magazine that people remember after I'm gone. I'd like to design one of the all-time great magazines. I don't know which one.

Title: Power to the People **Designer/Creative Director:** Patrick Mitchell **Publication:** Fast Company Magazine **Photographer:** Christopher Hartlove **Typeface:** El Dorado **Year:** 1998

Title: Greetings From Idea City **Designer/Creative Director:** Patrick Mitchell **Publication:** Fast Company Magazine **Photographer:** Burk Uzzle **Typeface:** Griffith Gothic **Year:** 1997

Title: Project: You **Designer/Creative Director:** Patrick Mitchell **Publication:** Fast Company Magazine **Illustrator:** Barry Blitt **Typeface:** El Dorado **Year:** 1998

A Life at Magazines

Title: Cannes Cover **Designer/ Creative Director:** Kelly Doe **Publication:** Washington Post Magazine **Client:** The French Embassy **Photographer:** Leo Mirkine **Typefaces:** Eagle, Palace Script, Didot **Year:** 1997

KELLY DOE
Art Director, *Washington Post Magazine*, Washington, DC

How did you get into editorial design?

I worked at various studios and agencies and by chance fell into a job designing and illustrating pages at the *San Jose Mercury News*. I was attracted to the nature of the content and the variety of interpretation that could be explored within a singular format. I loved working with illustration, photography, and typography to create a specific feel for material bound by a particular editorial framework. After that, I went to *Hippocrates* magazine and was lucky enough to participate in producing a magazine in the most civilized and highly creative environment I've yet experienced.

What makes a good work environment?

A good work environment is one in which everyone participating has respect for the work they're doing and each other and the opportunity to grow creatively within the job. We are living in a time where the economics of publishing have created an extremely unhealthy work situation in the industry; many designers are taken advantage of and generally treated as disposable. Worse, as magazines slowly turn to pleasing advertisers and statistics instead of a singular editorial vision, we all face a serious loss of decent intelligent material to work with.

So what makes it worthwhile?

The most fulfilling aspect of editorial work is, to me, working with the photographers, illustrators, and writers to solve the visual problems every week. The con-

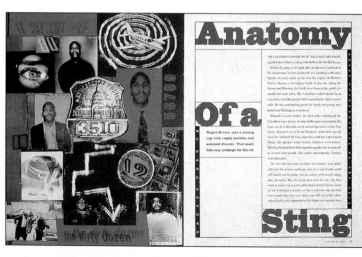

Title: Anatomy of a Sting **Designer/ Creative Director:** Kelly Doe **Publication:** Washington Post Magazine **Photographer:** Amy Guip **Typeface:** Egiziano **Year:** 1996

Title: Life As an Alien **Designers:** Kelly Doe, Lisa Schreiber **Creative Director:** Kelly Doe **Publication:** Washington Post Magazine **Photograph:** Courtesy of Author **Typeface:** Felix Titling, Weiss **Year:** 1998

Title: Holidays Made Simple **Designer/ Creative Director:** Kelly Doe **Publication:** Washington Post Magazine **Photographer:** Alan Richardson/ FPG Stock **Typeface:** Egiziano **Year:** 1996

stant dialog that goes on with such a varied, talented group is extremely gratifying. I am also happiest when I can come up with a solution that unites the visuals with the typography in a seamless, striking, and effective way so they all build on each other. Least fulfilling and most irritating has to be arguing with editors over little design details, and budget and production problems.

How much of your time is devoted to art direction and design versus business matters?
On a weekly publication like the *Washington Post Magazine,* it all depends on the complexity of the issue, but it can be a depressing figure. Often the art direction and design (a mixture of the conceptualizing of the story visually and typographically), takes only 40 percent of the time and the overseeing of staff projects, illustrators, budget, and prepress takes the other 60 percent.

How do you find designers and what do you look for?
The most usual way is through word of mouth. I ask every art director I know and I look up names on mastheads of magazines I consider to be well designed or photoedited and call people directly. I also keep the more promising resumes I receive in the mail. I interview people, and the editors they'll be working with interview them also, because their input at the beginning helps create a smoother, more cohesive working team later.

Title: Hypochondria **Designer/ Creative Director:** Kelly Doe **Publication:** Washington Post Magazine **Photographer:** David Peterson **Typefaces:** Grotesque Black, Weiss **Year:** 1998

Moments of Inspiration

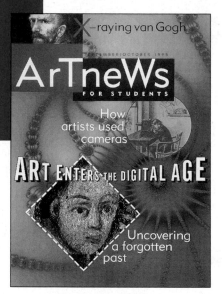

HELENE SILVERMAN
Founding Member, Hello Studio, New York City

Why editorial design?
I have never been very good at consciously directing the course of my work or my life. The closest I can come is staying away from the uninteresting paths. Making money was never a factor in what type of work I would do. Personal interest and the amount of satisfaction and fun I could have has always driven my direction. Publications remained a focus for years, but now I'm branching out into related areas.

How would you describe a good work environment?
For me, who does not like someone watching my every move, it is being my own boss. Ironically, that usually entails working harder and longer, but there is the illusion of autonomy. Besides all that, really nice people and a casual, fun group helps. It's also good to have people be happy with what their day-to-day job consists of, so there is a minimum of festering discontent.

Title: Art Enters the Digital Age **Designer/Creative Director:** Helene Silverman **Company:** Hello Studio **Client:** Artnews For Students **Year:** 1996

Title: Silencio = Muerte **Designer/Creative Director:** Helene Silverman **Company:** Hello Studio **Client:** Red Hot Organization **Illustrator:** Manuel Ocampo **Year:** 1997

Title: ladies' rooms **Designer/Creative Director:** Helene Silverman **Publication:** Metropolis Magazine **Photographer:** Elaine Ellman **Year:** 1988

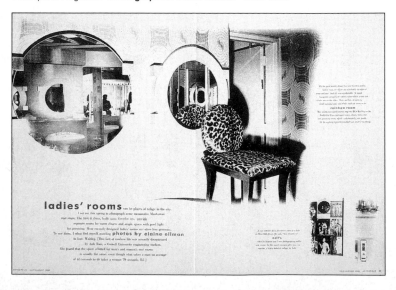

Title: Hats **Designer:** Helene Silverman **Creative Director:** Howard Klein **Client:** Clarkson Potter **Year:** 1991

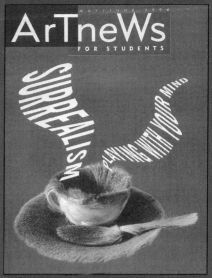

What is the most fulfilling aspect of your job?
As the years go by, surprisingly, the moments of most satisfaction come, when they do, in the early stages of a project. Sadly, very little fulfillment is usually gotten from the actual final piece. Usually, by that time, I am very tired of seeing it at all.

How have technological advancements affected your work?
Thinking about how work was done ten years ago, I am eternally grateful for the almighty computer. The freedom of type and color choices in the early stages of design is incomparable, to say the least. On the other hand, I have a sadness about the loss of how hard it was to physically get to where you wanted to be, and how easy and programmed it can be to get there today. There is a cloying smoothness and regularity to a lot of computer-generated work, whether or not it is germane to the work itself.

Do you have a specific approach to hiring designers?
I have had only one designer work for me and she actually talked me into it — for which I am eternally grateful. She was a student of mine at a school, which seems to be the usual way these days. I have rarely seen a person coming to me cold who seemed just right for me.

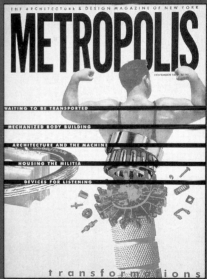

Title: Surrealism
Designer/Creative Director: Helene Silverman **Company:** Hello Studio **Client:** Artnews for Students **Year:** 1996

Title: transformations cover
Designer/Creative Director: Helene Silverman **Publication:** Metropolis Magazine
Year: 1987

Raised on Print

Title: Speak Magazine Cover
Designer: Martin Venezky
Client: Speak Magazine
Photographer: Unknown
Year: 1996

Title: Hot Rod Book Cover
Designer: Martin Venezky
Creative Director: Michael
Carabetta **Client:** Chronicle
Books **Photographer:** David
Perry **Year:** 1996

MARTIN VENEZKY

Art Director, *Speak* Magazine and Principal, Appetite
Engineers, San Francisco

Would you describe the kind of work that you're doing now?
I feel that my work has a lot in common with fine art. I take more
from fine art than from advertising or product marketing. I work with
photographers and artists in collaboration, which is actually what I
most love to do. I'm finding new ways of visually combining the image
with the text. Instead of creating a clear illustration of the text, I
make creative connections in the gap that occurs between the image
and the text. It's halfway between being a designer and an illustrator
and an artist. It sort of floats in that area.

Why did you turn to editorial design?
I really love print. To me, there's something about print that Web
design or multimedia design doesn't have. It could be just because
that's how I was raised — everything was print. Most of what I'm
known for is editorial design at *Speak* magazine. "Editorial" is a general term to describe my work because I just completed a book on
which I worked with a photographer and a writer. I guess that was
editorial, too, but I was given the opportunity to interpret the material, not just present it, which is unusual.

Title: "Cowboy" from Notes On the
West **Designer:** Martin Venezky
Client: Self-published at Cranbrook
Academy of Art **Year:** 1993

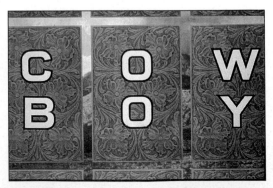

Title: Future Forward **Designer:** Martin Venezky **Client:** Q-Action **Photographer:** Martin Venezky **Year:** 1997

How do you use the computer to express your fine art sensibility?

I guess everything ends up having to be translated into a digital format or output — although it's funny, because with this brand-new issue of *Speak*, I am actually using a waxer, believe it or not. So I actually got to do some pages completely by hand that aren't even going to be put into the computer. They're going to be scanned with a digital camera.

Hand work is pretty novel at this stage in design?

When I was at Cranbrook, I did a lot of work with my hands. They had a stat camera there that no one had used for a long time, so I got it running and was actually going into the darkroom and making prints, all these things being hand skills. I really love doing that kind of thing, but the computer keeps luring me away. When I go to the art supply store, I often buy pens, ink, and paper just to remind myself of those materials. I try to allow time to play by hand. I cut up type with scissors and cut paper and tape them together with Scotch tape, which is how a lot of my form generation happens. Then I scan that into the computer and work it into a page or something. But I don't design all that much directly on the computer. It's always a way of juggling things that started out being done by hand.

What is the most satisfying aspect of your job?

Creating something where there's a certain magic, where the elements almost feel like they sprang to life themselves, became something didn't exist before I was there. I created this thing, whether it's a page in a magazine or a postcard with this wonderful image on it. The thing that I like the least is probably the thing that I'm weakest at, which is selling myself. Being a shrewd business manager is not the kind of thing that I am, but in a month from now I may be. It's just because I never had to do it, so I've been hesitant about the whole financial side. It's hard to manage all of those budgets.

What did you look for in your intern?

I teach at California College of Arts and Crafts, so I get interns from there. It's helpful to have them as students because not only do I see their work but also their work habits, their attendance, how alert they are, how conscientious they are, if they take instruction, if they take suggestions easily, or if they're belligerent, and all those other factors.

Title: Speak Promo Card **Designer:** Martin Venezky **Client:** Speak Magazine **Photographer:** Martin Venezky **Typeface:** Sign System **Year:** 1996

Consulting for Fun & Profit

WALTER BERNARD
Principal, WBMG, New York City

How did you know so early on that you wanted to do publication design?

I liked magazines so much and I liked the fact that something got published. I liked the fact that if you worked there your name was on it. I liked reading magazines. And even though I didn't know anything about them, it seemed very romantic to me. So I wanted to work in a magazine. The first one was *Ingenue*. It actually was nice and it was fun. I learned a lot. It wasn't a subject I was all that interested in, but still it was fun. And it got printed. One of our illustrators was Andy Warhol. We used a lot of good people.

Why did you partner with Milton Glaser to start WBMG?

I started to get a lot of work setting up formats for the *Atlantic Monthly* and *AdWeek* and was consulting on various magazines. I did some work on *Inside Sports* and then *Fortune*. I was working crazy. Even though I had an office and hired assistants, I didn't know how to set up a business. I was doing the books, I was designing the magazines, finding people office space. I was making money, but I was also just spending it like water, just to do the job. In 1982 I was at *Fortune* for three months as design director to launch the first issue and look for an art director. While I was there, I got a call from Ben Bradley at the *Washington*

Title: The Crushing Power of Big Publishing **Designers/Creative Directors:** Walter Bernard, Milton Glaser **Publication:** The Nation Magazine **Client:** The Nation **Photographer:** Matthew Klein **Typefaces:** Aurora, Century Old Style **Year:** 1997

Title: Psychiatry's Depression **Designer/Creative Director:** Walter Bernard **Publication:** Time Magazine **Client:** Time, Inc. **Illustrator:** Robert Giusti **Typeface:** Franklin Gothic **Year:** 1979

Title: Livres d'Occasion **Designer:** Walter Bernard **Creative Director:** Jean Pierre Cliquet **Publication:** Lire Magazine **Illustrator:** Mirko Illic **Typeface:** Caslon **Year:** 1989

Title: The Fortune 500 **Designers:** Walter Bernard, Milton Glaser **Creative Director:** Margery Peters **Publication:** Fortune Magazine **Client:** Time Inc. **Typefaces:** Times Roman, Franklin Gothic **Year:** 1997

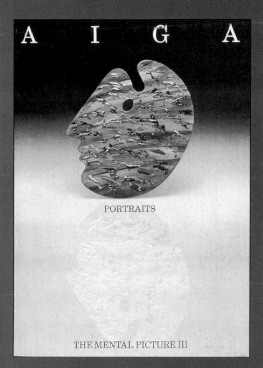

Post, about doing the *Washington Post Magazine*. It had been five years since I worked with Milton on *New York* magazine and we used to kid about how it was too bad that we weren't working together because we used to have a lot of fun doing magazines together. So when I got the *Washington Post*, Milton was also getting an inquiry from Sir James Goldsmith to do some magazines in France. And while Milton is very good at magazines, he has so much else going on that he doesn't have the patience to sit around, art-directing them and all that, so we formed a company together.

What is the most fulfilling aspect of your work?
I would have answered that question differently years ago, when the most satisfying thing was to design a magazine and actually have it come out. We're a little used to that now, so it's not as big a thrill. Now one of the the most satisfying things is really solving a magazine's problem and the other most satisfying part of my work is that I like the collaboration of working with smart editors. The least satisfying is endless meetings. When people come to us to redesign their magazines, they all have the same exact problem. The same things are happening to everybody and they think it's only happening to them.

How much of your time is devoted to design and art direction versus business matters?
We're small, so there isn't a lot of management. I do a lot in terms of getting new business. We don't sell, in the sense of going after things, but, on the other hand, there are a lot of meetings and inquiries that we follow up on. And we take calls and listen to people and sometimes it doesn't amount to anything. I would say that a third of my time is spent talking to people or speaking somewhere or doing something that is not a sales effort because we don't take our portfolio around, but it keeps our name out there.

Title: Portraits Catalog for AIGA Exhibit **Designer/Creative Director:** Walter Bernard **Client:** AIGA **Illustrator:** James McMullan **Photographer:** Roberto Broson **Typeface:** Century Expanded **Year:** 1997

Title: "He Can Still Save It!" **Designers/Creative Directors:** Walter Bernard, Milton Glaser **Publication:** ESPN Magazine **Client:** ESPN/Disney **Typeface:** Trade Gothic **Year:** 1997

Happy Accidents

Title: Jack Nicholson Cover
Designer/Creative Director:
Rhonda Rubenstein **Publication:** Smart **Photographer:**
Bonnie Schiffman **Typeface:**
Lucian **Year:** 1990

RHONDA RUBENSTEIN

Creative Director, *Mother Jones* Magazine,
San Francisco

You worked on *Smart*, the first magazine to be designed entirely on a Macintosh. What did you learn from this?
I had never worked on a computer before, so it was a whole new way of thinking about magazines and that had some influence on future work.

Do you feel that being ahead of the curve was an asset?
At the time, yes. That was definitely one of the advantages in going to my next job, *Esquire*; I had worked on a Macintosh and could help convert the magazine to desktop technology, but by 1991 a number of other designers in magazines were starting to use the Macintosh as well.

What are your thoughts on the computer and its effect on the design process?
There were times when more happy accidents occurred to combine type and images. For students, who have always used computers, it's not an issue. It would be like asking them, how does the X-Acto knife affect your work?

What was it like working at *Esquire*?
It was a pretty good time to be there; the magazine has definitely had its ups and downs over time. When I was there, we were still doing fairly experimental things. Some of the covers we did were definitely not as commercial as now. There was less pressure to follow the formula of a big face and lots of cover lines. There was more room for interpretation of story ideas, which was great for me as a designer.

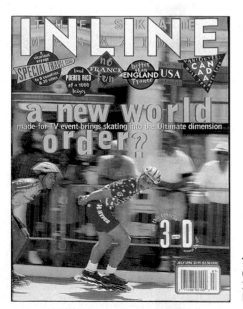

Title: Ultimate Inline Challenge Cover **Designer/
Creative Director:** Rhonda Rubenstein **Publication:**
Inline/Sports + Fitness Publishing **Photographer:**
Kris Ostness **Typeface:** Bell Gothic **Year:** 1996

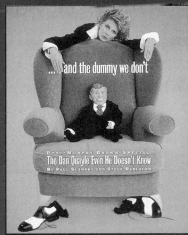

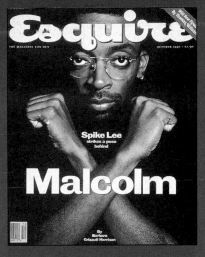

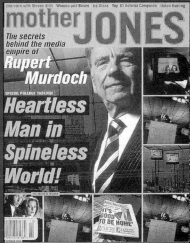

Is *Mother Jones* magazine very different from *Esquire*?
Mother Jones magazine is different from all the magazines I
worked for because it's run by the Foundation for National
Progress, an organization whose main goal is not necessarily making money. In that way they definitely try to be a magazine that is
doing something good. That's a very basic way of looking at it.
They are trying to make a positive social change. In the past, it's
been known for its muckraking stories on corruption in politics,
but it is also trying to look at other parts of society and figure out
better ways for people to live.

What is the most satisfying aspect of your job?
The most satisfying part of it is the ability to create new things,
to communicate new ideas that get published and seen by thousands of people. The least fulfilling aspect is seeing my ideas in
the trash bin or the recycling bin every month.

Have you ever felt the urge to move out of publication design?
When I had my own studio, I was doing other kinds of work besides
publication design. Probably half of it was editorial design and half
of it was Web sites, or I did some work on developments of CD-ROM,
some books, and I enjoyed that. I enjoyed the part about learning
the new technologies involved in producing Web sites. That was pretty exciting for a while. Then some of the limitations got to be rather
frustrating. There is something very accessible about publications in
that they get printed and they exist and you can carry them around
and you can throw them out if you want, but you can keep them for
years, and they don't change too much over time. You don't have the
problem where you go back two years later and find that you can't
open up the issue because you don't have the right software.

Title: Women We Love Cover **De-
signer/Creative Director:** Rhonda
Rubenstein **Publication:**
Esquire/Hearst Corporation **Photo-
grapher:** Peggy Sirota **Typeface:**
Bureau Grotesque **Year:** 1992

Title: Spike Lee **Designer/Creative
Director:** Rhonda Rubenstein **Publica-
tion:** Esquire/Hearst Corporation
Photographer: Frank Ockenfels III
Typeface: Bureau Grotesque **Year:**
1992

Title: Murdoch Media Cover (redesign
issue) **Designer/Creative Director:**
Rhonda Rubenstein **Publication:**
Mother Jones/Foundation for National
Progress **Photographers:** Amy Etra,
Nina Berman **Typeface:** Akzidenz
Grotesk **Year:** 1998

II. Corporate Design

THE GREAT PATRONS OF graphic design traditionally have been found among powerful businesspersons — for example, the Medici family of Renaissance Italy. Multinational corporations have the resources and wherewithal to fund interdisciplinary design and in many cases also to encourage progressive architecture, industrial, interior, and graphic design. Beginning in the 1950s, IBM, Westinghouse, Cummins Engine, General Dynamics, and Mobil, just to name a few of the biggest companies at that time, sponsored design programs that not only produced emblematic corporate identities but also modernized the very practice of corporate identity.

THE DISCIPLINE KNOWN as CI (corporate identity) began in the early twentieth century in Germany, where architect and industrial and graphic designer Peter Behrens developed the earliest inclusive, coordinated design system for the leading German electrical company, A.E.G. What Behrens did that no designer previously had done was develop a consistent design scheme consisting of standard typefaces, layouts, and colors, the application of which was governed by rules put forth in a design systems manual. This ensured a uniform approach to design regardless of who was designing the individual components of the corporate communications — catalogs, brochures, posters, instruction guides, etc. The touchstone of this identity was the logo or trademark — the three initials of the company designed in the form of a honeycomb — the typeface of which determined all other design forms. Behrens determined that a strong and consistent mark should be the anchor of any CI, and while such graphic identifiers were used in the past, never before was one so integral to the overall graphic system.

Since then many world-class identity systems have expressed a wide range of formal approaches, but they are almost always governed by the same fundamental concerns. For example, a corporate logo — which must identify the company clearly, instantaneously, and memorably — must be fairly reductive. In the nineteenth and early twentieth centuries, business trademarks were comparatively complex; like heraldic shields, different visual symbols were condensed into one square, circle, or triangle in order to illustrate the nature of the business or express some aspect of its history. The modern logo, as developed in Germany, was simplified to include only the initials of a company or abstracted into a kind of symbolic brand, that has a mnemonic effect (one associates the abstract form with the name of the business, which may or may not appear in conjunction with the mark itself).

Much has been written about the philosophy and psychology of logos and marks. Marks have value when associated with good companies and are valueless when attached to bad ones. The swastika is a case in point. Prior to its adoption as the Nazi party symbol in 1926 (and German national symbol in 1933) the swastika's history dated back to antiquity, when it signified good fortune. In the early twentieth century it was a very popular commercial mark used on scores of products. But once it was adopted by a heinous regime, it was inextricably wed to evil. The design of the swastika is simple, pure, and memorable, while its symbolic meaning is forever tainted.

The logo or trademark is the cornerstone of CI. The reason for developing a particular mark is often based on research into a company's mission and the synthesis of its ideals into a symbol or brand. The mark itself might be so abstract that no obvious connection can be made, but, simply, the imposed relationship between it and the company imbues it with meaning. The logo is usually the most charged design element of a company, sometimes inviolate, other times mutable, depending on the client's faith in the mark's symbolic power. Therefore, a logo or trademark might take a long or short time to develop and be accepted by the CEO, board of directors, management team, entrepreneur, or whomever else is empowered to make a final decision. Regardless of whether the company is large or small, the time it takes, from start to finish, to conclude the logo portion of the design process cannot be precisely projected; many rational and irrational concerns contribute to making logo design one of the most variable procedures. A logo must appeal to the client (and the public) on cognitive and emotional levels; it is not simply a graphic device to denote one business from another, but, like a national flag, a charged symbol of corporate philosophy. Therefore, it is treated as a kind of totem that does not come cheaply.

From In-House to Out-of-House

The corporate environment can offer invaluable experience. Working within conservative constraints contributes to professional discipline that will hold a designer in good stead, even if later one does more free-form work. Corporate experience from the inside is also a valuable credential when making the switch to the outside. Not all corporate work is done by in-house art departments. Quite a bit is commissioned to design firms that specialize in corporate communications, from public relations to environmental signage. In-house experience only contributes to networking capabilities but gives out-of-house designers a better understanding of what clients need.

Some designers present only one or two iterations of a logo; others bombard the client with many. While too many ideas might confuse a client, too few (unless the presenter has incredible self-confidence or charisma) may frustrate the client. Nevertheless, once the logo is decided upon, then designing the other elements of CI proceeds. This routinely includes the standards manual, which establishes the strictest do's and don'ts for the maintenance of the entire system, such as how, when, and where the logo will be used and what additional typefaces will represent the company. The manual further presents the grid, the invisible page architecture on which type and image is composed, which forms the infrastructure of any coordinated system. Grids are used for such quotidian items as stationery, business cards, mailing labels, hang tags, instruction manuals, etc. The manuals shows the permitted type sizes, weights, and colors.

A complete CI system is usually contracted to a consulting or external design firm working in conjunction with the internal design department of a particular company. These CI specialists are focused on every detail of the overall system infrastructure and consult with corporate leaders on its applications. The in-house designers strictly follow the manual and other guidelines to produce the lion's share of corporate materials — from business cards to annual reports, from newsletters to packages. Often, however, external design firms are commissioned to produce special components of the corporate communications program, such as advertising, promotion, and, notably, the annual report, which is a corporation's primary outreach to its stockholders. The annual report is often an elaborate piece of design and production that, while following CI system guidelines, is usually more conceptually elaborate. Because it is meant to stand out among the standard communications of a company, it is farmed out to design firms that specialize in conceptual thinking, visual creativity (smart and stylish photography and illustration), and high-end printing.

An internal (or in-house) corporate design department is referred to variously as the art department, the design department, and, frequently, the corporate communications department, among the most common names. A company that views design as integral to its success may also support an even more ambitious design laboratory or design center as a hothouse of experimentation in the service of its core mission. Entry- or junior-level designers are hired for these departments and labs based on the quality of their school portfolios; in-house design departments like to hire juniors immediately out of the better undergraduate and graduate design departments. Senior designers and design managers (art directors and design directors) are often hired through job placement services. Although it is possible to get a job in the corporate sector through referrals or recommendations, headhunters are often called upon to search for executive-level employees.

CI is not a design discipline that can be picked up on your own or acquired by osmosis. While a CI designer must not be void of imagination or intuition, knowing the procedures, rules, and standards of the profession is a prime requisite. Most American art and design schools do not provide exclusive majors in CI, but they do provide courses that focus on logo design and systems maintenance. Those who want the security of the corporate environment should pursue academic programs that focus on CI in the broadest sense. The portfolio that results from such a program is the foot in the door of an in-house art department. From then on learning the job from the inside is the most beneficial.

The Optimum Portfolio

Entry Level

School assignments should exhibit a well-rounded sense of design in general — typography, logo/trademarks, publications, posters. This is one area to show a broad range of talents as well as the ability to work within formulas. Present a balance of free-form and strictly formulated work. Do not include published pieces, even if you have them, if they are not of a high standard. A good student assignment is better than a bad professional one.

Contents

Ten to twenty samples:

a. Letterheads, to show both trademark design and application
b. Brochures with covers and interiors displayed
c. Conventional and unconventional typography
d. Miscellaneous school assignments showing a range of imaginative solutions

Junior/Senior Designer

Portfolios must include a large percentage of printed or fabricated three-dimensional work. The junior may retain a few of the better school assignments, but the senior should have only professional work. Both junior and senior should exhibit a keen ability to solve design problems and to develop design systems.

Contents

Fifteen to twenty-five samples:

a. Complete annual reports (or any part that was worked on)
b. Logo/trademarks (including letterheads and design guides)
c. Newsletters, in-house publications, and other collateral materials
d. Special presentation kits
e. Exhibition or display work
f. Audiovisual presentations for corporate meetings (if available)
g. Web pages (if available)

Format

35mm slides (in slide tray), 4×5 transparencies, dry-mounted proofs (lamination preferable), entire publications, digital work on CD-ROM or Zip disk.

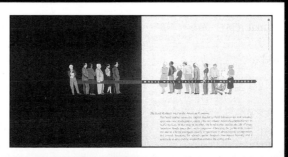

Title: Bond Brochure
Designer/Creative Director: David Barnett **Company:** The Barnett Group **Client:** PSA: The Bond Market Trade Association **Illustrator:** Guy Billout **Typefaces:** Berkeley, Meta **Year:** 1997

How Massimo Vignelli Influenced Me

Massimo Vignelli, a preeminent designer, founded Unimark, one of the early design firms devoted to corporate communications, and, later, Vignelli Associates. Some of today's leading designers worked for him. Here they talk about the impact he made on their work:

"I worked for Massimo for ten years. It was my first job out of school. Massimo was like a father to me. I learned three things:

1. Your work matters. Have a point of view and be passionate about it.

2. Although graphic design is ephemeral, you can never go wrong by striving for timelessness.

3. When in doubt, make something really big.

He never said these things to me exactly, but this is what I learned."

—**Michael Bierut, Pentagram, New York**

"Massimo has a perpetual passion for design and he has always been amazingly accessible, energetically engaging in discussion with anyone who shares his enthusiasm."

—**Katherine McCoy, McCoy and McCoy, Buena Vista, CO**

"After all these years, I still have Massimo's illustrated recipe for *Spaghetti Al (Presi) dente*, where he recommends cutting up the cheeses in little pieces about the size of 36 points uppercase letter *H*. He was always the consummate designer, even down to his attention to cheese size."

—**Tamar Cohen, Slatoff + Cohen, New York**

"Massimo is supremely confident in his own vision. He taught me to be clear, concise, and direct. He was and is intelligent, with a keen ability to quickly distill a problem. I'm grateful to have him as a teacher, model, and friend."

—**Michael Donovan, Donovan & Greene, New York**

"Vignelli's guiding dictum, 'Discipline, Appropriateness, and Ambiguity,' has influenced me continually in all my creative endeavors."

—**Allesandro Franchini, Crate and Barrel, Chicago**

Title: Lipton Teahouse **Project Team:** Nancye Green, Andrew Drews, Paul Soulellis, Vanessa Ryan, John Chu, Glennys Anglada, Thomas Thompson **Company:** Donovan & Green **Client:** Thomas J. Lipton Company

The Best of Times

Title: Barneys (Packaging Design System) **Designers:** Julie Riefler, Jenny Barry **Creative Director/Art Director:** Nancye Green **Company:** Donovan & Green **Client:** Barneys New York

MICHAEL DONOVAN
President, Donovan & Green, New York City

What constitutes the best of times at a corporate design firm?
A good work environment is one where everyone, myself included, is challenged and is happy in the challenge, where there is a real esprit de corps and a shared enthusiasm not only for whatever you're working on but for what the people around you are working on. I love it when we're really cooking on all twelve cylinders and people are working late and happy. I find that the most exhilarating situation in the world. It's particularly good when you have a client that is right in there with you. Sometimes you're working hard and doing a great job and the client takes it for granted. At other times you have an appreciative client and, of course, you work even harder, and everyone tries to solve the problem with the same enthusiasm. That's so cool.

And the worst?
If somebody says, "Here's your purchase order number. Mail in the solution." Frankly, I don't want to do the job if I feel like we can't make a difference and if the client isn't involved. I understand the situation at some large corporations where they're just trying to get the job done, but there is a big difference between just doing something and having people really engage across the board.

How long have you been in the business?
You really want to know? Probably about thirty years. I still love it and I'm still very enthusiastic and I'm still very challenged by it. But I don't get so worked up facing the problems. I have a cer-

Title: Corning (Exhibition) **Project Team:** Michael Donovan, Allen Wilpon **Company:** Donovan & Green **Client:** Corning Incorporated

Title: Lipton Teahouse **Project Team:** Nancye Green, Andrew Drews, Paul Soulellis, Vanessa Ryan, John Chu, Glennys Anglada, Thomas Thompson **Company:** Donovan & Green **Client:** Thomas J. Lipton Company

tain amount of confidence that we're going to solve this issue: We solved it before, we're going to solve this one. We've worked before with difficult clients — or with clients in difficult situations, to be diplomatic.

Do you think design is a good business, an ethical business?
Oh yes, I think so. By and large, people work very hard. Clients have historically gotten more than they've paid for, partially because people are always working for the challenge or for the kudos or because they need the experience. And, blessedly, there are large clients that recognize that they need experienced design firms that have done this for a while because their issues are big and important.

What qualities do you look for when you hire designers?
We look for intelligent people who have good skills both creatively and with people. Even though we have a large firm, we have a pretty flat organization. There isn't a triangulated structure where there's one creative person at the top and then a couple of assistants and then a whole bunch of production people at the bottom. The people here have a lot of personal interaction with the client, along with the partner or principal. I think it's a very positive environment. We don't have a lot of attrition as a result. So we have a tendency to hire carefully, and people have a tendency to stay a long time.

An Eclectic Mix

NANCYE GREEN
Chairman, Donovan & Green, New York City

What do you do, and what kind of business do you have?
My business is an eclectic mixture of professionals and projects. We started with the point of view that we wanted to do it all for a given client, but we ended up doing different things for different clients, because it was very hard for clients to understand how a person who did graphics could also do architecture. So we started Donovan & Green doing graphic design, exhibition design, interior design — showrooms and stuff like that — and we built our firm based on the principle that we wanted to tackle design projects and design problems irrespective of discipline.

Title: Lipton Teahouse **Project Team:** Nancye Green, Andrew Drews, Paul Soulellis, Vanessa Ryan, John Chu, Glennys Anglada, Thomas Thompson **Company:** Donovan & Green **Client:** Thomas J. Lipton Company

Have you accomplished that? Do you do almost everything?
Absolutely. We do almost everything. We have a firm of about fifty people, and the leadership is about a half-dozen people who represent fields from architecture and planning through graphic design. We were recently acquired by CKS, a very large company with 350 employees — a large New York office, eight offices in Europe — that does branding, strategy, graphic design — very high-level creative work. We do the environmental stuff in their projects. They do no environmental work. We are a completely separate brand from them but we have access to all their technology, and we are joint-venturing projects where technology has a major role to play and they are providing that aspect of it.

So early on, you decided to stay away from specializing?
Yes. Through a sorting-out process, I began to realize that my greatest gift was my ability to see the big picture and solve problems and set directions — in a sense, to be an art director — to really guide and critique and react to creative people and give them room to do what they did best. That's what I ended up doing.

What is the most satisfying aspect of your job? And the least?
I love thinking. Thinking is the best part. The beginnings of projects are the most exciting; all things are possible, and it's unclear what is going to happen. One has to sort through a lot to decide what this beast is. I find that stimulating and exciting. I love going through this process with other smart people. The other exciting part is how much I've learned about other businesses and industries. I feel like I'm paid to be highly informed, and I think that is really a gift. Think of all the people who sit and have to do one thing over and over and over at a manual job or even an office job. I get a chance to go out and learn something new every day. That is the upside, and that is why I love doing what I do. As for the least satisfying part, there are so many things, I don't know where to begin. I hate money. I hate budgets. I hate going over budget. I hate trying to stay on budget. I hate that part of it.

Title: Ronald Reagan Presidential Library (Public Exhibition) **Project Team:** Nancye Green, Michael Donovan, Susan Berman, Susan Myers, Stuart Silver, Steve Brosnahan, Alan Ford, Gabrielle Goodman, Patrick Nolan, Leslie Nowinski, Alexis, Siroc, Sheila Szcepaniak, Allen Wilpon **Company:** Donovan & Green **Client:** Ronald Reagan Presidential Foundation **Date Opened:** November 1991

How much of your time is devoted to design and art direction versus business matters?
Given what I do and how I do it, I'm just not a detail person. I care deeply about details and I'm a perfectionist, but I'm not the person to execute them. That's why I have to have a lot of good people around me. So what I do all the time is work as a broad thinker and as a person who brings focus to things and reacts to what I see. I also do that in dealing with my business and dealing with my clients. But I spend very little of my time doing administrative stuff. That is the real advantage of having a large firm: You can do what you want to do. In a smaller firm, there is usually more demand on you to deal with more things.

The Corporate Sphere

Title: Saks Fifth Avenue Annual Report 1996 **Designer:** Yu Mei Tam **Creative Director:** Kent Hunter **Company:** Frankfurt Balkind **Client:** Saks Fifth Avenue **Photographer:** Torkil Gudnason **Year:** 1997

Title: The Tech Museum Logo **Designer:** Stephen Fabrizio **Creative Director:** Kent Hunter **Company:** Frankfurt Balkind **Client:** The Tech Museum of Innovation **Year:** 1998

KENT HUNTER
Executive Creative Director, Frankfurt Balkind, New York City

How did you decide to go into corporate design?
Annual reports have always been a tangible form of design that I've enjoyed. They have high production values, and people were doing interesting work with annual reports when I was narrowing my focus and specializing. But I still consider myself a generalist. At Frankfurt Balkind we do everything from identity programs to annual reports to advertising to Web sites. What attracted me into the design profession is its breadth: You can design a showroom one day and an annual report or an album cover the next. I've always tried to be in a line that has variety in its day-to-day work.

What's the most fulfilling part of your job?
I think it's holding the piece in my hands after I've finished it — after all the long hours and the hard work — and it is this tangible thing that I can be proud of.

What's the least?
Holding that piece after it comes back from the printer and seeing everything that's wrong with it.

During a typical day, how much of your time is devoted to design and art direction versus business matters?
Unfortunately, graphic design is a service business, and a lot of what we do is deal with clients and deal with business matters and business issues. I see my role, as executive creative director here, is to hire great people and let them do what they do while directing, steering, producing the work so that the quality level is there and the thinking strategy is there. It's very much a team approach, but, unfortunately, I'm more the director than the cameraman.

Is it important that your firm have a distinct look?

No. As a firm, we do not have a look or a style. What we hope is common to our work is intelligence and a strategy and that the execution and the design of each piece is appropriate for the client and the strategy. Great people have a specific personal style, but they become designer brands, if you will. You go to that designer for that look. The integrated communication work we're doing for corporations is about the client more than it is about us. We feel like we shouldn't have a personal look. In certain categories of design, such as paper promotions and product design, certainly it's all about creating a look, and there are people who have done that very successfully. In the history of graphic design, as young as it is, there have always been people like Milton Glaser and Seymour Chwast, with great looks, who have become designer brands.

What do you look for in designers?

We look for brains rather than portfolio — brains over style. I want people who can communicate their ideas to me. The portfolio has to communicate as well as the person. The best designers are able to communicate their ideas to the client, first of all, and then do the work and communicate to the general public or whoever the audience is. If a student cannot express what the piece is about, what the thinking behind it was, then I find it difficult to see that person growing here. On the other hand, I think after you graduate that you're ready to learn. Your first job is a real learning experience, so what we've done for the past few years is hire two or three people from school as junior designers.

Title: Children's Hope Foundation Benefit Poster **Designer/Creative Director:** Kent Hunter **Company:** Frankfurt Balkind **Client:** Children's Hope Foundation **Photographer:** Ashton Worthington **Year:** 1998

Title: Pantone "Marigold" Ad **Designers:** Robert Wong, Kin Yuen **Creative Director:** Kent Hunter **Company:** Frankfurt Balkind **Client:** Pantone **Photographer:** Jordan Donner **Year:** 1996

Title: "Graphics - 2 - Go" Poster **Designer/Creative Director:** Kent Hunter **Company:** Frankfurt Balkind **Client:** Columbus (Ohio) Society of Communication Arts **Photographer:** Deena Delzotto **Typeface:** Trixie **Year:** 1997

The Competitive Market

Title: Skadden **Designer:** Carla Miller **Creative Director:** Ken Carbone **Company:** CSA — The Carbone Smolan Agency **Client:** Skadden Arps Slate Meagher & Flom **Photographer:** Erica Frudenstein **Year:** 1998

LESLIE SMOLAN
Principal, CSA — The Carbone Smolan Agency, New York City

What made you launch your own business? What kind of business is it?

I come from a family of entrepreneurs, so business is in my blood. Initially, I took a job at an annual report house in New York City but quickly left to start my own freelance business in Philadelphia. A year later I got a call from Ken Carbone, who had recently established a New York office for Gottschalk and Ash and was looking for a strong designer to collaborate with. When Fritz Gottschalk decided to return to Switzerland in 1980 we bought Gottschalk, and Ken and I have been together ever since. Our goal was to be design generalists — to be able to work on all media, and all industries. Twenty years later, we've managed to maintain a business that represents a full range of design disciplines: branding and corporate identity, marketing communications, architectural graphics, book publishing, packaging, product design, exhibits, and interactive design. Some of our work has now started to extend to video and advertising.

Has the business changed since you began?

In today's competitive environment, clients are no longer willing to make an investment in educating you about their business. They expect you to come to a project with a depth of expertise in their business and your design application. As a result, we have recently reorganized our business around four major business segments — luxury goods, children's products and services, financial services, and media and entertainment — and brought on senior marketing talent to provide an even greater internal resource for clients. This, coupled with our breadth of experience in all areas of design, has kept us a viable competitor as many design organizations grow to compete with both Web groups and advertising agencies.

Title: Putnam Investments **Creative Director:** Leslie Smolan **Company:** CSA — The Carbone Smolan Agency **Client:** Putnam Investments **Photographer:** John Still **Year:** 1993

MULTNOMAH FALLS

...collaboration in recent

...ent — how much they
...y are in their own role.

...wth that requires new

...ster rate. Technology has
...believe it will continue to
...e to learn new things every
...esting career.

...r as an employee?
...evel of intelligence and
...d with strong design aes-
...to be someone I enjoy
...think and see things in a

Title: NWQ **Designer:** John Nishimoto
Creative Director: Leslie Smolan **Company:**
CSA — The Carbone Smolan Agency **Client:**
NWQ Investment Management Company
Photographer: Dan Winters (brochure)
Typefaces: OCKB, OCRA, Bell Gothic, Letter
Gothic, Trixie

Title: PBS - The
Business Channel
Designer: Janette
Eusebio **Creative
Director:** Laurel
Shoemaker **Company:**
CSA — The Carbone
Smolan Agency
Client: PBS — The
Business Channel
Photographer: Doug
Menuez **Typeface:**
Thesis **Year:** 1998

Title: The Image Bank **Designer:**
Carla Miller **Creative Director:** Ken
Carbone **Company:** CSA — The
Carbone Smolan Agency **Client:** The
Image Bank **Typeface:** Thesis **Year:**
1998

It's the Budget, Stupid!

GREG SAMATA
Principal, SamataMason, West Dundee, Illinois

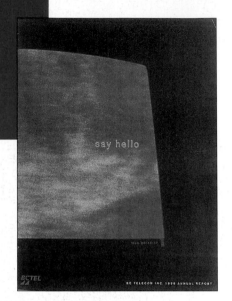

Title: BC Telecom 1996 Annual Report **Designers:** Dave Mason, Pamela Lee **Creative Directors:** Dave Mason, John Van Dyke **Company:** SamataMason **Client:** BC Telecom **Photographers:** John Kenny, Victor John Penner **Typefaces:** Bembo, AG Old Face **Year:** 1997

How did you decide to specialize in corporate work?
Pat, my wife and partner, and I knew that we needed to focus on an area of the business that was properly funded so that we could make a living. That was twenty-five years ago, and from the early days we focused on corporate identity and annual reports because most companies would allocate larger budgets for these types of projects.

Has there been a major influence on your design work?
Too many to document: designers, filmmakers, typographers, writers, photographers, musicians, architects, and more. John Heinrich, one of Mies's students who later went on to design and build Lakepoint Tower on Chicago's lakefront, was a driving influence and social misfit extraordinaire. Ralph Andre — one of my first clients and, later, best friends — became my mentor in marketing and great wine. My father and mother put me to work in the family restaurant when I was eight years old. My Great-Uncle Christ,

Title: Swiss Army Brands 1997 Annual Report **Designers:** Dave Mason, Pamela Lee **Creative Director:** Dave Mason **Company:** SamataMason **Client:** Swiss Army Brands **Photographers:** Victor John Penner **Typeface:** Neu Helvetica **Year:** 1998

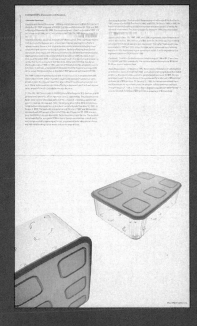

when I was fifteen years old, preached to me day in and day out that I must "leave the mark of my time." Saul Bass, who for years preceded me at just about every client I got in my early development, to me was everything good about the business. And many more. Most influences were personal relationships that became one part of a complex career path.

Have technological advancements affected your work?
What hasn't changed? Technology has allowed us the opportunity to expand our discipline and further our capacity as creative, communicating individuals. We are now typographers, filmmakers, software developers, Internet providers, songwriters, and animators, and have an unlimited capacity to put our imprint on every area of the media world. That is really exciting and a reason to get up in the morning. Has our worked changed? I hope not. If the typewriter never made anyone a better writer, a computer won't make us better designers. It is my determination to make sure the technology does not take the place of a good idea.

Title: Tupperware Corporation 1997 Annual Report **Designer:** Joe Baran **Creative Director:** Greg Samata **Company:** SamataMason **Client:** Tupperware Corporation **Photographers:** Mark Norberg, Victor John Penner **Typeface:** Univers Condensed and Bold **Year:** 1998

Title: The Florsheim Shoe Company 1997 Annual Report **Designers:** Dave Mason, Greg Samata, Brian Ehlers **Creative Director:** Greg Samata **Company:** SamataMason **Client:** Florsheim Group **Photographers:** Sandro, Victor John Penner **Typeface:** Clarendon **Year:** 1998

"I Don't Design Anymore"

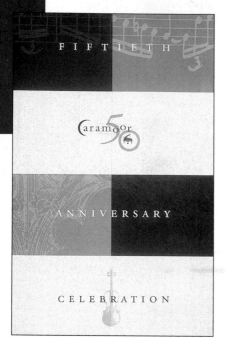

Title: Caramoor: 50 Years of Music **Designers:** David Barnett, Jeau De Angelis **Creative Directors:** David and Dennis Barnett **Company:** The Barnett Group **Client:** Caramoor Center for Music and the Arts **Typeface:** Garamond **Year:** 1996

Title: Public Issues **Designers:** David Barnett, Jade Lee **Creative Directors:** David Barnett, Jade Lee **Company:** The Barnett Group **Client:** MBIA (Municipal Bond Investors Assurance Company) **Typefaces:** Garamond, California, News Gothic **Year:** 1996

DENNIS BARNETT

Creative Director, The Barnett Group, New York City

As creative director of your firm, how involved are you in the design?

Well, I don't design anymore. When I first began in the business, I was a graphic designer. I had different staff jobs for about eight years, and after being fired from my last one, I decided to run the business and art-direct, which is what I do now. As the creative director of the firm, I come up with a lot of the concepts with the clients and I direct the designers, and that's my job. I never liked detail work, never had the patience for it.

What kind of clients do you have and what kind of design work you do?

Our clients are Fortune 200 — very top names. We specialize in corporate publications, marketing, and corporate identity.

How did you get to the point where you focused only on those areas?

I think we got stereotyped after a while. Dave, my brother, and I began to do museum book design. We did a lot of things for the Metropolitan Museum of Art, then more museum work. I tried to build a retainer-type business. I never wanted to become a project design firm; that scared the hell out of me.

You mean one-time deals?

One time, and you pray to get another one. I never wanted that. With a publication, you know it's going to happen again in a couple of months. So that's the way I built the business: I went after things that had regular frequencies. Once we had that as a base and we could afford to run a business behind it, we could then go after the one-shots, after the projects, and that's really the way we evolved.

What role does style play in your work?

I think a corporation needs an image. I think that a design firm needs an image. We don't impose a style on a client. Some design firms do that; they have a style and they sell it, and after three or four years they may be out of business. I think our niche is animated publication design. Even though we do work for very stodgy, very conservative corporations, they don't come to us for institutional-looking work. We do things — we call it layered design — where we know that a reader will not read the material unless he's teased into it, so we layer the design through the use of really great typography, sidebars, callouts, great photography, and illustration. You get the idea of an article before you read it and then get into reading it. That's where we differ from the more conservative firms. Clients come to us for more animated, energetic design work.

Most of your clients come from the corporate side. Do they understand and appreciate graphic design?

Our clients are mostly marketing directors, corporate communication directors, human affairs directors, editors, and publishers. This may sound arrogant, and I don't mean it to, but I don't like to work for art directors. I like to work directly for the clients. I think they appreciate us more than they appreciate design. They might not understand the design or what goes into it, but they understand what we're doing for them.

What is the most satisfying aspect of your job? And the least?

The most satisfying aspect of it? Solving a problem, whatever it takes, whether it's a concept or how to execute that concept, or how to package something. Coming up with the idea that works, that has lasting value. That's the most satisfying thing to me. Winning an account is extremely satisfying to me — not as a business thing, but as someone's acceptance of our work, especially if it's a bright person — a type that comes along more rarely these days. The least gratifying? Working with inexperienced clients. That's what I can't stand, having to educate them when they don't understand at all. I don't mind educating a client — I think that's part of my job — but at least respect what I'm saying. If we don't get respect, that really annoys me.

Title: Public Issues Designers: David Barnett, Jade Lee Creative Directors: David Barnett, Jade Lee Company: The Barnett Group Client: MBIA (Municipal Bond Investors Assurance Company) Typefaces: Garamond, California, News Gothic Year: 1996

Title: Inside Track Designer: David Barnett Creative Directors: David and Dennis Barnett Company: The Barnett Group Client: KPMG Peat Marwick Illustrator: Coco Masuda Typefaces: Times Roman, Univers Year: 1994

The Art of Involvement

Title: Steve Goodman Poster
Designers: Ken Fox, Fletcher Martin **Creative Director:** Dana Arnett **Client:** Old Town School of Folk Music **Photographer:** Goodman Archives **Typeface:** HTF Champion **Year:** 1997

DANA ARNETT

Partner, VSA Partners, Chicago, Illinois

What kind of work are you doing at VSA Partners?
We are gravitating toward what I would term *integrated marketing*. We still do a lot of traditional print communication, but about 40 percent of our work now is in the area of brand marketing, brand positioning, licensing products, and retail. We are even into event planning, whether it's a Harley rally or some large stage program for Potlatch Paper, which are clients of ours. Design today has a much bigger definition and a much more strategic activity.

What do you look for when hiring designers?
Generally, we're fortunate to be at a level where a lot of people are attracted to the work of the office, but it's still hard to find talented people. It's always been hard because our standards are high and we look for the rounded individual. Resumes don't carry a lot of weight. They are important and we need them as a level set, but when the person actually arrives for the meeting, if she doesn't have verbal skills, we nix her immediately. Applicants also have to present a portfolio that tells me that they are not sloppy. Most importantly, their design has to be absolutely arresting. We still give the most weight to solution-oriented work that's expressed in a powerful way. It does no good for us to see a book jacket if all that was solved were colors and the texture of the paper.

Do you hire interns?
We have two to three interns every summer. It's important that an intern learn how the production process works. By the nature of our structure, they get to see how teams work and how work is concep-

Title: Potlatch McCoy Logo **Designer:** Jason Eplawy **Creative Director:** Dana Arnett **Client:** Potlatch Corporation, Minnesota Pulp and Paper Division **Illustrator:** Jason Eplawy **Year:** 1997

tualized, and if there's time and room for their involvement on that side, we utilize them. I would say once every couple of years someone comes along who is good enough to contribute on a conceptual level, but what they really need to learn is the mechanics at that stage. We all had to cut our teeth. It is important for any young person to know that in this office at least, you don't walk right in and start designing your first day. As an intern, you walk in and you learn the mechanics and procedures of the practice.

How would you describe a good work environment?
One that always allows open participation in the process. We've kept a open environment where point of view is as important to success as getting here on time and getting projects done. I believe that if you've made a decision to hire somebody, you can't just slot them. You have to give them enough open ground when they start so that you can discover, as well as they can, where they are going to fit in and contribute. Our teams are set up so that there's very little rank. It's more like you bring as much as you can and are prepared and smart when you bring what you've got.

Title: Life/If Poster
Designer: Ken Fox
Creative Director: Dana Arnett **Client:** Diffa (Design Industries for AIDS Foundation)
Year: 1995

Title: Harley Davidson Eaglethon Poster
Designer: Dan Kraemer
Creative Director: Curt Schreiber **Clients:** Harley-Davidson and Muscular Dystrophy Association/copyright by Quadrillion Publishing
Typeface: Champion Gothic **Year:** 1997

Title: Tech Weenie **Designer:** Fletcher Martin **Creative Director:** Dana Arnett **Client:** Type Directors Club **Illustrator:** Max Cannon **Typeface:** Helvetica Condensed **Year:** 1997

III. Book Design

THE PUBLISHING industry is a major employer of graphic designers. Publishers use design to package and sell their merchandise, and while it may seem crass to discuss books as products, this is exactly how they are conceived and marketed. Despite the cultural significance of books, even the finest literature is nothing more than pages of worthless pulp until it is packaged in a form that attracts readers. It is the book designer's job to cast the text and images in an accessible and pleasing manner; it is the book jacket designer's job to create an alluring wrapper. Like any supermarket product, the jacket must attract the customer's attention and impart a message. Certainly, book and book jacket designers have more creative license than most food and hardware package designers, but the goal is the same: to move a product off the shelves.

THE BOOK design profession is divided into two basic categories — book interior and book jacket — that have a number of subsets. These two disciplines are traditionally separate but, depending on the nature of the publishing company, the roles can intersect. The book designer is responsible for the interior design of most textbooks (books with few or no pictures, such as novels and biographies). The jacket designer is responsible for the hardcover dustjacket, paperback cover, or paper-over-boards wrapper.

When introduced in the early nineteenth century, book jackets were unadorned protective coverings for leather book bindings. Later in the century, jackets were used as advertisements, routinely removed and discarded after purchase. Today, illustrated and typographic jackets are integral to the overall allure of a book and intensely scrutinized by marketing departments. Only purists still denounce book jackets as unwanted appendages. Indeed, most designers who seek jobs in publishing want to become jacket designers.

Book designers are typographers who understand the nuances of type and are skilled at presenting a page in the most elegant and accessible form possible. Interior design is a less glamorous job than jacket design, but without this design discipline a book would be anarchic at best. In addition to interior pages, book designers design bindings or casings (cover and spine) as well as endpapers (the decorative paper pasted inside the cover of some hardcover books). Book designers must also be skilled at production because a large part of type's success is how well it is set and printed. This cannot be learned from a manual — merely flowing type into a QuarkXPress template does not make a good book designer — but rather considerable study and often intense apprenticeship is needed to hone the designer's aesthetic sensibilities.

In some publishing houses, this job division is as it was a hundred years ago — the interior design and the jacket design have little relationship to each other. In other houses, the work intersects either from the outset or somewhere during the process. Increasingly, more nonfiction visual books are designed as total packages, with one designer responsible for the entire design. The book in your hands — the paperback cover and interior pages — was designed by one individual to ensure its cohesiveness.

Before discussing the roles of designers in the book industry, it is useful to explain the genres of publishing, for each requires a different kind of design. Industry sectors are conventionally categorized as follows: *trade* or *commercial*, which produces fiction and nonfiction books aimed at a general audience; *professional*, which caters its products to the specific needs of professional groups; *textbook*, which produces educational books for school or course work. Within these basic categories publishers might specialize in areas such as pop fiction, military biography, graphic design how-to books, etc. Perhaps the

Separation of Book and Jacket

Like church and state, there has long been a distinction between interior book design and cover design. Until recently, it was rare that the designer of one would cross into the other's territory. The reason: The book (cover, spine, endpapers, and text) was the essential entity; the jacket (the dust cover or wrapper) was advertising that sold the entity. Usually, the cover image and typography bore no relation to the interior typography — and, in some cases, the cover illustration exaggerated the plot and misled the reader.

Book designers come from a proud tradition of craftspersons with roots in the sixteenth century. The jacket designer is not only a johnny-come-lately (illustrated jackets did not exist until the 1900s) but is presumed to answer to a different set of qualitative standards. Today, the forms are increasingly merging. Interior book designers are a little less rigid in this distinction and jacket designers are more general in their skills and talents. Designers who do both are more common in publishing houses and useful to publishers.

largest publishing genre, however, is *mass-market paperback* — cheaply produced novels (romances, mysteries, science fiction, Westerns, etc.) that are marketed not just in bookstores but also in airports, drugstores, supermarkets, etc.

Marketing Schmarketing

Book publishing is a product-oriented industry and book jackets are the first line of persuasion in the attempt to win over the consumer. Therefore, jackets are often closely scrutinized by marketing departments and sales representatives. Don't think that just because you have designed a visually resplendent jacket that it will get printed. Sometimes the most original designs are deemed unsalable by individuals who know nothing about design but do know what sells. The constant complaints emanating from art directors, staff, and freelance designers include "The marketing people say the author's name is too small," "The marketing people say the color pink won't sell," "The marketing people say they can't see the image from twenty feet away." For the young jacket designer, the first encounter with marketing may be a shock. Often a savvy art director can save or salvage a good cover, but just as often the best work never sees the light of day. In this genre, however, there is always the next project.

Some publishers are known for highbrow content, others for middle- or lowbrow content. Some publishers are enormous conglomerates that release hundreds of titles in a season (usually fall, winter, and spring); others are comparatively small proprietorships with a limited number of books.

The approaches to graphic design used by different publishing enterprises are as different as the books they produce. Some publishers have a tradition of fine classical typography; others promote contemporary sensibilities, and a number do not have any house style or overarching design philosophy at all. Some publishers doggedly follow conventions imposed on their specific genre, while others are more inventive. When seeking employment in a publishing house art department, be familiar with the house's method (or lack thereof) in order to tailor your portfolio accordingly.

There are many ways to become involved in book design. The two most common are as in-house or freelance designers.

A publishing house art department includes a *creative director* or *art director* who manages other designers and also designs book jackets and interiors. In some houses there are separate art directors for interiors and jackets; in others, one art director manages both. In some publishing houses design services come under the aegis of the production department, where a production manager is responsible; in others the production manager only oversees prepress production. An average art department may employ two or more senior designers and two or more juniors. The seniors design the more critical books on a list. The juniors assist them and may design a few projects as well. At small publishers, the designers may also handle the production — the oversight of printers, color separators, typesetters, etc.

The larger trade publishing houses, such as

Making Book

Bookmaking is not as illicit an activity as it sounds — rather, it is a venerable craft that dates back centuries. Even with the computer as their tool, many interior book designers follow the same typographic traditions as the bookmakers of earlier centuries. Although technology and commerce have conspired to alter the book industry, one of the common methods of becoming a book designer is to produce handmade books in school, workshops, or on one's own. Learning typesetting (often by hand), bookbinding, and papermaking may seem somewhat arcane in this digital world, but the tactility of the process can inspire even the desktop practitioner to explore book design and production. While you should know the latest techniques, never underestimate the importance of learning about the past.

Knopf, Simon and Schuster, and Farrar Straus and Giroux, can release as many as 150 or more titles per season, each requiring interior and jacket design. In instances where the art director and staff designers cannot handle the workload, or the art director requires a unique or special approach, freelance designers are commissioned. The freelancer may be the principal or an employee of a design firm or studio or an independent contractor who specializes in book design. Most publishing houses maintain an expanding stable of freelancers, who are selected according to the appropriateness of their individual illustrative or typographic style. To become a freelancer specializing in book design, it is necessary to either show a portfolio or send a promotional mailer (each with mostly book-related work) to the art director. On average, almost 50 percent of all trade book interiors and jackets are done by freelancers. In fact, many smaller trade book publishers (who average between five and twenty books per list) use only freelancers.

Designers may be retained for a fixed number of books or seasons or hired on a book-by-book basis. It is therefore useful for freelancers to interview at or send promotional mailers to the full spectrum of large and small companies.

Mass-market paperback houses often produce three times as many books as the average trade publisher, usually on a monthly or bimonthly frequency. Their book covers are invariably more hard-sell than those of trade books, with screaming titles, authors names set large and in garish colors or metallic embossing, and seductive illustrations that leave little to the imagination. Most paperback art departments employ a few staff designers responsible for a specific number of covers on a list. Staff production persons routinely handle the interiors, which follow a more or less strict typographic format. Paperback designers often commission freelance illustrators to render cover illustrations and sometimes the lettering as well. Realistic or narrative paintings, mood photographs, and custom lettering are the

Title: The Boys of My Youth **Designer:** Barbara de Wilde **Creative Director:** Michael Kaye **Publisher:** Little Brown **Client:** The New York Times **Photographer:** Michael Wilson **Typefaces:** Vag Rounded, Hand-drawn **Year:** 1997

usual design components for mass-market paperbacks, and specialists in these areas are often in demand for fairly fast turnaround work. Again, a stable of freelancers is retained for this work. To be considered, your portfolio should show your understanding for and talent in this distinct publishing genre.

Publishing houses that produce professional, textbook, and subspecialty books more often than not use in-house art departments for the majority of design and production work. On the whole, these houses produce less adventuresome (creative) products but rather follow house styles and standards developed over time. For the neophyte, working in this environment offers considerable experience and perhaps an interesting assignment or two per season, but most of the work is fairly routine.

One other sector of publishing, book packaging, has exerted a strong influence on design. Book packagers are independent producers of books and related products who sell complete packages — text, illustration, design, and sometimes printed books — to publishers and distributors. Increasingly, large publishing houses purchase a certain number of book packages which are usually the visual books on their lists. The larger packagers are likely to have their own art departments staffed by a creative or art director, staff designers, and production persons. These positions are excellent opportunities to do creative work because there is little or no separation of labor; a visual book must be designed from jacket to index by a single designer to ensure the integrity of the package. Smaller book packagers use a fair number of freelancers and select candidates based on the quality of a portfolio and experience in total book design.

Any designer can design books or book jackets — the same fundamentals of design apply. But, in truth, not every designer can do book design well, just as not every jacket designer can create an effective or inspired interior. Different skills and talents are required, and although many designers have both, desire must be supplemented by knowledge. A book jacket is a mini-poster, but an interior is, in the case of text, a matter of knowing the nuances of type, and, in the case of a visual book, understanding the nature of visual flow. And flow is not as easy as following a grid in placing pictures on a page; it involves knowing what elements complement each other, which picture crops contribute to the dynamism of the page, and how the pages should flow to achieve melody, harmony, and dissonance. To learn this, sometimes on-the-job-training is adequate, but intensive study in school or a continuing education program is best.

Ultimately, a designer in book publishing might choose to stay in this specialty for a long or short time depending, of course, on the nature of the job. Many art directors and designers devote their lives to the field because challenges are ever-present; others find the specialties too limiting and, after a while, look for new opportunities in other creative media.

It is possible to get a book design job without having had experience. A smart portfolio with good samples may be enough to spark an employer's interest. Nevertheless, it is advantageous to include at least some book-related material. That said, the following is recommended.

Entry Level

School assignments should exhibit an ability to design book jackets and interiors. Emphasis on typography, photography, and illustration is important. Samples should exhibit both formal taste and conceptual acuity. They do not have to be published works, but should be fairly professional comprehensives produced as color lasers or Iris prints.

Contents

Ten to twenty samples:

a. The majority should be book jacket designs on a range of themes, both fiction and nonfiction, exhibiting typographic and pictorial skill and talent
b. A few interior book pages

Junior/Senior Designer

Junior designers may show exemplary school assignments but should include as much printed work as possible. Senior designers should only show printed book covers and interiors, as well as complete bindings, if available.

Contents

Fifteen to twenty-five samples:

a. The majority should be book jacket designs on a range of themes, fiction and nonfiction, exhibiting a variety of printing techniques
b. One or two speculative projects (self-generated comprehensives) to show a range of conceptual ability
c. Interior book pages (if available)
d. Two or three entire projects (interior, cover, jacket)

Format

35mm slides (in slide tray), 4×5 transparencies, dry-mounted proofs (lamination preferable), entire publications, digital work on CD-ROM or Zip Disk.

Title: The Black Book
Designer: Barbara de Wilde **Creative Director:** Michael Kaye **Publisher:** Farrar, Straus + Giroux **Photographer:** Bruno Barbey **Year:** 1994

Rant and Rave: Will the Book Survive?

The book's continuing vitality as a form of communication can be traced from the Good Book to the PowerBook, from the invention of movable type (Gutenberg's bibles) to the silicon chip (laptops). New media prosper because of the book — witness the success of Amazon.com. Books by or about media moguls and Silicon Valley sheiks such as Bill Gates and Andy Grove proliferate. Even media events, such as the O.J. Simpson trial, are summarized in books.

Today's book designers can trace their lineage to Gutenberg, for what is Quark or Pagemaker but a sophisticated typesetting technology? Designers have adapted to each generation of technology: to hand-set metal type, to Linotype, to phototype, to cutting and pasting on the desktop. Although tasks are now accomplished with a keystroke or mouse click, today's book designer still must observe traditions of book design such as copyright page protocol, folio placement, and indexing. There are potential pitfalls, however, for those designers who rely too heavily on page layout software. Long before Steve Jobs and Steve Wozniack invented the Macintosh, the nuts and bolts of text design — line length, line leading, text block proportion, margins, and kerning — were prerequisites to good critical judgment regarding legibility and readability. These elements of typographic style are not built into the software. No matter how fast or sophisticated the technology becomes, the computer is only a tool aiding the designer.

To its credit, some of the newer technology is more participatory in nature. For example, e-mail, interactive Web sites, and chat rooms may contribute to a renewed interest in communication in written form, albeit electronic. The lingua franca of technology has borrowed freely from that of typography, books, and printing: desktop *publishing*, *printer*, *fonts*, *kern*, web *page*, *bookmark*, and best of all, *PowerBook*. The computer has opened up opportunities for designers in new media. The difference between Web page and printed page may continue to narrow as the technology of one and the craft of the other evolve. If history is any guide, the book, in all likelihood, will survive.

— *Michael Carabetta*

Title: The Last Thing He Wanted **Designer:** Barbara de Wilde **Creative Director:** Carol Carson **Publisher:** Alfred A. Knopf **Photographer:** Katherine McGlynn **Typeface:** Alternate Gothic **Year:** 1996

Love for Books

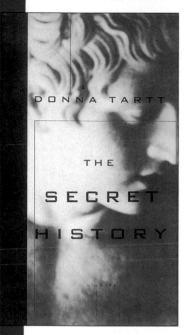

Title: The Secret History **Designers:** Barbara de Wilde, Chip Kidd **Creative Director:** Carol Carson **Publisher:** Alfred A. Knopf **Client:** The New York Times **Photograph:** Art Resources **Typeface:** Bank Gothic **Year:** 1992

Title: The Undertaking **Designer:** Barbara de Wilde **Creative Director:** Calvin Chu **Publisher:** W.W. Norton **Photographer:** Barbara de Wilde **Typefaces:** Engravers Bold Face, Engravers Gothic **Year:** 1997

BARBARA DE WILDE
Designer, Alfred A. Knopf Publishing, New York City

Why did you become a book jacket designer?
I came upon book jacket design because my best friend from Penn State got his first job at Random House. His name is Chip Kidd. That was ten years ago.

How do you feel about having a specific style?
I saw a documentary about John Adams, the composer, who said we are in a period of post-stylism. I agree. It is very liberating to design using any style appropriate. We live in a time when all styles exist at once and can be exchanged throughout the world in a matter of seconds. A style is just another element to choose from. Now, because I design primarily book jackets and readability is essential, there are some styles that are inappropriate.

What is the most fulfilling aspect of your job?
When the piece is finished, it's on a book, and I love books, I love to read. When I meet an author whose work I admire and I designed their book's jacket, I feel in a small way like a collaborator. When someone tells me that they bought the book because of the jacket, and that now they love this writer's work also, it's fantastic.

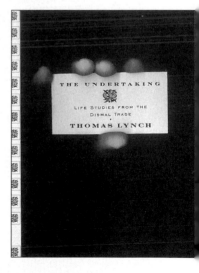

How has the computer affected your work?
Computers, we all have them now. They're fast, the type is a blessing and a curse. I love being able to control how I set it, I hate not having the variety of the type houses fonts, and I loathe the fact that they are listed alphabetically instead of by style. If I ever designed software, which will be never, but if I ever did I would design a program that would organize type by the stylist family it belongs to, like the old Photolettering book that I have on my shelf.

Do you have a specific approach when you are hiring designers? How do you find people and how does that work?
I often recommend students from a class I teach at SVA. I'm not looking just for good designers, but for people with a good work ethic and a good attitude. We often need designers who are very adept technically and who take initiative, but also designers who love to read.

Expressing Tradition

Title: The Mexican Empire
**Designer/Creative Director/
Illustrator:** Richard Eckersley
Company: University of Ne-
braska Press **Author:** Timothy
Anna **Typefaces:** Serifa,
Helvetica **Year:** 1990

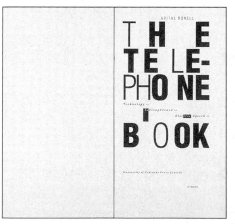

RICHARD ECKERSLEY

Senior Designer, University of Nebraska Press,
Lincoln, Nebraska

How did you decide to specialize in book publishing?
Initially, I wanted to do what my father did — graphic design,
poster design, particularly. But by the time I graduated, the poster was already disappearing as the principal vehicle for design. It
was partly accidental, I think, that the first job I got was with a
publishing house and a printer, working in a studio that was partly made up of work for printing clients as well as general graphic
design, and quite a large percentage of book design was involved.
So I went in a typography direction through that.

**The book design you do now — was this a natural evolution,
or did you have some sort of strategy?**
My interest in books really came through working on catalogs,
which is a much freer environment with general typography.

What is the most fulfilling aspect of your job? The least?
I think the most is being involved directly with the author and
dealing with a subject that's not essentially commercially driven. I
can take an interest in words and extend that through the visual.
It can be very tedious because there's so much checking of proofs
and that sort of thing involved, so the creative element is relatively short. And there are severe restrictions, of course, because
of the conventions and the size of the book. But conventions can
also be challenging and they also give one some feeling of connection to the tradition.

**Do you hire freelance designers? If so, how do you find
people? What do you look for?**
I would say 10 percent of our books are freelanced. The designers
are mostly people who have jobs at one of the university presses,

Title: The Telephone Book — Title Page **Designer/Creative
Director:** Richard Eckersley **Company:** University of Nebraska
Press **Author:** Avital Ronell **Typefaces:** Helvetica **Year:** 1989

and I suppose I choose them by being attracted to their work. Expressions are quite important. It is not simply a matter of going to a book shop; I would probably never find the people I wanted that way. But I think design competitions and books on design often have an index of people worth being curious about. Established relationships with freelancers tend to last a long time.

How has the computer affected your work?
I was terrified of the computer initially. I had one in my office for six months before I dared to use it. I was driven to it by a project that I simply couldn't have resolved in any other way — a text that I think reflected the society out of which the computer came, called *The Telephone Book*. It presents a deliberate challenge to convention as only an annoyance on occasion. But for that particular project I found the computer worked extremely well. The computer allows me to produce so many rough concepts that in some ways it actually makes it longer to design a book because I am tempted to explore all those options.

How have the shifts in media altered how you practice?
I don't think it's affected me, as a book designer, as much as it would have done designers in a general studio situation. So I'd say very little.

Working in a university environment, do you feel that you're more insulated from the mainstream business world?
Yes, I'd say isolated, actually. The advantage is that it's a fairly civilized existence. One is living in a community that promotes compatible interests.

Title: Stravinsky Retrospectives
Designer/Creative Director/Illustrator: Richard Eckersley
Company: University of Nebraska Press **Authors:** Haimo & Johnson **Year:** 1987

Title: Death to the Pigs **Designer/Creative Director/Illustrator:** Richard Eckersley
Company: University of Nebraska Press **Author:** Benjamin Peret **Typefaces:** Poetica, Joanna **Year:** 1988

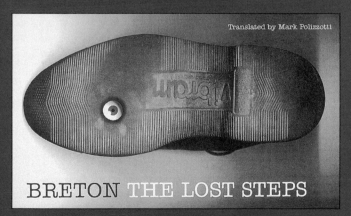

Title: The Lost Steps **Designer/Creative Director/Illustrator:** Richard Eckersley **Company:** University of Nebraska Press **Author:** Andre Breton **Typeface:** Serifa **Year:** 1996

Conception to Completion

MICHAEL IAN KAYE
Former Creative Director, Little, Brown,
New York City

Title: Fight Club **Designer:**
Michael Ian Kaye **Creative
Director:** Debra Morton Hoyt
Company: Michael Ian Kaye
Client: WW Norton **Photo-
grapher:** Melissa Hayden
Typeface: Dead History
Year: 1996

**Why did you decide to specialize in book jacket and cover
design?**
It was just luck. I landed in the book interior design department
at Penguin, and I didn't even know at that point that they
designed the interiors of books. I didn't decide on my specialty;
my specialty decided on me.

What is the most satisfying part of your job? The least?
The designing from conception to completion is the most satisfying
and exciting part of my job — reading a manuscript, conceiving
and executing a design, and following it through to production. The
business side of it is actually intrinsic and I don't hate it, because a
designer has to be good at it and has to be willing to do it. I think
the worst part about the job is in art-directing — communicating
absurd revisions based on either marketing decisions or odd author
interactions and having to explain why somebody's having to thumb
down a particular project. If I have to do it myself, I don't mind or
I'm much more capable of doing it because I understand that's just
the business, but when I'm dealing with what I consider to be very
talented people, it's almost embarrassing at times to have to communicate bad decisions on behalf of the corporate world. There are
times when I actually will give somebody a kill fee as opposed to
asking them to revise because I don't believe in the revisions that
are being asked.

How much contact do you have with the authors?
It varies. I like to have the contact when an author understands
what my job is and what I'm trying to accomplish. I think that
sometimes there's a tendency for them to become overinvolved.

Title: Pure Slaughter Value **Designer/Photographer:**
Michael Ian Kaye **Creative Director:** Mario Pulice
Hoyt **Company:** Michael Ian Kaye **Client:** Doubleday
Typeface: Trade Gothic Condensed **Year:** 1997

Are they ever free to approve your designs?
... ... have the right of approval if it's ... in their publication contract. The majority of Little, Brown authors have what we call consultation, which doesn't matter or amount to much. If it's a really important author, then obviously we have to please them.

How do you feel about not doing the interiors?
I would like to be involved a little bit more in the interiors, especially with the more complicated projects, or the more visually interesting projects, or where the visual aspects of an interior become a marketing hook.

When you're hiring designers, what do you look for and how do you find them?
I just recently hired somebody. It took me six months of looking to find that person. I care about the applicant's portfolio but more about his attitude and how he speaks about his work. And craft. I'm not looking for strong conceptual thinkers at an entry-level job. There's a difference. At the entry level, I don't want designers to be thinking too conceptually or to have what they consider to be a vision of design. I'm really looking for somebody who's open to learn and explore, focus in on what their vision could potentially be. Where upper-level people are concerned, I'm obviously looking for a nicely developed portfolio. I tend to like somebody that has a bit of range in their work but that's based on what I do, because I work for a company that publishes many different kinds of books. I need people who are multifaceted in their design ability and I try to steer clear of people who focus on trends of the moment.

Title: Elizabeth ... ...
Company: Little, Brown Client:
Photographer: ... Horst
Typefaces: ITC Garamond, Snell ...
Year: 1998

Title: U2 At The End Of the World
Designer/Creative Director:
Michael Ian Kaye Company:
Michael Ian Kaye Client:
Delacorte Photographer: Anton
Corbijn Typefaces: OCRB, hand
lettering Year: 1995

Title: Planet of the Blind
Designer/ Creative Director:
Michael Ian Kaye Company:
Michael Ian Kaye Client: The
Dial Press Typefaces: ITC
Century (photographed directly
from monitor) Year: 1997

The Children's Book Market

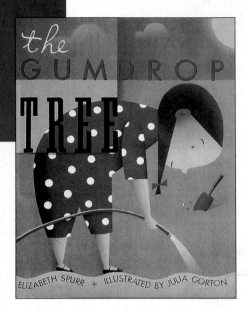

Title: The Gumdrop Tree **Designer/Illustrator:** Julia Gorton **Editor:** Howard W. Reeves **Publisher:** Hyperion Books for Children **Copyright:** ©1994 Julia Gorton **Year:** 1994

HOWARD W. REEVES

Director, Children's Books and Senior Editor, Harry N. Abrams Inc., New York City

How did you become a children's book editor?
Both my parents are educators, so I heard a lot of discussions about early childhood development and the history of education over dinner. But primarily I love stories — I love make-believe. I was working at Rizzoli Publishers editing adult books and convinced the publisher that we could develop a line of illustrated children's books.

Where does your interest in images come from?
As a child, I was a big fan of Dr. Seuss. His wild, fantastic images and characters really drew me in. My sisters used to read to me at night — all kinds of books. My parents also had several books on the coffee table that I remember: *Michelangelo's Cappella Sistina* and collections of artists like Dali and Bosch. I would go through them over and over, especially the Bosch and Dali.

How does an illustrator break into children's books?
Breaking into the market is tough. Primarily, illustrators need to route their portfolio to either editors or art directors that they feel will respond to their work. Sending it out without a plan yields the least results. There are a lot of publishers out there. I suggest going to a children's bookstore and seeing which books you like. Where does your art style fit in? Call the publisher and find out who designed or edited a book you like. Send them your portfolio. Target your audience. An idea to round out your portfolio is

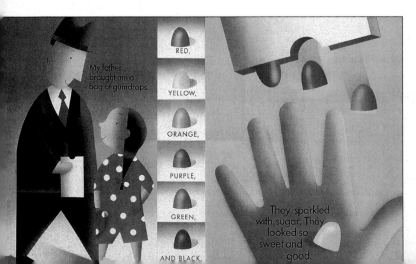

My father brought me a bag of gumdrops.

RED,

YELLOW,

ORANGE,

PURPLE,

GREEN,

AND BLACK.

They sparkled with sugar. They looked so sweet and good.

to take a favorite fairy tale or other story and illustrate a scene or two. That way publishers can get a real handle on what your style for children will be as well as how you contribute to the telling of the tale.

More and more children's books are being designed in playful and sophisticated manners. When did this start? How does a graphic designer become a children's book designer?
The newest surge in such design began in a big way in the 1980s, with such illustrators as Maira Kallman and Lane Smith. A graphic designer interested in doing children's design should do some sample layouts. Take some artwork you like and add text. Work it in different ways and send these samples to art directors. The catch is that most houses do most of their children's book design in-house.

What do you look for in the design of books? Legibility? Excitement? Novelty?
Legibility is key. If a tired parent at bedtime or a teacher or librarian in front of a large room of children has to figure out a book — squint at the pages, turn the book upside down — then they will not want to read it again and again. Successful books are those that aren't read once, but over and over.

What differentiates a children's book designer from the adult counterpart?
Nothing other than formats, font size, and age-appropriateness. In the same way artists can create illustration for both groups. What is important is to consider the age group intended.

Title: John Jeremy Colton
Designer: Higashi Glaser
Design **Editor:** Howard W.
Reeves **Publisher:** Hyperion
Books for Children **Illustrators:** Byron Glaser, Sandra
Higashi **Year:** 1994

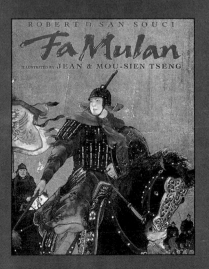

Title: Fa Mulan **Designer:** Ellen Friedman
Editor: Howard W. Reeves **Publisher:** Hyperion
Books for Children **Illustrators:** Jean and Mou-
Sien Tseng **Year:** 1998

Books Last Forever

Title: La Fete des Enfants
Designer/Creative Director:
Rita Marshall **Company:**
Marshall & Delesert **Client:**
Editions Script **Photographer:**
Marcel Imsand **Year:** 1984

RITA MARSHALL
Partner, Marshall & Delesert, Lakeville,
Connecticut

Why did you decide to go into book design?
I worked for four or five years as a graphic designer in a limited
market in Colorado, then I went to Denver and got a job in an
advertising agency. I worked in the design studio for two years,
and then I worked for about six or seven years as an art director.
I think that really taught me how to think and how to come up
with ideas and how to sell ideas. Then I moved to Europe and I
got a job in advertising, but it was almost impossible to do that
in a foreign culture. I quit and started designing books on a freelance basis.

What is the most satisfying aspect of your job? The least?
The most satisfying is that when you produce a book, it lasts forever, whereas in advertising you do a TV commercial and you have
a great time in Hollywood working on it, working with a lot of
nice directors, models, but the commercial runs for two weeks. A
few weeks in different markets and it's gone, or becomes a print
ad. But a book can really influence a lot of people for many, many
years. So I think that's the most satisfying. The least satisfying is
that now the publishing industry, almost internationally, has been
so taken over by marketing people that a lot of the creativity is
getting lost.

How much of your work is educational books?
The company that I'm doing a huge percentage of my work for
does publish school and library books, but they're not necessarily
textbooks. They have a small percentage of trade books and a

Title: Dance **Designer/Creative
Director:** Rita Marshall **Com-
pany:** Marshall & Delesert
Client: Creative Editions **Type-
faces:** Copperplate, Piranesi
Year: 1994

large percentage of school and library. I imagine quite a lot of those. They can be short stories, or illustrated books, a series of nature books. There's a lot of children's book stuff, but they're not necessarily textbooks.

Do you work closely with illustrators?
Yes. There's a huge collaboration. I would like to start writing books because, in a way, I'm writing them already. Many of the books I'm working on began because the illustrator came to me to help them work out their ideas. By the time I work out the storyline or the pictures, I feel like I've contributed to that book as if I were an editor. The same is true for the text. A lot of illustrators now don't have many outlets. The magazines are really cutting back on the use of illustration. A huge percentage of book jackets are now being done in Photoshop with stock photos. But I think that there is still this glorious illustrated children's book market for illustrators.

Does it take a certain personality to work well with illustrators?
I think it does. Once again, you have to be able to have an idea of how you want this book to tell the story. If the illustrator also has an idea, you have to work with her to get it right. It's basically her book. After many years of doing that I've gotten better at it.

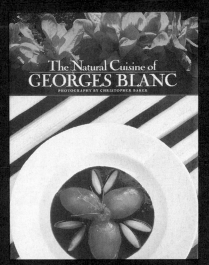

Title: The Natural Cuisine of
Georges Blanc. Design/Crea-
tive Director: Michael Mabry.
Company: Michael Mabry
Design. Design: Michael
Mabry. Photographer: Christo-
pher Baker. Publisher: Chronic-
le Year: 1987.

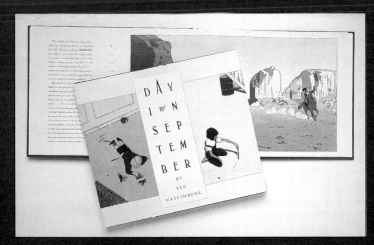

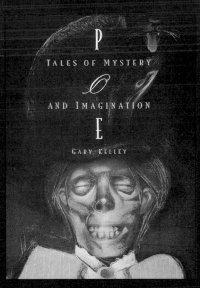

Title: A Day in September. Design/Creative Director: Mi-

Trials of Trade Publishing

Title: Star Wars Chronicles
Designers: Earl Gee, Fanny
Chung **Creative Director:**
Michael J. Carabetta **Company:**
Chronicle Books **Client:**
Chronicle Books **Typeface:**
Centaur **Year:** 1997

Title: The Blues Album Cover Art
Designers: Sarah Bolles, Michael
Carabetta **Creative Director:**
Michael J. Carabetta **Company:**
Chronicle Books **Client:**
Chronicle Books **Photographer:**
David Gahr **Typeface:** Bell
Gothic **Year:** 1996

MICHAEL J. CARABETTA

Creative Director, Chronicle Books, San Francisco

As the creative director of a primarily illustrated book publisher, what are your primary concerns?
Chronicle Books is a publisher of illustrated books. My criteria, and those of our designers, are twofold: practicality and aesthetics. Practically speaking, we strive to communicate what the book is about: its title, its content, and its spirit. Aesthetically speaking, we aspire to design books with captivating, original visual content. In the crowded world of book retailing, where the eye encounters scores of titles in seconds, it's imperative to arrest the browser's eye. In the case of a bestselling name author with a stack of books on display, this alone will catch your attention. But what about the unknown first-book author? This is where design can provide the means to get your attention, compel you to pick up the book, read the flap copy or back cover blurbs, and take it to the cash register. It's by design that this last bit of marketing is accomplished and the sale made.

You have a full-time staff, but you also commission freelance designers. How is that division of labor accomplished?
The first division of labor occurs when books are assigned to our designers on staff. We divide the book projects to balance the workload and see that our designers have an opportunity to work on different types of books of varying levels of complexity. Next, the designers can decide, based on their workloads and preferences, how they would like to proceed with a given project, either as sole designer or as project director, which entails hiring a freelance designer, photographer, illustrator, or other talent.

What do you look for in a designer's portfolio for a staff job?
The qualities we look for in a designer's portfolio, whether for a staff position or freelance assignment, are essentially the same: namely, originality and a sound approach to the basic elements of design — in particular, typography. A book, above all, is meant to be read. We're looking for a designer's proven ability to compose

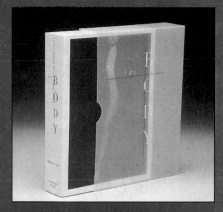

Title: Chronicle Books Trade Show Booth **Designer:** Earl Gee **Creative Director:** Michael J. Carabetta **Company:** Chronicle Books **Client:** Chronicle Books **Photographer:** Andy Caulfield **Typeface:** Copperplate Gothic **Year:** 1992

text and visuals into an integral whole, to give the book a sense of continuity and personality. A working knowledge of materials and printing processes is a given.

With new media as a major aspect of design, do you see the role of the book, and book design, changing in any significant manner?

It is obvious when you think about it, but we often forget that the book has withstood the innovations of radio, movies, TV, VCRs, CD-ROMs, and now the Internet. With each successive medium, the doomsayers predicted the book's demise. Long before the development of new media, books were fought over, collected, burned, banned, and passed down from century to century. Books remain the backbone of education, reference, literature, and, ironically, technology. Virtually all computer and software manuals are printed in book form because they offer what no hardware can — comfort, accessibility, and absorbability of highly technical literature.

Title: The Body **Designer:** Lucille Tenazas **Creative Director:** Michael J. Carabetta **Company:** Chronicle Books **Client:** Chronicle Books **Photographer:** Tono Stano **Typeface:** Bodoni **Year:** 1994

Title: Bordertown **Designer:** Martin Venezky **Creative Director:** Michael J. Carabetta **Company:** Chronicle Books **Client:** Chronicle Books **Photographer:** David Perry **Typeface:** Univers **Year:** 1998

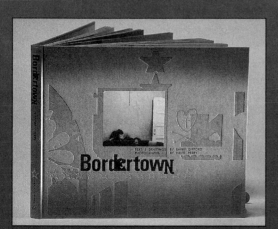

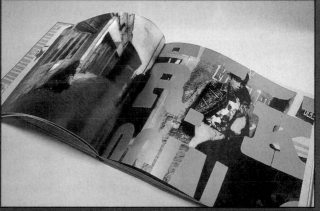

The Medium Is the Style

ERIC BAKER

Principal and Creative Director, Eric Baker Design,
New York City

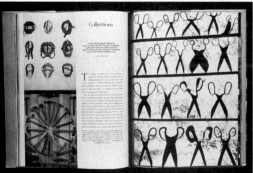

Title: Zona Home **Designers:**
Eric Baker, Greg Simpson
Creative Director: Eric Baker
Company: Eric Baker Design
Client: Zona **Typefaces:**
Bodoni, Geo Metrica **Year:** 1996

Why did you choose book design as a primary speciality?
Early on I did a lot of different things — corporate, medical, film, and music work. About ten years ago I fell into publishing through a back door and produced a little book of my own called *Trademarks of the '20s and '30s*, a Chronicle book. I realized then that I wanted to concentrate on work that wasn't so client-related. In other words, I wasn't interested in selling tennis shoes or bicycles, and I feel selling is what graphic design is about.

Do you have a personal style in your design? If you do, how would you describe it? Do you think that a personal style is important?
I've really struggled with that for a long time. I don't think of myself as having a personal style. In a way, I've kind of avoided one because the projects that we work on are so diverse that to apply a single style to them would be a mistake. I try very hard to look at a project and find the design direction within it. We worked on a book a few years ago on the history of North American Indians that was tied into a television documentary that Kevin Costner produced. It was called *Five Hundred Nations*, and I couldn't apply a design style to that. I had to find a quiet, appropriate voice to implement that work. Other projects we can apply more of a design direction to. But when we were beginning the *Five Hundred Nations* project, I was looking at a lot of portfolios to hire some new designers, and a lot were from Cranbook and from people that had worked at *Ray Gun*, and I was thinking, what are they going to do with this book on the history of North American Indians? Are they going to apply this Cranbook style to it? To me that would have been inappropriate and disrespectful.

What is the most fulfilling aspect of your job? The least?
I think the most fulfilling is working on a project that meets all of its objectives, whether it's a commercial project helping a client

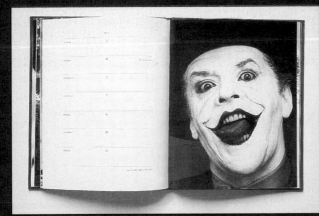

Title: Herb Ritts
Calendar Designers:
Jason Godfrey/Eric
Baker Creative
Director: Eric Baker
Company: Eric Baker
Design Associates
Client: Twin Palms Photo
Graphics Publishers
Printer: Gardner
Year: 1994

to bring a new product to the market or whether it's designing and producing a book that you walk into Rizzoli and one day there it is on a big pile of books. I think that the worst part of design is special manner in which some clients treat design as if it is a commodity.

How do you hire designers?
Sometimes I'll use a headhunter, sometimes I'll just use word of mouth. I'll call my friends and colleagues and tell them I'm looking. I hire from people right out of school as well as people who've been working five, six, seven years.

What do you look for when you're hiring people?
I look for intelligence. I look for somebody who can express themselves visually, of course, but orally and in writing, too. There is tremendous communication that of you can't articulate your ideas, if you're not communicating very well, I look for people who can bring a distinct cultural perspective to the work. We've had designers in here from England, France, Germany, Holland,

Exterior Man

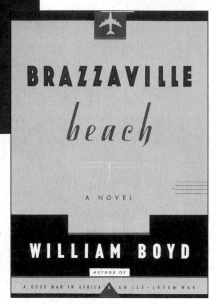

Title: Brazzaville Beach
Designer/Creative Director:
Chip Kidd **Publisher:** William
Morrow **Year:** 1994

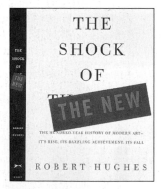

Title: The Shock of the New
Designer/Creative Director:
Chip Kidd **Publisher:** Knopf
Publishing **Client:** The New York
Times **Typefaces:** Bodoni, Trade
Gothic **Year:** 1996

CHIP KIDD

Senior Designer, Alfred A. Knopf Publishing and
Principal, Chip Kidd Design, New York City

**You are known as a prolific book jacket and cover designer.
Have you done many interiors of books?**
I've only done a handful of interiors. In terms of text and novels,
I've done several, including *The Secret History* with Barbara de
Wilde. In terms of picture books, I did a book with Chuck Close,
the artist, that was an overview of his work since 1988, when he
became a paraplegic.

How do you feel about doing covers and not interiors?
I think the interior designers at Knopf get beaten up a lot by editorial, far more than I do. They are considered the ugly step-
children of design here, which is really a shame. But every once in
a while somebody there does something really nice and really
wakes me up to what is possible. What usually happens is that I
get a jacket approved very early on, something that I am really
excited about, and I have to go through all of the political chan-
nels in order to be able to design the interior. But personally, I
think the two should be unified; there's no reason for the jacket
to have one kind of personality and the inside to have another. It
just doesn't make any sense.

Do you have a personal style?
I don't consciously try and design that way. People have said, "I
can tell if you did something in the bookstore but I can't really
put my finger on why." You don't need to define it; not being able
to put it into words suits the medium of graphic design perfectly.
Certainly I can say I prefer that things are usually on a straight
line instead of curved — the simpler the geometry, the better.
The publisher here thinks I'm a minimalist. But I think I'm a minimalist only in the sense that I look at a jacket and ask does this
element need to be here? If I can put my thumb on it and not
miss it, then I get rid of it. But certainly I think I've done jackets
where there's a lot going on. Sometimes that is needed.

How has the computer affected your work?

It's allowed me to do a lot more in a much shorter amount of time. It's seductive, and I have to fight it in order to keep reminding myself that it doesn't have to be the starting point of everything. It can be involved somehow, but going from doing everything by hand to doing everything by machine makes you have to remind yourself that you can do things by hand again, if you want. I think the computer is great and has completely changed everything, but if I was in charge of the graphic design program at a college, I would make all the kids spend their first year not using it at all.

How involved are you in the final production of your work — the separations, paper, printing? Do you get involved in that aspect at all?

I get involved only to the extent that I can deal with. One of the really nice things about working someplace like this is that we have a really terrific production department, and I would much rather defer to them on this stuff. This is why when I'm sitting around designers and they're talking about paper stocks and things like this, I'm really at a disadvantage because I have no idea what they're talking about. Which is probably bad for me, because I'm not always going to be here.

Title: American Illustration Annual #14 Designer/Creative Director: Chip Kidd Publisher: American Illustration Illustrator/Handletterer: Chris Ware Year: 1995

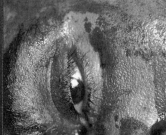

Title: The New Testament Designer: Chip Kidd Creative Director: Michael Ian Kaye Publisher: North Point Press Photographer: Andres Serrano Typeface: Times Roman Year: 1996

Title: Print Magazine - Cover Designer/Creative Director: Chip Kidd Publication: Print Magazine Year: 1995

IV. Music/Record Design

GRAPHICALLY DESIGNED album covers were not used by the recording industry until the late 1930s, but from that moment on original cover art changed the courses of design and music history. The first record album designed by pioneer Alex Steinweiss for Columbia Records increased record sales by an incredible 800 percent over non-designed covers. After the first year or so, sales no longer depended entirely on the quality of album design, but during the ensuing decades graphic design for LP and now CD covers has contributed to the overall allure of the music package as well as the identities of musicians. Indeed, certain recording artists are forever remembered as much for their emblematic album art — for example, The Beatles' *Sgt. Pepper's Lonely Hearts Club Band* — as for their performances. Although the quality of the music (and the airplay it gets) ultimately determines whether a record succeeds or fails in the market, album design definitely tips the purchasing scales. Creative packaging is an integral component of the marketing equation.

THE RECORDING INDUSTRY is such a wellspring of graphic design that it is among the field's most viable career niches. Although various codes are imposed on the design for different kinds of music, within these constraints is great potential to do innovative work. In addition, the recording industry offers the designer a modicum of cultural cachet and public visibility.

Large record labels, such as Sony Music, Atlantic, Reprise, Capitol, etc., have sizable art and creative services departments that are responsible for CD and tape cassette packaging as well as all collateral material (including lyric booklets, special collectors' packages, and in-store displays).

A typical design department is supervised by a *product manager* or *creative director*, who may or may not have a background in design. If a recording company has multiple divisions and separate labels (such as classical, pop, rock and roll, hip-hop, etc.), a single design director may oversee individual art directors assigned to each division. Within this hierarchy, in-house designers are assigned to work on projects within either one division or a few. These designers are usually responsible for typography and imagery (they may commission freelance illustration and photography or execute it themselves). Sometimes freelancers are temporarily hired to assist senior staff designers. Additionally, the seasonal release of many new and repackaged records often necessitates commissioning seasoned freelance designers with studios or firms to design entire record packages.

The recording industry operates much like the book industry. New records are scheduled for release during a selling season, which must be coordinated with promotional materials and performances. Designers must strictly adhere to these schedules lest the coordination of release and promotion be sacrificed. Nonetheless, design and conceptual packaging ideas are always subject to change, sometimes owing to the whim of a recording artist, who may not like a particular solution, or the marketing department, which may prefer an entirely different approach.

The ease or difficulty of designing record albums and collateral material can be measured in direct proportion to the star quality of the recording artist(s). The most popular not only retain the contractual right to approve or reject design but can also recommend a preferred graphic designer, artist, or photographer. This is not rare, but neither is it common practice. Most record albums are designed in a routine manner without the recording artist's interference. Scheduled releases are determined by product managers, who transmit the monthly or seasonal list to the art director, who, in turn, makes specific design assignments to the staff or freelancers. Once budgets are determined, these designers develop ideas that must be initially approved by the art director and, after comprehensives (or dummies) are completed, go to the product manager and marketing departments for final acceptance or rejection. Unfortunately, the process does not always stop there. Graphic design is not an exact science — it is not even a science — and various non-design-savvy people in the recording industry, like any industry, sometimes weigh in with opinions that can affect the final outcome.

In a large recording company, this kind of interference is fairly common; in a comparatively small company, where low budgets prevail, more creative license is often the rule. The recording industry has long included many small or independent companies that cater to a wide range of musical tastes and talents. Of course, the job hierarchies in these precincts are not as strict as in the larger companies; in fact, many independents employ only freelance designers to fulfill their design needs. Some freelancers work on a project-by-project basis, while others are hired on retainer to give consistency to an entire record label's particular identity. Small record companies' budgets are invariably tight, which challenges the enterprising designer to develop innovative approaches and allows for more ambitious solutions. Moreover, independents are not always tied to conventional marketing presumptions and, therefore, encourage designers to take chances that larger companies would not even consider.

Owing to the relative economy of manufacturing CDs these days, numerous small independents may release only one or two albums a year (in fact, there is a curious trend among a few digital type foundries to produce music CDs), while so-called alternative indie labels release 7" × 7" vinyl records with sleeve covers. Designing for these companies offers little remuneration in exchange for invaluable freedom. The work done for these companies offers a good entry point into the album design field.

Designing for a standard CD package means that the designer is confined to a square plastic jewel box (or, in some cases, a cardboard sleeve that is protectively wrapped in plastic). The box is usually clear, but occasionally colored plastic is used. A small multipage booklet inserted between the front of the box and the CD serves as the album cover. On the front of the booklet is emblematic cover art or a photograph with the typeset or custom-drawn album title; inside are the liner notes describing and crediting the music, artist, producer, etc., along with lyrics, photographs, and other pertinent information. The verso side lists the contents of the album and is also a continuation of the design motif. The front side of the disk itself is also usually emblazoned with type or image.

Increasingly, recording companies are releasing boxed sets, containing two or more CDs, that comprise many more printed materials than a single album, including printed inserts that are often ambitiously designed and produced. In addition, the box that holds the CDs is often fairly unconventional — for example, a casket-shaped box for Goth music, a guitar case for Elvis Presley's entire oeuvre. This kind of assignment offers great opportunities to test a designer's skill with two- and three-dimensional media. Although product managers usually determine when and for whom these packages are produced, an enterprising designer can suggest and experiment with approaches that might be accepted.

The key to being a good designer for music packaging is to have passion for music regardless of style or form. One can approach music as just another job, but the results usually betray such indifference. Also, one should appreciate the musical genre that is being packaged. An effective design must somehow underscore the essence of the musical content, help to project the ideas therein, and apply an emblematic image to the sounds. This can derive from individual interpretation or conversations with the musicians. Whatever the means, a record album design must not be a set of rote solutions. Of course, the demands of marketing are at odds with the instincts of art. But designers must nevertheless begin each project with confidence that their proposed design is indeed the best way to graphically frame their subject.

Artist versus Artist

The most popular recording artists often retain the contractual right to approve their album covers and promotion. The really big stars may also have the power to decide who designs their record packages. For example, the Rolling Stones have total control over their identity, and Mick Jagger and Keith Richard act as art directors. This can be frustrating for the record company art director whose input is thus limited, yet who is still responsible for the production of the total package. But it can, at the same time, be a tremendous opportunity for the anointed designer to work with legendary musicians.

Sometimes, however, the collaboration between recording artist and graphic artist is not satisfying in the least, particularly if the latter is on staff at a recording company.

Because it can be difficult to get a good idea passed through the marketing department in any case, when it is for a high-visibility act, the stakes are even higher. Having to negotiate ideas with the musicians or their managers can be a further stumbling block. And then ego kicks in. Graphic design is not an anonymous endeavor, and no matter how much a designer might appear to believe that her work is solving someone else's design problem, in the end the designer has to have some ego satisfaction, too. In the record industry, the balance between individual ego and professional responsibility is often tough, but in the end it must be reconciled in a professional manner.

It is possible to get a design job in the music industry without previous experience designing album packages. A portfolio that exhibits stylishness and conceptual intelligence may entice a potential employer. Nevertheless, it is advantageous to include at least some music-related material, even if that includes comprehensives.

Entry Level

School assignments are useful. Emphasis on typography, photography, and illustration is important. Samples do not have to be printed, but they should be fairly professional comprehensives produced as color lasers or Iris prints.

Contents

Ten to twenty samples:

a. CD packages on a range of musical genres to show versatility and interest in music

b. Two or three compilation or gift boxes, to indicate an ability to think conceptually and employ printing variations

c. One or two non-music-related pieces

Junior/Senior Designer

Junior designers may retain a few school assignments but should include as many printed pieces as possible. Senior designers should show a variety of printed pieces representing a range of music genres.

Contents

Fifteen to twenty-five samples:

a. CD packages (and one or two cassette packages) exhibiting a variety of printing techniques

b. One or two speculative projects to show a range of conceptual ability

c. As many special packages as available

d. A range of collateral materials — posters, flyers, point-of-purchase displays.

Format

35mm slides (in slide tray), 4×5 transparencies, dry-mounted proofs (lamination preferable), entire publications, digital work on CD-ROM or Zip Disk.

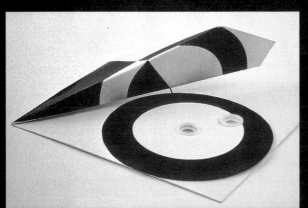

Title: Record Playing Postcard **Designer/Creative Director:** Stefan Sagmeister **Company:** Sagmeister Inc. **Client:** Sagmeister Inc. **Typeface:** Spartan **Year:** 1993

Eclectic Style

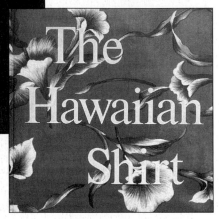

Title: The Hawaiian Shirt
Designer/Creative Director:
Tommy Steele **Company:** Capitol
Records **Client:** Abbeville Press
Photographer: Tommy Steele
Typefaces: Times Roman/Caslon
Year: 1984

Title: Leaning Tower Pizza
Designer: Andy Engel **Creative
Directors:** Tommy Steele, Andy
Engel, Jim Ludwig **Company:**
Capitol Records **Illustrator:**
Andy Engel **Photographer:** Larry
Dupont **Year:** 1990

TOMMY STEELE

Vice President, Art and Design, Capitol Records,
Hollywood, California

Why did you decide to specialize in the music industry?
My friends were leaving Art Center and going to work for ad agencies in Manhattan and Chicago and Los Angeles, but I opted for the creativity and freedom of the music industry. This is the closest thing we get to fine art in the commercial art world.

Do you have a personal style?
I describe my style as eclectic. I try to solve each problem in a unique way. Ideas and concepts are important to me, not simply decoration.

How much of your time is devoted to design and art direction? How much to business matters?
Art direction takes up the bulk of my time these days. There are hundreds of projects that flow through this creative services area. Setting the direction, honing the ideas, then letting go and delegating is my approach to most projects. I collaborate on the design aspects. I have two new people in my department who help keep the business side to a minimum, an accountant and a photographic coordinator, but managing the business is as important as the creative to the company. I look at this creative services area as a freestanding design firm that just happens to be housed within a record company. What I've learned, and am still learning, is how to run a design business from every aspect — design, production, legal, accounting, media buying, etc.

Title: Ultra-Lounge **Designer:** Andy Engel
Creative Directors: Tommy Steele, Andy Engel
Company: Capitol Records **Illustrator:** Andy
Engel **Photographer:** Don Miller **Year:** 1997

How have technological advancements affected your work?

In the last five or six years, the computer has changed what we
do and how we do it in almost every way. We are sending jobs
via ISDN to vendors across town and across the world daily. We
are viewing work on freelance designers' Web sites in an instant
rather than waiting for the next day's FedEx. We own a huge
library of type fonts that used to reside at typesetters. We're
viewing separations via dedicated lines on our computer networks.
Digital photography is being used more often to meet stricter deadlines. But still, it comes down to people — communicating to each
other, selling to each other, interacting with each other.

Title: The Beach Boys **Designer:** Andy
Engel **Creative Directors:** Tommy Steele,
Andy Engel **Company:** Capitol Records
Illustrator: Andy Engel **Photographer:**
Capitol Archives **Year:** 1993

What do you look for in a designer?

Great work rises to the top, but chemistry is equally important to
the workings of a design team. I'm looking everywhere to find talented people — promotional mailers, design schools, referrals
from friends, work that I've seen, design annuals, magazines, etc.
I've never hired interns because our company has yet to implement a policy. In these days of scaled-down headcount in corporate America, everybody counts and I need to hire the best I can
for every position.

An Artist's Vision

STEFAN SAGMEISTER
Principal, Sagmeister, Inc., New York City

How did you become such a specialist in music packaging?
I thought that it would be a great combination of my two favorite things: design and music. I get a bigger kick out of meeting some of my musical heroes than sitting in meetings with marketing directors (which I did a lot before I opened my own specialized studio). I love record stores. I love coming up with an idea just by listening to music.

What challenges or obstacles are involved in music packaging?
• The package is small; like most challenges, this can be turned into an advantage.
• The format never changes but still should be filled with something new every time.
• In general, the budgets are smaller than in regular graphic design.

What were some of your most challenging projects?
As in general graphic design, the bigger the project, the more people involved, the harder to get anything through, the wetter the tears, the louder the cries, the bigger the challenge.

Title: Jazz Festival "Konfrontationen" **Designer/Creative Director:** Stefan Sagmeister **Company:** Sagmeister, Inc. **Client:** Nickelsdorfer Konfrontationen **Mechanical:** Christian Hochmeister **Year:** 1990

Title: Rolling Stones' Bridges to Babylon **Designers:** Stefan Sagmeister, Hjalti Karlsson **Creative Director:** Stefan Sagmeister **Company:** Sagmeister, Inc. **Client:** Promotone B.V. **Illustrators:** Kevin Murphy, Gerard Howland, Avan Auers **Photographer:** Max Vadukul **Typeface:** Hand type, Mrs. Eaves **Year:** 1997

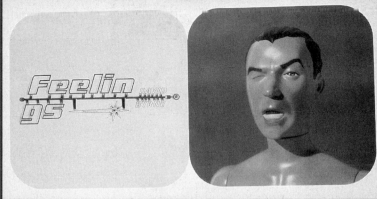

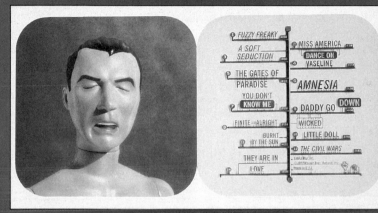

Title: David Byrne Feelings **Designers:** Stefan Sagmeister, Hjalti Karlsson **Creative Directors:** Stefan Sagmeister, David Byrne **Company:** Sagmeister, Inc. **Client:** Luaka Bop, Warner Bros. Music **Model Maker:** Yuji Yoshimoto **Photographer:** Tom Schierlitz **Typefaces:** Hand Type, Franklin Gothic **Year:** 1997

Do you have to answer to the artists or an in-house art director or both?

We present to the artists. In-house art directors are often helpful (they are designers themselves and know that it's counterproductive to have one more opinionated person on the project) but occasionally there are other groups involved: on the record company side, product managers, marketing people — if the band is very important, the president or CEO; on the management side, band manager, business manager, tour manager.

In the face of the artist's creative vision, how do you maintain your own?

We try to take on jobs only from artists whose visual sense we admire — David Byrne, for example.

Do you want to continue in this specialty or do you foresee a much more general practice?

I want to continue; there are still quite a number of CD covers to be designed.

Title: H.P. Zinker **Designers:** Stefan Sagmeister, Veronica Olt **Creative Director:** Stefan Sagmeister **Company:** Sagmeister, Inc. **Client:** Energy Records **Photographer:** Tom Schierlitz **Typefaces:** Peignot, Franklin Gothic, News Gothic, Hand Type **Year:** 1994

Staying in Tune

Title: Bruckner Symphony No. 4, Salonen **Designer/Creative Director:** Roxanne Slimak **Company:** Sony Music **Photographer:** Mark Hanauer **Typeface:** Didot **Year:** 1998

ROXANNE SLIMAK
Senior Art Director, Sony Music, New York City

Why did you become involved in music packaging?
After nine years of working at the Push Pin Group, a general design studio, I felt I was ready for a radical change. Another world of design had been exposed to me that involves gifted performers and their music and shaping a look or image for them.

Obviously, formats have changed from LPs to CDs. What are the latest changes in record packaging to affect design?
It seems what we are asked to do continues to grow. We now adapt our designs for cassettes, VHS boxes, DVD packaging, the menus that accompany the programs so they are all graphically connected, laser discs, and now Web sites. I have designed sites for individual new releases that will tie in with the artist's complete catalog as well as what we call supersites, which include historical information, tour schedules, chat sessions, bulletin boards, etc.

What challenges or obstacles are involved in music packaging?
• I suppose working with the five-inch-square format, satisfying our marketing team's needs for shelf impact and my need for something done well. It is everyone's dream to have the package scream for attention; however, I prefer to create something beautiful, tasteful, and appealing, perhaps with a little mystery so the consumer is curious and wants to pick it up.

Title: The Tango Lesson **Designer/Creative Director:** Roxanne Slimak **Company:** Sony Music **Photographer:** Christopher Porter, Adventure Pictures **Typeface:** Futura **Year:** 1997

Title: Vocal Masterworks Series
Designer/Creative Director:
Roxanne Slimak **Company:** Sony
Music **Photographers:** Valerie
Clement, Erika Davidson, Don
Hunstein **Typefaces: Agenda,
Futura Year:** 1998

• Never having enough time!
• Too many layers of people to satisfy, all of whom have an opinion.

In the face of the artist's creative vision, how do you maintain your own?
For most packages, a dialog is established that keeps designers attuned to the final result, with no surprises. Often, if the artist or the label wants something that is just awful, we meet to work out the situation. There are times when people insist and you must just go on. Each and every project is different, and I couldn't say any two were alike in their outcome or the road traveled during the course of the assignment.

Do you want to continue in this specialty or do you foresee a more general practice?
I very much like working in music — the best is meeting the artists and hearing their thoughts, listening to their music, and thinking of how to create a package or style that describes to consumers what the music is about before they hear it. All of this does not happen only in my office; I have the good fortune to work with talented photographers and illustrators who often deliver much more than one might think possible.

Title: Masterworks Heritage
Highlights **Designer/Creative
Director:** Roxanne Slimak
Company: Sony Music **Photographers:** Various **Typeface:**
Bureau Grotesque **Year:** 1996

From LP to CD

Title: Mitakuye Oyasin Oyasin
Designer/Creative Director:
Greg Ross **Company:** A&M
Records **Client:** Neville Brothers
Illustrator: Christian Clayton
Year: 1996

GREG ROSS

Senior Art Director, A&M Records, Hollywood,
California

How did you decide on music as a design speciality?
Like many design students, I wanted to go into the music field for
two reasons: I love music and I thought that the music industry
would allow me the space for the greatest experimentation in
design. I also felt that I could be sympathetic to design within
the music world because I had studied music and music theory for
a number of years.

What is your role at A&M?
My title is Senior Art Director. I work directly under Jeri Heiden,
who is the creative director of the company. My main responsibility is to create CD packaging as well as merchandising and advertising campaigns for the recording artists that I am assigned to. I
am also responsible for a number of administrative duties within
the department, annual reviews of the other art
directors and designers, offering con-

Title: Q's Jook Joint **Designer/Cre-
ative Director:** Greg Ross **Company:**
Qwest Records **Client:** Quincy Jones
Illustrator: Nate Giorgio **Photogra-
pher:** Annie Leibovitz **Typefaces:**
Block/New Berliner **Year:** 1995

Title: Smitten
Designer: Greg Ross
Creative Directors:
Jeri Heiden, Greg
Ross **Company:**
Polydor Records
Client: Buffalo Tom
Hand Lettering: Elvis
Swift **Photographer:**
Jacques-Antoine
Moulin, Courtesy of
Musee D'Orsay, Paris
Year: 1998

structive criticism, and signing off on all the work that leaves the department.

Do you have a personal style in your design?
I do not think that I have a strong personal style, although, in general, my work tends to lean to clean, simple layouts. For me, a personal style is not important. I enjoy approaching my projects differently, giving to each what is most appropriate. Working in an in-house art department, I think it is important to be able to change styles to fit the project.

Obviously, formats have changed from LPs to CDs. What are the latest changes in record packaging to affect design?
Although it is not a new packaging format, there is still a lot of debate about the digipak, the main alternative to the jewel box. It is made of cardboard and paper, except for the tray that the disc fits in. It is a fairly common form of CD packaging, but it is unclear whether or not the public likes it. There is also a problem at the retail level; most stores prefer the jewel case, but designers love the digipak because it offers possibilities that the jewel case does not. Other than that, there are no across-the-board changes in CD packaging, except for the special packages that we create for certain artists.

What distinguishes a good from a great record cover designer?
Because a good amount of the portfolios that I look at are those of recently graduated students, the first thing that I look for is whether or not they know how to use type. I see so many books that have very interesting imagery and use of photography but the type is not thought out at all. I think to become a sucessful record cover designer one has to be able to conceptualize, to turn an idea or an emotion into something visual. I am most interested in the designers whose portfolios show that they are thinking, not just trying to make something look good.

What do you see as the growth areas in music for the designer?
I do not think that printed packaging is going away any time soon. I think there is tremendous opportunity for the music business on the Internet. Designing pages for the A&M Web site has been added to the in-house designer's responsibilities. A number of our CDs are now being released with enhanced material. Videos, photo libraries, and interactive material are now being created for this portion of the CD. There is much room for growth in the area.

Title: Behind the Eyes **Designer/Creative Director:** Greg Ross **Company:** A&M Records **Client:** Amy Grant **Lettering Artist:** Lilly Lee **Photographer:** Kurt Markus **Typeface:** Engraver's Gothic **Year:** 1997

Title: Avenue A **Designer/Creative Director:** Greg Ross **Company:** Rocket Records **Client:** Daniel Cartier **Photographer:** Tom Tavee **Typefaces:** Franklin Gothic, Clarendon **Year:** 1997

Art and Commerce

Title: Farenheit 451 **Designer:** Christopher Austopchuk **Creative Director:** Roger Black **Client:** The Limited Editions Club **Typeface:** News Gothic **Year:** 1982

CHRISTOPHER AUSTOPCHUK
Vice President, Creative Services, East Coast, Sony Music, New York City

How did you become involved in the music industry?
Let's just say that it picked me and I foolishly, youthfully went along. I have since grown into my career.

What is the most fulfilling aspect of your job? The least?
The most fulfilling aspect is seeing potential realized — seeing good students become the good designers that you knew they would be, then good art directors and so on. I suppose the most fulfilling aspect is teaching or mentoring. The least fulfilling aspect has got to be how much commerce takes precedence over art.

How have technological advancements affected your work?
Technological advancements have changed to the core everything that we do, in both positive and negative ways. I feel that this is an over-discussed topic, however, and may be a meaningless one to designers graduating from school today.

Do you have a specific approach to hiring designers? How does it work? Where do you find people? Do you or have you hired interns? How does that work?
I like to hire students of mine, or former students, the reason being that it is terribly important to know how someone reacts to situations when a job isn't on the line. I find job interviews mostly unsatisfying and misleading, although I do a lot of interviews and have hired people for major jobs after one twenty-minute interview. Am I overstating when I say that someone's personality is perhaps even more important to me than their work? We work with interns all the time and have hired interns that we like ("we" being myself and my management staff; I rarely make unilateral decisions about a staff hire).

Title: Bartok **Designer/Creative Director:** Christopher Austopchuk **Client:** CBS Masterworks **Photographer:** Photo courtesy Melodiya Records **Typeface:** Wood Type **Year:** 1980

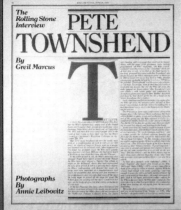

Title: Pete Townsend, the Rolling Stone Interview **Designer:** Christopher Austopchuk **Creative Director:** Mary Shanahan **Publication:** Rolling Stone Magazine **Photographer:** Annie Leibovitz **Typeface:** Clearface **Year:** 1979

Title: The Outfield, Bangin **Designer/Creative Director:** Christopher Austopchuk **Client:** Sony Music **Photographer:** Chip Simons **Typeface:** Alternate Gothic Condensed **Year:** 1989

Title: Tom Wolfe, the Rolling Stone Interview **Designer:** Christopher Austopchuk **Creative Director:** Mary Shanahan **Publication:** Rolling Stone Magazine **Photographer:** Annie Leibovitz **Typeface:** Bulmer **Year:** 1979

Title: Smash Palace **Designer/Creative Director:** Christopher Austopchuk **Client:** CBS Records **Photographer:** Duane Michaels **Year:** 1988

Title: Nils Lofgren, Flip **Designer/Creative Director:** Christopher Austopchuk **Client:** Sony Music **Photographer:** Steve Borowski **Typeface:** Helvetica **Year:** 1985

V. Information Design

YOU MAY ASK, isn't all graphic design about packaging information? In a word: no. Graphic design is about framing ideas, projecting attitudes, promulgating styles, *and* managing information, but not always at the same time. We have already touched on those disciplines, such as editorial and corporate design, where presenting information is a key but not the only concern of the designer. Yet in recent years, information design, or what architect/designer/author Richard Saul Wurman calls "information architecture," has grown not only in importance in these particular media but also into a specialized discipline under the graphic design rubric. Although information architects argue that theirs is a field unto itself, far from being subsumed by graphic design, it is discussed here as a graphic design sub-genre with its own defining characteristics.

INFORMATION design, at its most rudimentary, employs type and graphics to clarify and concretize mostly nonvisual information, such as facts and figures. This is not an entirely new form; after all, pie charts and fever-line graphs have been used throughout the century in all kinds of arcane and public documents, from scientific reports to high-school textbooks. Yet usually these visual aids have been minimally designed, if designed at all. Over fifty years ago, however, a movement began to improve such material by making it more visually accessible. What has been called the pictograph revolution launched by German designer and social scientist Otto Neurath in the late 1920s, introduced universal graphic symbols that stood for common words, terms, or concepts and were used in charts, maps, and graphs to represent specific ideas and notions. These images evolved into what are known today as *pictorial sign symbols*, the icons used in public spaces like malls and airports to identify restrooms, restaurants, telephones, etc. But even more important, they developed into an extensive lexicon of icons used to clarify all kinds of data, from television listings to annual corporate profit and loss statements. Thus they have become the proverbial picture that speaks a thousand words.

Pictorial sign symbols are used in graphic

design disciplines – editorial, corporate, environmental, etc. – and are ubiquitous on computer screens and as Web site navigational buttons. But the sign symbol is only one small part of information design. Type and image are the primary tools of graphical information management. As in any design discipline, information designers must have a mastery of these fundamental tools, but unlike in decorative design, the focus is not on style and fashion but rather function and utility. The role of the information designer is to guide users away from confusion into understanding, regardless of subject.

Information can be communicated in many ways. For example, introduced in the post–World War II era, the Swiss School or International Style of graphic design proffered the reduction of graphic design to a few typefaces built on tight grids and based on mathematical proportions. All text and visual information fit into strict formats void of nonessential or decorative graphic accoutrements. Breaks in text indicated by added space or different type weights relieved daunting masses of text and generous amounts of white (or negative) space lessened the clutter of most high-density visual material. It was correctly assumed that the reader would focus on the essential aspects of the printed matter and, in the end, simplicity wed to rigidity would enable greater comprehension of what was usually dry information.

The International Style continues to hold sway when designers have to assemble massive amounts of textual information for publication, but owing to the sharp increase in the volume of information during this "information age," concurrent with the decrease in available time for the average user to digest these data, additional presentation alternatives have been introduced to both ease and simplify information flow. The current information design specialist must be fluent in all methods of presentation and expert in decidedly visual or graphic approaches.

This is not an area that a designer can acquire only through instinct (although some people are better suited to visual organization than others). Yet this does not mean that instinct does not play a part in the day-to-day process of design. Information designers are in various proportions typographers, statistical analysts, mapmakers, and reporters, and must constantly draw upon their instincts in these areas to make correct design decisions. However, while the combination of all or some of these attributes is important, to become an information designer one often begins as a renderer of others' ideas. Most designers start as, and many continue to be throughout their careers, translators of writers', analysts', or reporters' nonvisual material into graphic form. To do it well — to make intelligent interpretations — is invaluable because often what passes for information design is merely the overlay of a few decorative graphics that may relieve eyestrain but fail to add substantive cues that help the user obtain or retain the information.

Effective information design looks good, but it also adds an intellectual dimension to the subject that increases the user's understanding. It must eliminate, again in the words of Richard Saul Wurman, "information anxiety." The ability to achieve this goal takes time and practice. Although information design is an expanding area of graphic design and practitioners are always in demand, an even greater demand exists for those with outstanding qualifications. The way to attain these is, first, to pursue a good education; second, to start practicing at any level and in any medium that is available; and, third, to explore different ways of presenting information — to not follow tired formulas.

For the Public Good

Title: Master of Architecture Poster **Designer:** David Peters **Client:** Nova Scotia Technical College **Typeface:** Helvetica **Year:** 1976

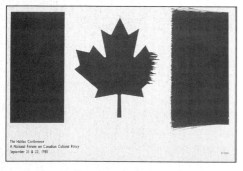

Title: Conference Flag and Postcard **Designer/Creative Director:** David Peters **Company:** GDA, Inc. **Client:** The Halifax Conference: A National Forum on Canadian Cultural Policy **Year:** 1985

DAVID PETERS
Project Director, Meta Design, San Francisco

What are your responsibilities as project director at Meta Design?
I put together creative teams to solve problems. I work simultaneously in the role of creative director and producer in that I help clients understand what problems design can solve and then put together the editorial resources and the visual resources and the design resources to execute them.

What kind of clients do you have?
I've been involved with publishing clients as well as clients in software development, principally for network environments. These are two very different kinds of clients, but representative of my interests in design, in that I'm interested in all kinds of things as opposed to any one thing in particular.

What is the most fulfilling aspect of being a graphic designer specifically involved with information design and management?
The consequences of the work that I do. I think I help people do things for themselves. As a designer, to do that means being sensitive to the things that people want to do for themselves, the choices people would like to be able to make, and giving them the tools or the resources to do those things. Also, not pushing my agenda of what is hip or cool, not making presumptions of how to do that, but actually listening to clients and working with them.

Would you give an example of this?
Helping people who are blind to use ATMs through the software that I've developed. This is really satisfying because I know that I've given them a freedom that they didn't have. They had to be reliant on others to handle their money for them. I like doing projects that are about empowering people, using design to give people choices in their lives and giving society choices about where it goes.

Is it difficult to get your ideas fulfilled?
The most frustrating thing for me is the time it takes to explain what we're doing and why users and people in general are important enough to treat with respect and dignity. The least fulfilling thing is realizing that we have to go down that road again and again with clients, that many businesses, institutions, corporations are so caught up in their own internal dynamics that the relationship they have with the public is a byproduct of what they do. It is exasperating to go through this education process because I feel like somehow society has failed if it hasn't helped managers and people who have authority and responsibility to serve others.

The computer has obviously changed the way we work. How has it affected you in a field of design intended to inform?
The most significant change is that it allowed me, through my work in software development, to get into real-time relationship with my audiences. When I was designing annual reports and corporate identities and posters for the theater and programs and such, I was unhappy with the lack of feedback that I could get as a designer about how well these information products were serving their purposes. When I was introduced to developing interface projects and interaction design, a part of me woke up to the impact that this is going to have on traditional graphic design and its availability to the public. Something special is going to go on as people interact with these devices, something that has become branded as the discipline of interaction design. The conversion process that I went through was a consequence of developing design studies for software and being allowed to take those into research settings and watch people in real time use them and see the extent to which people understood the cues that I was trying to provide them. This completely changed the way I work as a designer.

Do you have a specific approach when you're hiring designers?
I want to meet them in person. Looking at their portfolio is not enough for me. Reviewing a portfolio can be a powerful stimulus to meeting someone, but I think that design is a frame of mind, it's a discipline that one learns to exercise or practice, and many of the details about how one practices design can be learned in a healthy environment. For me, the right frame is an awareness of how communication happens in society, commitment to one's work, to be constantly working, producing material, and doing projects, because this kind of drive is the sign of a willing and eager designer. I can only discover that through meeting someone.

Hello - May I help you?
Please dip your card in and then take it out so we can begin.

XXXXXXX © Citicorp 1987, 1992   xx

Title: ATM Touchscreen Interface
Designer/Creative Director: David Peters **Company:** Two Twelve Associates, Inc. **Client:** Citibank, N. A. **Year:** 1992

The Optimum Portfolio

This is a comparatively new field, but one with fairly rigorous standards. Portfolios should be tightly edited and professional.

Entry Level/Junior

School assignments should emphasize the marriage of research, reporting, and design. Samples need not be published, but they should be quality laser or Iris prints.

Contents

Ten to twenty samples: Charts, maps, and graphs that show drafting and conceptual strengths

Senior

Printed work showing a wide range of problems and solutions designed for periodical, textbook, audiovisual presentations, and annual reports is preferred.

Contents

Fifteen to twenty-five samples:
a. Charts, maps, graphs, and information graphics that exhibit typographic acuity and conceptual strength
b. On-line or CD-ROM graphics (if available)

Format

Printed work, laser or Iris prints, digital work on CD ROM or Zip Disk.

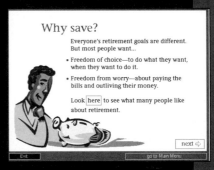

Title: Decisions Retirement Savings Software **Designers:** Casey Reas, John DeWolf, Andrea Koura **Creative Directors:** David Peters, Julie Marable **Company:** Two Twelve Associates, Inc. **Client:** T. Rowe Price **Illustrator:** Matt Foster **Typeface:** Berkeley **Year:** 1996

Title: Tommy CD-ROM (unpublished) **Designer:** Jerry Lien **Creative Director:** David Peters **Company:** Two Twelve Associates, Inc. **Client:** Kardana Productions **Illustrator:** Jerry Lien **Year:** 1994

VI. Advertising

THERE IS NO BIGGER mass communications producer than the advertising industry. More than any other discipline, advertising is so completely intertwined with American life that one cannot even peel a banana without confronting a "Got Milk?" ad. With the exception of public television and radio (which do feature sponsor advertisements), advertising is indeed everywhere and on virtually every surface. While television and radio command the largest budgets and address the highest audience share, print (publications, flyers, brochures, direct mail, and billboards) is the most ubiquitous of the advertising media. Before entering the advertising profession, therefore, it is important to know both the divisions of labor and distinctions among approaches.

THE CENTER of advertising production is an advertising agency (or shop, as it is colloquially called). Mega-agencies, midsized agencies, and small agencies sometimes vie for the same accounts as well as service different niches. Some agencies are so big they can afford to accept only megaclients, while others, the so-called boutique agencies, handle lower-billing accounts. The mega-agencies are often media-capital-based conglomerates that also own subsidiary advertising agencies in several cities and around the world. Some of these agencies own graphic design firms that service the creative needs, and produce the collateral materials for, the clients of the larger agency. The midsized agency usually handles midsized accounts, those that do not have tens of millions to spend on saturated national media blitzes but rather have a few million to spend on targeted areas. The small agency usually gets local accounts with limited budgets (but may have one or two highly visible accounts as well). In addition, countless smaller all-purpose agencies serve small local businesses. Finally, some graphic design firms also handle advertising for their own clients.

The size of an agency is determined by the number of its clients divided by its annual billings. Without getting deeply into the complex financial structure of advertising agencies, which is a book in itself, the larger the agency, the more money it spends on placing advertisements in mass media; the more money it spends, the larger its commission or return. For each ad placed on, say, network TV during the Super Bowl, the agency will get a larger fee than at other less visible time periods. These fees or commissions are tied to the amount it costs to buy ad space. In a sense, the creative services of an agency are a loss leader. The number of employees in an agency is directly proportional to the number of clients that it services as well as the number of accounts that it is attempting to add to its roster. The largest amount of staff work is devoted to existing accounts, but in many agencies some staff is devoted to attracting new business, which often involves creating entire spec (or proposed) campaigns. An agency, regardless of size, may spend hundreds of thousands to capture a prized multimillion-dollar account.

The size of agencies varies from a few hundred employees (and additional freelancers) to two or three persons (and freelancers). An agency is typically headed by two or more *partners*, who are the names on the shingle (for example, Lord Geller Federico and Doyle Dane Bernbach). Whereas a design firm need only have one creative principal, an advertising agency routinely has creative *and* business partners. Under the creative rubric is typically an *art director* and *copywriter*; under the business rubric is an *account executive*. An advertising art director is the arbiter and creator of the visual message or style (either for print or television); the copywriter develops the themes and creates the words that sell the message or product. These "creatives" often work in tandem, in creative teams, and constitute a symbiotic entity. The account executive manages the account. Sometimes this is the person who sold the agency to the client in the first place; at other times this is the liaison between the client and the creative team. This three-way combination is integral to the workings of the agency.

Below the partner level are various jobs and job categories. The principal level is the *creative team*, which is assigned to an aspect of or an entire account. A team may include three or more principals; the number is determined by the scope of the account. Below this level are *creative* and *production assistants* who fabricate the work. In addition, creative teams may call upon freelancers and subsidiaries to attend to the diverse components of the basic campaign. For certain kinds of printed matter, for example, an agency might subcontract to a subsidiary or independent graphic design firm. For television commercials, an independent production house might get the call. The larger agencies employee their own graphic designers, while the smaller ones may not. The larger agencies may have a house director for TV or radio, but most hire freelance directors from a large pool of itinerant talents. Some agencies directly handle only one aspect of a campaign, like national TV spots, and routinely subcontract all other components to independent firms or studios. There are, obviously, many places for a graphic designer to get a foothold in the advertising industry.

Legend has it that art and copy people are not the best collaborators — in fact, sometimes they are too concerned with their turf to meld into one. In advertising, the copywriter once ruled supreme, but for decades art and copy have been more or less balanced in importance — depending, of course, on the nature of the product. Yet a memorable jingle or tag line — something that forever sticks in the consumer's head — is quantifiably more valuable than the smartest layout or wittiest picture. So, it is important for art directors and designers to pursue writing as well. A talent for writing crisp copy invariably makes the visual idea much stronger. Most schools that teach advertising wed the two disciplines. Incidentally, it is rare that entry-level advertising designers are hired without some kind of formal education.

In the agency hierarchy, television is the pinnacle. Print is, as agency people say, "below the line." Nevertheless, designing for print is a good way to enter the agency structure. Print art directors are usually responsible for a large percentage of creative output, and art and design schools continue to emphasize print as the most important component of a campaign. If an advertising campaign is seen as a strategic military action, television and radio are the first wave of attack, but owing to the expense of mounting such an offensive, print is the second wave of land troops. After saturation bombing to soften up the audience through electronic media, print captures the high ground by providing constant reminders in the manner of a continual assault on the consciousness of consumers.

Starting out in advertising requires some historical deep background. At root is knowing the function of advertising and how its goals are attained. But the neophyte's true calling card is the portfolio, and this important container must, like an ad itself, contain enough material to convince the interviewer that the interviewee is devoted to making smart advertising. A few years ago, art directors wouldn't even look at portfolios that were not dedicated entirely to advertising campaigns. In fact, graphic designers were thought of as people who make letterheads. However, graphic design is integral to the look and feel of contemporary advertisements. Indeed, a large percentage of advertising today is less about the so-called big idea, driven by the marriage of terse copy and stark image, than about mood, feeling, and attitude. Graphic designers and, specifically, skilled typographers, are routinely hired as staff or on a freelance basis to massage components of or to develop entire advertising campaigns.

Whether or not an agency employs its own graphic design specialists or subcontracts to independent firms, there is no doubt that the graphic designer's role in advertising has measurably increased during the past decade. Among the most typical assignments (for which samples should be represented in a portfolio) are promotion pieces (booklets, flyers, mailers, press kits, etc.), point-of-purchase displays, (easel-back standups, countertop objects, etc.), and package designs. This last has emerged because more agencies are not only selling already conceived products but also packaging and repackaging old and new products. The value of the so-called full-service agency to a client is its capacity to engage in many advertising and design services.

Designers have a significant role in the advertising industry, but it is nevertheless important to caution that this is a very volatile profession. Even the fortunes of established advertising agencies may tumble when clients pull their accounts — and they invariably do. A client engages in agency reviews when it feels the performance of its current agency is no longer selling the goods, or when it simply wants a change. Moving a multimillion-dollar account can be a devastating blow — if not to the agency as a whole, then at least to many of its employees. Entire creative staffs, including veteran employees who worked years for the same agency, are laid off when accounts are switched. Sometimes the competing agency will hire them — often not. Advertising is a high-pressure profession; its practitioners must creatively serve the client's whims and needs. Many creatives are, therefore, peripatetic, frequently moving from agency to agency. Given this uncertainty, the entry-level designer might be wise to consider starting at a midsized or small agency, one with a variety of relatively stable clients, and spend a few years learning and experiencing the advertising business before moving on.

Advertising is a multimedia industry, and designers and art directors are sought after for print, television, and on-line work. A typical advertising design portfolio is not very different from a general graphic design portfolio, yet there must be due emphasis on ads and promotion materials.

Entry Level

School projects, including entire ad campaigns for real or imagined products, are useful for showing insight into advertising methods.

Contents

Ten to twenty samples:

a. Two complete campaigns (three or more ads showing headlines and visuals), including logo, print advertisements, and collateral material. (Additionally, show the product, if that was part of the school problem.)

b. Single ads or posters for different products

c. Marker-drawn storyboards, to show technical skill

d. Web example, whether or not done for an advertising project

Art Director

Show samples that exhibit experience with a firm or agency.

Contents

Fifteen to twenty-five samples:

a. One speculative campaign (for school or otherwise)

b. Print ads done individually or as part of a team (two people)

c. One or two storyboards, to show technical and conceptual skills

d. Various ads done by you alone

e. Web examples, whether or not done for advertising clients

f. Examples of logos, packaging, and branding (if available)

Format

35mm slides (in slide tray), 4×5 transparencies, dry-mounted proofs (lamination preferable), entire publications, digital work on CD-ROM or Zip Disk.

Title: "NYC" **Designer/Creative Director:** John C. Jay **Company:** Weiden & Kennedy **Client:** Nike **Year:** 1995

212 575–Yoke

Adman Designer

JOHN MARTINEZ
Principal, J & M Martinez Ltd., Watermill, New York

What differentiates advertising design from graphic design?
I've done advertising, design, and illustration. Everything in advertising has to contribute specifically to the one message, goal, concept. In graphic design, there is often more flexibility and independence.

Are there more compromises in advertising than other areas of design?
There is more collaboration. Everything is carefully considered and tested because, usually, much more is at stake. A lot of capital and many livelihoods can be tied to a campaign for a large enterprise.

As a freelance art director, what kind of clients do you have?
In advertising, hit and run. We're brought in to solve particular problems quickly. The clients are mostly luxury goods, image campaigns. In design, there is more time, less pressure, and the clients are mostly publishers or manufacturers.

What is the most fulfilling aspect of your job?
Having clients who give good guidance and trust me implicitly.

And the biggest problem?
Short deadlines; not having sufficient time and budget.

How much of your time is spent on design and art direction and how much on business matters?
All to the first and none to the second (I have a good agent and a willing partner). Thanks to FedEx, time and distance have been completely altered. Except for production, I work entirely from home now. I no longer need full-time assistants. I e-mail much of my work. Clients expect fewer meetings and replace them with faxes, e-mail, and conference calls (I usually attend only for presentation or if a briefing is particularly involved).

Title: Noritake - Rehearsal Dinner, Coffee, Takeout **Art Director:** John Martinez **Advertising Manager:** Floyd Sullivan **Copywriter:** Nancy Tag **Company:** Dentsu **Client/Copyright:** Noritake **Photographer:** Alan Richardson **Year:** 1994

What do you look for when you do hire designers?
I look for people who have ideas and understand concepts; design skills are secondary. We have hired students and beginners but always pay them. Even if they are learning on the job, they are getting work done for us.

Tough Advertising

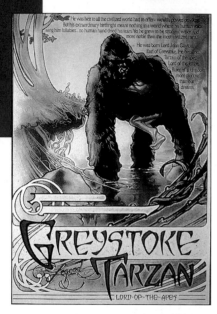

Title: Greystoke Tarzan **Designer/Creative Director:** Mike Salisbury **Company:** Salisbury Communications **Client:** Warner Brothers **Typeface:** Hand Lettered **Year:** 1989

MIKE SALISBURY
President, Salisbury Communications, Venice, California

How did you get involved in advertising and design?
I first designed logos in trade for surfboards (which are still being used today). I also painted flames on hotrods and designed the yearbook and newspaper in school. But my first real job was as the art director/reporter/cartoonist/ad designer of *Surfer* magazine. My first advertising employer was Phil Lansdale, a no-bullshit communicator at the Lansdale Agency. I learned from the agency's illustrator how to make a livelihood with ideas. Style comes and goes but ideas always communicate. The 1960s style of New York advertising and design was my design school, as were the European magazines *Twen* and *Nova*. Today I'm influenced by things like the Guerilla Marketing Seminars.

So you decided to specialize in advertising?
I've been an advertising creative director on accounts like Levi's, an editorial art director who redesigned *Rolling Stone*, a designer of corporate identities, as for Hasbro Toys, a photographer whose work is in the Museum of Modern Art, a corporate art director who won a Grammy — I don't have a specialty. What I do is make complex ideas simple. I communicate with universally understandable visual communications. How did I decide what to do? I just wanted to have fun. I wanted to do it all: print, TV, film. Now I am also a writer for *Forbes*, *Men's Journal*, *Print*, and other magazines.

What are the most and least fulfilling aspects of your job?
The most satisfying aspect of work, besides getting paid, is having clients who work with us as part of the team. Hasbro is like that. Our agency clients are like that. Our Rollerblade client is like that. We took a surfwear company from a little garage at the beach to over two million dollars a year in retail sales. Working as a team, it was fun. Our work environment here at Mike Salisbury Communications is totally open, like the newsroom of a paper. We are a team. We have no offices. The sun comes in all day and we are near the

beach. That is not too shabby a place to toil. But the most fun of all is being all alone on the road with no place to go and no particular time to have to be anywhere, with just a couple of bucks, some film, and any old camera. The least fun is hassling with clients and having employees who do not try.

What's it like working with film clients?
Tough. Very tough. Only tough guys and gals can make billions gambling on the public's likes. Movie people are demanding and tough. But they do pay their bills, and with a lot of money.

Title: Goonies **Designer/Creative Director:** Mike Salisbury **Company:** Salisbury Communications **Client:** Kaleidoscope Film **Typeface:** Hand Lettered **Year:** 1987

How do you run your shop?
Simple. I am the boss. Keep simple files. Take notes. Try. Do not overpromise. Laugh.

How much of your time is devoted to design and art direction? How much to business matters?
Ninety to ten. Guess which is the 90 percent part?

What do you look for when you hire designers?
I hire on my instincts. It has worked better for me than the traditional methods of looking at a prospect's past performance, etc. If people didn't hire based on their instincts rather than job history or experience, I would never have gotten a job.

What do you look for in designers' portfolios?
A lot of promise and a sense of irony. It is not all that serious of a world creating ephemera, is it?

Title: Streets of Fire **Designers:** Mike Salisbury, Tom Nikosey **Creative Director:** Mike Salisbury **Company:** Salisbury Communications **Client:** Universal Pictures **Typeface:** Hand Lettered **Year:** 1990

What advice would you give to someone who wants to be a graphic designer?
Study art, design, literature, history, office skills, typing, speaking. But most of all, learn to write it down: Make lists, take notes. Learn from company presidents, CEOs, salespeople, and lawyers.

At this stage in your career, are you looking to expand?
If I had his skills and his talent, I would try to have as small an operation as Paul Rand had. I have repositioned this firm to take on fewer but bigger clients. With a small staff, we are doing good work but hard work for appreciative people.

Nonstarving Art Director

ABI ARON SPENCER
Senior Art Director, DeVito Verdi, New York City

How did you get into advertising design?
I received a B.F.A. from the School of Visual Arts, and as an SVA undergraduate, you get exposure to the major communication fields. I took a strong liking to advertising.

Do you have a strong personal style? Is it important to have one in advertising design?
The agency I work for has a style, but I try to avoid being pigeon-holed into any one style. Madonna would be a great art director.

How would you describe a good working environment?
One that is open to new ideas: an environment where people are not threatened by the unfamiliar, an environment where people are willing to take chances.

What is the most fulfilling aspect of your job? The least?
Having your ad stand out among the millions. Having an ad remembered and appreciated by people not in the industry. Least fulfilling is having an ad you know is great never see the light of day.

Title: T-Shirt **Designers:** Aaron Eiseman, Abi Aron Spencer **Art Directors:** Abi Aron Spencer, Aaron Eiseman **Publication:** People Magazine **Client:** Daffy's **Photographer:** Steven Hellerstein **Year:** 1996

Title: Multiple Personalities **Designers:** Aaron Eiseman, Abi Aron Spencer **Art Directors:** Abi Aron Spencer, Aaron Eiseman **Client:** Digital City **Year:** 1998

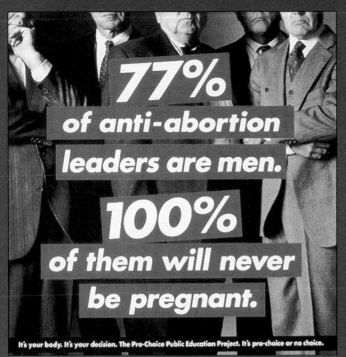

77%
of anti-abortion leaders are men.
100%
of them will never be pregnant.

It's your body. It's your decision. The Pro-Choice Public Education Project. It's pro-choice or no choice.

How much of your time is devoted to art direction versus business matters?
You never get enough time to design an ad. I currently work at an agency that's more concept-driven than it is driven by design.

What do you look for when hiring designers?
It helps to have connections, but a great portfolio is a great portfolio. Good agencies don't have to look for art directors; art directors have to look for good agencies.

What advice would you give to someone interested in becoming an advertising art director?
My advice to anyone who wants to be an advertising designer is to either do great ads or don't bother. The field is already saturated with mediocre art directors. The good advertising designer remembers that an advertisement is more than a piece of art — it must clearly communicate an idea. An overdesigned ad can be worse than an underdesigned ad. Knowing this is more important than any skill.

What would you like to attain in your career?
Money, power, respect. Let's not forget, this isn't a career for people aspiring to become the next Mother Teresa.

Title: 77% (Inspired by Barbara Kruger) **Art Directors:** Abi Aron Spencer, Aaron Eiseman **Client:** Pro-Choice Public Education Project **Year:** 1998

Title: Siskel & Ebert **Art Directors:** Abi Aron Spencer, Rob Carducci **Client:** Time Out New York **Year:** 1998

Title: Beer Can **Designers:** Aaron Eiseman, Abi Aron Spencer **Art Directors:** Abi Aron Spencer, Aaron Eiseman **Client:** Esquire Magazine **Year:** 1997

Designing Advertising

RICHARD WILDE

Principal, Creative Director, Wilde Design; Chair, Advertising & Graphic Design Departments, School of Visual Arts; and President, Magical Monkey, New York

How did you decide to go into advertising design?
I've always been influenced by great design and advertising work. Also, I'm influenced by humor in virtually any form it takes. As strange as it may sound, people do not select a profession; the profession selects them. I've had the good fortune of being a graphic designer, advertising art director, and educator for the past thirty-three years, where each discipline has influenced the other. Getting back to the question of how I got into advertising design, it simply presented itself, and although I like to think I chose it, it chose me.

Is there a fundamental difference between working in advertising and other forms of graphic design?
There are fundamental differences between advertising and graphic design. Generally speaking, in creative ad agencies one works collaboratively with a writer. The initial focus is developing a concept, which in turn dictates the form and content of the ad. In graphic design, the formal concerns for the most part are paramount, and the concept lies

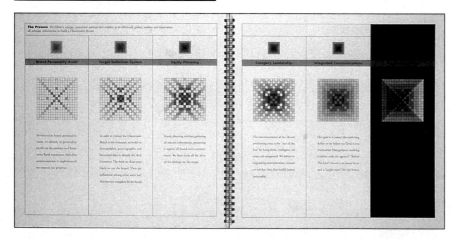

Title: Ad Agency Philosophy and Identity **Designers:** Richard Wilde, Roswitha Rodrigues **Creative Director:** Neil Drossman **Agency/Client:** Ryan Drossman + Partners **Typefaces:** Futura XBold, Garamond **Year:** 1998

in this formalism. Although design problems need a strategy, it ultimately comes down to, not what you do, but how you do it.

It sounds like you're saying that just as in the past, copywriters rule the roost. Is that right?

The relationship between the copywriter and the art director is dictated by each specific agency. In top ad agencies throughout the United States, copywriters and art directors have equal footing. Generally speaking, in the less creative shops, copywriters still have the edge.

How much of your time is devoted to design versus art direction?

Currently, I'm senior vice president at Ryan Drossman and Partners, which is an advertising agency where I work on both advertising and graphic design projects. I'm also a principal of Wilde Design, where we only do design projects. In all, 50 percent of my time is devoted to design while the other 50 percent is devoted to advertising art direction.

At the agency, do you use much freelance work?

I use freelancers all the time: photographers, illustrators, model makers, type designers, producers, and directors. Recently, the agency created a design department that hires designers as projects dictate. Because I'm also chair of both the advertising and graphic design departments at the School of Visual Arts, I hire several student interns throughout the year.

What do you look for in a graphic design portfolio when hiring a designer or art director for the agency?

When I hire for advertising work, I'm not interested in seeing graphic design portfolios. My interest is in portfolios made up of ads that show conceptual thinking and original art direction, that focus on campaigns for specific products or services. I review graphic design portfolios only when I'm hiring someone to do promotional work for the agency. Then, I look for innovative thinking coupled with first-rate design executions. Today, the student who has expertise in graphic design and advertising and is well versed in the computer has a marked advantage in securing the more creative job.

What advice would you give to someone who wants to be an advertising designer?

I choose not to use the words *advertising designer*. For the most part, people in the art end of advertising are called art directors. They conceptualize and design ads. If one wishes to be an art director today, it is essential to study in an art school that offers advertising as a major, such as the School of Visual Arts or the Art Center. This affords one the best opportunity in terms of getting into the field. Concerning employment for graphic designers, the same holds true.

Title: Total Delivery Service **Designer:** Richard Wilde **Creative Director:** Neil Drossman **Client:** Total Delivery Service **Typeface:** Futura Condensed **Year:** 1998

Title: Poster - Neil Drossman **Designer:** Richard Wilde **Creative Director:** Neil Drossman **Client:** Ryan Drossman and Partners **Illustrator:** Judith Wilde **Typefaces:** Garamond, Futura Book **Year:** 1998

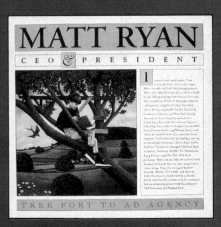

Title: Poster - Matt Ryan **Designer:** Richard Wilde **Creative Director:** Neil Drossman **Client:** Ryan Drossman + Partners **Illustrators:** Martucci + Griesback **Typeface:** Garamond **Year:** 1998

Strong Collaborator

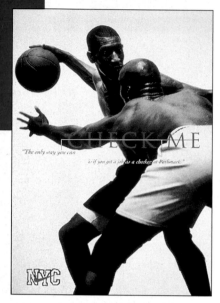

Title: "NYC" **Designer/Creative Director:** John C. Jay **Company:** Wieden & Kennedy **Photographer:** John Huet **Client:** Nike **Year:** 1995

Title: Tempo D'Italia — television advertisement **Designer/Creative Director:** John C. Jay **Company:** Wieden & Kennedy **Client:** Bloomingdale's

JOHN C. JAY
Creative Director and Partner, Wieden & Kennedy, Portland, Oregon

You worked for a number of years as creative director at Bloomingdale's and were responsible for their brilliant in-store marketing programs. How did that prepare you for work in advertising?

Although I had no experience in fashion, advertising, or retail, my second job was at Bloomingdale's, first as senior art director, then as creative director for ten years, and then as executive vice president and director of marketing for another two-and-a-half years. It was an amazing time to be at the store. We built one of the most unique creative departments in the country and recruited talent from all over the world. With Kal Ruttentstein and his fashion office, we created projects like no retailer had ever seen before or since. Despite all of the acclaim, in the minds of most of the so-called elites in the advertising agency world, in-house retail creative departments such as ours were still at the bottom of the food chain. Thus, it is with great irony that today I am a partner and creative director of one of the world's most respected creative agencies. I owe a lot to all of my associates from that in-house shop.

Under the leadership of Bloomingdale's former chairman, Marvin S. Traub, we were given the world to learn from. No other job on earth could have prepared me better for my future career in advertising at W&K. That includes any job at any other agency in the world. For over a decade, I traveled to all parts of the world on both research trips and shoots. We worked in China, France, Spain, Brazil, Italy, Ireland, India, Japan, and many other countries to develop the famous country promotions at the store. On these trips, I was able to learn firsthand about product development; we married Bloomindale's design and product marketing expertise with the skills of artisans from around the world.

This learning experience is the backbone of my career and style of work. It was the total fusion of research, product design, advertising, public relations, event planning, and graphic design. This kind of training and learning experience simply doesn't exist today. The Marvin Traubs of the world have been pushed aside as the gritty and financially tough times of retail bankruptcies and consolidation continue to take their toll. Traub not only encouraged us to learn more about our specific areas but made it practically mandatory to learn about each culture's food, politics, history, and art. This school was not simply about advertising or design — it was about life, taste, culture, and diversity. It was truly extraordinary.

What is the fundamental difference between working in advertising and other forms of graphic design?

The major difference is the partnership — and I stress the word *partnership* — of copywriter and art director. Together, they work on concepts first and think about execution second. There is a general mistrust of graphic design in advertising — a suspicion that its priority lies in the decoration of communications, not in ideas. Where there is smoke, there usually is fire, but we must be careful of such sweeping generalizations. There is good and bad in both disciplines. It is a shame that they have been separated into different skill sets.

You mentioned the partnership between copywriters and designers. In the past, copywriters ruled the advertising roost. Has this changed markedly?

Sad to say, this hasn't changed all that much, and it is still a bit perplexing to me. Sometimes it's a matter of how you were socialized by the industry's internal politics and culture. In the ad world, the writer has somehow been more associated with the concept. This may be the fault of the art director, and I've noticed that some young art directors fall into that support role all too quickly. Art directors need to be articulate in expressing the ideas to the clients; the best ones can often write very well, and they all need to live in a world much bigger than advertising or design. Graphic designers point to advertising's gross commercialism when, in fact, they may simply be suffering from a case of budget envy. I laughed in school when my Professors of Purity deemed advertising to be "the closest thing to prostitution" while case studies on corporate identity programs, designed to sell a major corporation's image, were viewed as noble. Historically, designers have been guilty of treating copywriters as an outside service like typesetting, retouching, and separation instead of an integral part of the conceptual process.

Advertising's television-oriented art directors are supported by a lot of outside specialists who can make their lives easier. They are supported by a director's vision, the production designer's creativity, an editor's vision for storytelling, and a sound and music designer to add emotion. Need to kern out the type? No problem, hire a type-on-film specialist. Everything is a bit less hands-on. It's no wonder that basic skills and taste in typography and photo direction have eroded in the ad world.

Title: Urban Attack
Designer/Creative Director: John C. Jay **Copywriter:** Jimmy Smith **Company:** Wieden & Kennedy **Illustrator:** Moshino **Client:** Nike **Year:** 1998

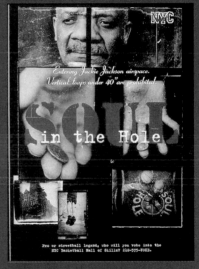

Title: "NYC" **Designer/Creative Director:** John C. Jay **Company:** Wieden & Kennedy **Photographer:** John Huet **Client:** Nike **Year:** 1995

Combining Talents

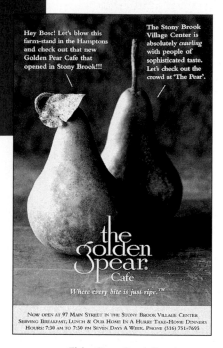

Hey Bosc! Let's blow this farm-stand in the Hamptons and check out that new Golden Pear Cafe that opened in Stony Brook!!!

The Stony Brook Village Center is absolutely *crawling* with people of sophisticated taste. Let's check out the crowd at 'The Pear'.

the Golden Pear. Cafe

Where every bite is just ripe.™

Now open at 97 Main Street in the Stony Brook Village Center
Serving Breakfast, Lunch & Our Home In A Hurry Take-Home Dinners
Hours: 7:30 am to 7:30 pm Seven Days A Week. Phone (516) 751-7695

Title: Stony Brook Grand Opening **Designer/Creative Director/Copywriter:** Jean Govoni **Company:** Jean Govoni + Partners **Client:** The Golden Pear Cafe **Photographer:** Lou Spitalnick **Typeface:** Bembo **Year:** 1998

Title: Yar Logo **Designer/ Creative Director:** Jean Govoni **Client:** YAR Communications **Company:** Jean Govoni + Partners **Year:** 1990

JEAN GOVONI

President and Creative Director, Jean Govoni + Partners, Sag Harbor, New York

How did you get involved in advertising design?

In the fall of 1969 at Syracuse University I had an art history professor ask me what I was planning to major in (as I had done such a bang-up job with my "Neoclassicism and Romanticism" oral and written report). When I told him advertising, he recoiled in horror and tried to steer me toward a career in art history with the goal of ending up at some big museum or something. Fortunately for the world of business, I stuck to my guns and stuck with advertising.

And what made an impression on you?

At the time, I was gaga over George Lois's work and Helmut Krone's. I had the opportunity to meet George Lois when I was still in school, which is a whole story in and of itself. My aunt had a dear friend who knew George Lois, so they arranged a meeting with him. On the day we were to meet, I set off on foot for my 8:00 A.M. appointment and within a few minutes, a torrential rainstorm materialized. In true New York it's-raining-like-crazy fashion, there was not a taxi in sight. So I had to walk the whole way and needless to say, showed up at George Lois's doorstep looking like a wet rat. I remember George asking his secretary for a towel so he could wipe off my book and I could dry my hair. Anyway, I was totally awestruck. The offices were very modern, beautifully designed — everything an ad agency should look like. He was very nice, gave me a few suggestions on things I could do to my book, and that was the last I saw of him. Except I do remember him commenting in *Adweek* on a campaign I did for Yoplait Yogurt (way back when), and it gave me a bit of a thrill to read he gave it a thumbs-up.

So you specialize in advertising now?

As I look back over my career, I have combined both my graphic design and art direction skills. I have designed logos, packaging, displays, all kinds of things as well as conceptualizing the Big

Ideas and blowing them out in TV, print, direct mail. So, by being a bit "ambidextrous," I can really think and execute in a totally integrated way. I used to feed lines to copywriters and eventually I started just doing some of it myself. So at this point, I don't consider myself a specialist. I am most definitely a generalist — or, more accurately, I consider myself a true communicator.

What is the most important aspect of your work?

I guess the one thing I can say about my work is that I like to make people smile. Even if it's something serious and practical, like banking, I like to inject something that will make people smile — make them like the product. Overall, I believe it's my job, as a communicator, to tap into people's emotions, humor being one of those emotions. If I can stir you emotionally, make you cry, make you think, make you feel warm inside, then I have gotten through to you. Let's face it, most of what I do is not the number-one thing on people's minds. I have to catch their eye, grab their attention away from what is going on in their life, to present something to them in the hope that they will ultimately buy it. So, whimsical, humorous, likable, accessible, clean, and up-market is how I like to describe my style.

Do you have a specific approach to hiring designers?

When I need to find art directors or designers, I usually call a couple of headhunters who I like and respect and fill them in on what I'm looking for. What I look for in a designer is usually 80 percent represented by their book and by their resume. I don't necessarily mean what's in the resume — I'm talking about how they design their resume. I like to see advertising campaigns, generally about four or five of them, with three executions per campaign. I also like to see outdoor boards because they encapsulate so much of the idea and the execution into one single-minded piece. I also look for examples of graphic design projects — logos, packaging, collateral, that sort of thing. I look for a sense of typography; this is very important to me. I look at how the book itself is put together. If it is sloppily put together, then I know that they don't care about how things look. If it's clean and professional-looking, then it tells me that the person behind the book is probably going to be the same.

Title: Art Directors Club - Awards Invitation Designer/Creative Director: Jean Govoni Company: Jean Govoni + Partners Client: The Art Directors Club Typeface: Trade Gothic Year: 1995

Title: History Page Designer/Creative Director/Copywriter: Jean Govoni Company: Jean Govoni + Partners Client: The Golden Pear Cafe Illustrator: Clip Art Typeface: Bernhard Modern Year: 1998

Title: Soup Designer/Creative Director/Copywriter: Jean Govoni Company: Jean Govoni + Partners Client: The Golden Pear Cafe Photographer: Lou Spitalnick Typefaces: Bernhard Modern, Bembo Year: 1998

VII. Environmental

GRAPHIC DESIGNERS have engaged in some aspect of what is currently known as *environmental graphic design* since the 1800s. Back then it was called *sign painting* — which is not to imply that the new discipline is exactly the same as the old but rather suggests that it evolved from a venerable craft into a sophisticated specialty (that employs sign painters, among other craftspeople, in the process). Today, environmental graphic designers are involved in a wide range of design activities, from billboards to wayfinding to interactive kiosks. Indeed, virtually every aspect of design that deals with an outside or inside physical environment is fair game for the environmental designer. For those with an interest in architecture and interior design, this specialty is a point of intersection. Environmental graphic designers are routinely included in design and planning teams that must solve problems endemic to defining and marking cultural, commercial, and residential space.

ON THE MOST rudimentary level, environmental designers are concerned with the look and feel of signs, which might include anything from a simple retail shop shingle to an entire directional system for a hospital, theater, or museum. The former might be one board that bears little or no relationship to the rest of the architectural or interior design, while the latter is often a major component of a coordinated overall identity — an institution's logo and related graphic elements are carried through the environmental aspects of an entire program. To achieve success at this kind of design is not as easy as flipping a switch that causes one or two dimensions to become three. Rather, it involves a keen ability to make something that is ostensibly flat into dynamic three-dimensional objects. Moreover, this is not an abstract process; the environmental designer must have experience with and current knowledge of numerous new materials and fabricating processes that transform ideas on paper into functional objects.

Urban Blight/Advertisers' Rights

Critics argue that billboards are a blight on the environment, but this is not always true. While roadside beautification is a cause célèbre that few would argue against, billboards and electronic spectaculars are also invaluable means of mass communication. A billboard in the middle of a sylvan setting certainly has an adverse impact on the sanctity of nature, but on the urban streetscape, in areas zoned for such things, these signs are perfectly acceptable, particularly when environmental graphic designers exercise responsibility. Times Square would be a drab canyon if not for the spectaculars that give the Great White Way its glimmer and sheen. Likewise, commercial strips around the nation benefit from well-designed outdoor advertising that both sells a product, conveys a message, and provides entertainment. Not all these displays are blights when designers make it their business to act responsibly.

Title: Walt Disney World, Orlando, Florida **Associate in Charge:** Robert Cordell **Designers:** Scott Cuyler, Corky Retson, Kyoko Tsuge **Creative Directors:** Deborah Sussman **Company:** Sussman Prejza **Client:** Disney Development Co. **Photographer:** Timothy Hursley **Year:** 1990

Two-dimensional graphic design is a decidedly utilitarian applied art, but environmental graphic design demands even more attention to function because of the direct impact it has on the public. The old saying that graphic design, unlike architecture, will not collapse and therefore never harm an individual is not necessarily true in this genre. A badly built or installed sign can do considerable physical damage. In fact, official ordinances and codes govern at least the minimum requirements for this kind of design, so environmental designers — many of whom begin their careers as print designers — must have extensive training and apprenticeships with design firms that devote the better part of their time to practice in this area. Most art and design schools include environmental courses within a graphic design curriculum, but for those who want to seriously pursue this specialty, more rigorous course work should be sought out.

Environmental graphic design is an umbrella term for various design activities, of which wayfinding is among the most common. Everyone has found themselves lost within a sprawling confine where, most likely, directions were either confusing or nonexistent. Without a map (and even with one), successful navigation relies on a system of integrated signs. This is the job of wayfinding, and the graphic designer's responsibility (often working with environmental planners) is to devise systems that are not only easy to follow but aesthetically pleasing within the environment. It is not enough to design a sign with an arrow pointing in one direction if no complementary signs are spaced at just the right intervals as further guides. Wayfinding is as much about engineering efficient traffic flow as it is making functional design. Yet wayfinding is also often just one component of a larger scheme.

The environmental designer is responsible not only for directing traffic but also for education and illumination. Take a zoo, for example: Not only must the public be directed where to go in the maze of displays and attractions, but it must also be informed about the contents of the displays. The job of creating informational signs and panels often resides with the environmental designer. This, like any graphic design activity, is not as simple as stapling a piece of paper with a block of text to a wall beside an attraction. Because individuals read differently — and some do not read at all — it is important to present information in an engaging and aesthetically pleasing manner consistent with the overall identity of the zoo. Sometimes the designer builds a format typographically; at other times, type and image are combined. Sometimes illustrators are employed to render details of the flora and fauna; sometimes photographs are the principle visual ingredient. Of course, maps and charts play important roles in showing where species derive and migrate. The smart designer knows how to marshal these elements and who to commission to do the best possible work (often within a tight budget).

Creating information graphics in a physical environment is fundamentally not all that different from doing it in a print environment. However, three-dimensional space allows for more media options than does print. Among the most

common are interactive displays — kiosks with touch-screen computers, videos, or CD-ROMs — that can be effectively employed to complement the more traditional text media. Environmental designers must be trained to determine which of these is most effective in a particular context (and within a concrete budget).

In addition to education, environmental design involves creating and establishing an aura or mood for events, places, and institutions, such as baseball stadiums, Olympic arenas, theme parks, commercial malls, industrial parks, and urban arts and culture zones, as well as entire city and town business districts. The materials employed may include banners and flags, signs and guideposts, stands and kiosks, billboards and electronic spectaculars — both temporary and permanent. Working in tandem with architects and planners, the environmental designer does not just provide a service but contributes to the content of project.

Some corporations hire in-house environmental designers under the rubrics of graphic, interior, or architectural design but, more often, outside design firms are commissioned on a project basis. Some of the larger architecture firms maintain environmental design divisions, but the medium- and small-sized offices also commission outside design firms. Some graphic design firms include environmental design as part of their repertoire, while other firms dedicate themselves exclusively to environmental design. Finally, some environmental design firms subcontract parts of a job (interactivity, for example) to specialist firms. To enter this field, you are advised to identify a design firm, office, or studio where environmental design represents a significant amount of the work and tailor a portfolio to this growing specialty.

Graphic designers who work in this area must have two- and three-dimensional acuity. An effective portfolio shows a variety of typographic and problem-solving skills, as well as an ability to design effective wayfinding and navigational systems.

Entry Level

School projects including signs and graphics for real or imagined buildings, shops, and events are useful in showing insight into how design works in the environment.

Contents

Ten to twenty samples:
a. Two sign ideas
b. Two to three drawings of signs, banners, etc. in the context of the environement
c. One to three coordinated sign systems

Advanced

Show samples that exhibit experience either assisting or initiating environmental projects

Contents

Fifteen to twenty-five samples:
a. One speculative campaign
b. Any work that exhibits prowess with three-dimensional media
c. Plans for signage or wayfinding systems
d. Real or prospective exhibition or event design materials

Format

35mm slides (in slide tray), 4×5 transparencies, dry-mounted proofs (lamination preferable), entire publications, digital work on CD-ROM or Zip Disk.

Title: Central Park Zoo Signage and Graphics Program **Designers:** David Gibson, Juanita Dugdale, Sylvia Harris **Creative Director:** David Gibson **Company:** Two Twelve Associates, Inc. **Client:** The New York Zoological Society **Architects:** Kevin Roche, John Dinkeloo & Associates **Photographers:** Jim D'Addio, Peter Aaron/Esto **Typeface:** Bodoni **Year:** 1987

Vision Matters Most

Title: East Washington Boulevard Revitalization **Associate in Charge:** Scott Cuyler **Designers:** Sharon Blair, Holly Hampton, Paula Loh **Creative Director:** Deborah Sussman **Company:** Sussman Prejza **Client:** Culver City Redevelopment Agency **Photographer:** Jim Simmons, Annette Del Zoppo Photography **Year:** 1998

DEBORAH SUSSMAN
President, Sussman Prejza, Culver City, California

How did you decide on environmental design?
A natural evolution from fine art to visual communication and a feel for environmental (dimensional) work.

Do you have a personal style in your design?
A personal standard and vision matter most. Style is to be avoided; one's imprint is what counts. My approach is contextual, free, tending toward boldness. I thrive on large-scale programs, collaboration, and teamwork.

How much of your time is devoted to design and art direction and how much to business matters?
Art direction: 25 percent; design: 15 percent; conceptualizing: 25 percent; dealing with clients and collaborators: 25 percent; business matters: 10 percent.

What would you like to accomplish in your career?
Permanent civic and cultural aspects of the urban landscape or streetscape. The best product for the most people, accessible to all.

Title: 1984 Olympic Games **Designers:** Debra Valencia, Mark Nelsen, Scott Cuyler, Luci Goodman, Susan Hancock, John Johnston, Charles Milhaupt, Charles Reimers, Corky Retson, Stephen Silvestri, Eugene Treadwell, Fernando Vazquez **Creative Directors:** Deborah Sussman, Paul Prejza **Company:** Sussman Prejza **Client:** Los Angeles Olympic Organizing Committee **Photographer:** Jim Simmons, Annette Del Zoppo Photography **Year:** 1984

Title: Walt Disney World, Orlando, Florida
Associate in Charge: Robert Cordell
Designers: Scott Cuyler, Corky Retson, Kyoko Tsuge **Creative Directors:** Deborah Sussman
Company: Sussman Prejza **Client:** Disney Development Co. **Photographer:** Timothy Hursley **Year:** 1990

Title: City of Santa Monica **Designers:** Deborah Sussman, Debra Valencia, Paula Loh **Creative Director:** Deborah Sussman **Company:** Sussman Prejza **Client:** City of Santa Monica **Photographer:** Jim Simmons, Annette Del Zoppo Photography

Effect On the World

Title: Irvington Gateways
Designers: Michael Manwaring, Bruce Anderson, Jay Claiborne
Company: The Office of Michael Manwaring **Client:** City of Fremont, California **Typeface:** Futura **Year:** 1993

MICHAEL MANWARING

Principal, The Office of Michael Manwaring, San Anselmo, California

You do print and environmental design. What is the difference?
In general, environmental graphic design (EGD) is a slower process than print or digital graphic design. Most of the people in the field right now are early to late middle age. Of course, it does not have to be this way. If you want to create graphic design that hangs around for a longer time period, and you love craft and materials and have some degree of patience, then EGD might be for you. EGD can be as simple as choosing wall colors or adding a sign on the front of a store. It can be more complex if you change the position of the walls to redefine the space, or make the walls into shapes, or make the space into figures, or make the walls a sign, or make the space a sign, or make the whole front of the store a symbol that then becomes known as its sign. It can also be how a store relates to the public space in front of it — landscaping, street furniture, lighting, paving patterns, lighting shadow shapes, sounds, and smell.

Title: Silicon Graphics Signage Program **Designers:** Michael Manwaring, Tim Perks **Company:** The Office of Michael Manwaring **Client:** Silicon Graphics Computer Systems **Typeface:** Univers family **Year:** 1996

What about this interests you?

What interests me is working in public space. This can involve street signing, trail maps, history walks, exhibits, memorials, monuments, and design of festivities. Working in public space means being engaged in the world; it can shape space, perceptions and consciousness. There is so much potential here for designers to have a useful and positive affect on the world and simultaneously feel that they are part of it.

What advice would you give to someone who is interested in environmental design?

Even though I feel EGD has not really defined itself clearly, to me there are a few things that should be canon:
- Whatever you create, you should think of it in a cultural sense: Are you contributing to your culture, or are you making things worse?
- Make things well. Nurture a love for materials and how things are made. Think of tectonics.
- From time to time, make something with your hands — preferably out of doors.

Title: Downtown Plaza Signage **Designers:** Michael Manwaring, David Meckel, Tim Perks **Company:** The Office of Michael Manwaring **Client:** The Hahn Company **Year:** 1991

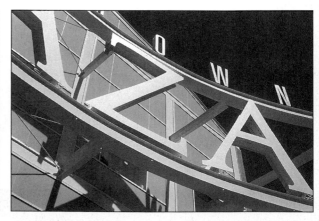

Designing in Public Spaces

Sheila Levrant deBretteville has a special interest in the environmental design of public spaces that give something to the community. A recent project, funded by the Department of Cultural Affairs of the City of New York, for a library in Flushing, Queens, is called Search: Literature. "I searched for a visual metaphor that would have to combine a basic and immutable aspect of Library," she says, "as well as a major aspect of the Flushing Community — historically a place where immigrants come in search of freedom, in search of a better life. I identify with this quest as I am the daughter of Polish immigrants for whom reading and education were the path to becoming viable citizens." Her idea involved placing the titles of what she refers to as "search narratives" at the base of the new library. Narrative literature, stories in which a person seeks out a truth, exist in every culture and are handed down by grandparents, parents, or read in school. DeBretteville talked to many people in the neighborhood serviced by the Flushing Library and each related a story that they said was known to virtually everyone in the community.

DeBretteville chose titles commonly known to the people of the country in which they were told and written. She then etched the titles into the granite risers of the stairs in much the same way names of famous thinkers are cut into the stone of civic buildings. Her hope was that at least one title would be recognized by pedestrians and that their interest in the titles they did not recognize would lure them into the library. "Each title I chose because of an aspect of search in the nature of the story told," deBrettville explains. "Searching for something you do not have at home appeared to me to be an apt metaphor both for immigration and for the experience of going to a library. Many of the people in the street do not come from cultures with public libraries but all of them either recognize their language or the names of one or more of the stories whose titles I had cut into the stone

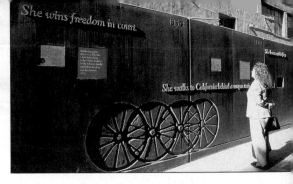

Title: Biddy Mason: Time & Place
Designer: Sheila Levrant deBretteville
Client: Community Redevelopment Agency, Los Angeles, Power of Place
Photographer: Annette del Zoppo
Typeface: Goudy **Year:** 1990

steps when they were still in the Georgia quarry."

Regarding design for public spaces, deBretteville says, "I do permanent public work now, usually at the edge of cities, and usually involved with immigrant populations. As my parents were immigrants and I grew up in an extended family of many aunts, uncles, and grandparents, I have an affinity for the experience of immigrant populations. And I like to talk to people about their neighborhood's history. It is a terrific opportunity for me to be able to go to a site and propose what it is I think makes sense both to me and to the neighborhood."

Architecture and Design

Title: Gateway Sign **Designer:** Jennifer Bressler **Creative Director:** Wayne Hunt **Company:** Hunt Design Associates **Client:** City of Pasadena **Photographer:** Jim Simmons/Annette del Zoppo **Year:** 1998

Title: Airport Welcome Sign **Designer:** John Temple **Creative Director:** Wayne Hunt **Company:** Hunt Design Associates **Client:** McCarran International Airport **Photographer:** Jim Simmons/Annette del Zoppo **Year:** 1998

WAYNE HUNT
Principal, Hunt Design Associates, Pasadena, CA

How did you decide to become an environmental graphic designer?
I've always loved architecture and have a sense for three-dimensional spaces and design. I'd rather read an architecture magazine than any graphics publication. Environmental graphics is the logical result of marrying architecture and graphic design — signage, exhibit design, placemaking, and wayfinding design. At Hunt Design, we practice environmental graphics with an emphasis on entertainment spaces.

Is it more difficult doing environmental work or print?
Each has good and bad points. Some designers are good at both. However, as each discipline grows more technical, it is less likely that any one person can be effective at both — there's just too much to know.

How do you go after clients?
The best is when they go after you. That doesn't happen too often, especially at first. We try to be a source that is automatically considered for the good EGD projects, certainly in Southern California. That's a result of reputation, public relations, being active in the field. Of course, we go after specific projects, architects, and clients. We contact them and try to wangle an interview. It's pretty basic, really.

Do you have a personal style in your design?
I hope not. We try to avoid it at all costs. Graphic designers generally should not have a personal style.

What is the most fulfilling aspect of your job? The least?
I enjoy the dialog with enlightened clients (when we have them) — presenting, selling, promoting, persuading. The best part of all is bringing good work, work I believe in, to a meeting of sophisticated, demanding clients. I also enjoy broad overviews, strategy, and organizing complex situations. I'm not good at the details.

The least fulfilling part is the ever-increasing noncreative part of large environmental graphics projects: mountains of paperwork and reports, insurance, legal issues, recordkeeping, etc. I also don't enjoy firing people — so I hire extremely carefully.

What does someone who is interested environmental design need to know?
It helps to love architecture, cities and neighborhoods, museums and theme parks, airports and public spaces of all kinds. It helps to love maps, systems, and complex communication challenges. However, if you're an uncompromising perfectionist, EGD may be frustrating for you.

Title: Children's Zoo Exhibit **Designer:** John Temple, Christina Allen **Creative Director:** Wayne Hunt **Company:** Hunt Design Associates **Client:** LA Zoo **Photographer:** Jim Simmons/Annette del Zoppo **Year:** 1996

Title: Panda Panda Restaurant Identity **Designers:** Jennifer Bressler, Christina Allen **Creative Director:** Wayne Hunt **Company:** Hunt Design Associates **Client:** Panda Management Inc. **Photographer:** Jim Simmons/Annette del Zoppo **Year:** 1998

Title: View of Rocket Plaza at Apollo Saturn File Center - Exhibit Design **Designers:** Brian Memmot, Christina Allen **Creative Director:** Wayne Hunt **Company:** Hunt Design Associates **Producer:** BRC Imagination Arts **Client:** NASA **Photographer:** Jim Simmons/Annette del Zoppo **Year:** 1997

Network and Teamwork

Icons developed as landmarks to identify interpretive overlook stations.

Taylor Park Riverwalk
Newport, Kentucky

Sacred Hunting Grounds
Boy Scout Trail
Turn of the Century Newport

Newport Barracks
Barrels of Beer
Bridging the River

Down by the River
Raging Waters
Steel Town

Title: Newport Riverwalk
Designers: Robert Probst, Heinz
Schenker, Kelly Kolar **Company:**
Firehouse Design Team **Client:**
City of Newport, Kentucky
Photographer: Robert Probst,
Heinz Schenker **Year:** 1996

ROBERT PROBST
Principal, Firehouse Design Team, Cincinnati

How do you define environmental graphic design?

Environmental graphic design is defined as the planning, design, and specifying of graphic elements in the built and natural environment. These elements are used to communicate specific information in the environment — for example, they identify, inform, direct, interpret, orient, regulate, or decorate. Environmental graphic design is multidimensional, utilizing materials that withstand the elements as well as time. Examples of environmental design applications are seen in zoos, museums, airports, hospitals, commercial events, sports facilities, cities. Teamwork is essential in this field. Practicing environmental graphic design requires a more collaborative effort than does graphic design. Its multidimensionality usually necessitates and involves a variety of professionals: engineers, landscape architects, artisans, administrators from municipal bureaucracies, etc.

How do you go after clients?

Networking and teamworking with architects, interior designers, urban planners, engineers as well as public and private institutions is essential. Large-scope environmental graphic design work is almost always awarded through a competitive process and often to multidisciplinary joint venture teams.

What is the most fulfilling aspect of your job? The least?

The most fulfilling aspect of my job is that I am free to create, usually restrained only by time and budget. That freedom gives me the energy to passionately invent, strategize, develop, and create solutions for design problems. This activity comes from the heart — therefore, it seems effortless. On the other hand, it can easily consume my entire life and put a strain on relationships and family. The least fulfilling aspect for me is the constant calculation of my creative output against the estimated financial worth of a project. I have a hard time assessing creativity by giving it a monetary value and almost always feel exploited. The true reward is usually the creation, not the paycheck.

Title: Sinclair Community College **Designers:** Robert Probst, Heinz Schenker, Kelly Kolar **Company:** Firehouse Design Team **Client:** Sinclair Community College Administration, Dayton, Ohio **Photographer:** Robert Probst **Typefaces:** Frutiger, Clarendon **Year:** 1996

How has the computer affected your work?

The computer has affected my work only in that production is done differently — on the surface, quicker and slicker. The computer is a seductive tool. Its speed allows the rapid generation of endless variations, but any given software program places limits on the design solution. The computer provides opportunity for better visualization and more effective communication. It surely makes a lot of things easier, but also opens the door to a whole new dimension of increased complications.

What do you look for when hiring designers?

A creative personality with integrity, honesty, and humility. Because I am also a professor at a highly respected institution, I do not have to look far to find the right talent. I have hired many interns from our own institution. We are set up as a cooperative education program in which students alternate school and work at three-month intervals. Practice informs education and academia inspires industry.

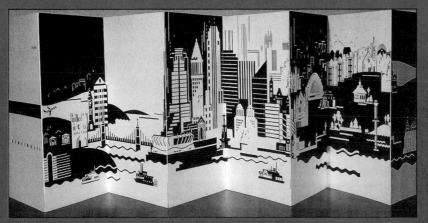

Title: Cincinnati City Identity **Designers:** Robert Probst, Kelly Kolar **Company:** Firehouse Design Team **Client:** DCI, Inc. — Downtown Cincinnati Incorporated **Illustrators:** Robert Probst, Kelly Kolar **Year:** 1994

The Built Environment

Title: Baltimore Waterfront Promenade Signage Program **Designers:** David Gibson, Doug Morris, Julie Marable **Creative Director:** David Gibson **Company:** Two Twelve Associates, Inc. **Client:** Baltimore Harbor Endowment **Architect:** Cho, Wilks & Benn **Photographer:** Jake Wyman **Typeface:** Futura **Year:** 1992

DAVID B. GIBSON
Principal, Two Twelve Associates, New York City

What is environmental graphic design and how is it different from graphic design?
Environmental graphic design is graphic communication in the built environment, a.k.a. signage. Environmental graphics is a confusing term; people often assume it refers to something ecological, which it does not. It is quite different from classic two-dimensional (and four-dimensional) graphic design. The projects are usually much bigger, the client teams more complex, the issues more diverse, but the sensitivity to design and good typography and layout is similar. The key is to understand communication in three-dimensional space and the creation of three-dimensional objects.

How competitive is the field of environmental graphic design?
EGD is a less mature field than conventional print graphic design. As such, fewer firms are doing the work, and even fewer are working on the big high-profile projects. This is quite unlike the situation where countless smaller print design specialists compete for a standard print project. On the other hand, for high-profile and large-budget projects, there may be a national search for a design firm and therefore competition from the key players across the country. As a result, as many as ten or fifteen firms may go after such a project. Getting the job requires a submission of qualifications, possibly a visit to a remote site, the preparation of a detailed proposal, and the conducting of an interview with the client. This can be a lengthy and expensive process over several months. To get these big fish, you have to get it all right.

Is it more difficult doing environmental or print work?
EGD are more complex to me, not more difficult.

Title: Chicago Park District Signage Program **Designers:** David Gibson, Andrew Simon, Cesar Sanchez **Art Director:** David Gibson **Company:** Two Twelve Associates, Inc. **Client:** Chicago Park District **Maps Illustrator:** Gerald Boulet **Photographer:** Erik Kvulsvik **Typeface:** Scala **Year:** 1998

There seem to be many fingers in this kind of pie.
There are many, many fingers in the EGD pie. The client group can include the architect of the building and the owner or institution that is the ultimate client. These both may have several representatives on the project. An owner's representative may be managing the project. Presentations to ten or fifteen people are not unusual.

How do you go after clients?
Mostly we answer the phone. We're not proactive enough, but many great opportunities come to us because we're now well known and have been around for almost twenty years. A good deal of our work comes from the architects of the buildings and developments that need signage. We keep in touch with those that are actively giving us work right now.

Do you have a specific approach to hiring designers?
We get resumes all the time; we're in some great books about design; we have contacts with the schools.

What do you look for in new designers? Where do you find people?
I look for a sense of personal vision and commitment to design and am also interested in a personable, poised individual who can collaborate with her peers in the office and deal with clients. I assume the designer has a graphic design education.

What does someone who is dedicated to environmental design need to know?
Patience to deal with long-term projects, an interest in complexity, and, most importantly, an understanding of the third dimension — how communication works in space rather than on a two-dimensional surface.

Title: Chicago Streetscape Signage **Designers:** David Gibson, Jill Ayers **Creative Director:** David Gibson **Company:** Two Twelve Associates, Inc. **Client:** Chicago City Government **Maps Illustrator:** Gerald Boulet **Photographer:** Erik Kvulsvik **Typeface:** Transit **Year:** 1999

Title: Massachusetts General Hospital Wayfinding System **Designers:** David Gibson, Cindy Poulton, Sylvia Harris **Creative Director:** David Gibson **Company:** Two Twelve Associates, Inc. **Client:** Massachusetts General Hospital **Architect:** Stubbins Assoc. **Typeface:** Minion **Year:** 1998

VIII. Interactivity

THE TERM *new media*, which represents Web site, PDA, and CD-ROM interface design, is neither precise nor accurate. What was indeed new a decade ago has become commonplace. Now the operative term is *interactivity*. Virtually all businesses and nonprofit institutions have dedicated Web sites, which means that many design studios and firms are engaged in designing and maintaining them. Although a large percentage of Web sites are designed by freelancers or design consultancies, in-house staffs are employed where they never existed before. Businesses that have small sites usually rely on freelancers to revise and update them regularly; larger companies with continually changing contents require consistent, daily design attention. This may not be *new* anymore, but it is a burgeoning field. For those who seek jobs in this area, working for a dedicated Web design firm, a graphic design studio with a Web design component, or at an in-house staff position in a corporate Web design department are all viable options. The better your experience, the more competitive you are for the most challenging jobs.

A FEW YEARS ago, the population of designers involved in new — or what practitioners call *multi-* or *time-based media* — was comparatively low. The only way to get experience was on the job. Today, virtually every significant art and design school includes courses on Web design and other digital media. A large percentage of student portfolios include at least the requisite home page designs and, usually, fully developed Web sites with advanced navigational systems and links to supplementary pages. A few years ago, the technology did not allow for sophisticated design nuances. Today, advanced software programs have increased the potential to such an extent that stu-

Too Many Cooks?

Multimedia requires multiple skills and talents. Even if you have been a desktop Web designer in your own home and of your own site, that does not mean that in the real world you can do it by yourself. Once in the professional arena, many people are required for, and often imposed on, a multimedia project. In addition to the interface designer are directors, producers, programmers, and other technical support staff. While it is useful to be well versed across the board, total authorship in the digital realm is rare. The best work is a mixture of different chefs with distinct ingredients. Of course, this could mean too many cooks — but with the right collaborators, the project will turn out fine.

dent work is sometimes on a par with professional accomplishment. In addition, a growing number of students are launching actual sites as virtual portfolios, both to show off their talent and to develop content on their own.

New, advanced programs have made it relatively simple for a nondesigner to master this medium. In an age when even grade-school children can effortlessly create their own or classroom Web pages, adults without design training do some suprisingly competent layouts, but these must not be confused with skilled and professional designs. As is the danger with desktop publishing, it is not enough to know a few type fonts or to be able to import a picture onto a page — this is not designing, it is constructing. A Web designer must have the talent to bring aesthetic taste and navigational acuity to the construction site. The designer is often both bricklayer and architect — but more often, these days, the designer is solely an architect, leaving the mechanical aspects of Web page construction to pro-

gramming and production experts.

Because this is a highly technical medium, designers must know, or at least understand, the technological parameters and potentials involved in making site, PDA, or CD-ROM interfaces. While it is also true that print designers should understand prepress and printing limitations, a print designer can actually make do without ever seeing the inside of a press room. The multimedia designer, however, must work directly with the technology to achieve results. While the Web and CD designer does not have to be fluent in programming code, it is useful to be able to converse in this language, if only to ensure that designer and programmer are on the same track. Numerous intermediate and advanced design and programming courses are available for virtually every level of multimedia activity, from brief intensives to extended graduate studies. Those who are interested in becoming proficient in this field should explore investing in one or more of the available courses.

Within the Web site and CD-ROM job market, the possibilities are vast. All the major mass-media corporations — newspapers, magazines, television, book publishers — have Web site divisions. While the Internet is still considered a complement to the primary media, and, with most companies, on-line content is taken directly from the newspaper or television programming, nevertheless, more original material is being developed every day. Web creative departments are also growing. The Internet offers media consumers many more options than the conventional outlet, including interactivity, archiving, and purchasing capabilities. Some Web sites are solely informational, while others are designed to engage the consumer/viewer/reader in specific activities and offerings. With such a large variety of uses, designers are constantly challenged to develop interfaces that are aesthetically and functionally alluring — and rapidly changing to retain the audience's interest.

All graphic designers must work collaboratively. Some designers may have personal styles, but none can be islands without bridges to clients, production personnel, or other designers. Web and CD-ROM design require even more intense collaboration. Like movie and television producers, multimedia designers cannot achieve their goals without writers, producers, programmers, and technicians. A single designer can take on many of these roles and act as an auteur, but the completion of the project would require unlimited time. Owing to the immediacy of the medium, Web design (and, to a lesser extent, CD-ROM)

is rarely afforded a leisurely schedule. With so much competition for attention, a site must be launched quickly and revised frequently for it to be a destination of choice.

Web sites are governed by demographics, which means that each is aimed at specific segments of the on-line population. This also means that Web sites do not conform to the same few design codes. As in print design, some designers are better suited for one type of content than another. Designers for the *New York Times* site may not be qualified for the Cartoon Network site; the aesthetics and sensibility required for each style are certainly incompatible. Therefore, designers looking for work in this area should show prospective employers their most relevant work.

Web and CD-ROM design hierarchies are not very different from those in the print environment. Depending on the makeup of the firm, studio, or in-house design department, the designations are the same: *design director, art director, senior* and *junior designer*. Most Web offices also employ a large number of *interns*. Internships offer the best way to get hands-on experience in a real-time situation. Freelancers are routinely hired to fill out the creative and production teams; often, a good freelancer is permanently hired. A few years ago, Web design directors and art directors did not necessarily need to have prior Web experience. Today, however, the proliferation of the medium makes it necessary for designers on every level to be trained in the tools of the trade. But, if ever there was a graphic design industry that was welcoming of newcomers, this is definitely it.

The Optimum Portfolio

This is one of the fastest-growing media for the graphic designer and, therefore, the standard for good work is fluid. Those looking for jobs as Web site or CD-ROM designers are encouraged to present work in both printed and digital forms to at once show the quality of the graphic interfaces and the intelligence of the navigational system.

Entry Level

School assignments and personal projects are expected. Because this medium can be practiced by anyone with access to the appropriate software, it is presumed that mastery even at this level is higher than comparable print forms.

Contents

a. Various printout versions of user interfaces
b. Working screens on Zip Disk or CD-ROM
c. Links to sites already up and running (if available)
d. Photographic and illustration styles

Advanced

Projects should be fairly advanced. Not only is the design of the interface, agents, and navigational tools important, but examples of navigational systems should be prominently displayed.

Contents

a. Printout versions of user interfaces (a wide range of approaches from a signature to a utilitarian style)
b. Working screens on Zip Disk or CD-ROM
c. One or two speculative projects (if available)
d. Typography, either in digital or print formats
e. Links to sites already up and running
f. Related multimedia projects

Format

35mm slides (in slide tray), 4×5 transparencies, printouts in binder, Zip Disk, CD-ROM. The best format is your own Web site.

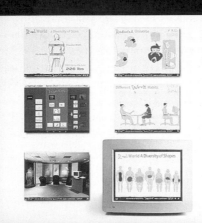

Title: The Aeron Chair
Designers: Clement Mok, Claire Barry, Paula Meizelman **Creative Director:** Clement Mok **Company:** Studio Archetype **Client:** Herman Miller **Illustrator:** Ward Schumaker **Photographers:** Stan Musleik, Terry Heffernan **Year:** 1995

I Was a Digital Psycho

Title: "Solutions for a Small Planet" Web site **Designer/Creative Director:** Ron Meckler **Company:** Re:Design **Client:** IBM **Typefaces:** IBM Bodoni, IBM Helvetica **Year:** 1996

RON MECKLER
President, Re:Design, New York City

What influenced you to become expert in the digital realm?
In 1984, I moved to New York to art-direct a music magazine for teens called *Star Hits*. After four months, *Mademoiselle* hired me as a design director. A year later, the publisher of *Star Hits* hired me back to start up *Mac User* magazine. I had played around on his Apple Lisa computer and became enthralled with the technology. Even though it was in its infancy, designing with the Macintosh reminded me of producing in a recording studio. It gave me the opportunity to try different type, graphics, and effects easily. I could see how they looked without committing to them until I was happy, affording me a lot of control. It was a lot like building music tracks — a natural evolution for me. I was such a believer that after the first six issues, I quit to start my own studio.

What new skills were needed to become a Web designer?
I learned all the new software as it came out. I was a psychopath; I spent twenty hours a day learning all the nuances, exploring the potential I felt was inherent in the new media. Understanding multiple applications, what they do and how they work, their strengths and limitations, is vital. More important, besides looking good, a Web site has to work for and be navigated intuitively by the user. Understanding how a computer can manipulate the many kinds of data and organize them for presentation is a vision every great Web producer must have.

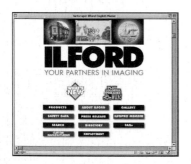

Title: Ilford Web site **Designers:** Ron Meckler, Michael Davis **Creative Director:** Ron Meckler **Company:** Re:Design **Client:** Ilford **Typeface:** Futura **Year:** 1996

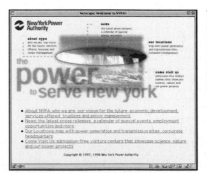

Title: New York Power Authority Web site **Designers:** Ron Meckler, Liam Sherman **Creative Director:** Ron Meckler **Company:** Re:Design **Client:** NYPA **Year:** 1997

What is different about the Web and print?

So many times I see amazing-looking sites designed by great print designers that fail due to the lack of consideration the designer has given to the Web experience. The user and his perception of the use of the site are critical. Conversely, I've seen sites that have brilliant interactivity, navigation, content, and data presentation but are unbearable because they are designed by a tech person without any knowledge of design. If those people work together on the site, they'll probably end up with something spectacular. It helps a great deal to excel in both of those disciplines so you can apply your knowledge of one while creating the other.

Are there greater opportunities for a Web designer than a print designer?

With the enormous boom in the Internet over the past few years, it seems logical that there would be many more opportunities for Web designers than print. However, print will be around for a long time, at least until all the trees are gone, so I don't think print designers need to start worrying yet. These days, clients and employers expect the print designer to be multidisciplined and have working knowledge of print-oriented applications. It's not unusual for a single designer to be responsible for a project from design through color separation or even to prep files for a print-on-demand color printer. Both disciplines have their own headache set. I happen to enjoy the set for Web design more. I think you should go for the medium that suits you.

Title: Viacom Web site
Designer: Ron Meckler
Creative Directors: Ron Meckler, Chris Hough
Company: Re:Design
Client: Viacom **Year:** 1997

Title: Pantone Web site
Designer/Creative Director: Ron Meckler **Company:** Re:Design **Client:** Pantone
Typeface: Letter Gothic
Year: 1996

Working with Concepts

Title: A+W Web Site **Designers:** Robert Altemus, Janet Waegel **Creative Director/Illustrator:** Robert Altemus **Company:** Altemus+Waegel Design **Client:** Altemus+Waegel Design **Typeface:** Magnito **Year:** 1998

Title: Altemus Collection Web Site **Designer/Creative Director/Illustrator:** Robert Altemus **Company/Client:** Altemus Collection **Typefaces:** Cushing, Empire, M Script Bold **Year:** 1998

ROBERT ALTEMUS

Partner, Altemus+Waegel Design, New York City

About your shift to new media from print — was it difficult to adjust to new forms and paradigms?

It has not been difficult for me to make the transition to the new media. I've always been a bit of a tech head, which helps, and that's probably because of my lifelong love of science fiction. The new media share the basic tenets of design and aesthetics that all print work demands and layer upon that the concerns of time, motion, and navigation. Although I had gotten deeper into print and magazines specifically in the years since college, I can refer to my experiences with film and TV. I have always approached design based on my illustrative training — that is, how do I tell the story? Not just, How do I decorate the page?

What training was required?

Much of my illustration training comes into use and, of course, I had to learn Web-specific software, including the ability to hand-code advanced HTML. Working with HTML is a rather abstract way to design. The work I do for the Internet has required learning the restrictions that this medium has; those restrictions are a moving target.

What are your specialities now?

I tend to work on the concepts and the look and feel of a project; however, I do get down and get pixels under my fingernails doing some of the actual construction.

How has the physical makeup of your studio changed in terms of plant size, staff, etc.?

The most dramatic changes occurred with the changeover from traditional magazine design and production process to desktop publishing. Ten years ago, to produce a sixty-four-page editorial product I needed three designers, two pasteup people, a type house, a stat house, a color separator, and a lot of wax. Now I can do all those jobs with just me and my Mac.

What changes do you foresee in the digital environment?

The changes will come on the user end and include a reduction of desktop clutter; the current mass of equipment in some ways still inhibits many designers. What we will move toward is something like smart, touch-sensitive high-definition drawing boards. The Internet will morph into an enhanced broadcast metaphor. We see much more influence on print design from disparate sources. The disciplines of TV design and print used to be very distinct, their looks divergent. Now each discipline seems to feed the other, as does the Internet. How many beach culture–type collages do we now see on TV commercials and intros? How many World Wide Web looks do we see on TV or in print? It's a feeding frenzy of metaphors.

Title: ABC Satellite Services **Designer/Creative Director:** Robert Altemus **Company:** Altemus+Waegel Design **Client:** ABC **Typefaces:** Bureau Agency, Helvetica Neue **Year:** 1998

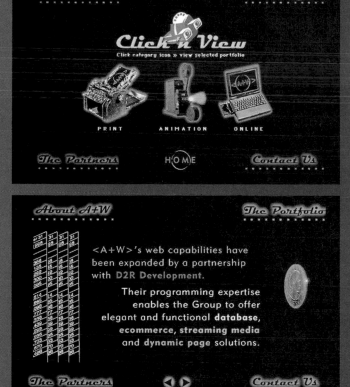

Title: Get a Clue CD-ROM **Designer/Creative Director/Illustrator:** Robert Altemus **Company:** Altemus+Waegel Design **Client:** Lyceum Communications **Typeface:** Totally Gothic, Magnesium **Year:** 1998

Title: Batman Returns CD-ROM **Designers/Creative Director:** Robert Altemus **Company:** Altemus+Waegel Design **Client:** DC Comics **Photographers:** Various **Typefaces:** Matrix Script Agency Bureau **Year:** 1998

An Immature Medium

Title: ups.com **Designers:** Matt Coulson, Guthrie Dolen, Samantha Feutsch, Gregg Heard, Mark Liguameri, Michael Vizzina **Creative Directors:** Samantha Feutsch, Gregg Heard, Clement Mok **Company:** Studio Archetype **Client:** United Parcel Service **Year:** 1997

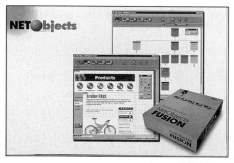

Title: NetObjects Fusion **Designers:** Vic Zanderer, Sal Arora **Creative Directors:** Clement Mok, Sal Arora **Company:** NetObjects, Inc. **Client:** NetObjects, Inc. **Year:** 1996

CLEMENT MOK
Principal, The Office of Clement Mok,
San Francisco

What made you choose new media as a focal point?
My introduction to graphic design was through technology. The printing press was the new medium for an impressionable fifteen-year-old kid twenty-five years ago. Since that first encounter, the graphic design industry has gone through continuous changes and realignments. I don't see the new media focus as unusual; it is a continuation of my self-learning process.

How would you describe new media in relation to print?
To date, the new media resemble a game rather than a book where structured discourse or opinions can be presented. There are no rules. The arena is immature, incredibly restrictive, and driven primarily by technology. It's addressing these weaknesses that I find compelling. It's in these weaknesses that a designer can have the most profound effect. This is the area where one can establish standards and develop new benchmarks for others to follow. The new media truly engage all aspect of design thinking.

You have often talked about the changes in graphic design since entering the field. What are these changes?
The changes are both in processes and in the things we create. The visual differences are self-evident. The most notable changes have to do with the overall characteristics of the work.

Would you explain?
Implicit vs. explicit: Print graphic design is a mature medium with an established lexicon between the author and the reader. Structures and systems are well established, so deviation from the norm is expected if the work is to challenge and to compel. Implicit is good and explicit is common or everyday — done by amateurs. Screen-based graphic design is still in its infancy. The

The Visual Symbol Library

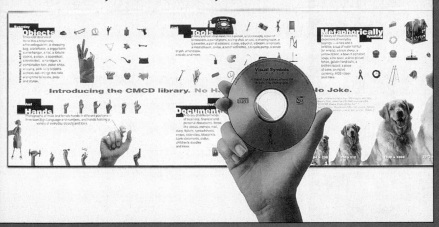

Title: The Visual Symbol Library **Designers:** Joshua Distler, Clement Mok **Creative Director:** Clement Mok **Company:** CMCD, Inc. **Client:** CMCD, Inc. **Photographers:** Mario Parnell, Steve Underwood **Year:** 1994

medium has many interdependencies and functions that are inherently absent from print — for example, hyperlinks, searches, and animation. The aesthetic is both visual and functional.

Without an established lexicon that's understood by many, graphic design in the new media has to work at a more explicit level than its print counterpart. For computation and processing needs, graphical user interface principles drive the aesthetics, leaving very little room to inspire, compel, and engage. For ephemeral thoughts, the new discipline of typokinesis and the language of film have been coopted into this medium to compensate for the design requirements of functional needs.

Text is difficult to read off the screen, hence graphics is the driver. Graphics has to carry a larger burden of distilling large, complex ideas than when text and graphics were equal partners in the print world. Only when audio is used are words and pictures on the same footing.

Control vs. influence: Except with editorial projects, the ink does not dry in the new media. Ideas, thoughts, and product features are updated, upgraded, and revised continuously. Absolute is a moment in time. The designer's notion of absolute control over the user experience does not exist in the liquid new media. Context and usage are often broad — hence a tailored approach to design is rare, if not inappropriate. The variables are numerous and cannot be accounted for in advance. An ideal solution for digital media is a design that is flexible and able to scale and adapt with change. Providing all things to all people is a dangerous edge designers are skating on — we either succeed or fail miserably.

Do you still consider yourself a graphic designer? Does another term better apply to your work?
How about *designer*? My firm now competes with advertising agencies, Web development firms, and system integrators.

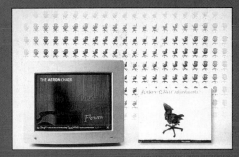

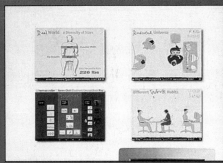

Title: The Aeron Chair **Designers:** Clement Mok, Claire Barry, Paula Meizelman **Creative Director:** Clement Mok **Company:** Studio Archetype **Client:** Herman Miller **Illustrator:** Ward Schumaker **Photographers:** Stan Musleik, Terry Heffernan **Year:** 1995

Digital Melting Pot

CHRIS CAPUOZZO
Art Director, Funny Garbage, New York City

Why did you decide to be an interactive designer?
I was really taken with the type of communication happening in the interactive world. When you're designing for interaction, there's this heightened sense of two-way communication. There's a tangible audience out there. Interactive media still have this pioneering sensibility in that every day you see major developments. This is a field where we need artists steeped in other disciplines.

Do you have a personal style or are you wed to certain conventions?
It's all communication to me, a melting pot — that's the convention. I am involved in too many types of projects for my work to develop a personal style — yet when a look or style is being used for a project, I get passionate about it. One of the things I love about graphic design is that in it there is opportunity for the work to be the sum of the many disciplines I'm interested in.

What is the difference between print and the Web?
There are technical limitations in all design. For the Web, the technical aspects are more wedded to the design process: color palettes are limited; image size is important to the viewer's ability to see a whole page. We are constantly aware of time — how much time something takes to draw in a browser, which browser is being targeted; if the pages can have animations on them, then it's a different animal. At a certain point in print work, the page is concrete. This can't happen on the Web. Web design looks different on different monitors and machines. We address a different level of technical considerations as we design.

Title: Luaka Bop Web site and On-line Catalog **Designer/Creative Director:** Chris Capuozzo **Company:** Funny Garbage **Client:** Luaka Bop Records **Typeface:** Rosewood **Year:** 1997

How much of what you need is creative versus production?
With these projects, the creative boundary is blurred. I rely on a great production team. I need producers to coordinate the myriad issues that arise daily. I need programmers who actually like the medium and approach projects creatively with the code they write. It's really a collaborative medium. The design is useless without the technical implementation.

What do you look for in the portfolio of a prospective Web designer?
I need to see the ability to work in different contexts. I look for passion in the work. If I'm seeing different jobs done for different clients and the work looks the same, I immediately know that this isn't someone I can use. I look for a familiarity with typography. I see a lot of work that imitates David Carson, Designers Republic, and Tomato. This work, while high in passion and quality, leaves me numb.

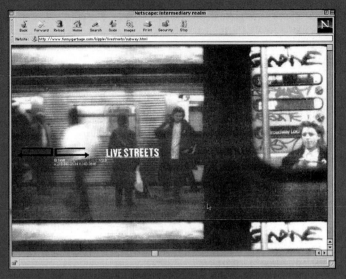

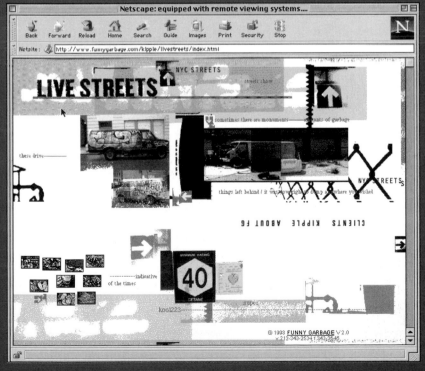

Title: Funny Garbage
Web Site: Live Streets
Designer/Creative Director: Chris Capuozzo
Company/Client: Funny Garbage

User-Centricity

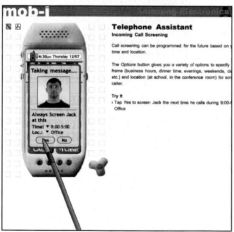

Title: Mob-I, an affective icon representing a mobile device Assistant **Designers:** Luke Ball, Junghwa Lee **Creative Director/Producers:** Eugene Chen, Aaron Marcus **Client:** Samsung Electronics, Seoul, South Korea **Year:** 2000
Figure courtesy of Aaron Marcus and Associates, Inc., www.AMandA.com, and used with permission.

AARON MARCUS
President, Aaron Marcus and Associates, Inc.
Emeryville, California

How do you define *experience design*?
The term *experience design* seems a bit grandiose. Experience design seems to imply that the entire set of mental states (thoughts and emotions) and physical actions of the consumer, customer, end-user, viewer— in short, the experiencer— will be significantly under the influence of the designer through some set of artifacts.

So, is experience design analogous to team-driven design?
Yes. A team of people is involved in developing all contacts a consumer has with a company, its products, services, staff, architecture, ads, vehicles, marketing literature, and news stories. Yes, the team is enormously complex, like the staff list after a movie has completed its presentation, full of strange terms like *gaffers* and *continuity monitors*. But it seems more useful to remind ourselves that particular designers are responsible for particular artifacts, particular products, particular services, while others are concerned about overall brand, which comprises brand promise, brand experience, and brand perception/conception.

You are involved in very detailed projects that are designed to make experiences on the Web more accessible to average users. What is the role of a graphic designer in this work?
Even though AM+A's origins, and my own professional education, lie in corporate graphic design for printed publications, AM+A has been engaged in user-centered, information-oriented, visually oriented design of computer-based communication since 1982. Even in our earliest years, we were concerned with the larger issues of understanding a user's context, not just the laser-printed page or screen design.

And what is the goal of user-centered design?

To provide designed products and processes that reflect what users need/want to learn or do, as determined by anecdote, observation, and interviews as well as business, marketing, engineering, and design professionals' considerations. The better we meet the users' objectives, the better their experiences will be. What is crucial is to gain deeper insights into the users' objectives beyond what they say and do in the short term, or from statistical long-term studies.

How is this done?

The role of a visually oriented designer in this work is of group visualizer. To be effective in a group, the graphic designer, or visual designer, must understand the terminology and concepts of his/her colleagues in other disciplines and to produce sketches or final presentations that are appropriate at each step of development, sometimes conceptual and general, at other times highly detailed. Showing displays that are too finished too early, or showing displays that are too rough too late can be equally distracting or dysfunctional to the group attempting to solve complex challenges. The audience for these presentations may be team members or other stakeholders: users, customer purchasing agents, funding groups, executives, business managers, marketing managers, engineering managers, or other design professionals.

What must graphic designers learn to be more attuned with experience design?

Good designers already have the user in mind when they do their work, and that is half the battle. To the extent that the desired user experience takes place over a period of time, or in a complex information space, as is the case with the Web, graphic designers must be prepared to provide information or tell stories that users can experience via their own paths.

If experience design includes information-design and user-interface design, then graphic designers must understand that they are designing systems, not just one individual image or composition, and that these systems may be changed by the user.

Designers also must become comfortable working in multi disciplinary teams and adept at explaining, persuading, and compromising with their own team members and with the client's team members. Designers must also involve users in the design process as informants and as participants.

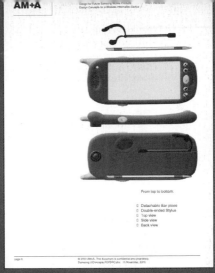

Title: Mob-I, the mobile device assistant, in various states of announcement conveying alerts, messages, warnings, etc.
Designers: Luke Ball, Junghwa Lee **Creative Director/Producers:** Eugene Chen, Aaron Marcus **Client:** Samsung Electronics, Seoul, South Korea **Year:** 2000

Title: Chart of product strategies for combined cellphone and PDA products, placing them in a context of pleasure vs. productivity and simplicity (special purpose) vs. complexity (do everything). **Designers:** Eugene Chen, Luke Ball, Junghwa Lee **Creative Director/Producers:** Eugene Chen, Aaron Marcus **Client:** Samsung Electronics, Seoul, South Korea **Year:** 2000
Figure courtesy of Samsung Elecronics Corporation, Korea, and used with permission.

Leveraging Intuition

Title: Nickelodeon's Wave Rave™
Designers: Todd Calvert and
David Vogler **Creative Director:**
David Vogler **Client:** Nick-
elodeon Online **Year:** 2000
©2001 Viacom International Inc. All
Rights Reserved.

Title: Nickelodeon's Wave Rave™
Designers: Todd Calvert
Creative Director: David Vogler
Client: Nickelodeon Online
Year: 2000
©2001 Viacom International Inc. All
Rights Reserved.

Title: TeenPeople.com **Designer:** David Ehlers **Creative
Director:** David Vogler **Client:**
TeenPeople Online **Year:** 2000
©2000 TIME Inc.

DAVID VOGLER
Principal, David Vogler, Inc., New York City

**The Web has changed considerably since you first produced
sites for Nickelodeon and Disney. How has it changed for you?**
One thing is for sure, what's consistent about the Web is the in-
consistency. But alas, the more things change, the more they stay
the same. The authoring tools designers use change rapidly. But a
practical Internet business model remains consistently elusive.

What role does design play in your current business?
A big role. We define *design* as being more than just graphics.

**Are the traditional elements of graphic design still key to
making a good site, or is concept really more important?**
We believe concept is always king. If you don't have a solid concept, then all the graphics are simply shallow eye candy. The concept and the overall story need to drive the project. Concept
dictates everything you do. It's the creative blueprint that informs everything else— the content, the navigation, the graphics,
the typography— everything. Any designer who just makes brain-
dead Web sites dressed with pretty pictures, pointless rollovers

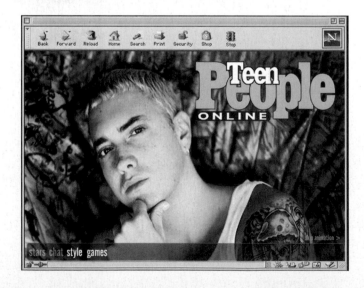

and gratuitous ambient techno music should be put in jail. Every mark you make should contribute to a greater whole and the project's communication. Designers have a responsibility to themselves, the client, and the profession not to be a cake decorator. And that applies to any medium, whether it's in print or pixel.

Dot-coms have come and gone. What is the future of the Web, particularly for the designer?
Out of the zillions of harebrained dot-com ideas that have launched, only a handful have created a viable business. So as Web businesses fail, it spells trouble for studios that serve them. Luckily, my Web clients are extensions of traditional media (print and cable television, for example). They have never been pure-play Web efforts, so they have weathered the tech sector's economic storm better than most. A designer who can work in diverse media stands the best chance of survival and growth. Print isn't dead yet. The Internet is great, but it's not the only place to be.

Compared to print, are the aesthetics of the new media quite different?
The end-user experience is, of course, wildly different. One of the nice things about print is the warmth of the finished product. There is a timeless beauty to ink on paper. Graphics on a page feels honest, humble, and, perhaps, quaint. The very same graphics displayed on a glass CRT computer screen can feel cold and aloof. Perhaps I'm being nostalgic for the tactile qualities we've lost on the Web. Web sites are sexy, but even the most hard-core digital designers agree that nothing can top the thrill of touching an exquisite blind emboss or a funky die cut.

How important is intuition versus logic in the Web environment?
Communication and navigational solutions that leverage a user's intuition always produces the best results. Look at the Mac OS, for example. It is based on smart, intuitive principles. The Mac interface has remained virtually unchanged for fifteen years because the Apple designers got it right from the get-go. They created a Graphical User Interface (GUI) rule book that was militantly consistent, simple and intuitive. A GUI is a pointer-driven interface with movable windows and icons. The very heart of the Mac experience comes from the artistry of an enlightened designer. By comparison, Microsoft's Windows is the result of a programmer. In its early versions, Windows had a lot of logic but no intuition. That's a lesson to folks who design for the Web. Like any piece of software, a Web site serves its audience best when it's easy to operate and doesn't frustrate the user.

Title: Handshadows **Designer:** Mark Pagano **Creative Director:** David Vogler **Client:** Nickelodeon Online **Year:** 2000 ©2001 Viacom International Inc. All Rights Reserved.

Title: Rude Toot Noisemaker **Designer:** Mark Pagano **Creative Director:** David Vogler **Client:** Nickelodeon Online **Year:** 2001 ©2001 Viacom International Inc. All Rights Reserved.

Title: Busted Rhymes: A Bohemian Poetry Reading **Designer:** Mark Pagano **Creative Director:** David Vogler **Client:** Nickelodeon Online **Year:** 2001 ©2001 Viacom International Inc. All Rights Reserved.

Pushing the Medium

Title: MoodLogic: Magnet Browser **Designers:** Pascal Wever, David Young, Triplecode **Programmer:** Lindi Emoungu, Triplecode **Client:** MoodLogic **Year:** 2000

DAVID YOUNG

Cofounder and Partner, Triplecode, Beverly Hills, California

What inspired you to be a designer for the Web?
I've always been interested in computers and design, but it was my experience at the MIT Media Lab with Muriel Cooper that really got me excited. Not for the Web specifically, as that didn't exist when I was there, but for interactivity with the computer as the medium. And then, through teaching at Art Center, I started to explore how design research could be finished and made usable by the real world.

What do you bring to Web design that you feel is unique to your personality and sensibility?
I think that my background in computer science and programming gives me a unique approach. But it's combining that with my interaction design education and visual design experience, that makes me feel unique. The creativity in organizing content and data and in developing programmatic approaches to dynamics, interaction, and content— especially when combined with more visual design skills— is what this medium should be about.

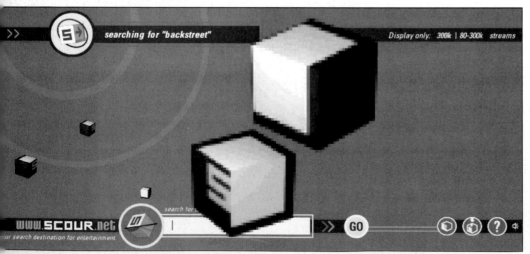

Title: Project Nile **Designers:** Pascal Wever, David Young, Triplecode **Creative Director/Producer:** Daniel Tsai - Scour, 44 Phases **Back-end Programmers:** Kevin Smilak, Ilya Haykinson, Mike Todd, Scour **Product Developer:** Lawrence H. Leach, Scour **3-D Animator:** Mike Frantum **Music Composer/Sound Designer:** Robert Casady Jr. **Client:** Scour **Year:** 1999

What is the most important design attribute in this medium?
One hears so much about "usability"— as if that were the most important criterion for evaluating a project. But for something to be merely usable is for it to be pretty boring. I'd argue more for experimentation, exploration, and innovation. Each project has the ability to push the boundaries of the medium.

How much of your work is dictated by clients, and how much is woven from whole cloth?
I think we need clients to help give shape and direction to our work. But we are always trying to find new ways to explore and

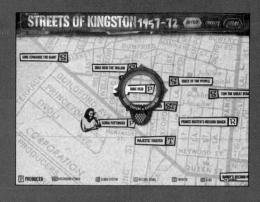

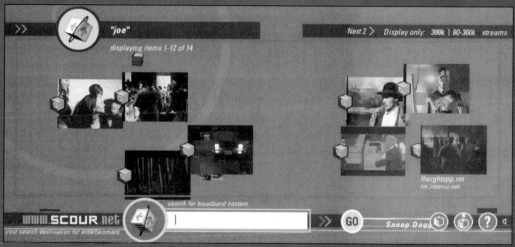

push the medium. In each project, we want to learn something new and to try something that hasn't been done before.

Do you allow yourself time for experimentation?
While there's less time for undirected experimentation than I'd like, we do give each new project a large amount of initial exploration time. During this phase, we explore ways of organizing content, methods of interaction, and visual form. It's when we find the intersection of all three that we know we've found a solution. This often results in a redefinition of the client's assignment— not only in a direction that better matches our approach, methods and interests but often one that gives the client more than they might have initially asked for.

Have you developed a style? Or is style unimportant in this realm?
Style seems to have negative associations. An "approach" might be closer to what we do. But it doesn't sound very flexible. If anything, we treat each project as if it were the only one (or our first? or last?) and give it our full creativity and enthusiasm.

Title: Streets of Kingston, 1957–1972 **Designers:** Wolfgang Geramb, Pascal Wever, David Young, Triplecode **Creative Director/Producer:** Jasen Emmons - Producer and Writer, EMP **Programmer:** Lindi Emoungu, Triplecode **Art Director:** Brooke Mackay, EMP **Client:** Experience Music Project (EMP) **Year:** 2001

Title: Project Nile **Designers:** Pascal Wever, David Young, Triplecode **Creative Director/Producer:** Daniel Tsai, Scour, 44 Phases **Back-end Programmers:** Kevin Smilak, Ilya Haykinson, Mike Todd, Scour **Product Developer:** Lawrence H. Leach, Scour **3-D Animator:** Mike Frantum **Music Composer/Sound Designer:** Robert Casady Jr. **Client:** Scour **Year:** 1999

Grand Master Flash

Title: Adobe.com **Designers:** Hillman Curtis, Ian Kovalik, Grant Collier, Matt Horn **Creative Director:** Hillman Curtis **Producer:** Homera Chaudhry **Art Director:** Ian Kovalik **Client:** Adobe Systems Incorporated **Year:** 2000

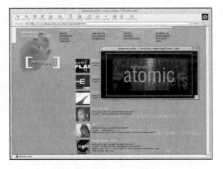

Title: Sky, a poem by Christina Manning **Designer/Creative Director:** Hillman Curtis **Client:** Born Magazine **Year:** 2000

HILLMAN CURTIS
Principal and Chief Creative Officer, hillmancurtis.com, Inc., New York City

What do you like most about working on the Web?
It's constantly changing and offers so many opportunities for growth as a designer. Perhaps not everyone will agree with me on this, but I also think it's a very nurturing environment for designers. There's a pretty supportive community out there. Plus it offers that great combination of the visual and the technical. Sometimes it can drive you crazy— bandwidth, CPUs, new/old browsers, different platforms, css, Java, JavaScript— all of that stuff you have to at least understand on a basic level, but it appeals to me because you have to design things that work. Web designs have to work at communicating first, but they have to function, and how well they function directly impacts the communication. It's this great big ball of form follows function bouncing around in a constantly changing environment. And so much of the functionality appears to be invisible. I often find myself explaining excitedly about how small a file is, how quick it loads, even though the client is on a T1 (a high speed telephone connection) and, at least on the surface, doesn't seem that concerned. It all matters, though. If you use the limitations of the Web to your advantage you become, like I did, a better designer.

What do you need to know now about Web design that you did not need to know, say, last year?
Usability has always been important, but for the last year and a half there was a trend that favored wild experimentations in usability. You know— floating, gravity-sensitive navigation

Title: Manifestival **Designers:** Hillman Curtis, Ian Kovalik **Creative Director:** Hillman Curtis **Producer:** Kiley Bates **Client:** Manifestival **Year:** 1999

elements, palettes that you can drag all over the browser, rollovers for the sake of rollovers, browsers that maximize and take over your desktop with no clear way to minimize back. Some of it was brilliant. Then you had these ridiculous debates between academics and punk designers, one waving the flag of standardization and the other innovation. It's still happening, but now I feel the collective focus now seems more firmly fixed on finding the simplest way to design navigable, functional, and compelling environments. The other thing you have to be aware of is making the Web sites think, making them remember the user's name, likes/dislikes, interests. That's where it's all headed now.

Some sites today are text heavy, which seems to be what a lot of clients want. What kind of design do you feel yields the optimum site?
I hope clients don't want text heavy and if they do, they should call me. I would try hard to steer them away from that. It's not an effective use of the medium— don't believe anyone who claims it is. Very few people turn off graphics while surfing and if they do, the chances are they are interested in research, academic or otherwise. The very people who promote text only also acknowledge that most users don't read on the Web. Instead, they scan and grab the last few sentences of any given paragraph. Graphic design exists for a reason. It's a visual language that everyone understands and it offers the opportunity for communication that speaks deeper than words. Colors mean something, typography means something, layout communicates, choice of motion communicates, an image can impart a deep emotional impression— and the Web is such a wonderful place to communicate this way— simply because it knows no borders.

How much of your business revolves around the Web? How much around design? And how much technology?
About 75 percent Web, the rest a combination of broadcast, film design, and print. And it's about the same ratio for design (75 percent) and tech (25 percent). While we can program as well as the next guy and certainly can expertly work the software, we're committed to and focused on becoming a great design shop across all media.

Title: Roger Black's Interactive Bureau teaser **Designer:** Hillman Curtis **Creative Directors:** Roger Black, Dan Roam **Client:** Roger Black's Interactive Bureau **Year:** 1999

Title: Contagious Pictures Web site **Designers:** Hillman Curtis, Ian Kovalik **Creative Director:** Hillman Curtis **Producer:** Kiley Bates **Client:** Contagious Pictures **Year:** 1999

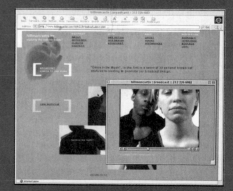

Title: hillmancurtis, Inc., Web site **Designers:** Hillman Curtis, Ian Kovalik, Matt Horn **Creative Director:** Hillman Curtis **Producer:** Homera Chaudry **Client:** hillmancurtis, Inc. **Year:** 2000/2001

Web as Theater

Title: Newsweek Online - Web Prototype **Studio:** Jessica Helfand / William Drenttel **Designers:** Jessica Helfand, Jeffrey Tyson **Art Director:** Jessica Helfand **Client:** Newsweek Interactive **Typographer:** Jessica Helfand **Year:** 1998

Title: National Design Awards Credits - Web site **Studio:** Jessica Helfand / William Drenttel **Designers:** William Drenttel, Jeffrey Tyson, Dan Bowen **Art Director:** William Drenttel **Client:** Cooper-Hewitt National Design Museum, National Design Awards Identity Program **Typographer:** William Drenttel **Year:** 2001

JESSICA HELFAND

Principal, JHWD Studio, Falls Village, Connecticut

How much of your work is now Web based?
About half, but it fluctuates, and I would have to say the Web-based work is always better when we are doing a substantial amount of print work, or exhibition work, or film work. I would add, too, that of the Web-based projects, many are experimental and/or self-initiated. We did a big design exploratory site for the National Design Awards that turned into a fairly comprehensive and collaborative site involving a number of outside designers and illustrators. And we're hoping to collaborate with Michael Morris and Yoshiko Sato, the architects who worked with us to renovate our studio, to create a similar site— similar in the sense that it allows for an exploration not only of the product but also of the process that preceded it.

In the early days of the Internet, technology prohibited fine typography. Indeed, you are a fine typographer. How have things changed, and does the medium allow you to address your design passions?
In my view, the most exciting thing to happen to typography in time-based media is the fact that it can now assume new and unusual kinetic properties. These are properties that involve movement and change, cadence and nuance — the elements of pure theater. Conflict! Denouement! Mystery! I had an early and brief career as a television writer a number of years ago, and for me, this opportunity to merge the diagnostic (logic, clarity, the stuff of information design and design principles) with the dramatic (passion, tension, the stuff of theatrical writing and dramatic paragigms) is exciting. Recently, I have written at some length about what I see as choreographic tendencies on the Web (I call it *choreo-typography*) which depends as

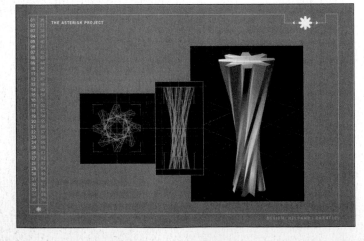

much upon sequencing and orchestration as it does leading and kerning. Certainly, type on-line competes with an enormous quantity of dueling media types, sound being the most obvious one. In this environment, type's need to reinvent itself, or at least to reposition itself within the context of such graphic and sensory complexity, is critical. But it is also exciting. Take the typographic rollover, for instance. In a purely formal sense, what was previously parenthetical in print terms (think footnotes and other forms of typographic marginalia) can now assume certain cinematic conventions: dissolves, fades, pans, and tilts. But now type can be used to reveal its subtext, whereas you once turned to the bottom of the page or the end of a

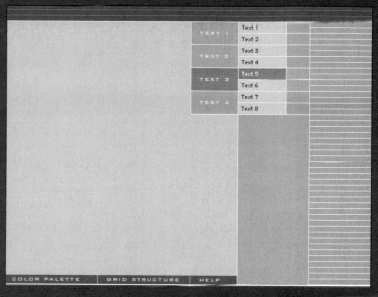

chapter, you now roll over a word and it shifts its meaning or unveils a secondary narrative right before your eyes. This is instant and seamless and, in many cases, enchantingly seductive. And dramatic! Time-based media offers a kind of richly enhanced canvas for typography, and while I would not argue for relaxed standards as far as our classic definitions of "good" typography are concerned (there will always be a need for good kerning), such dynamic opportunities are full of endless promise.

Title: Cablevision Interactive Study Guides - Web Prototype **Studio:** Jessica Helfand / William Drenttel **Designer:** Jessica Helfand **Art Directors:** Jessica Helfand, William Drenttel **Client:** Cablevision **Typographer:** Jessica Helfand **Year:** 1999

What is the value of this medium for designers? What can designers offer the medium?

Given the complex, kinetic nature of new media, design educators would do well to consider some element of dramatic training in their visual curricula. It is arguable that the degree to which shaping narrative and sequencing information in time-based media will necessitate more than purely formal design skills. This is, in my view, an issue of serious and timely concern for design educators. While there are applicable skills common to, say, sequencing a sixteen-page book and crafting the site architecture for a small Web site, what equips the young designer with skills that allow for the successful migration to screen-based media — media that involve complex layers of storytelling, character building, plot structuring, and revealing their relative exposition over time? What about sound and editing, lighting and writing — where is the intersection of the script, the stage, and the computer screen? The merits of good design notwithstanding, this medium is really all about theater. And that's the really big pradigm shift — and only a few of us have really had the guts, so far, to accept.

The Vision Thing

Title: shape.com (Shape Magazine) **Designer/Creative Director:** Karen Barranco **Client:** Weider Publishing, Inc. **Year:** 2001

Title: Evenson Design Group Web site **Designer/Art Director:** Karen Barranco **Client:** Evenson Design Group **Year:** 1998

KAREN BARRANCO

Designer and Creative Consultant, Los Angeles

You began in the print realm designing identities and logos. Was the change to Web work one of natural evolution?
Designing identities and logos poses consistent challenges throughout any medium — in essence, there is no difference in applying identity to the Web. The Web is just another publishing medium in which the identity/brand is applied.

My interest in the Web began with the challenge to extend the off line brand into an interactive on-line experience. With growing demands for businesses to develop an online presence, it became necessary to rapidly expand into Web design and make it a part of my skill set. I cannot say the evolution was "natural" in that many of the ideals that were previously learned no longer applied. Aesthetics became almost secondary to functionality and content. As I became more adept, the struggle to enlighten colleagues and clients alike became what I later learned was a perpetual uphill climb.

What about these two media is different? What is the same?
Print and the Web, are both communication vehicles. Print focuses on telling the story in a linear, planned, and intentional, visual way. For the Web, telling the story is different. Depending on the goal of the site, there are more obstacles to encounter. Web design influences the functionality of the way the user interacts with the content.

It's tempting to reinvent the wheel, throw in bells and whistles, and apply all the great skills a print designer knows instinctively because you feel you need to give the client something special. But in order to design Web sites effectively these days, you must concentrate on solving visual problems and exceed at organizing information in a graphically functional way. Working closely with the Web development team is important to make sure you get what you set out to do.

How much of your vision do you contribute to the client's need?

As a creative director, I often play a big role in contributing the vision to address the client's needs. However, it is also my job to remind the client that the user is preeminent, as the goal of the designer doesn't always mirror the goal of the client, which doesn't match the goal of the user. I work with the client to find out their business objectives. I suggest solutions, and together we determine the best option.

What have you always wanted to do on a Web site? What would you never do, for whatever reason?

Wanted to do: To throw out all the limitations and rules and bring a richer visual interface to the Web.

Never: To assume the design will look like I designed it to look like. However, I know what to do to make it look the best I can for all platforms. On the Web, speed and functionality are valued, although good design can be so transparent the user doesn't realize it's there.

Is designing for the Web ultimately satisfying to your typographic and other design sensibilities?

Good design is based on problem solving, on-line or off-line. There are definitely some trade-offs. My typographic and design sensibilities are appeased in other ways that collectively contribute to the system as a whole.

Designing for the Web is still dependent on a traditional understanding of design, strategic thinking, and knowing your audience. The creation of a compelling and memorable Web site is just as gratifying as creating a great poster, as long as the message is delivered in a clear and concise way.

What do you want out of a client?

I appreciate when clients trust me to do what they hired me to do. I admire sophisticated clients who understand the basics of what makes a Web site work. I appreciate it when the number of people involved in the process is limited, as a lot of Web site projects are muddied by internal politics. I encourage the client to test the site to potential users and get their opinions. I also have my clients add white space as a design element must-have on the pages.

Title: centertheatregroup.com
Designer: Eric Brown **Creative Director:** Karen Barranco
Client: Red Ant Media Group
Year: 2000

Title: redantmediagroup.com (now Brandforia.com) **Designer:** Eric Brown **Creative Director:** Karen Barranco
Client: Red Ant Media Group
Year: 2000

Through the Back Door

Title: The Later Days of Paul Bunyan (comic strip) **Designer/Art Director/Illustrator:** Patrick Smith **Client:** The Ganzfeld, Issue 1 **Year:** 2000

Title: Levers (web page) **Designer/Art Director/Illustrator:** Patrick Smith **Client:** Vector Park **Year:** 2001

PATRICK SMITH

Designer/Illustrator/Programmer, New York City

You came to Web design through a back door. Tell me how this influenced your current work.
Well, I should start off by saying that I don't really consider myself a designer. My background is as a painter and sculptor, and so I think my approach is different than that of most designers. I've found that I'm better at thinking of things structurally than graphically, so the best way for me to approach a Web site design is to think of it as an object rather than as a flat layout. As a result, the Ganzfeld Web site behaves like a little machine.

Your Web site for The Ganzfeld (www.theGanzfeld.com) is delightful for its hand-hewn look and sketchy sensibility. What is your conceptual thinking behind the site?
The concept of the Web site changed a number of times. It was originally intended as little more than an on-line sales mechanism for the [small, self-published] magazine of the same name. Then the Ganzfeld editors Dan Nadel and Tim Hodler, and I decided it could be a sort of on-line counterpart to the print magazine, but with its own set of contents. At first, it was going to be full of regularly updated features, and we got our friend Mike Reddy to come up with a really nice design for us. However, it became clear after it was up for a few weeks that we had neither the time nor the energy to maintain an on-line magazine, and so we had to abandon that design. Hopefully, Mike has forgiven us. We decided that a better idea would be to make the Ganzfeld site an on-line archive of drawings, pictures, and comics. I had been learning Macromedia Flash, so by that time I was comfortable enough with the ins and outs of the software to begin to see how something like that could be built.

How did the Web site take shape?
The new design was literally conceived on a napkin at Tom's Diner in Brooklyn. The idea I came up with was of an unfolding, branching structure, that would allow as much or as little of the content to be available as the visitor chose. The resulting design was a

kind of cross between a blooming tree and an elaborate display cabinet, with secret drawers and compartments. Once the idea was worked out, it took about two weeks to build the site.

It is truly a branching tree, with many suprises coming to the fore as the tree blooms, so to speak.
Thanks! I wanted the way it functioned to be completely intuitive, and I tried to make its organization as clear as possible. Which I think it is— it essentially functions as its own site map, and it unfolds in a manner dictated by the visitor. And its design is modular, so it can be expanded easily. We will be trying to add to it semiregularly, and so as time passes, the content will accumulate. The hand-drawn aspects are intended to soften the mechanical feel — and it seemed to fit, because the site is about drawings, comics, and pictures. I originally designed the Ganzfeld letterhead for the print magazine. It was somewhat based on Pablo Ferro's lettering for the Talking Heads' concert film *Stop Making Sense*— a hand-drawn font created by a rigid set of rules, so it's both organic and highly structured— which I think complements the mechanically unfolding limbs.

Did designing for the Web surprise you in anyway? Were you prepared for all it offered and prohibited?
At the time I made the site, I was just beginning to become interested in the Internet. For some reason, I had always found HTML a little bit discouraging, but once I started playing around with Flash (a vector-based animation program), I started getting a lot of ideas for things to do with it. Once I began learning some programming, I was really hooked.

With print work, the challenge for me has usually been to figure out how to deal with (or overcome) the limitations of the medium. With the interactive work I'm doing now, it's a matter of trying to figure out how to build things. I get a chance to be an inventor, which is a lot of fun.

Now that you've tasted the digital, what do you prefer, print (drawing) or Web (narrating)?
That's hard to answer. I like working on different kinds of things, and I think that a lot of my ideas feed from one medium to the other. I'll probably keep focusing on working digitally for at least a little while longer. The number of things you can do still seems enormous to me, and there is a lot of open territory. It's also very easy to have work available and accessible to other people, which is important to me.

In any case, whatever medium I'm working in, I try hard to make things that are not only engaging and clear but beautiful as well.

Title: The Ganzfeld (Web site) Designer/Art Director/Illustrator: Patrick Smith Client: The Ganzfeld Year: 2001

Title: Independent Film Channel (internet) **Creative Director:** Chris Capuozzo **Art Director:** Matthew Canton **Senior Designer:** Jesse Alexander **Designers:** Andrew Pratt, Kiki Lavigne, Peter Hamlin, Yi Liu, Matthew Girardi **Sound:** Andres Levin, Sohrab Habibon **Programming:** Brett Webb, Kim Howe, Randy Weinstein, Asya Prikster, Jeff Jackson, Russel Simpkins **Executive Production:** Kristin Ellington, Hope Moore **Producers:** Susanna Graves, Dan Latorre **Year:** 2001

Title: Comedy Central (Web) **Creative Director:** Peter Girardi **Art Director:** Jeff Tyson **Designer/ Illustrator:** Todd Hulin **Client:** Comedy Central **Year:** 2001

PETER GIRARDI
Principal, Funny Garbage, New York City

What about the Web creatively excites you?
It's not specifically the Web that excites me, it's the whole range of design for new platforms and media. The Web is an early example of what the future will bring for designers— issues of usability, interface design, information design, application design. There are a lot of possibilities for design in all these new areas. It's a challenge for younger designers and a real kick in the ass for older designers. I also really love the idea of design not being a sovereign gesture sent from the designer to the audience. These new media allow people to customize and sometimes change designs according to their preferences and needs. This can be scary to some designers.

What about the Web makes you want to smash your computer?
Lots of things make me want to smash my computer. I cut the Web a lot of slack; it was sent out into the world when it was too young. It's growing up in public. The real problems I have with the Web are mostly inherited from general interface and application standards that have been problematic with computers and human-computer interaction for a long time. I also think it's important to make a distinction between the problems people have with browsers and browser-based technology and with the Web itself. The Web is a great location for information and resources of all kinds; the browsers and other technology to view the Web can really suck.

Are there any viable comparisons between the Web and print, or must you design in unique ways for each medium?
You must design for each medium in a unique way. Every medium has its own pros and cons. Designing for pixel-based delivery is quite different than designing for print-based or film/TV-based. A lot more technical issues must be considered in designing a Web site or other forms of interactive experience, both from the users point of view and the designers. That said, good design is good design regardless of medium. There are plenty of commonsense design lessons that should be remembered no matter what medium you are designing for.

What is the most challenging aspect of teaching design in the digital environment?

Separating the teaching of design principles from the teaching of the software. You have to know all of the software to really be able to design for this medium, but knowing all the software doesn't make you a good designer. Sometimes the opposite. It's also hard to teach all the skills it takes to be a successful interactive media designer. You have to be part graphic designer, part information designer, part interface designer, and part programmer.

What have you learned about designing for the Web that is a total revelation?

How difficult it is to be part graphic designer, part information designer, part interface designer, and part programmer.

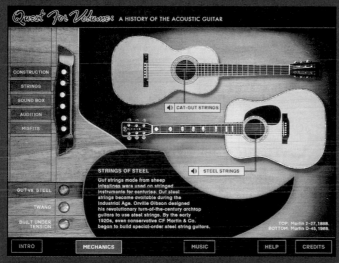

Title: Raptoons (Animation) **Directors:** Mark Marek, Ric Heitzman **Illustrator:** Todd James **Client:** Funny Garbage **Year:** 2000

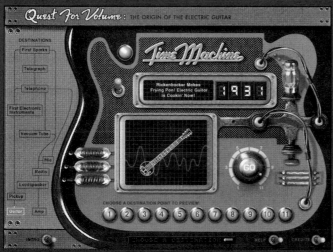

Title: EMP (hard media/kiosk) **Executive Producer:** John Carlin **Creative Director:** Peter Girardi **Producer:** Sarah Shatz **Associate Producer:** Alec Bemis **Programmer:** Colin Holgate **Art Directors:** Agnieszka Gasparska, Matthew Canton **Designers:** Todd Hulin, Jesse Alexander **Production:** Sharon Spieldenner, Angela Martini, Darleen Hall **Client:** Experience Music Project **Year:** 2000

The Right Balance

Title: PBS Kids **Designer:**
Richard McGuire **Creative
Director/Producer:** Lee Hunt
Associates **Client:** PBS
Year: 1999

RICHARD MCGUIRE
Principal, Work Is Play, New York City

As an illustrator, did you always want to see your work animated?
I think if you grew up watching as many cartoons as I did, maybe
you would. I watched a lot of Warner Brothers and Fleischer
Brothers cartoons. I would make flip books and shoot short Super
8 animations with my dad's camera. Much later, I worked at a few
animation studios, starting at the lowest level painting cels and
eventually moving up to inking. Every project that came in had its
own look or style, and the job became more about being a really
good forger than anything else. I wanted to be more in control of
the work I was doing, so I put a portfolio together and became an
illustrator. This led to doing children's books, and eventually that
led to having my own work animated. Once you've had the experience of seeing one of your ideas moving around, it's hard not to
get hooked and want more.

**How has the computer influenced your work in a kinetic
sense?**
The computer has given me more control. It makes it a
whole lot easier to create animation entirely by myself. I'm interested now in getting a better understanding of the interactive
side of programs like Flash. I want to create experiences that are
deep and rich and, hopefully, entertaining. In the case of the TRY
site, I don't think the concept would have occurred to me if it
was a print job. You are using a different set of tools, so they
suggest different ideas. Even if the same idea was adapted to
print it wouldn't be half as effective. Magic happens when you
see the transformation trick in real time.

Are you more interested in telling stories or creating effects?
I'm developing different things. One thing I'm interested in doing
is creating a longer book project that will have an animated Web
component and could possibly be adapted for TV as well. When I
look back at my work and see the pattern of my interests, it has

never really been about story. I like systems and structures. I want to create experiences that make you see the world a bit differently after the experience. I'm also interested in pure play — making things that are for fun, with no real goal. I like the idea of creating virtual toys.

What are the most important components in animation for TV and the Web?

The most important thing about the Web is the fact that you can create something, post it, and there are potentially millions of viewers. Word of mouth can be enough. My TRY site got half a million hits with no advertising, and that amazes me. I'm always trading interesting sites with friends in the same way you pass along a good joke. It's unlike any other medium because of its direct link to an audience.

It's also cheaper than any other way of communicating to the masses. Of course, the TV audience is bigger; millions of people see my PBS Kids logos everyday. Technically, TV has different sets of problems. The broadcasting system in this country is actually pretty crude. It hasn't changed at all since color TV was introduced in the 1960s. Things like having color against color can cause shadows and vibrations unless there is a trapping line, for instance. There are color problems with the Web, too, where you have to use a limited Web palette. Then there are also the restrictions of connecting speeds with modems.

Do you work differently for TV and the Web?

Yes; they are completely different. The Web is about navigation and structure and is more like architecture, really. It's about being able to move around spaces where things happen. I can work with a small crew and there are, in general, fewer people to answer to. With TV, it's about advertising, shows, or branding. A lot more people are involved because the budgets are bigger. You would think this would translate to better quality, but everyone usually wants the cheapest, quickest solution. If the budget allows for a really good animator, someone who understands how to make an object look like it has weight and knows something about anatomy or the timing of a joke, it's a luxury.

What is the most challenging aspect of working in a kinetic environment?

The most challenging thing is creating the right balance. The content is crucial, but finding the right people to nurture it is also crucial. Animators are like actors interpreting the work, and their personalities show in the work. Getting the right soundtrack is crucial. The voice of a character or the music is so important it can change the feeling of everything. In Web design, I think a big challenge is to make a site inviting enough that users stay to explore it.

Title: www.willing-to-try.com
Designer: Richard McGuire
Creative Director/Producer:
Funny Garbage **Client:** TRY
Year: 1999

The Power of Interactivity

Title: Building Flash
Presentation UCON99
**Designer/Copy Writer/Sound
Producer:** Todd Purgason
Client: Macromedia/self
Year: 1900

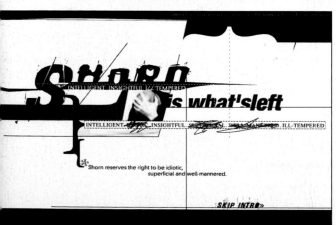

TODD PURGASON
Creative Director, Juxt Interactive,
Newport Beach, California

Why and how did you start designing for the Web?
I used to be an architect and had a love for visual design and computers. I got involved with graphic design and soon learned that this pursuit was much more rewarding for me personally. Eventually, I got my hands on (Macromind) Director software, and when I found the power of interactivity, I knew I had found my future. Being able to design and then bring that to life was magic to me. Soon after this, the Web came on the scene and a previous employer decided to start a shop doing home pages, as he called it. This was back in 1995. He hired me as the art director, and I worked along side my now partner, Steve Wages. We saw the Web bloom and we wanted to be a part of it not just as bystanders but as part of its evolution. This compelled us to create Juxt Interactive and to focus on trying to push the envelope of the medium.

Some of your work is wildly kinetic; some is more quiet and staid. What determines how you will approach the design of a project?
The client's brand and the audience are the two major factors that drive the design. We design objective-driven projects, not style-driven projects as such. It all boils down to solving the particular needs of the client. We do have clients asking us to refer to some of our previous work as inspiration for their project, so you can see veins of style running through many projects. We also love typography— all of us do, even our programmers— so that influences our work as well.

Title: SHORN Prototype **Designers:** Todd Purgason, Ryan Holstein, Kristian Olson, Paul Nugyen, Jenn Redmond, Eva Au **Art Director:** Ryan Holstein **Creative Director:** Todd Purgason **Photographers:** David Tsay, Todd Purgason **Sound Design:** Todd Purgason **Copy:** Dave Fraunces, Itay Dankner, Jordan Berman **Project manager:** Steve Wages **Client:** Shorn LLC **Year:** 2000

Title: IPPA June 1999
Screen Calendar Designer:
Todd Purgason Client: IPPA
Year: 2000

How much of what you do on the Web is informed by film or TV? Or is there no relationship among the media?
I have not had TV for fifteen years. I hate it, it is insulting, and I'm stupid enough to watch it when it is around me, so I avoid it. But I do love film. I watch a lot of videos— probably not as many as people without children but enough to fill my mind. I love film titles, especially from the 1960s and the last five years. My wife thinks I'm a total design geek. I sit in the darkness of the theater and name the fonts in the titles and man, if I see a font I don't have and want, I can't focus on the movie— obsessive-compulsive, I suppose.

What is the most challenging design problem with new media?
Browsers; they are so inconsistent, and the makers have released some real bad versions that were only published for weeks or days even that have their own obscure incompatibilities. We love Flash (although it is not totally immune to browser bugs); it is much more self-contained and consistent.

Title: Juxt Interactive's The
Process Designer/Copy
Writer/Sound Designer: Todd
Purgason Programmers: Brian
Drake, Shaun Hervey Client:
Juxt Interactive Year: 2000

"What do you look for in a designer?"

When hiring motion designers I look to see if they can tell a story. I don't care how slick their reel is. In fact, the more slick and polished it is, the more I get suspicious. I ask myself, "Can this person get the job done when he has specific constraints? Can he think beyond of formulas to really engage an audience? Can he create work that is relevant and not just self-indulgent?"
　　—Mathew Mulder

A thinker or conceptualizer who has not yet been contaminated by "sophisticated" design trend.
　　—Garson Yu

I would hope for the same thing that I would hope for from Wim Wenders, Ingmar Bergman, and Charlie Chaplin. Just knowing Photoshop and After Effects isn't enough.
　　—Benita Rephan

Good taste in music and type and a goofy sense of humor.
　　—Julie Hirschfeld

I look for passionate designers who are great typographers and problem solvers. Our studio comprises multi disciplined individuals, including ex-surfers, skateboarders, architects, and musicians, who've combined other fields of study with their passion for design. In brief, I seek out people that have completely different life experiences and influences than my own, people who can add a unique perspective to our company.
　　—Chris Do

Someone who has great ideas, is a good communicator and a team player, and last, but not least, has good design skills.
　　—Bob English

Basic design and thinking skills. I like designers to do their homework before the design phase begins. To know the product as well as the client does. The Web designer should understand aesthetic limitations and that simplicity goes a long way.
　　—Karen Barranco

The ability to communicate one's ideas is very important. So is a cool head. In a smaller studio such as ours, it is an absolute requirement that each designer be technically multi-faceted. It is not unusual to start the day editing on the Avid and end it coding Action-script in Flash.
　　—Paul Schneider

Intelligence. Creativity. Courage. The willingness to satisfy a client's requirements but also create something that goes beyond them. Perhaps most important is the ability to intelligently talk about and to justify design ideas.
　　—David K. Young

I've seen demo reels that consist of only several spots that are beautiful. I've seen reels that consist of every job a designer has worked on. I like to see a variety of work, a range, but I don't like to see everything an artist has ever done. Editing one's work is important. I'm interested in seeing print and Web as well as

motion design. Good design is good design. Experimental and personal work is important to see as well. I like to see how a designer thinks through her work without client restrictions.
—**Michael Uman**

Good oral language skills for interiewing users, explaining ideas to clients, and writing reports. Curiousity about the world and enjoyment of learning about new disciplines of knowledge. Significant skills in manipulating dynamic typography, color, layout, signage, and sequencing to convey content appropriately and effectively. Ability to work with peers in teams effectively: to organize efforts and to be responsible in carrying out tasks thoroughly and on time. Comfort with technology. Comfort with people from a mixture of cultures, from marketing to mainland China. Generally good academic skills (verbal, mathematical, and visual literacy).
—**Aaron Marcus**

I look for ideas, and I don't really care about background or technique unless it influences the designer's ideas. Ideas span across all media and cause a designer make his own decisions.
—**Jonathan Notaro**

First she has to be a good designer. Then she has to have a good knowledge of the medium and all the skills a good designer needs, but mostly a passion for the future, good collaborative working experience, and a lot of patience.
—**Peter Girardi**

That look that says, "I have a lot to learn and am grateful for it." That's the look we all have here, and when we interview for new designers, we recognize that quality— and it is a quality— immediately. Then it's a matter of skills. We're not drawn to resumes but to URLs. We want to see that the designer can design effectively for the Web, and the only way to find that out is to experience the work. We aren't a "wow" shop, so we also look for designers who don't feel the need to blow you away with gimmicks but rather stick to a consistent theme.
—**Hillman Curtis**

I look for designers who embrace the future but respect the past. Specifically, I look for designers who are equipped with the skills to operate modern authoring tools but also have an understanding of old-world techniques (like actually sketching a concept on paper or kerning letterforms). I think

that more than ever, digital designers need to understand the design history that paved the way before them and how their craft is an extension of this history.
—**David Vogler**

Intelligence, creativity, skills in design and in the tool set, confidence, solid work and team ethics, self motivation, the desire to learn, and a great passion for design. Not too much really.
—**Todd Purgason**

I assume he knows the technology but also has a feeling for and knowledge of the past. I don't care for the "filter of the day" look.
—**Mirko Ilic**

Intellectual curiosity. Lack of pretension. Flexibility. A willingness to experiment, collaborate, and occasionally throw caution to the wind. Forgiveness. Humor. And a tolerance for the occasional interruptions of two very young children who, in spite of their minimal scale, can display a surprising lung capacity. (Mercifully, however, they're pretty cute.)
—**Jessica Helfand**

IX. Motion

IN RECENT YEARS, with the advent of cable TV and an increase in the number of both Hollywood and independent movies being made, graphic designers have become more integral to film and television production. Both industries have traditionally employed graphic and advertising designers to promote their wares in print, but a current surge in the use of motion designers has developed into a popular specialty.

MOTION IS THE generic term for a discipline practiced by designers who create movement on either silver or cathode-ray screens. The former create film titles (the graphic cinematic sequences that introduce a movie) and trailers (promotions used to advertise a film prior to release), while the latter develop station or network identifiers, interstices or bumpers (short promotional sequences between programs), and program openers (the main titles for a TV show). Some designers work with live action, others with animation, and most integrate type with kinetic imagery. Some work exclusively for the film or broadcast industries, but most are generalists within this specialty. Some designers are on the staffs of film studios or television stations; others are independent contractors with studios or firms. Some firms are small — based on the vision of one or two designers — and a few are very large and handle a wide variety of motion-related projects. For those with an interest in movement, this is a creatively challenging yet highly pressured field that requires considerable collaboration.

FILM

WHEN HOLLYWOOD WAS in its infancy and movies were silent, generic title cards were the means to introduce a film and to caption scenes. With the subsequent advent of talkies and color, titles were designed in more ambitious and dramatic styles befitting the content of the movie. In the early 1950s, Saul Bass, a graphic designer, directed the first abstract title sequence for the Otto Preminger film *The Man with the Golden Arm*; it showed the animated development of a crooked, serpentine arm and hand twisting around the names of the cast. Influenced by the art of German expressionism, this unprecedented symbolic approach was used to indicate the raw, drug-related theme of the movie. Not only did the sequence present the title and cast billing in a novel way, it established the tenor of the film through allusion rather than a live-action scene. From this touchstone, Bass and other title designers began to direct very short films. Although not all title sequences are as ambitious, the best are indeed films within films and used as shorthand introductions that ease the viewer into the story or plot of the movie.

Many classic examples are currently found on video — *Vertigo, North by Northwest, To Kill a Mockingbird, Around the World in Eighty Days, The Pink Panther*, and *Dr. Strangelove*, just to name a few of the best. And in recent years, numerous future classics have been produced — *Seven, Men in Black, Casino, Clockers*, and more. Everyone interested in this design discipline should watch these again and again.

In most cases, film titles are budgeted into an overall production estimate; they are also often the first thing to be jettisoned when costs run over. Low-budget films are routinely bereft of designed titles, while high-budget and blockbuster films, which can afford them, go all out. Of course, this is not a consistent rule; sometimes young designers work at cost in order to experiment with titles for independent films — but "at cost" can be costly. Title sequences are usually commissioned by film directors or producers and, depending on their level of involvement, they either micro- or macromanage the sequence. Regardless of how little or how much freedom is allowed, the title sequence designer is not hired to create an independent film but to complement, as creatively as possible, the main story.

Various optical houses based in Hollywood, which once did almost all the title work, specialize in main and end titles and employ staff designers and technicians who work anonymously on specific projects. Quite a few well-known title designers got their early training at these optical houses. However, after Saul Bass created his first title sequence, the conventions changed to include freelance designers, working alone or in studios, who were commissioned on a project basis. Today, the most inspired and memorable title sequences are designed by independent firms and studios that have their own creative and production components. Most are headquartered in Los Angeles in close proximity to the major film studios, but New York is home to others. Indeed, as more film pre- and postproduction is done in New York, it is no longer necessary to live and work in L.A. to get good film title assignments. Moreover, in addition to the dedicated film title firms, generalist graphic designers are commissioned to do the occasional film title as one part of their overall practice.

Film title assignments are commissioned in various ways. Specialists are known for their work and hired based on their portfolio (or reel) and reputation. If both director/producer and designer have a good experience, the likelihood of repeat business increases. Although the well-known specialists get the lion's share of the work, small and even untried design firms are continually tapped by directors looking for novel approaches.

Designing a title sequence is not for the neophyte. If a designer is not well versed in the techniques of filmmaking, a strong support/production team is necessary to translate a storyboard into celluloid. The designer must, however, be able to think in terms of movement and create narrative or abstract sequences that fuse into a graphic entity. The designer should understand as much of the process as possible, which means a fairly extensive apprenticeship at an optical house or design firm. Training in (or exposure to) film and sound editing and cinematography is recommended, if only to have a sense of the medium and its potential. Because an increasing number of effects are done on computer, the designer should also have experience with editing programs (Director, AfterEffects, and others) for the Macintosh, Media 100, and Silicon Graphics hardware.

Film titles are concept-driven but work-intensive and require much collaboration from the design/production team. For those who want to direct sequences, it is prudent to become members of these teams. The neophyte should create both storyboards and computer-generated samples as principle portfolio components — then, once in the door, learn as much as possible. More knowledge means more options that can be brought to the screen.

Some designers who specialize in film titles also do collateral print work for the movie industry, including posters and press kits, but most of this work is done by designers in advertising agencies or design firms that specialize in promotion.

TELEVISION

DESIGNERS WHO WORK primarily in film may also work in television (and vice versa). Although the aspect ratio (the size of the image on the screen) is quite different, the basic technology is the same. Of course, a TV program introduction is rarely as long as a film title sequence, and a television bumper is no more than thirty seconds, but the creative energy and production invested in each is similar.

Once, when only three major networks reigned and a few local stations operated in regional markets, all television work, from broadcast design (such as the graphics seen behind the talking heads on the news) to on-air motion design, was stratified and restricted. In-house art departments were responsible for the majority of the work, or it was farmed out to production studios that specialized in them. However, with the advent of cable TV networks, the demand for unique approaches (rather than network clichés) led cable creative directors to commission independent designers to supplement in-house design staffs. Although this genre is not as huge as publishing, advertising, or corporate design, opportunities have increased, and the number of dedicated practitioners is growing. When one stops to think how much broadcast air has to be filled with distinctive graphics, it is clear that this is not a slacker industry.

From the 1950s through the 1970s, CBS was the major influence on television graphic design. From its iconic logo — the CBS Eye, designed by William Golden — to its print advertising and on-air promotion, designed by Louis Dorfsman, all the graphics for the "champagne network" were elegant, creative, and memorable. In addition, NBC had its peacock, ABC had its Paul Rand logo, and these were the cornerstones of design achievement. Early in the 1980s, computer technology entered the graphic arena and with it a not altogether welcome trend called the *flying logo*. State-of-the-art imaging systems, such as Paintbox, allowed designers to dimensionalize and kineticize their graphics with such ease that every network and regional station made their identifiers jump, bounce, and otherwise speed across the television screen. Soon the practice was ridiculed inside the profession as a substitute for original thinking. Today the trend is lessened, although not entirely gone. Instead, MTV was launched in 1979 and with it an entirely new approach to on-air graphic identification. The original logo was not a simple, elegant form but an inelegant *M* with a scrawled *TV* beside it. Not only was this akin to graffiti, the mark constantly and animatedly changed its form — color, pattern, context — on the air. In addition, over time, the logo was included in bumpers and interstices that were miniature animated movies. With the busting of television graphic convention, the floodgates were opened to a wide range of creative possibilities throughout the cable industry. Today, diverse approaches contributed by a new generation of TV designers are found on Nickelodeon,

This area includes any kind of film- or television-based media. While some motion designers also engage in Web or CD-ROM design, others do not. The emphasis should be on film or television title sequences, television interstices, bumpers, videos, and other related practice.

Entry Level

School and speculative assignments are acceptable, along with any design or artwork that contributes to sequential motion graphics.

Contents

a. Printout versions of on-screen designs
b. Screen grabs on Zip Disk or CD-ROM
c. Video cassette (if available), featuring motion graphics, animation, pencil tests, etc.
d. Two or three storyboards

Advanced

Projects should be fairly advanced. Individual or collaborative live assignments should be combined with speculative work.

Contents

a. Printout versions of on-screen designs
b. Screen grabs on Zip Disk or CD-ROM
c. One or two speculative projects as storyboards or realized
d. Videocassette with professional-quality work
e. Two or three storyboards or preparatory work

Format

35mm slides (in slide tray), 4x5 transparencies, printouts in binder, Zip Disk,

Title: Mimic — Dimension **Designers:** Kyle Cooper, Karin Fong, Dana Yee, Scarlett Kim, Kimberly Cooper **Art Directors:** Kyle Cooper, Karin Fong **Director:** Kyle Cooper **Company:** Imaginary Forces **Client:** Dimension Films/Miramax [Director: Guillermo Del Tor] **Digital Photographer:** Keith Coop **Director of Photography:** Juan Ruiz Amchia **Year:** 1997

Lifetime, American Movie Channel, Comedy Central, E!, and Bravo.

Television or broadcast design employs numerous skills and talents. Some designers specialize; others do not. Here is a brief summary:

1. **In-house graphic designers or graphic artists for news broadcasting:** These are the designers who produce breaking news and generic graphics that highlight or introduce a news subject and are most commonly seen behind the newscaster's talking head. These designers are proficient in drawing and graphics software.

2. **In-house graphic designers or graphic artists for station identifiers:** All large and most small broadcast operations employee staff designers to create on-air bumpers, promos, and common identifiers. The more ambitious work might be contracted to independent design/production firms.

3. **In-house art departments for program openers:** Most of these are contracted to independent designers but, in some larger design departments for stations or networks that generate their own programming (like certain public broadcasting stations), this is considered something of a perk. It usually requires an art director working with a production crew (cameraman, animator, etc.), depending on whether the film is live action or animated. Program openers are not restricted to type on a screen.

4. **Independent design firms for on-air promos and identifiers:** Graphic design studios are getting an increasing amount of choice on-air assignments, and the ratio of experienced film or broadcast designers to those without track records in this area is fairly balanced. MTV Networks (including Nickelodeon, Nick at Nite, and Cartoon Network) have turned to young designers, illustrators, and animators in an effort to tap unknown talents. In turn, this has launched new subspecialties for firms and individuals who may have been exclusively print-oriented.

There is also a great need for advertising and program *content*. This is the prime area for animation studios, a few of which combine graphic design and illustration. Although traditional animation studios are routinely subcontracted by television and advertising art directors to produce predetermined storyboards, there is also a rise in creative animation/design firms that specialize in developing their own ideas. For some of these, it is important to have experienced animators, producers, or directors, while others supplement a core staff of experts with neophytes who are unfettered by constraints. With more advertising spots using animation, and with the advent of cable programming devoted to new animation (experimental programming) as well as a desire among the funkier stations to push the limits of on-air identification, creative animation teams are finding a receptive clientele.

To enter the motion design discipline, it is useful to have some film and television training, which can be obtained in special school courses or through internships (even local low-power TV stations are a good place to begin, if only to become acquainted with broadcast technology). Today, it is not as daunting or difficult to enter the field, as it used to be. Indeed, knowledge of key programs (which change frequently, so stay informed) allows you to try your hand at this medium and to determine whether or not you have the talent to pursue a career.

In the Ink Tank

R.O. BLECHMAN
Creative Director, The Ink Tank, New York City

You are known as a creator of animated films and commercials, and you run an animation studio. Does this make you a specialist?
I have no area of specialty in design, except that I favor incorporating my illustrations in a graphic format. I do this primarily to maintain an identity.

With your different approaches, how much of your time is devoted to design, art direction, and business matters?
I wear at least three hats: illustrator, animated film director and studio head, and graphic designer. Of the three, the least worn is that of graphic designer. I don't solicit design work, so I don't receive many commissions for it. (I almost forgot my fourth hat: business manager. That's a hat permanently cocked on my head.)

Do you have a specific approach when you are hiring designers?
My design operation is too small to hire designers on a staff basis, so I use freelancers exclusively. I usually find people through word of mouth. Somebody calls me and says, "I have this great intern leaving me" or "You must see this person's portfolio!" I hire interns for my animation studio, and they usually work themselves into a staff position in my firm.

Title: Story; various covers **Illustrator:** R.O. Blechman **Company:** The Ink Tank **Client:** Story **Years:** 1992, 1994, 1995

Title: Take a Walk Through History **Illustrator:** R.O. Blechman **Company:** The Ink Tank

Lights, Camera, Design

Title: The Big Lebowski
Designer: Randall Balsmeyer
Client: Working Title Films
Typefaces: Mesquite, Magneto
Year: 1997 **Copyright:** ©
Polygram Filmed Entertainment

Title: Jungle Fever **Designer:**
Randall Balsmeyer **Client:** 40
Acres and a Mule Filmworks
Year: 1991 **Copyright:** © 1991
Universal City Studios, Inc.
Courtesy of Universal Publishing
Rights, A Division of Universal
Studios, Inc. All rights reserved.

RANDALL BALSMEYER

Secretary/Treasurer, Balsmeyer & Everett, Inc.,
New York City

How did you become a film title designer?
I was working as a graphic designer when a friend asked me if I
could design the titles for a documentary she had just made. It
sounded like fun, so I gave it a try. Next thing I knew I was
designing more titles, which led to learning about animation, cinematography, and opticals. It was the first time that my interests
in photography, design, film, and computers all clicked together.
It was very satisfying to create these kinds of images. I've always
been both left- and right-brained, and this was the first time that
both sides were happy.

What is the key difference between designing for film and TV?
The principal difference between film and TV (aside from aspect
ratio) is pacing. TV is about getting through material as quickly as
possible, before the viewer clicks his remote control. It's also
about selling the show. The goal in TV is to grab the viewer's
interest and hook him into watching the rest of the show. Films
are a bit more leisurely. You can take the time to set a mood,
build a rapport with the viewer. You don't have to sell the movie
because the viewer has already bought his ticket and has committed to watching the picture.

What about the difference between motion and print?
In both TV and film, designers dictate the pace at which the piece
is seen. In print, the viewer controls the pace and chooses
whether to explore the piece in depth, skim for meaning, or just
turn the page.

Is this field open or closed to newcomers?
Film graphics is now more open than it ever has been. The techni-
cal changes of the last few years have taken design out of the
Iron Age and made it more accessible to anyone with a good idea.
The downside of this is that a lot of really terrible work shows up

because now anyone can do it. We now frequently see technique masquerading as an idea.

How much technology must you know to achieve your goals?
I live with one foot in the design world and one foot in the visual effects world. By necessity (and choice), my inclination is to be fluent in the available technology. On one hand, I try not to think about the means of execution when I'm coming up with ideas. On the other hand, I need to know how to actualize something once a design is agreed upon.

We invented a character, my alter ego, the Technoslut (someone who is easy for technology). We gave him a tongue-in-cheek slogan, "Complicated Is Better," which we hope communicates the sense of humor with which we view the technology we're so dependent upon.

You work with assistants; what do you look for in a portfolio?
The work should be idea-centric. It should not be about its own means of production. It should be bold, not precious. It should be a strong, original means of communicating an idea. If it breaks rules to do that, great! But the work should not be about breaking rules, because it then becomes self-referential. If it's a thesis on kerning, don't bother sending it.

Title: Naked Lunch **Designer:** Randall Balsmeyer **Client:** Recorded Picture Company **Typefaces:** Futura **Year:** 1991 **Copyright:** © 1991 Twentieth Century Fox

Title: Short Cuts **Designer:** Randall Balsmeyer **Client:** Short Cuts Productions **Typefaces:** Journal **Year:** 1993 **Copyright:** © 1993 Fine Line Features. All rights reserved.

Title: Kundun **Designer:** Randall Balsmeyer **Client:** Refuge Productions **Typefaces:** ITC Viner Hand Italic **Year:** 1997 **Copyright:** © 1997 Touchstone Pictures. All rights reserved.

Title: The First Wives Club **Designer:** Randall Balsmeyer **Typefaces:** Hairspray, Cafeteria **Year:** 1996 **Copyright:** © 1996 Paramount Pictures

Animated Art

Title: Tango **Designer/ Illustrator:** J.J. Sedelmaier **Production Company:** J.J. Sedelmaier Productions **Creative Director:** Andrea Janetos Hyett **Company:** Foote Cone Belding **Client:** Pacific Bell **Year:** 1996

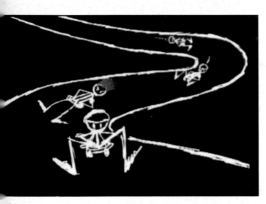

Title: Larry the Luger **Designer/Illustrator:** J.J. Sedelmaier **Creative Directors:** Hal Rosen, J.J. Sedelmaier **Production Company:** J.J. Sedelmaier Productions **Company:** North Castle **Client:** Slim Jim **Year:** 1997

J. J. SEDELMAIER

President and Director, J.J. Sedelmaier
Productions, Inc., White Plains, New York

What motivated you to become an animation producer/director?
Nothing specific. I've become what I am through the normal growth process of acquiring more and more experience and developing my talents toward having as much control of the final product as possible. I naturally like to know as much as I can about the process of anything I am involved in. I guess you can say that close to twenty years of coming up through the animation ranks and being a sponge is what has brought me to where I am now.

Do you consider yourself a designer or an illustrator?
I pattern my involvement as I feel it's needed in any project. Sometimes I actually design characters and the look of a spot; other times I art-direct with a very heavy hand. And there are instances where I merely help keep things graphically on track. Because I often work with artists and illustrators in translating their style to animation, my involvement is never the same because the requirements of projects always differ. I am a filmmaker who also designs and illustrates.

As an animation producer/director, do you have a personal style?
My personal style and the studio's reputation surround a sensibility, whether it's a sense of humor or simply the level of entertainment. I simply pattern my style for each and every project.

You hire many people— animators, storyboarders, etc. What do you look for in a portfolio?
When people show their work to me, I look for an approach or feel to the work that I've never seen before. I am also receptive to people who come in with enthusiasm and a can-do attitude. The animation process is a collaborative effort and depends on contri-

Title: Buy Low
Production Company:
J.J. Sedelmaier
Productions
Designer: David
Levine **Creative
Directors:** Bob
Hoffman, J.J. Sedel-
maier **Company:**
Gearon Hoffman
Client: Brown &
Company **Year:** 1995

bution from and harmony among everyone involved in the process.
I can see a beautiful portfolio filled with ground-breaking images,
but if the person appears to be overconfident, I'll have second
thoughts about making her a part of the studio. It's also possible
that a portfolio's content might not be up to a level where I think
it should be, but there is something about that person's personality
that still makes her attractive as a potential member of the group.

How has the computer affected your work?

Computer technology has allowed us to work faster, which is obviously good and bad because it only makes deadlines shorter. But it
has also freed us from tasks that historically have been tedious.
The ink and paint process has been revolutionized by digital computer technology. Our involvement in projects like Beavis and
Butthead and the Saturday Night Live cartoons would simply not
be possible at all because of tight schedules. New techniques of
animation production make it feasible.

Title: Speed Racer in "Sabo-
tage" **Production Company:**
J.J. Sedelmaier Productions
Creative Directors: Ron
Lawner, Allan Pafenbach,
Lance Jensen, J.J. Sedelmaier
Company: Arnold Advertising
Client: Volkswagen of America,
Inc. **Year:** 1996

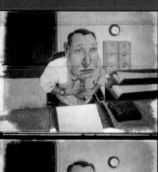

Title: Heartburn **Production
Company:** J.J. Sedelmaier
Productions **Designer:** C.F.
Payne **Creative Directors:** J.J.
Sedelmaier, Harry Azorin
Company: Klemtner Advertis-
ing, Inc. **Client:** Astra Merck
Year: 1997

Title: Psycho Training II
Production Company: J.J.
Sedelmaier Productions
Designer: Gideon Kendall
Creative Directors: Mickey
Paxton, J.J. Sedelmaier
Company: Houston Herstek
Favat **Client:** Converse
Typeface: Bernard Maisner
Year: 1995

The Art of Storytelling

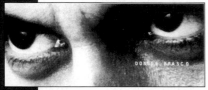

KYLE COOPER

Executive Creative Director, Imaginary Forces,
Hollywood, California

What have been the major influences on your work as a film title designer?

Saul Bass's main titles for *The Man with the Golden Arm*, *Take a Walk on the Wild Side*, and *Seconds*, which I saw in 1985. I was also influenced by R/Greenberg's titles for *Altered States*, *Goldfinger*, by Robert Brownjohn, and *To Kill a Mockingbird*, by Stephen Frankfurt. Of course, I also loved *Star Wars*, but what impressed me the most was the editing and the juxtaposition of images. Paul Hirsch and George Lucas really made an impression on me. George Lucas seems very aware of the editorial aspect of a film and what that can bring to the movie.

Do you have a personal style in your film titles?

I heard someone say once that having a style is like being in jail. I do not agree, but I try to approach each design differently; one style is never appropriate for all jobs. The visual approach I take for a main title sequence should establish a tone, encapsulate, and generate excitement in people about what they are about to see. My work is sometimes seen as experimental; I do like to keep up to date with what is new in graphic design and film, but I think that under everything I have done is an attempt to solve a specific communication problem. With each title sequence, a problem has to be solved. I need to understand the content of the film. The type is often like an actor, always behaving in a way that would help explain the small story.

What is the most fulfilling aspect of your job? the least?

The most fulfilling aspect of my job is being able to combine my

Title: Donnie Brasco **Designers:** Kyle Cooper, Kurt Mattila, Adam Bluming, Olivia D'Albis **Company:** Imaginary Forces **Clients:** TriStar Pictures, Mandalay Entertainment **Year:** 1997

Title: Sphere **Designers:** Olivia D'Albis, Mikon Van Gastel **Creative Director:** Kyle Cooper **Art Directors:** Mikon Van Gastel, Kurt Mattila **Company:** Imaginary Forces **Client:** Warner Bros. **Deep-sea Photographer:** Norbert Wu **Typographer:** Mikon Van Gastel **Year:** 1998

interests in film, typography, technology, and storytelling. There are limitless options in the production process. I can integrate almost every medium imaginable. The least is probably when we try to do too much work at once or go into something without a plan. I also do not like when people try to separate the main title from the movie and critique it as a separate piece. A main title, ideally, should seem like an integrated part of the film.

How have technological advancements affected your work?
A great deal. Technology allows us to do complex things more simply and in less time. Take *The Island of Dr. Moreau*, for instance. We used Adobe Illustrator to do things with type — stretching end points to create violent shards, sharpening, deconstructing, reconfiguring. It's the kind of graphics that would have to have been hand-painted ten years ago. Technology allows us to execute almost anything we imagine.

Do you have a specific approach to hiring designers?
We look for people who are good thinkers, typographers with a good film sense first. I do lean toward good typographers, however. I like to give people a chance to try something they may not have done before. Often this means bringing in incredibly talented print graphic designers and introducing them to motion graphics. It is really an ongoing process of constantly being open to meeting and seeing the work of interested designers and interns.

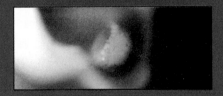

Title: Mission Impossible **Designers:** Kyle Cooper, Jenny Shainin **Creative Directors:** Kyle Cooper, Peter Frankfurt **Company:** Imaginary Forces **Client:** Paramount **Year:** 1996

Title: The Island of Dr. Moreau **Designers:** Kyle Cooper, Karin Fox, Chris Do, Scarlett Kim, Vince Abogado **Art Director:** Karin Fox **Company:** Imaginary Forces **Client:** New Line Cinema **Typefaces:** Mason, Caslon **Year:** 1996

Narrative Design

EMILY OBERMAN
Cofounder, Number Seventeen, New York City

As a graphic designer with a print background, what do you think is fundamentally different about working in the television medium?

Well, the most obvious answer is music and sound design. That is a huge challenge because even though moving type is obviously different from setting it on a piece of paper, it still works under the basic principles of design. You are still trying to get your audience's attention by using scale, placement, and visual stimuli. With motion, you also have the added layer of sound, which is something I didn't learn in school, so my approach to it is basically instinctual.

Do you find that working in sequential media requires story-telling ability?

Being a good storyteller is important in any art or entertainment work, be it commercial, fine art, music, literature, babysitting, or cooking, to name a few. Success is all in the timing and the delivery.

Are you more concerned with the narrative or the design?

The narrative is definitely the thing that drives the work. It is from the narrative that the idea is born and, as far as we are concerned, the design can only come from that, not the other way around. You are trying to connect with your audience, and the narrative helps you do that.

How many fingers are in this particular pie?

Hmmmm? All of them?

Title: Saturday Night Live **Designers/Creative Directors:** Emily Oberman, Bonnie Siegler **Company:** Number Seventeen **Client:** Saturday Night Live **Typeface:** Engraver's Gothic **Year:** 1997

Title: MTV Animated Logo **Designers:** Keira Alexandra, David Israel **Creative Directors:** Emily Oberman, Bonnie Siegler **Company:** Number Seventeen **Client:** MTV Productions **Year:** 1996

Title: Calvin Klein In-Store
Display **Designer:** Keira
Alexandra **Creative Direc-
tors:** Emily Oberman, Bonnie
Siegler **Company:** Number
Seventeen **Client:** Calvin
Klein **Year:** 1997

Title: American Dreamers
Designers/Creative Directors: Emily
Oberman, Bonnie Siegler **Company:**
Number Seventeen **Client:** Schaffer
Typeface: Clarendon **Year:** 1997

What has been your most challenging on-air project, and why?
Our most challenging project was not exactly on air in that it was
made for high schools across the country. We were hired by the
Josten's Corporation to make a short film about the millennium.
The directive was to give kids a sense of why the year 2000 should
be important to them and to do it by showing the history of the
past thousand years and the possibilities of the next thousand
years, and to do it in a way that was smart, funny, hip (but not
too hip), inspiring, entertaining, cool (but not too cool), global,
and local, and able to be shown in every high school in America.
Oh, and it should be about six minutes long. We made a moving
timeline and are very proud of the piece.

Can you describe the perfect marriage of design and motion?
The scene in *Take the Money and Run* where Woody Allen plays the
cello in the marching band. Also, almost anything by the Basses,
Maurice Binder, Pittman Hensley, Bureau, and Buster Keaton.

**Doing this must require senses that are unnecessary in print
— music and sound, for example. Was this something you had
to learn, or was it an innate talent?**
Sound design is hard. As I said earlier, it's not something we
learned in school. But over time, you get a feel for how to work
with music and sound, so it is both innate and learned.

**Would you say that time and space require considerably more
skill than print?**
Nope. Just slightly different skills. And the difference is narrowing
every day.

Ready for Her Closeup

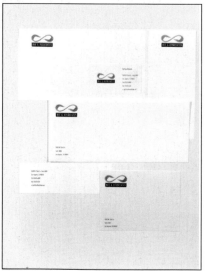

Title: BCC + Associates Brochure and Logo/Letterhead **Designer:** Robert Vega **Creative Director:** Deborah Ross **Art Director:** Marilyn Frandsen **Company:** Deborah Ross Film Design **Client:** BCC + Associates **Photographer:** Arthur Tress, Shinichi Eguchi (Photonica) **Typeface:** Bodega Sans **Year:** 1997

DEBORAH ROSS

Art Director, Deborah Ross Film Design, Culver City, California

What made you launch your own film title design business?
I'm a very independent person and have always followed my own course. I like the freedom of being able to come in and work on something when the creative juices are flowing for me rather than punching a time clock. Of course, along with the responsibilities is the satisfaction that it's all my baby!

What is the key difference between print and the film and TV work that you do?
Many of the design issues are similar. For example, I give the same kind of attention to detail, in terms of research and approach, to logos, whether they be for film, TV, or print. But I'm aware that some type designs work better on the printed page than on film, so I compensate for that. For instance, if a font I'm using is on the thin side, it may break up on film, so I might thicken it before shooting it onto film.

Is this a field that is open to newcomers?
A few years ago, I would have said film graphics was a pretty tight field to break into, but that has changed because of computer technology. The field is breaking wide open, with young designers being snapped up right and left. However, I still believe a sound training in design provides a tremendous advantage over those who may be a whiz at AfterEffects but who haven't bothered to learn the basics of good design, concept, and typography.

What are the biggest challenges in working in this medium?
New technology is always coming out, and there comes a point when you realize a certain diminishing return on investing time in learning every little facet of each new version. Unless, of course you want to have a total hands-on approach. That's valid for some

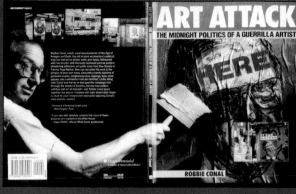

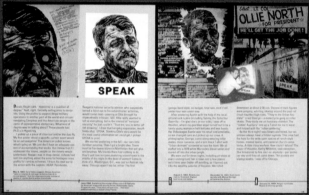

Title: Art Attack: The Midnight
Politics of a Guerilla Artist
Designer: Christina Chang
Creative Director: Deborah Ross
Company: Saxon/Ross Film
Design Client: Harper Perennial
Photographer: Alan Shaffer
Year: 1992

people, but it doesn't work for me because my time is spread out
over many areas of my business.

How much technology must you know to achieve your goals?
I have to keep the big picture in mind at all times. I'm more concerned about finding the right person to execute my concepts than
I am in learning the programs available to do it. I know enough
about the programs to ask intelligent questions and give sensible
direction when faced with problems. It helps that I have a background in animation as well because I understand what I want a
particular design to achieve and can usually figure out how to
make that happen.

You work with assistants. What do you look for in a portfolio?
Besides neat, beautifully presented storyboard designs, I'm looking
for someone who understands what narrative is: good storytelling,
the ability to create some mystery, or a question that needs to be
answered — and then the answer. I like a sense of humor or irony
too. Of course, it really doesn't hurt to have strong type design
sensibilities as well.

Title: WGBH Clock **Designers:** Chris Pullman, Louis Alvarado **Creative Director:** Chris Pullman **Company:** WGBH Boston **Client:** WGBH Design **Typeface:** Univers **Year:** 1989

CHRIS PULLMAN
Vice President for Design, WGBH, Boston

Why did you decide to enter broadcast design?
It was an accident. At the time, I didn't even own a TV, and the only thing in my university town more derided than advertising was television (this was 1973, when TV had been rightly tagged as "the vast wasteland"). But I was able to see a distinction between what WGBH (public television in Boston) was up to and what television in general was up to.

While a career in broadcast media was not something I had anticipated, WGBH offered me an environment that suited many of the personal and professional values I had gradually self-selected in the ten years since I had entered the field. It was nonprofit, with a prosocial purpose; its mission was to bring ideas and information to a huge audience at low cost; its content was eclectic (science, history, home improvement, you name it); and it expected a designer to express this content in every imaginable medium (print, film, and video, and, now, new media and the Internet).

What is the most fulfilling aspect of your job?
Being part of an effort to help people understand things better — that's the big payoff. The smaller one is doing something satisfying with my own hands, finding the clever, apt, and efficient solution to a tricky problem. Which brings me to the least satisfying aspect of my job: In my role as a manager, I constantly tussle with the paradox that if I really do my job well, I should give all the juicy jobs to everybody else on my staff and then help make sure that they make something wonderful. By not being in the trenches, I

Title: Joy **Designer/Creative Director:** Chris Pullman **Company:** WGBH Boston **Client:** Corporate Communications **Typeface:** Univers **Year:** 1990

Joy!

Title: Africans in America Funding Document **Designers:** Chris Pullman, Alison Kennedy **Creative Director:** Chris Pullman **Company:** WGBH Boston **Photographers:** T.P. Pearson, Louis Agassiz **Typeface:** Baskerville **Year:** 1993

Title: Masterpiece Theater Title Sequence **Designers:** Chris Pullman, Alison Kennedy **Creative Director:** Chris Pullman **Company:** WGBH Boston **Typeface:** Times Roman **Year:** 1993

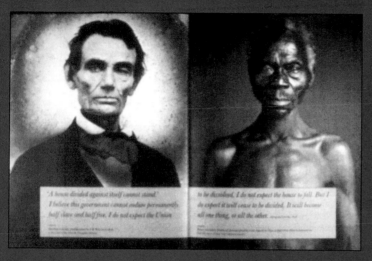

have allowed myself to become less skilled, technically, than the people who work for me, something that was not true when I came to WGBH twenty-four years ago (and for many years after).

How have technological advancements affected your work?
Greatly. Our method of working has shifted dramatically since 1985, when desktop computers first came into the WGBH design room. Unhappily, the complexities attendant on software have tended to force specialization; it is harder, rather than easier, to slip from Web to video to paper. Your investment in mastering motion, for example, makes you best suited for the next motion job. You quickly fall into the trap of not being able to get hired to do something unless you can show that you have already done it. Students come into our group already focused on one medium, right at a time when, theoretically, they suddenly have the potential to move horizontally across the discipline.

What makes a good WGBH designer?
A person who is confident and worldly (rather than narrow); someone who can say what is going on in their work, who is more interested in the other guy's problem statement than in his own need to express himself; who values the values and mission of our organization and is willing to deal with the (relatively) measly money to be made here; whose work shows a range of expression based on the content of the problem; who can draw and speak clearly; who has a sense of humor.

Designing on Air

Title: On-Air Design Sequence
Designer/Art Director: Cather-
ine Chesters **Creative Director:**
Jeffrey Keyton **Company:** MTV
Design **Client:** MTV

JEFFREY KEYTON

Vice President of Design and On-Air Creative, MTV,
New York City

What is your role at MTV, and what are your responsibilities?
I'm responsible for all on-air graphics and show opens. I do all
the packaging for the channel and for shows, and I'm also in
charge of all the print work, which ranges from business-to-
business stuff to consumer stuff to licensing and consumer products. I have currently about thirty-five people on my staff. It's a
big in-house group.

**MTV is the hot medium; how do you address the problems you
are given?**
I think the biggest challenge is constantly trying to have a philosophy, as much as possible, and to reinvent yourself and trying
to keep moving, and to not get caught up in visual redundancy. In
that way, whether people see your work on air or in the print
materials, they feel that there's a continuity but also an evolu-
tionary process going on. Sometimes we live in a world of fashion
and pay attention to what's going on, but you have to change
with the times, too.

**Being in the vortex of the most fashionable designing for a
youth culture, do you lead, follow, or echo?**
It's a combination. We really don't want to echo but at the same
time, we have to pay attention to what's going on and what kids
are reacting to and what their world is about. We really can't
impose our own visual agenda on them. We tend to look at fashion trends and pay attention to music kids are listening to. In the
time of Nirvana, when everything was grunge, the graphics had a
little bit more of that type of look and feel, but now, with the
current fragmentation in music, a youth might be listening to the
music of Puff Daddy and Celine Dion. You can get away with more
eclecticism and probably go a little cleaner and more minimal, as
it seems to be a more conservative time. That's just in the last
couple of years.

Sometimes I feel if I look at too much stuff it could affect me subconsciously. I'll skim enough to know what's going on; I don't want to feel like I'm out of it. I think it's important to know what your peers are doing, but not to the point where you study it. So if I am following, it's more fashion and music trends than design trends.

When hiring designers, do you have a specific approach?
First and foremost, we're always looking for someone with basic design skills and at how well she can decorate. We'd prefer someone with an interesting, slightly unusual approach rather than a classical, traditional approach because that's not necessarily the most appropriate style up here. Being an in-house department in a corporation, we are influenced by interpersonal skills. Is she going to be a good communicator? In small studios, you can get stuck in a back room and not come out. You can't really get away with that in a corporation. And, of course, conceptual thinking is always good, too.

Title: American Illustration 16 **Designers:** Jeffrey Keyton, Stacy Drummond, Tracy Hoychuck **Company:** MTV Design **Client:** Amerulis, Inc. **Illustrator:** Geoffrey Gran **Typeface:** Helvetica

Title: On-Air Opens for Sports and Music Festival **Designer:** Greg Hahn **Creative Director:** Jeffrey Keyton **Art Directors:** Todd St. John, Greg Hahn **Company:** MTV Design **Client:** MTV **Illustrator:** Packorn Buppahavesa

Typographic Justice

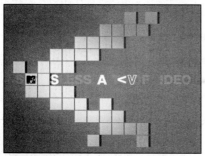

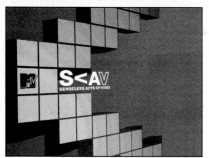

Title: Senseless Acts of Video—show package **Designer:** Jonathan Notaro **Creative Director/Producer:** Jonathan Notaro **Producer:** Casey Steele **Client:** MTV Networks **Year:** 2000

JONATHAN NOTARO

Principal, Brand New School, Santa Monica, California

Why did you decide to work in new media?
I'm a designer of things. I don't necessarily work in new media. Sure, I've done plenty of "new media" projects for companies and self-promotion, but I guess I'm a graphic designer who just happens to be working in motion right now, until something else interests me, or I get bored, whatever comes first.

How much does typography play in your design scheme?
Typography plays a huge role in my work. On the page, typography is one thing, but it goes so far beyond that. I explore its relationships in space and environment—how it reacts, mimics, or negates identifiable relationships in physical space. Ultimately, I suppose, it carries a whole new set of connotations, not to mention an evolution of form. The majority of work I do is for ad agencies: they love to see their precious copy receive typographic justice.

Do you integrate design for the digital realm with print?
We've seen so much of this lately, where the constraints of Flash [vector-based image making] influence the print aesthetic, and things start to carry a poor 1970s lithograph nostalgic vernacular. The mysticism of the digital realm has been unveiled, so I think its design has become much easier. Or has it? It's always interesting to see what spills over to the other side, formally and conceptually. The old limitations of the Web have forced designers to think simply yet still attempt to be interesting with information. I think the biggest fear designers should have is managing aesthetic differences based on the functional differences of variation in media.

Do you allow enough time for research, development, and experimentation? How so?
That's one of the perks of owning my own company. As a design director, part of my job is choosing the right projects, determining how much time to allocate for research, development, experimentation, and assessing what resources the project may demand.

Ling
Satin blue stretch top by DKNY
Pinstripe blue pants by DKNY
Leather belt by DKNY

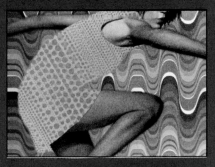

Mystikal
Camouflage double duty hat by Coogi
Embroidered knit sweater by Paris Blue for Coogi
Australian taco tee by Coogi

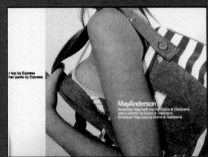

AlekWek
Diagonal sequins halter top by Express
Lizard tongue pink leather pants by Express

MayAnderson
American flag tank top by Dolce & Gabbana
Zebra shorts by Dolce & Gabbana
American flag bag by Dolce & Gabbana

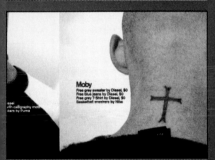

Moby
Free grey sweater by Diesel, $0
Free blue jeans by Diesel, $0
Free grey T-Shirt by Diesel, $0
Basketball sneakers by Nike

AlexLundqvist
Basic black V-neck by Hugo Boss
Deep blue jeans by Levi's

NoDoubt
Black dirt shirt that looks like I spilled on it
Teal chain stitch pants by Anja Flint

Mystikal
Camouflage double duty hat by Coogi
Embroidered knit sweater by Paris Blue for Coogi
Australian taco tee by Coogi

Title: MTV fashionably loud
week— show package **Designers:** Jonathan Notaro, Jens
Gehlhaar, Sean Dougherty
Creative Director/Producer:
Jonathan Notaro **Producer:**
Angela de Oliveira **Client:** MTV
Networks **Year:** 2000

Designing over Time

Title: Couleur 3 Poster Series
Designer/Art Director: Matthew
Mulder **Agency:** WGR Lausanne,
CH **Client:** Swiss State Radio
Year: 1999

MATTHEW MULDER AND PAUL SCHNEIDER,
WIDEOPENSPACES, Los Angeles, California

How does your firm integrate print, Web, and motion into a holistic practice? Or are these totally separate activities?
Mulder: They are not totally separate activities. They just require separate considerations. For example, broadcast design work general exists in a low-resolution format like NTSC. The way you can handle type and line is very different from what is possible in print. Therefore, your visual solutions have to be flexible enough to change for each medium. Doing work in all three genres is challenging. It usually takes a day or so to switch gears when going from a large motion project to a print project. But I think it keeps us on our toes because we are influenced by that many more people and ideas.
Schneider: Creatively, these factors all seem to melt together. Of course, sensibilities change with each media type but, often, one creative solution will spur ideas in other areas. This seems particularly evident in dynamic on-line media such as Flash and its comparisons to Film/Broadcast. It's becoming quite cyclical.

As graphic designers, did you have to acclimate yourselves to motion? What was the learning curve?
Mulder: I did for sure. Because of the greater freedom that designing over time gives, you need to be a better manager of time and assets. It was really overwhelming at first. You have the ability to vary an infinite amount of factors in seemingly infinite numbers of ways at infinite points in time. Technically, there is a learning curve of specialized knowledge for broadcast and film work. But the technical knowledge isn't any more or less complex than you would find for print or interactive; it is just different.

What is the most important design issue for film?
Mulder: The single most important design issue for film or any other motion-based medium is understanding narrative and dramatic structures. This is completely overlooked in graphic design education currently. We should look to our film school brethren, for whom understanding an audience and how to engage them is beaten into their brains as students. I also think that the concept of editing is important. In the beginning, I would try and fit every-

thing into a single moment because that was what I was used to doing in print.

Schneider: Telling a story over time utilizing conflicts created between imagery, sound, and graphic. It is important for a designer working in such media to realize this in order to react/interact in a desired manner.

How important is a typographic or cinematic style?

Mulder: I believe that each project should develop its form based on its context and goals, so I wouldn't place a relative value on one style. It all depends. Hopefully, you can avoid relying on a single style to drive your designs. Of course, this is a catch-22 for all creatives. If you have some success with a certain piece, then, often you are approached to provide a client with the same treatment. Personally, I try to avoid doing too much of the same thing. Working in a variety of media helps.

Schneider: The thought process for different media is varied, so identifying original style becomes a dubious proposition.

Title: I AM **Designers/Directors:** Matthew Mulder, Paul Schneider **Client:** CODEX 3 **Year:** 2001

Title: Rossignol Snowboard Video 1999 **Designer/Director:** Paul Schneider **Client:** Rossignol Skis and Snowboards **Year:** 1999

Title: WIDEOPENSPACES Postcards **Designers:** Matthew Mulder, Paul Schneider **Client:** WIDEOPENSPACES **Year:** 2001

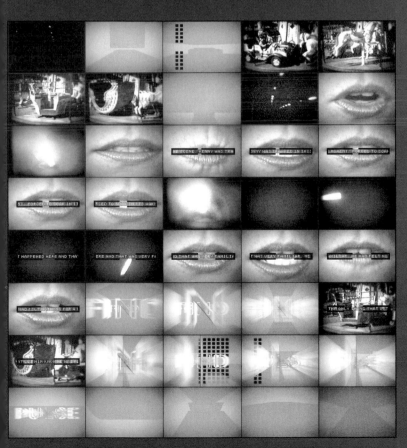

Title: The Pulse Lets Me Know I Am Alive **Designers/Directors:** Matthew Mulder, Paul Schneider **Client:** Belief Studios **Year:** 2001

Closer to Clarity

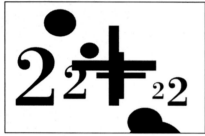

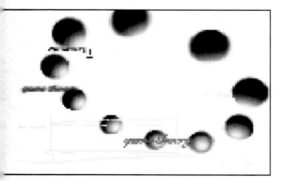

Title: 2+2 **Designer:** Benita Raphan **Codirectors:** Benita Raphan, Clayton Hemmert **Typographer:** Benita Raphan **Clients:** Destined for Channel 4 Television, UK, and Public Television, USA **Year:** 2001

BENITA RAPHAN

Filmmaker, Flame Artist/Broadcast Designer, New York City

Are there similarities between print design and film, or are these two distinct activities?

If you are a good print designer, it can certainly make an impression on your film work, but the reverse is almost never the case. And most directors are never going to care if they can design a nice poster for the opening of Issey Miyake's first American boutique at Bergdorf Goodman. Financially speaking and ego speaking, we are talking about apples and oranges. If you can direct a feature film for millions of dollars, with big stars and special effects and a shoot on a sound stage and have ten assistants at your beck and call, why would you want to design a book cover?

You make expressionistic films and documentaries. Which is your preference?

All of my films have been documentaries. The last one, the current one on Noble laureate John F. Nash, Jr. is known to the wider public. The prior three are known only to those people familiar with the subjects. The John F. Nash, Jr., I am codirecting with a man named Clayton Hemmert from a bicoastal company called Crew Cuts. I call him the Clarity Guy. He keeps me from getting too far away from the expressionistic and closer to the clarity. Sometimes he has to use a hard ruler to do so.

How do you design a film?

You just create a storyboard or a loose concept and find a nice person like Clayton who in this case also doubles as a capable and award-winning editor and keeps you on track. I have found a team of people, including Marshall Grupp, a great sound designer, who always manages to work within my *Rocky IV*–type budget. As we get about 75 percent finished, we begin showing the film to people we know and respect and ask if we are getting across the message we wanted. This is different, of course, from the European tradition, where this would be the only thing we do all day, in addition to taking coffee breaks, as in France, or tea breaks, as in England. Here, we do this in addition to more than full-time, very demanding jobs.

What is the goal of your filmmaking?
To do something that I exist for, quite simply—and wish I could get paid for, instead of having to do logo replacement from Pepsi to Cherry Pepsi, or having to work at Dean and Deluca or at Barnes & Noble—not to say that that is not noble work. I just think that others do it better than I do. And with less angst.

How difficult is it to get the funds to do the films that you do?
Impossible. But having the back door of working in advertising, I am able to find people who make commercials for a living who would rather be making short films, if they lived in Europe and had the eternal dole and didn't have to pay rent and feed families in a way that always seems impossible here in the States— but seems possible in Europe.

Title: Bravo Arts for Change **Designer/Art Director/Director/Typographer:** Benita Raphan **Client:** Bravo Network and @radical.media **Executive Producer:** John Kamen **Year:** 1996

Title: Absence Stronger than Presence **Designer/Art Director/Director/Typographer:** Benita Raphan **Clients:** Channel 4 Television, UK; and The Sundance Channel, USA **Year:** 1996

Title: Rockefeller Grant Award **Designer/Art Director/Director/Typographer:** Benita Raphan **Client:** Rockefeller Grant Award **Year:** 1999

Motion Control

Title: A&E Biography - show open **Designer:** Dana Yee
Creative Director: Bob English
Client: A&E Network **Year:** 1998

Title: 48 Hours - show open
Designer: Chun Chien Lien
Creative Director: Bob English
Director: Bob English **Client:** CBS **Year:** 1997

BOB ENGLISH
Creative Director, Media and Entertainment, Razorfish, New York City

What changes in the broadcast environment have you experienced that affect your design?
More than I could reasonably mention here. I began my career in the BBC graphic design department in a nondigital age. As I look back on those years, I have cause to think how primitive it all was. Whilst we did not have the bag of tricks that are now available, we certainly had to be very creative with not much at all. The basic principle of idea first and technique second has provided me with a fantastic grounding.

So what specific changes have affected my work? I will list them in more or less chronological order. Don't forget this list represents changes over approximately twenty years. Most of the changes have happened within the last five to ten years.

1. Motion Control: This meant we were able to shoot multiple passes on a subject. Each pass matched exactly, so we were able to achieve effects not previously possible.

2. Computer Graphics: Although poor at the beginning, CG became another way of creating original images for designers wishing to explore the third dimension. Many CG techniques have been developed over the years.

3. Telecine Steadygate: This got rid of film weave and allowed for multiple layering.

4. Digital paint systems: Suddenly, design is pitched into the spotlight. No longer did we have to create artwork traditionally, then record it onto film or tape. Paint systems like Quantel Paintbox revolutionized the TV design world.

Title: CMT - channel relaunch
Designer: Stephen Fuller
Creative Director: Bob English
Director: Chris McCumber
Client: Country Music Television
Year: 1999

5. Digital editing on-line: Multiple passes can now be achieved without the degradation caused by analog editing. These early machines were developed from digital paint systems and allowed bad directors to save their careers with retouching!

6. Digital editing off-line: Suddenly, the world of cutting a film together is revolutionized. No more strips of film stuck together with tape. More alternative cuts can be worked in a much quicker time.

7. Desktop software: Suddenly, a simple Apple Mac is able to do the job that the previous generation of expensive high-end paint and digital editing systems did. A single designer working from home is able to do what an army of specialists previously did.

8. Internet: We can send still and moving images from one continent to another instantly. This has allowed me to more easily work for international clients.

What is more important, the narrative or the effects?
That deserves an unequivocal answer: The narrative.

Do you feel that you have developed a style? An approach? Or do you roll with the problems that are given to you?
I see myself as a chameleon. I try to avoid a specific style, because each client's requirements are different. I tend to work at a much more conceptual level, in any case, and enjoy collaborating with people who have the unique talent and style that I think is appropriate for each project.

How would you like to see motion design progress in the near future?
I would like to see motion designers given the flexibility to work in different media. Broadband will offer many possibilities for the future. I would like motion designers to be a little more open to different techniques. Too many designers are designing on computers. This, in my mind, is dangerous. Free thought and inspiration should be allowed to evolve away from the confines of a screen.

How much of your work is determined by client intervention? How free have you been to develop on your own?
This is a difficult question to answer, as I regard myself as a designer, not a fine artist. I would prefer to have a relationship with a client that allows for work to develop in partnership. In reality, this doesn't always happen and depends on the mindset of the client. Occasionally, I have been asked to do my own thing. These times are wonderfully liberating and, I suppose, have produced my most innovative work. I tend to do my own thing outside of TV design to truly express myself.

Title: Arte - channel redesign
Designer: Bob English **Creative Director:** Bob English **Directors:** Thierry Rajic, Sylvie Pere
Client: Arte **Year:** 2000

Title: ZDF - channel rebrand and relaunch **Designers:** Bob English, Reg Squires, Jason Fisher Jones, Jodelle Reed, Thom Hallgren **Creative Director:** Bob English **Directors:** Jurgen Bolmyer, Jason Fisher Jones, Wolfgang Jaiser, Jodelle Reed, Thom Hallgren
Client: ZDF **Year:** 2001

Title: Court TV - Channel rebrand and relaunch **Designer:** Kylie Matulick **Creative Director:** Bob English **Photographer:** Chris Amaral **Client:** Court TV **Year:** 1999

Sequential Format

Title: Archipelago **Design Director:** Chris Do **2-D Animators:** Nic Benns, David Ko, Calvin Lo **3-D Animators:** Colin Strause, Brian Bell, David Ko **Agency:** Fallon McElligot, MN **Agency Art Director:** Bobby Appleby **Agency Creative Director:** Scott Vincent **Client:** Archipelago **Software:** Maya, Flame, Inferno **Year:** 2001

CHRIS T. DO,
Blind Visual Propaganda, Inc., Santa Monica, California

Why did you open a firm devoted to motion design?
Motion graphics is an extremely challenging and compelling field, adding a dimension to design that is fertile for discovery. It combines the principles of graphic design, typography, film making, animation, and photography. Working and thinking in a sequential format opens up new variables and opportunities not available in traditional two-dimensional print design.

What were your influences in this field— film, type, animation, or all?
I think it is important for designers to draw from a pool of experience, ideas, and images outside of the design world. For this reason, my influences come from all fields of study. I am inspired by other designers and artists, including Robert Rauschenberg, the Starn Brothers, Herbert Bayer, Marcel Duchamp, David McKean, Jan Tschicold, Tadeo Ando, The Brothers Quay, Joseph Muller-Brockman, Paul Rand, Joel-Peter Witkin, Andy Warhol, Joseph Cornell, John Pawson, Morphosis, and Bradbury Thompson.

Do you feel that you've developed a style or an attitude in your work? Can you explain what either is?
Our philosophical approach to design is centered around the notion that all problems are different and require and appropriately unique solution. Only by examining a particular project and its parameters can we determine the merit of a solution. This fundamental belief is used to guide our design and thinking.

Title: LAFF **Design Director:** Chris Do **Designer/Director/Animator:** Tom Koh **Editor:** Erik Buth **Composer:** Adam Sanborne **Director of Photography:** Joe Maxwell **Client:** IFP/West Los Angeles Film Festival **Medium/Software:** 35mm Film, After Effects, Flint, Media Composer **Year:** 2001

What is the most important aspect of design that you bring to motion?

Our love of letterforms and typography in both its formal and symbolic application, our uncompromising pursuit of creative expression, combined with our unique brand of design.

Is storytelling a key part of what you do? Or are effects more central?

Great design occurs when an idea and a design are inseparable. They are naturally complementary components. In essence, the solution comes from the content. We use design, images, and typography as a means to communicate an idea or to tell a story.

What does the future hold for motion design?

Motion graphics is still far from reaching its potential. As tools become more powerful and affordable, designers are more liberated to express their creative vision, unbound by the machines they use. Small design boutiques are able to produce incredibly experimental and interesting work. At the same time, the general public is much more visually aware and sophisticated. As a result, companies are more receptive to new ideas that may help them connect to their audience. Motion graphics is still relatively contemporary in that rules and boundaries haven't been established; we like to push that envelope.

Title: Ultimate TV **Design Director:** Chris Do **Directors:** Steve Pacheco, Tom Koh **Editor:** Chris Do **Effects Photographer:** Rick Spitznass **Animators:** Lawrence Wyatt, David Ko **Agency:** Foote, Cone & Belding, SF **Agency Art Director:** Jay Gnospelius **Client:** Ultimate TV - Microsoft **Software:** After Effects, Henry, media composer **Year:** 2001

Title: Dogtown **Design Director:** Chris Do **Designer:** Tom Koh **Animators:** Tom Koh, Calvin Lo, David Ko, Wilson Wu **Animation Editors:** Chris Do, Tom Koh **Firm:** Agi Orsi Productions **Client:** Stacy Peralta **Software/Medium:** After Effects, 35mm, 16mm, super 8 film elements **Year:** 2000

Film Is Storytelling

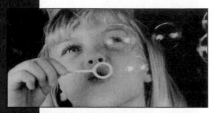

Title: Hanging Up **Creative Director/Designer:** Garson Yu **Designer/Animator:** Ying Fan **Producer:** Jennifer Fong **Client:** Columbia Pictures **Year:** 2000

GARSON YU,
Yu+co, Hollywood, California

Did you start as a filmmaker or a graphic designer?
I came from a traditional graphic design background. If I were a film maker, my works would be very different. As a graphic designer, it is important to have diverse knowledge of different disciplines, such as architecture, art, film, and music. I was always interested in art and architecture as well as graphic design when I was in design school. But ever since one of my classmates introduced Eisenstein's film montage theory to me, my interest and passion in film has grown exponentially. After I graduated, I worked as a freelance designer at RGA in New York. I have been learning more about film making since then.

Does designing film titles draw upon your traditional design training or require all new skills?
Design is about problem solving. It is also about communication. Film is storytelling. Conveying a thought, to me, is communication. We still need to design in our mind before we communicate to others. Most people think film title design is just dealing with fonts, which is not totally accurate. Typography is only a minor part of film title design; the main part is storytelling, setting up the tone and emotion. When we say traditional graphic design, does that mean two-dimensional design? In that case, do we deal only with sharps, colors and all pictorial formal issues? When we deal with images transforming over time, then we need a different mindset and require all new skills because we need to make an image into an event: What's before? What's after? And what's the beginning? How does it end?

PRODUCTION DESIGNER PIERRE-FRANÇOIS LIMBOSCH

PRODUCTION DESIGNER PIERRE-FRANÇOIS LIMBOSCH

Title: Passion of Mind **Creative Director/Designer:** Garson Yu **Designer/Animator:** Ying Fan **Producer:** Ty Van Huisen **Client:** Paramount Classics **Year:** 2000

A title sequence is often a film within a film. How do you view your role as title designer?

Although it is often a film within a film, a good title sequence should seamlessly blend into the film. It is the title designer's job to tell the background story, setting up the tone and letting the audience get ready for the film. I am particularly interested in using animated title sequences to reflect or hint what the film is about.

How much do you actually have to know about the technology with which you work?

Everything is possible nowadays because of the technology. It is all about imagination. If I don't know how to do something, I will surround myself with good, knowledgeable people. Technology gives me possibilities and options. But the key is the concepts and ideas. Knowing the technology will surely broaden my options.

As you continue to work in motion, can you see a new design form emerging? How would you describe it?

Motion is the fourth dimension that we are dealing with in design in the context of time and space. In the twenty-first century, things are getting virtual, and artificial intelligence has become a major topic. What those contribute to are interactivity in design. We always want to find ways to control the behaviors of images. Images respond and react to what we like them to in real time. It is quite exciting to see this new form of design emerging.

Title: Enemy of the State **Creative Director/Designer:** Garson Yu **Designers/Animators:** Ying Fan, Steve Kusuma **Producer:** Grace Huang **Client:** Touchstone Pictures **Year:** 1998

Title: Mission Impossible 2 **Creative Director/Designer:** Garson Yu **Designers/Animators:** Bryan Thombs, Aki Narita, Stephan Kurle **Producer:** Jennifer Fong **Client:** Paramount Pictures **Year:** 2000

Message Matters

Title: Fresh Poster **Art Directors/Designers:** Stefanie Barth, Julie Hirschfeld, Joan Raspo **Firm:** Stiletto NYC **Illustrator/Photographer:** Lisa Carville **Client:** AIGA **Year:** 2001

Title: 9.9.99 **Designer:** Julie Hirschfeld **Creative Director:** MTV - Jeffrey Keyton **Art Director:** MTV - Romy Mann **Animator:** Bennett Killmer **Client:** MTV **Year:** 1999

STEFANIE BARTH, JULIE HIRSCHFELD, JOAN RASPO
Principals, Stiletto NYC, New York City

How and why did you form a studio that deals in multiple medias?
Some things just happen. When we met, we were working in different media and countries, but we connected creatively and wanted to work together. The studio evolved out of that.

Of these media, what are your primary tools?
Well, right now, we are back to handcrafting and using things like crayons. But tool number one is still our computer.

How do you handcraft in this digital environment?
It's about going back to precomputer methods— replacing the mouse with the pencil.

To do motion design well, how much do you rely on narrative versus technical skill?
For us, narrative drives every project. The idea drives the execution. We try not to let technical skill drive the concept. First we come up with the idea, then we figure out how to do it.

What is your most ambitious narrative to date?
Joan co-created and directed the animated series "Avenue Amy" on Oxygen.

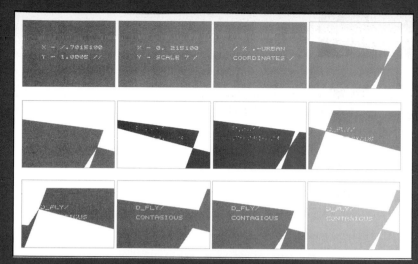

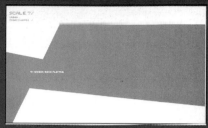

Title: Scale 7 Web site and Corporate Identity **Designers/Art Directors/Illustrators:** Stefanie Barth, Sandra Singer **Client:** Blue-c/Scale 7, Vienna **Client Creative Director:** Mirela Abadi **Year:** 2000

Do you try to have a studio style? Or do you flow with the needs of the commission?
We tend toward a certain sensibility because we relate to the same things and look at the same influences. We hope that we never develop a signature style. Our aim is to continue evolving and not be defined by anything described as Stiletto style. It would suck if a client wanted that certain thing we did in project x for client y.

What is the greatest challenge for you as a designer in today's new media?
Outsmarting the young designers.

What is more important for you— message, attitude, or effects? Or are these completely interconnected?
We'd say message matters. Effects are the least relevant. They feel dated really quickly and seem kind of cheap.

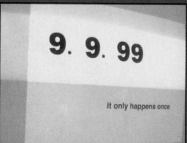

Thinking Through Motion

MICHAEL UMAN
Creative Director, FDG, New York City

How did you get involved in motion and film design?
In 1987, I took an internship in a postproduction facility. For six months, three or four nights a week (I interned during the grave-yard shift), I learned the Quantel Paintbox and Harry systems, at that time the standard in composing and video paint systems. I had previously been a freelance airbrush illustrator/designer working primarily in the music biz (album graphics, music industry stuff). I also did quite a bit of comic/cartooning work. I had studied anima-tion and film from the age of twelve (super 8 movies, animation courses through high school and college). After learning the basics of postproduction, I became a freelancer doing post work. I still continued doing print but, as I got busier in video, I took on less print, only taking on jobs that I thought would be cool or fun.

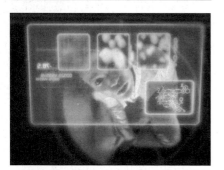

Was a career path in sight?
Broadcast design as an industry/career really didn't exist. If you wanted to design a title sequence, it was usually design by the hour. After several years of honing my skills, I eventually got frus-trated and bored retouching product packaging and executing lame boards from ad agency hacks.

It's 1992. The previous year and a half, I had been experiment-ing with programs like Photoshop and Director, immersing myself in the technology and befriending local animators and designers who were pushing the early desktop programs. In particular, there

Title: Sci Fi Beverly **Director:** Michael Uman **Designers:** Michael Uman, Martin Koch, Violet Suk **Art Director:** Todd Mueller, Sci Fi Channel **Director of Photography:** Eric Schmidt **Client:** Sci Fi Channel **Year:** 1999

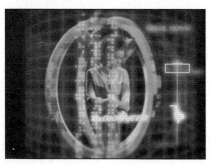

was this new, amazing animation program from a software company named Cosa. This program was named After Effects and it changed the industry and my life. I realized that, given enough time, I could produce the same results as a Paintbox and Harry. I could afford to own the equipment and do everything myself. Time to reinvent myself again. I used my life savings to buy the latest and greatest Macintosh computer, a Quadra 800. Over the course of the next year, I continued doing post work but concentrated on selling myself as a broadcast designer working with a Mac. It was a long and hard uphill battle.

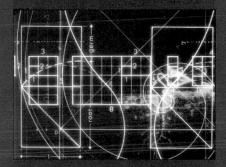

How would you define the role of the graphic designer in motion design?

A good motion designer is someone who wears many hats. Part marketer, part film maker, part animator.

What do you look for in designers? Must they have film or TV experience?

My preference is working with what I term *designamators*—designers who can animate their own work. I think it's important for a designer to be able to think through and execute the motion. It's not just about a pretty layout. You need to be able to think through the storytelling aspect. This said, I also like to experiment with teams and combinations of creatives. I'll team someone who has a mostly print background with someone who is stronger in animation or pure production. I've worked with photographers who have a great eye and have a designer animate and work with their photos. I don't like to necessarily limit a designer to whatever their skill sets are. I usually encourage designers I work with to think in terms of the design and the creative, and if need be, we reinforce them with the appropriate backup talent. I also like my designers to have an interest in film making, music, and pop culture. Design is about pop culture. Sometimes it leads, sometimes it follows. Half of a design job is the audio. You can have a beautifully designed spot that will totally suck if you have the wrong sound design and music.

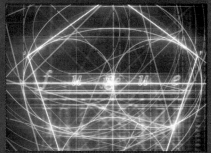

Title: Fugue **Designer/Animator/Senior Creative Director:** Michael Uman **Creative Director:** Peter Burega **Client:** Peter Burega **Year:** 2000

Illustrating with Film

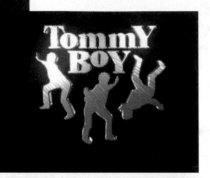

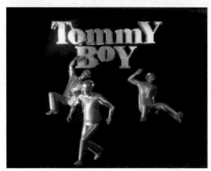

Title: Tommy Boy **Creative Direction:** Mirko Ilic **Motion Design:** Lauren DeNapoli **Design Studio:** Mirko Ilic Corp. **Client:** Tommy Boy Records

MIRKO ILIC
Principal, Mirko Ilic Corp., New York City

You began as a pen and ink illustrator. Why did you turn to the computer?
As a traditional illustrator and designer, you are always looking for new tools. Something new and dramatic comes along only every ten or fifteen years. Seeing the development of the Macintosh, I bought my first computer in 1990 or 1991. I figured out that it would allow me to operate in the capacity of a studio (combining the roles of typographer, keyliner, etc.) and still remain an individual.

What influenced you to turn to motion design?
In the 1970s, I was publishing a lot of comics while working at Zagreb Films as a freelance animator. As an illustrator and as a designer, you must tell a story in a single image. But in comics, I found my first opportunity to tell a story in multiple images, a visual essay. The computer is the next logical step. It condenses to a few the once large array of roles necessary to produce traditional cell animation. In 1992, I bought my first Silicon Graphics computer. But for most of the time, in the beginning, I used it only to create illustrations. From the narrow U.S. corporate point of view, you are only able to produce things like you've already done, so I was commissioned for editorial illustration only. It took time to make the transition.

As an illustrator, you work by yourself; with movie titles you must collaborate with many people— directors, programmers, etc. How does this affect what you do as an artist?
Tell me in what country an illustrator works without collaborating, and I'll move immediately there. From my experience in the United States, illustrators 99 percent of the time must collaborate with art directors, designers, editors, and even writers. Being an illustrator, in most cases, means constant compromise. It's true that in movie titles, a few more people are involved, but it's a more expensive and complicated procedure. It's a logical extension that more people are required; the dynamic is essentially the same.

What do you need to know to work in this medium that you did not have to know before?
The thing you really need to know is that the technology is constantly advancing. It's important to know when to get new equipment and, more importantly, when to stop. You could spend your whole life buying new equipment.

What do you think is your most valuable asset in terms of motion design?
I didn't come to motion design from the usual path: from graphic designer to motion designer. I came to it from both this and an illustration base. I think about motion design differently. If graphic design was my only experience, I would take photography or illustration and place type over it in Illustrator or Photoshop, then using whatever filter is most up to date, I'd manipulate the forms. But coming also from an illustrator's point of view, I consider type in a more illustrative way, as a character on the stage, so to speak, fusing this with the narrative. In the case of the title for *You've Got Mail*, we created the whole environment on the computer, and made it into a little story. I was able to do this because of my illustration skills.

How difficult is it to get good commissions?
It's extremely difficult to get any commissions in such a narrowly divided, compartmentalized field. Moving from one genre to another (in this case, movies) is hard. Every movie studio has its own system. Different people make decisions. With most key people in California, it's a big challenge finding the right person's hands to put your reel into.

Title: Scout's Honor **Art Direction:** Walter Bernard and Mirko Ilic **Design Office:** WBMG, Inc., and Mirko Ilic Corp. **Client:** Neil Leifer

Title: Zen Stories **Creative Direction:** Mirko Ilic **Motion Design:** Mirko Ilic and Hillman Hillman Design Studio, Mirko Ilic Corp. **Client:** IMG Media

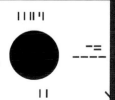

X. Type and Lettering

NOT TOO LONG AGO, type design was almost an airtight profession. Only the very skilled and highly motivated were allowed entry. One reason was the intense amount of time that it took to design a typeface in its various weights and point sizes. Another was the expense involved in making metal fonts. A third was that type foundries were major industrial operations, and although they commissioned a fair number of novelty typefaces to supplement the classics, they relied on either proven and experienced staff designers or respected freelancers. Breaking into this realm of design required years of apprenticeship.

TODAY, THE COMPUTER has changed all that — some argue for good, others for ill. Type design software has increased the capability of serious type designers to create many more custom and proprietary typefaces and has made it possible for neophyte and fly-by-night designers to develop personalized type. Somewhere between these two extremes, graphic designers who are interested in or passionate about typefaces have entered the field, either developing the occasional face, which they then sell or license to a digital type foundry, or establishing their own digital type foundries. The computer has broken down the barriers between designer and craftsperson and the Internet (shareware, free programs offered on the Web) has democratized the distribution networks. Of course, today more laypeople know the once arcane term font than ever before, and many even know the names of a few typefaces (as if they were rock groups).

And yet, type design is definitely not a profession for amateurs. Indeed, many of the novelty faces are too eccentric and quirky for continued use. These faces may be fun to use as display type for the occasional poster or advertisement, but it is unlikely that they will have legs over the long haul and for diverse applications. For type to work effectively, it is not enough to simply draw an alphabet; rather, it is necessary to know how the letterforms will function together on both aesthetic and utilitarian levels. Although it can be enjoyable to invent a typeface, to make it functional remains the province of the trained type designer.

So what is a trained and skilled type designer? There are two answers. A type designer is someone who has devoted the better part of a professional life to knowing the history of type, drawing letterforms precisely, having aesthetic values *and* practical savvy, and a vision of the overall application of type in the print environment. A type designer is also someone who is gifted with a keen sense of aesthetics and function *and* can draw with complete precision. The former takes many years and considerable practice (internships, apprenticeships, and scholarly study); the latter comes at birth and yet requires all of the former to make a truly effective type designer. This is not to say that the generalist designer cannot design one perfectly utilitarian typeface — and never design another. Bertram Goodhue, an architect, designed Cheltenham in 1896, one of the most commonly used American typefaces. But the majority of good typeface designers are dedicated to their field — and dedication is exactly what it takes.

For those inclined to choose type design as a career choice, the best idea is to seek a position at a digital type foundry (or type shop) that both licenses other designers' and produces its own typefaces. In the 1990s, many such foundries were established and can be found listed on the Internet. Even an entry-level job at a good foundry provides exposure to and, perhaps, hands-on experience with the entire type design process, from inspiration to distribution. (Incidentally, those foundries that are *not* good are the ones that routinely pirate other designers' original work or license inferior typefaces without first testing their viability.) Another entry point is an apprenticeship with an experienced type designer; here

you can learn as much as possible before either becoming a freelance type designer or joining a company. Yet another approach is to enroll in a type design class with a master type designer and then attempt one or all of the above.

At the same time, the technology is available for a neophyte to experiment at designing typefaces on the desktop and then testing its applications in real documents. Never before in the history of type design and type founding has this been so technically and financially accessible.

Lettering is another indispensable component of graphic design. Lettering is the design of one-of-a-kind, often limited-use, typographic or calligraphic compositions. The letterer is not necessarily a type designer, and vice versa, but the skills of one are certainly useful to the other. Letterers are most often used to develop signs, logos, book titles, package labels, and other custom needs. Lettering classes are common in most art and design schools and are the only efficient way to learn the methods of the craft. Although much lettering begins as hand drawing, the computer is used as a tool for detailing and finalizing work.

Type design is an extremely time-intensive field; the designer may work for many months on a single family, style, or even weight. Type designers who create custom faces for publishing, corporate, or institutional clients also spend a large sum of time in revisions as well. The letterer works on a specific project, usually for a fixed period of time. This is not to imply that one field is more satisfying than the other, but if type and lettering are desired specialties, it is important to evaluate the investment required for each of these.

Type design is fairly straightforward. Full or partial alphabets and the drawing that go into making them are the ideal portfolio contents for both entry-level and advanced typeface designers.

Entry Level and Advanced

School assignments and personal projects, either drawn or composed on the computer, are ideal samples.

Contents

a. One or more complete alphabets

b. Example of typefaces application

c. Drawings used in the development of a typeface or family of faces

Format

High-resolution printouts or digital QuickTime movies.

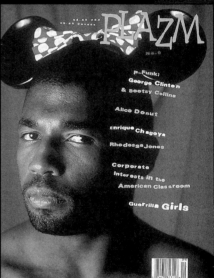

Title: Truth **Designer/Creative Director:** Patric King **Company:** Thirst **Client:** Gary Fisher Mountain Bike **Illustrator:** Patric King **Year:** 1997

Title: Plazm 6 Cover **Designers:** Joshua Berger, Niko Courtelis, Greg Maffei **Creative Director:** Joshua Berger **Publication:** Plazm **Client:** Plazm Media **Sculpture:** Bruce Conkle **Photographer:** David Potter **Typefaces:** New Hamburger, Twiggy **Year:** 1995

Title: Plazm 9 Cover **Designer:** Denise Gonzales Crisp **Creative Director:** Joshua Berger **Publication:** Plazm **Client:** Plazm Media **Photographer:** Christine Cody **Typeface:** Inky-Black **Year:** 1996

A Font of His Own

PATRIC KING
Designer, Thirst Type, Barrington, Illinois

Why did you decide on type design?
Simple: I couldn't ever find a font I liked when I needed it, so I designed my own.

With so many typefaces extant, what determines what faces you devote your time to?
I try to concentrate on the works that could transcend their original context.

How much time, on average, do you devote to designing new or reviving old faces?
I spend about a year and a half per face in a stop-and-go manner: Initial design takes about two weeks, refinement of forms takes about three months of repeat visits, and the rest is refinement and development of weights within a family.

Title: Voice Keepsake Book **Designer:** Patric King **Creative Director:** Rick Valicenti **Company:** Thirst **Client:** Gilbert Paper **Illustrator:** Patric King **Photographer:** William Valicenti **Typeface:** Smile **Year:** 1996

Title: Princess Died **Designer:** Patric King **Creative Director:** Rick Valicenti **Company:** Thirst **Client:** Thirstype **Illustrator:** Patric King **Typeface:** The Royal Family **Year:** 1998

Title: Scrabble **Designer:** Patric King **Creative Director:** Rick Valicenti **Company:** Thirst **Client:** Gary Fisher Mountain Bike **Illustrator:** Patric King **Typeface:** Cooper Black **Year:** 1997

Title: Interstate **Designer/Art Director:** Tobias Frere-Jones **Company/Client:** The Font Bureau **Year:** 1993-94

TOBIAS FRERE-JONES

Senior Designer, The Hoefler Type Foundry, Inc., New York

How did you decide to be a type designer?

I was always fond of geometry; it was one of my favorite classes in high school — aside from the art classes, obviously. Drawing type lets me indulge my fascination in ratio, interval, curvature, etc. Although I love to draw, I was never very good with perspective or color. Happily for me, type design rarely involves either of those.

As a type designer, do you exhibit a personal style?

I'm sure I do, though I prefer not to think about it too much. Ruminating on one's own style can be a dangerous activity. I prefer to just draw what pleases me and let someone else describe the style. Being a hardcore believer in self-education, it seems that the more styles and motifs I work in, the more I'll learn.

With so many typefaces extant, what determines what faces you devote your time to?

Generally, those ones that attract me are the ones that satisfy me. I have no delusions about changing the course of design in any significant way — I do this because I think it's fun. For my personal projects (that is, the ones with no client directly attached), my own enjoyment always comes before potential sales. Some of the faces I've drawn sank like a stone in the retail market, but I don't care that much, because I enjoyed the design process. It may be simply having some entertaining forms to draw, like Stereo or Reiner Script, or it may be the challenge of taking on something new, like Poynter Oldstyle and Gothic.

Title: Poynter Oldstyle **Designer:** Tobias Frere-Jones **Art Directors:** Tobias Frere-Jones, Mike Parker, David Berlow **Company/Client:** The Font Bureau **Year:** 1997

How much time, on average, do you devote to designing new or reviving old faces?

This is a tricky one to answer, as the line between purely original and straight revival is not sharp. Besides, I don't think it's possible to say that one kind of work is better or more valuable than another. I'm always drawn to projects that will educate me but also to ones that will offer users new options. If I can show that the old standards aren't the only way of getting a job done, I'd find that very pleasing. In that context, I don't worry so much about what category of sources I'm working with.

Is there room in the business for more type designers?

That's hard to say, because the number of designers and the number of users are expanding simultaneously. One hundred years, or fifty years, or even fifteen years ago, nobody would know what to do with so many type designers. Having said that, I think there are two general classes of designers: ones that work in a careful, measured approach, and those that work only in the mode of the moment. In other words, there are ones that ignore the fads and others that are driven by them. If there's room for more, it's with the classicists.

Title: Stereo **Designers:** Karlgeorg Hoefer, Tobias Frere-Jones **Art Director:** Tobias Frere-Jones **Company/Client:** The Font Bureau **Year:** 1993

Title: Reiner Script **Designers:** Imre Reiner, Tobias Frere-Jones **Art Director:** Tobias Frere-Jones **Company/Client:** The Font Bureau **Year:** 1993

Title: Niagara **Designer/Art Director:** Tobias Frere-Jones **Company/Client:** The Font Bureau **Year:** 1994

Building Blocks

Title: Plazm 11 Cover **Designers/Creative Directors:** Joshua Berger, Niko Courtelis, Pete McCracken **Company:** Plazm **Client:** Plazm Media **Torching:** Robert Irwin **Photographer:** D×J×C Studio 3 **Typeface:** Censor **Year:** 1996

JOSHUA BERGER
Art Director, Plazm Fonts, Portland, Oregon

What is Plazm?
The word *plazm* is taken from plasm, or protoplasm — the building blocks of the universe. Plazm Media Collective consists of three interlinked divisions, with a fourth in development: *Plazm* magazine, Plazm Fonts, Plazm Design Group, and Plazm.com.

What are your most popular typefaces?
Some of the most popular fonts, in terms of sales, include Retrospecta, by Christian Kusters, Inky-Black, by Pete McCracken, and Rocket Science, by Lotus Child. In terms of positive feedback, Widows, by Marcus Burlile, Pulsitallia, by Dave Henderlieter, and Superchunk, by Charles Wilkin, have all been well received.

How do you get and generate typefaces?
We have a core group of talented font designers on our roster who develop new faces for market. New designers regularly submit samples to us. Most of the faces are generated digitally on the Macintosh. Some faces are rendered by hand, then converted to digital format.

How do you market your faces?
We produce new type catalogs at six-month intervals. A limited PR effort, articles in magazines, and word of mouth are all used as marketing tools.

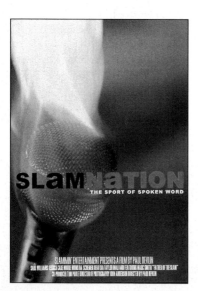

Title: Slamnation **Designers:** Joshua Berger, Pete McCracken, John Kieselhorst **Creative Directors:** Joshua Berger, Pete McCracken **Publication:** Plazm **Client:** Slammin' Entertainment **Photographer:** Bob Waldman **Typeface:** Ariel, Interstate **Year:** 1998

Title: Submit Poster **Designer/Creative Director:** Niko Courtelis **Company:** Plazm **Client:** Plazm Magazine **Photographer:** Bob Waldman **Year:** 1996

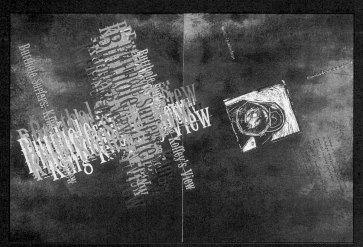

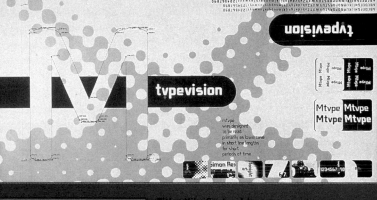

Title: Nike Santos Ad
Designers: Joshua Berger,
Niko Courtelis, Pete McCracken
Creative Director: Niko
Courtelis Company: Plazm
Client: Wieden and Kennedy
Photography: Mark Ebsen
Year: 1998

Title: MTVPE Designers: Joshua
Berger, Niko Courtelis, Pete
McCracken, Riq Mosqueda
Company: Plazm Design Client:
MTV Networks Typeface: MTVPE
Year: 1997

Title: Butthole Surfers Spread
Designer/Creative Director:
Joshua Berger Company: Plazm
Client: Plazm Media Illustra-
tion: Jerry Johan Typeface: State
Bevel, Onyx Year: 1995

Title: Shop Talk Designers/Cre-
ative Directors: Joshua Berger,
Niko Courtelis, Pete McCracken
Company: Plazm Client: Plazm
Media Year: 1995

Type Is Passion

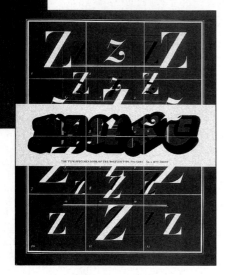

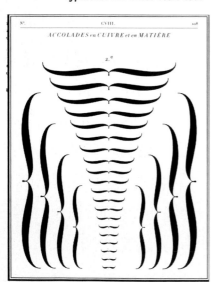

Title: Muse **Designer/Creative Director:** Jonathan Hoefler **Company/Client/Illustrator:** The Hoefler Type Foundry **Typeface:** HTF Didot **Year:** 1997

JONATHAN HOEFLER
Director, The Hoefler Type Foundry Inc.,
New York City

Why did you decide to become a type designer?
I recognized early on that an infatuation with typography isn't really enough to make a good graphic designer. A series of book jackets where I paired immaculately lettered titles with boxes marked "author photo to come" didn't really endear me to my publishing clients, and the fact that I'm red-green color blind suggested that art-directing photo shoots might not be in my future. But I've also always been fascinated by the history of design, the history of typography specifically, and as a practicing graphic designer I suspected that I wouldn't have the opportunities to dwell on the things I find so rewarding. Research is an important part of type design and writing is an important part of running a foundry; I'd miss these things too much if I were a graphic designer.

With so many typefaces extant, what determines what faces you devote your time to?
My clients, for one. When I'm commissioned to develop a new typeface, it generally means that someone has spotted something lacking in existing faces, and the opportunity to address some of these lacunae in typography is what keeps me going. There are

also areas of personal importance to which I try to devote some time; there are always things I'm coming across that I think warrant further investigation, discoveries that sometimes result in a pretty good idea for a new typeface.

Is there room in the business for more type designers?
Of course. But I hope that both working graphic designers and future type designers will recognize that rampant font piracy is seriously threatening the industry. I hope that anyone who's enthusiastic enough about typography to consider a career in it might start by recognizing that collecting fonts on disk — how a lot of us get our most rudimentary education — is a dangerous pastime that endangers the livelihood of practicing designers and encourages the benighted idea that fonts are somehow free. Type designers are already regarded somewhat suspiciously by art directors, and that we're now fighting a rising tide of passed-around fonts makes it even harder to do what we do. You're welcome to join the party, but enter at your own peril.

Title: Catalogue of Typefaces, No. 2
Designer/Creative Director:
Jonathan Hoefler Company/
Client/Illustrator: The Hoefler
Type Foundry

The Rise of Fontographer

CHESTER
Designer, Thirst Type, Barrington, Illinois

Why did you decide to become a type designer?
Type design is but one of the things that I do. In the service of communication, I find myself a designer, writer, photographer, and sometimes type designer. Often I just tweak a typeface for a given project. But when the type design muse does pay a visit, I abide by her, whatever she may ask me to do. As a result, I do not have an area of type design. I do whatever comes, when it comes.

As a type designer, do you exhibit a personal style?
There are probably hints in each of my typefaces that would allow a typo-archaeologist to trace them all back to the source. It may be the way that my ampersands look, or the placement of accents over lower case *i*'s. Perhaps once I have a proper, sizable body of work to analyze, I will be able to link it all up.

With so many typefaces extant, what determines what faces you devote your time to?
I have been working on some titling caps faces, both sans and with serifs. One is being used in its unfinished state in signage and other stuff for the Lyric Opera of Chicago. There is also a face based on a typo-joke based on real-life events: Shirley Temple, and its companion heavy face Shirley Temple Black. (Have you ever seen *The Bachelor and the Bobbysoxer*? It's a great movie with Cary Grant, Myrna Loy, and the teenage Shirley Temple.)

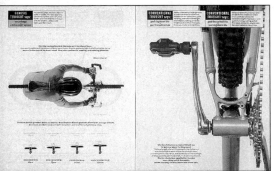

Title: Change Is Good **Designer:** Rick Valicenti, Chester **Company:** Thirst **Client:** Gary Fisher Mountain Bikes **Photographer:** Rick Valicenti **Typeface:** Interstate **Year:** 1997

Title: You Gotta Start Somewhere **Designer:** Rick Valicenti, Chester **Company:** Thirst **Client:** Gary Fisher Mountain Bikes **Photographer:** Rick Valicenti **Typeface:** DIN, Zeus's Hammock **Year:** 1996

Title: Past, Present, Futures: 1997 Annual Report **Designer:** Rick Valicenti, Chester **Company:** Thirst **Client:** Chicago Board of Trade **Illustrator:** Thirst, William Harrison, Ann Evanson **Photographer:** Rick Valicenti, ARCHIVE **Typeface:** Traitor, Rheostat **Year:** 1998

Is there room in the business for more type designers?

I kind of liked it in the old days, when I was just getting started designing type and there were perhaps a few hundred professional type designers. Now that the world has discovered Fontographer, a lot more type amateurs are playing at being professional. But there are also the real talents who, thanks to access to Fontographer, are able to get their ideas out into the world. If I may draw an analogy, type designers are like musicians. The world is full of music, but a new voice, a new musical style comes along from time to time, and it enriches a lot of lives. We do not actually need more typefaces, but a fresh new idea is wonderful to behold.

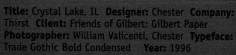

Title: Crystal Lake, IL **Designer:** Chester **Company:** Thirst **Client:** Friends of Gilbert: Gilbert Paper **Photographer:** William Valicenti, Chester **Typeface:** Trade Gothic Bold Condensed **Year:** 1996

Title: Unpublished Typefaces **Designer:** Chester **Company:** Thirstype

Title: Whuzzat? **Designer:** Chester **Company:** Thirst **Typeface:** Info Text **Year:** 1996

WHUZZAT

Fonts Online

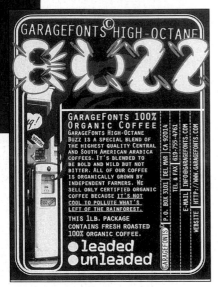

Title: GarageFonts High-Octane
Buzz Coffee Label
Designer/Creative Director:
Betsy Kopshina
Company/Client: GarageFonts
Typefaces: Oak Magic Mushroom, Pure **Year:** 1996

Title: GarageFonts Catalog
Designer/Creative Director/
Photographer: Betsy Kopshina
Company/Client: GarageFonts

BETSY KOPSHINA
Partner, GarageFonts, Delmar, California

What made you focus on type design?

Working as a freelancer with David Carson's studio introduced me
to type design. Many of the fonts he used were sent to him by
students and professionals. He also did a few of his own, both
new designs and distortions of old designs. It was very appealing.
I started designing a few of my own. Then we started Garage-
Fonts, David Carson, Norbert Schulz, and I. (Since David moved to
New York City, he is no longer a partner, due to time restraints.)
Now I spend more time fixing and testing other designers' fonts
that we sell, which is good practice. When I get back to my own
fonts, I will be a better font designer.

How did you start and set up your foundry?

We placed a number of ads, mostly for trade at first, made a catalog, and started a mailing list. We wrote contracts for a number of
font designers to give us the rights to license their fonts. And we
were off.

What are the challenges in being a proprietary business in
such a competitive field?

Keeping up the testing and posting of fonts online. We continually try to get better and a larger variety of type designs in our
library. Even though most fonts are designed by other designers,
in-house we spend days testing each one. It is very tedious.

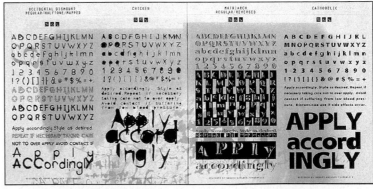

What distinguishes GarageFonts from other font companies?
How we got our start, for one. Having David involved really
helped. Many of the fonts we sold he used in his designs. We still
do work together from time to time and GarageFonts are thrown in
there somewhere. Plus, we try to be creative and cost effective
with our marketing. The "In Search of the Next Whatever" contest
with Macromedia was a way for Macromedia to advertise Fontographer and for us to include new fonts in our library and get good
promotion at the same time. The great judges helped too.

What do you see as the future of the type font business?
The majority of small foundries that stick it out will continue to
make better fonts, both technically and designwise. Some will drop
out of the race, because creating good fonts that work on all platforms will get too demanding without enough monetary return. It
is not an easy business, and it can be downright tedious — but if
you enjoy it, rewarding.

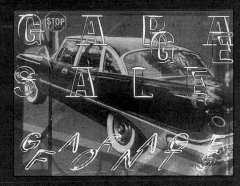

Title: Garage Sale Brochure **Designer/Cre-
ative Director:** Betsy Kopshina
Company/Client: GarageFonts **Photographer:** Norbert Schulz **Typefaces:** Bigfella,
Teenager **Year:** 1996

Title: Swimsuit Edition Catalog
Designer/Creative Director: Betsy Kop-
shina **Company/Client:** GarageFonts
Typefaces: Oak, Magic Mushroom, Gladys's,
Bigfella **Year:** 1996

Title: In Search of the
Next Big Whatever
Contest Brochure
**Designer/Creative
Director:** Betsy
Kopshina
Company/Client:
GarageFonts **Photog-
rapher:** Norbert Schulz
Typefaces: Out,
Teenager **Year:** 1997

Type for Now and the Ages

Title: Glide **Designer:** Jeffery Keedy **Company:** Cipher

Title: Hardline **Designer:** Jeffery Keedy **Company:** Cipher

JEFFERY KEEDY
Designer, Cipher, Los Angeles

Why did you become a typeface designer?
I was designing two posters and related collateral for a promotional campaign for a fashion school. In order to tie all the pieces together and express the theme of the event, I wanted a unique typeface, but I couldn't find anything that came close, so I designed the typeface I needed. After that I was hooked. I wanted to see if I could design typefaces that reflected contemporary ideas, attitudes, and emotions. I like the challenge: A typeface can be as simple or complex as you want to make it; you can design one in a few minutes or a few years.

Do you have a personal style?
I think all designers exhibit a personal style to some degree. I am sure I do too, but I am probably not the best judge of what it is or what its merits may be.

With so many typefaces extant, what determines what faces you devote your time to?
It takes a lot of time to develop and refine a typeface, so the last thing I want to do is design one that is too similar to one that already exists, particularly if it's not an improvement. So if I know the face is sufficiently distinctive, the next thing I ask is, Would anyone want this? Does it fill a need? or create a need? Would I like to use this and see it on the streets, in magazines, on television? In the end, it comes down to being committed or obsessed enough to see it through to the end.

How much time, on average, do you devote to designing new or reviving old faces?
Technically, all typefaces are revivals, in that they are all based on existing typefaces and the alphabet. I'm not very interested in designing revivals that are copies of old typefaces that have fallen out of use or fashion. In designing new typefaces, I know they

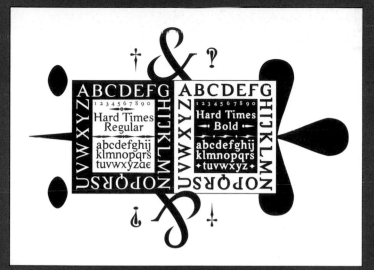

Title: Hard Times **Designer:** Jeffery Keedy **Company:** Cipher

Title: Jot **Designer:** Jeffery Keedy **Company:** Cipher

Title: Keedy Sans **Designer:** Jeffery Keedy **Company:** Cipher

Title: Manu Sans **Designer:** Jeffery Keedy **Company:** Cipher

will become old soon. I'm interested in expressing our current era in all of its complexity and contradictions.

Is there room in the business for more type designers?
There is always room in this business for more type designers, but it is not easy to make a living on type design alone. Unless you have continuous commissions and a way to sell a lot of typefaces directly, or you get royalties from a big distributor, you won't make much money. Only a few designers survive on type design alone. For most graphic designers, type design is an excellent skill that helps improve typography and logotype design, and a few popular typefaces can be good for self-promotion.

Don't concentrate on technical skills. Learn to see. Learn to think. Learn to listen to everything going on in the world around you. Design follows from ideas, not the other way around. The best design does not come from knowing two thousand typefaces and six Macintosh programs by heart. It comes from having a life and being observant and involved in the world at large.

—Randall Balsmeyer

Be culturally literate, because if you don't have any understanding of the world you live in and the culture you live in, you're not going to be able to express anything to anybody else. And don't become a designer unless you're good. We don't need any more mediocre designers.

—Paula Scher

Learn the basics of typography. I know a lot of students are not getting a great education. You just really need a strong foundation.

—Tamar Cohen

In my experience of interviewing people, what I look for has more to do with their connection to the universe than with their talent.

—Nancye Green

Try and eke out some fun. This is supposed to be a creative job. If it ain't, then why the hell are you doing it. Go out and get a real job that pays well, one for which you won't have to sit up late at night answering questionnaires. What do designers need to be successful? What is successful? They need to figure that out.

—James Victore

Unless you are a terrific self-motivator and terribly insightful and wise, I think it's a good idea to go to some art school and get a degree in communications. At school you'll get the tools and skills you need to get a job. School is where all of your competition is getting their skills and tools. I see personal communication as being the single most important skill.

—Christopher Austopchuck

Publish, publish, publish! There's nothing like a real assignment to focus one's energies and force a job to completion. For someone breaking into the field, if this means working on spec, my advice is to take it. The most important virtue for any creative person is dogged perseverance against all self-doubts.

—R.O. Blechman

Look at a range of design possibilities. Investigate and explore where graphic design can fit in, so that if you have interests besides doing brochures, you find a way of bringing that into what you do. I think you should investigate the whole world, read widely, see lots of things, collect things. I'm a collector, always have been. Now I let my collecting be part of my process. It's natural to me.
—**Martin Venezky**

Start your career in a multi-disciplinary firm that does a broad range of projects. Try to work on as many different assignments as you can and decide which kind you like best. Specializing right out of design school is the kiss of death, from a career standpoint. Study the field, learn as much as you can about which firms are doing good work, and make every effort to secure at least some freelance work with them.
—**Ken Carbone**

Choose the places where you want to work very carefully. That means forget about the money. If there's a good designer there or someone that you admire to work with, that's important. Work with good people; it really elevates you.
—**Walter Bernard**

When going for an interview, do your homework: Know what that firm has done in the past, what kind of work they do. Be very familiar with who you're talking to.
—**Kent Hunter**

Look at cultural history, really look at art history and understand it. Anything anthropological is a valuable reference for a graphic designer, so I'd say really hit that world in a big way. I would also look at the history of architecture, anything in the history of printing, anything that provides the map of how people solved problems in the past.
—**Michael Patrick Cronan**

Have money behind you, because the design field is very, very tough to break into.
—**Dennis Barnett**

Talk to professional designers about the actual day-to-day experience of the business. I feel there is a great disappointment upon entering the workplace and finding out the reality of creative parameters, client interaction, boredom, frustration, and the lack of satisfaction and respect that are the hallmarks of this odd field.
—**Helene Silverman**

I find, as an educator, a lot of students don't really have the comprehension of what good design is. It's kind of scary. Sometimes I think the computer has something to do with this. Everyone's getting so caught up in decoration, just making stuff look good, that a lot of young designers today forget that we are communicators.
—**Jeffrey Keyton**

It is difficult to give advice in general; patients should be cured individually. However, we think that graphic design is the organization of information in a sensitive, exciting, and creative way. Therefore, we do not think that graphic design is a second-class art form and we try to clarify that in students' minds. I think the most important skill in a graphic designer is the capability of a quick diagnosis that gets to the core of the problem.
—**Massimo Vignelli**

Find somebody that you really respect, then just swallow your pride and be around them, even if you're making Xeroxes. You'll learn more from making Xeroxes with a genius for a year than you will being an associate art director someplace where it's not really you.
—**Yolanda Cuomo**

Look at everything for influence and inspiration; don't limit yourself. It is also very important to have an understanding of the history of art and design. And it is very important not to let people discourage you.

—Kyle Cooper

In a college situation, I don't think it's important if somebody decides after a couple of years to drop out and do an entirely different subject. I think art school is a splendid general education for anybody. At the same time, if you are serious about continuing after two or three years in college, you need to start meeting designers and, if possible, spending time on an internship or something of that sort, actually meeting circumstances in the environment.

—Richard Eckersley

A designer needs a broad education that is not too narrowly focused on design. A designer needs to have a skepticism about design, a slight sense of remove from it, or it will swallow him up.

—J. Abbott Miller

To be a graphic designer is fundamentally to be in the service of others. It doesn't mean to be blindly in the service of others, but it does mean that we play a role in society for which we are trained to think, to analyze communications problems or social problems, and to provide options, and so if someone is considering graphic design, the perspective that I offer them is: Are you willing to serve? And if their goal, their desire is other than to serve and to learn what it means to serve, then I think that they are really misconstruing what design does in society.

—David Peters

Be aware, very early on, of what your life's work is going to be. Don't let the career define your path. You define the path. The single most debilitating aspect of designers that I've seen is that they've let the career define their life for them and they have had neither the energy nor the vision to overcome how demanding this work can be. And don't wait for it to happen. Respond the day you enroll in college or the day you discover you have a talent. Respond to it and devour it. Don't let it devour you. Because it will.

—Dana Arnett

Seize any design opportunity to make the best of any situation where design skills can be utilized. Always make the effort to take things one step beyond.

—Michael Ian Kaye

Try different areas of design and find whatever best fits the way you work, be it books or newspapers or multimedia. Develop a portfolio that solidly reflects your area of interest. The problems and conflicts that arise in any area of design are only worth solving if you can be completely invested in the projects you're working on.

—Kelly Doe

I get the feeling that some people go into design because they like playing on the Mac and they end up just fooling around with that, and personally I think the Mac is pretty easy to learn and I think they should concentrate on more specific things or imagery — what kind of imagery best communicates what they're trying to get across and really look at lots of photography, lots of art, lots of design, design history. So many young people don't have any sense of design history.

—David Slatoff

1. Fire in the belly
2. Intellectual curiosity
3. Visual sensitivity
4. Guts of steel
5. Thick skin
6. Stamina
7. The ability to listen
   —**Deborah Sussman**

I would recommend students to carefully select a design program that includes a range of design fields under an umbrella structure. While it is important to train deeply in one design specialization, students should also participate on interdisciplinary design projects while in school. It is interesting to note that Illinois Institute of Technology requires all its undergraduates to devote one semester to an interdisciplinary project; on these teams designers have interacted with engineering, science and business majors. To participate and communicate effectively with other professionals, the broadest possible education is important, including the humanities, social sciences and communications, as well as business practices. Because of this, I recommend a broad university undergraduate education over a specialized studio program in an art school. And it is often wise to pursue a liberal undergraduate education followed by a highly focused graduate study in a design specialization.
—**Katherine McCoy**

Read, write, and draw, which will give you the means to express your ideas and a broader sense of how others express their ideas. You must be accepted and respected for your intelligence if you want a chance for important work.
—**Don Morris**

Unless you have a huge flair for self-promotion, it's going to be tough to get recognized. It's hard for somebody who's just getting started. I guess I would say that you should look at every possible magazine and book and European publication, to try to see everything that's being done, now and in the past.
—**Rita Marshall**

A good graphic design education or a real apprenticeship is still a preferred starting point. Selecting the best school is not an easy task, as so much has to do with the focus of the program and the faculty at the time. More than anything else, I believe a designer needs to have an enormous curiosity and interest in life, an appetite for problem-solving. If intelligence is a skill, I would say that it is most important.
—**Steff Geissbuhler**

Be as smart and as well read and as talented and as hard-working as you possibly can be, and have a burning passion. Otherwise, don't bother. I think passion is a real, real important thing to have. Otherwise, you sell insurance or something. Not all designers have passion for it. They work for a big insurance company doing newsletters or report covers or whatever. You don't need a passion for that. But to drive your own bus, you better be passionate about it.
—**Eric Baker**

The most important thing designers need is an appetite for solving problems posed by others. Of course they need the skills to express themselves in the tools of our trade, but beyond that, the more you know about anything, about life in general, about business, about how people tick, the better. For this reason I advocate getting into the field later rather than sooner. An undergraduate degree in something else, then art school.
—**Chris Pullman**

The fundamental design skills are still the most critical: typography, composition, symbol design, page layout. I can tell immediately if a portfolio reflects these basics.
—**Wayne Hunt**

Businesses

The recommended first step to getting started in the design business is to find an internship or staff job in one or some of the areas outlined in the preceding section. Learn as much as possible, do as much hands-on work as you can, and become an experienced practitioner in your chosen field(s). Pretty simple, right?

Right! Yet not every young designer is content to be an employee – or at least to be employed at the same job for an extended period of time. Nonetheless, it is prudent to have the experience of a staff job. Before deciding on an opportune time to leave it, you should make certain that you have developed the talent and acquired enough skill to move forward. If there is no such forward movement after a year or two, the situation should be reexamined and questions like these should be asked: Is there more to be learned in the present position? Does the job offer opportunities for advancement? Does this situation provide enough challenges? Am I taking advantage of the challenges? If the job does not equal your ambitions, it is time to move on. If your ambition is to be more directly responsible for the work being done, then it is possible that working for someone else will never satisfy you.

The graphic design profession is comprised of staffers, freelancers, and proprietors. The first category is discussed throughout the previous section. The second includes hired hands who work independently but may be employed as either temporary (or casual) staff (without the benefits and perks of a full-time staff member) or on a job-by-job basis based on need. The third group is designer-managers who are proprietors of small, medium, or large studios, firms, or offices. Work done in this category is developed and produced on the proprietor's premises and using the proprietor's staff. The following are more detailed descriptions of the common divisions of labor.

FREELANCERS: WORK FOR HIRE

NOT ALL INDEPENDENT contractors are called freelancers, but all freelancers are independent contractors. They may be specialists in particular disciplines or generalists hired for various jobs. They may have formerly held staff jobs and decided that they are better suited to being their own bosses (with all the freedom and limitations that this implies). Freelancers may work in a home office, small studio, or on the client's premises. Often a freelancer's workweek is spent shuttling among several work environments. Freelancers may rent a studio with other freelancers and share basic utilities and hardware (such as copier and water cooler), or may lead a solitary existence without the benefit of sustained human contact. A freelancer may employ other freelancers to help produce certain projects but, more likely, she works without assistance.

Freelancers are hired as production support for identified assignments. They are hired to design or art-direct specific projects (newsletters, letterheads, posters, magazines, etc.) — moreover, freelance advertising art directors are a staple of that industry. Virtually every kind of design operation uses freelancers in at least one of these capacities: In-house art departments employ them to supplement insufficient full-time staff, and independent design studios hire them when particular projects demand more attention.

The graphic design profession relies heavily on freelancers with both creative and production experience. In turn, highly skilled freelancers command relatively substantial hourly rates. For the less experienced freelancer, this is an excellent opportunity to be tested prior to being hired in a full-time position (or used regularly as a freelancer). Some young designers use their freelance status as a way to sample options and determine which jobs they prefer. Some designers simply prefer working as freelancers because they are not locked into predetermined schedules.

For the freelancer with the ambition of opening a proprietary design studio, firm, or office, this is a very effective way to establish a reputation and develop the beginnings of a solid client base. Most designers do not open offices straight out of school but allow some time wherein they acquire experience and contacts. Freelancers who develop numerous clients put themselves on a good trajectory for the next professional stage. More clients equals more work, and more work usually requires an overarching management structure—which in turn, means opening a studio, firm, or office.

SMALL STUDIO: BUSINESS BABY STEPS

THERE IS NOTHING mysterious about starting up a small studio. It is essentially a natural outgrowth of being a freelance practitioner who already works out of a home or outside office. The requirements are minimal: computer (with modem), telephone, copy machine, flat files, desk(s), and an ergonomic chair. Oh yes, and a title, which can be a proper name (Jane Doe Design), a clever name (World Domination Design), a corporate-sounding name (Apex Communications), or an enigmatic name (TypeSet Ltd.). A freelance or full-time assistant is commonly employed to help with production and traffic as well as design. It is also prudent to retain an accountant or bookkeeper to keep track of income and outlay and to help formulate a business plan.

The first question to ask is not "How do I set up a small studio?" but "Why?" Some freelancers are much better suited to working alone on a job-by-job basis than running a small business. Most designers are interested in making design, not worrying about the pressures of business, while others are capable of (in fact revel in) both. For those freelancers who are so endowed, the desire to start a small studio is the result of need—*and* success. More work equals more demand on one's time equals the need to have an assistant (or more). Thus a studio is born.

The term *studio* suggests a primarily creative group, often working in general practice. *Firm* indicates a fusion of creative and business and may very well be a multidisciplinary or specialist practice. *Office* is a more brisk-sounding way of describing a studio or firm. Generally, a small studio consists of a principal (or a couple of partners) and approximately one to three employees. This number may include senior and junior designers, a production artist, and an intern. The team might also include a receptionist to answer phones and manage traffic.

The reasons vary for why small studios are started. Here are a few typical possibilities:

Experience: A designer at a company or design firm who has gained enough experience as a staffer decides to become an independent practitioner.

Clients: A freelancer develops one or more regular clients and, therefore, enough income to make a studio financially feasible.

Ambition: A designer with only a few years of experience decides that independence is the key to success, and a studio is a way to achieve that goal.

Partnerships: Two or more like-minded individuals agree that by pooling their talents and skills (for example, creative and business) they can achieve success as a single entity.

Getting those all-important initial jobs is accomplished in a variety of ways. Here are a few common scenarios:

Existing clients: The designer is given hand-me-down jobs from a former employer (which is different than the unethical practice of stealing clients); this may include being subcontracted certain aspects of a job that the primary designer is no longer interested in doing.

Referrals: The vast amount of job-getting is done through word of mouth. A potential client may not have a large enough budget or does not have the right kind of assignment for a larger studio or firm and is therefore referred to another. (Hence it is always a good idea to keep on good relations with former employers as some important early referrals may come from this direction).

Advertising/Promotion: Promotional kits and advertisements featuring samples of past work serve as the first line of attack in making contact with clients. Frequent mailings are recommended and entry to design annual competitions is an excellent idea.

Reviews: Potential clients may approach many studios (the names of which are obtained through referrals, promotional materials, and work found in the design annuals). Bidding and proposals (a itemization of costs and services rendered) are usually solicited if the client is fundamentally interested in the studio's work.

Representation: Some small and many larger studios or firms use representatives or salespersons (who often work on a commission basis) to approach clients. When properly managed, this is a good way to make initial contacts—if not for a specific job, then for future possibilities.

The small studio may be an end in itself or a stepping stone to the next professional stage, which may be a medium-sized studio or larger firm. Some studio proprietors prefer not expand to the degree that additional clients demand the hiring of more employees, which requires greater overhead. Growth also means that the principal spends more and more time managing than designing. Therefore design commissions are scrutinized and weighed (as much for profit and loss as for time expended and ultimate satisfaction) before acceptance.

However, if a small studio is a stepping stone, the principal(s) seek out the most demanding and ambitious commissions in order to lay the foundation for the larger studio or firm. Those designers with good management skills make the transition from small-to medium-sized firms without difficulty. The problem to avoid is becoming overextended; the solution must be an individual business decision.

In deciding to go from small to intermediate or large studio, various decisions must be weighed. How much design versus management is required? How much of that is within the principal's ability? Will it require additional assistance? At this juncture it is also useful to consider whether a sole proprietorship or a partnership is a more effective direction.

PARTNERSHIPS: MARRIAGE WITHOUT CHILDREN?

A YOUNG DESIGNER can build an independent business either as a sole proprietor or in conjunction with one or more partners. Partnerships are often an efficient way of easing into the

What Not to Name Your Studio

A studio by any other name is not the best maxim. Not every name is a suitable or smart way to win clients and influence people. A studio should be given a name that represents its mission not only to other designers but to clients. Some studios use clever names simply to be clever, without an eye or ear to the real world. Depending on the quality of the work, this may not be a problem, but a name like Boo Poo Bee Doo Studio usually defeats the purpose of attracting long-term, intelligent clients. Hair salons can afford cute names but serious design studios cannot. The rule of thumb is to think hard before committing resources (letterhead, mailing labels, promotion) to a name that you may want to change in a year's time.

Which is not to say that something offbeat is entirely taboo. Many design firms have metaphorical or symbolic names that are conceptually smart. So let *smart* be the watchword. If you can't think of a name that expresses a characteristic of your practice, or is a play on or anagram of your name or your partners' names, then go the conservative route: Call your studio by your name. You can always add an identifier (Jane Doe Design, Jane Doe Communications, Jane Doe Office, Jane Doe Visual Communications, Jane Doe Graphics, Jane Doe Limited, or Jane Doe and Associates).

business of graphic design by sharing responsibilities in a collegial environment. This is certainly among the best ways to mitigate the inevitable insecurity of starting a new business. Partnership is also one of the most difficult relationships to engage in, short of marriage. In fact, it is somewhat analogous to marriage.

Partnerships are based on the common interests of two or more individuals. They often grow from design or art school friendships or collegial relationships made at staff jobs. Some even involve married couples who manage, often against the odds, to balance home and office life. Some are marriages of convenience — acquaintances whose particular specialties complement each other and add value to the overall business. The reason for a partnership to exist is that the sum of the parts equals a whole that is potentially greater than each of the individuals alone could achieve. If one partner is better at editorial work, and another is best at multimedia work, then the result is a more diverse studio or firm. If one partner is the creative engine and the other is more talented at sales and promotion, then the result is combined strength in those areas. Partnerships come in many configurations and sizes, depending on the perceived needs of the whole.

Of course, the wedding of two or more personalities is potentially problematic, but the best partnerships are based on mutual respect for each other's talents, mutual tolerance for each other's weaknesses, and mutually shared goals that allow individuals to forge respect and tolerance (and perhaps even a certain amount of fondness) into a viable business.

In any partnership, the strengths of each partner must be funneled into the reputation of the studio or firm, while at the same time the individual must be able to preserve his uniqueness. Invariably there are alpha and beta partners (suggesting dominance and subservience). Because an individual may be subsumed by the partnership, accommodations must be made (and there are no established guidelines for this; they each must be addressed individually). Some partnerships grow into long-term, well-balanced associations, while others unravel in time. Like any human relationship, the partnership should be nourished for mutual gain, but when, if ever, signs of distress appear, the issues should be addressed immediately. Although no definitive statistics are available, many partnerships face problems within the first three years.

Partnerships are found in all strata of the design business, in small, medium, and large studios, firms, and offices. Some partnerships are intended to remain small and easily manageable; the partners complement one another nicely and form a tight, self-contained unit. Others are more ambitious and spin off into many directions wherein the partners take on different tasks and responsibilities in the management of the larger entity. Medium- and large-sized firms may involve a managing partner or office manager who oversees the daily operation.

All business arrangements, especially partnerships, should be built on a solid legal foundation. Partners must consider safeguards to ensure that

Image Isn't Everything, But It Helps

A graphic designer must prove his capabilities through work. Nonetheless, it helps to have sophisticated promotion that presents a postitive image. Clients are impressed by quality and the way in which the work is presented enhances the image. You can promote yourself in print, on CD-ROM, and, on the Internet, and can employ both novel and traditional formats, including booklets, posters, and portfolios. A promotion piece serves two immediate functions: It presents a current sampling of work, and it reveals taste and imagination. The former is obvious, but the latter requires investment. To present a memorable image, create an unforgettable promotion designed in accordance with your aesthetic and conceptual values. Do not skimp on promotion, but do not be ostentatious, either. This piece is possibly the most revealing work you will ever do.

the emotional needs of each are seriously considered, but equally important is the legal and financial structure of the business, which must be protected from problems that may (and probably will) arise between the partners. While great mutual benefit is to be gained from the marriage of talents and energies, neophyte partners must be aware that this kind of business requires maturity.

Learns While She Earns

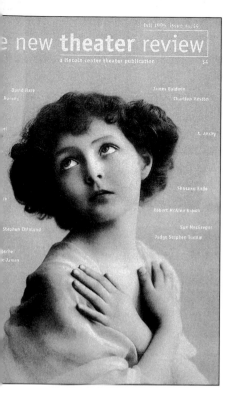

Title: The New Theater Review
Designers/Creative Directors:
Tamar Cohen, David Slatoff
Company: Slatoff + Cohen
Partners Inc. Client: Lincoln
Center Theater Photographer:
Unknown Typeface: Officina
Sans Year: 1995

TAMAR COHEN

Principal, Creative Director, Slatoff + Cohen
Partners Inc., New York City

You are principal of a two-person partnership. What kind of work you do?
Slatoff + Cohen started out doing mostly print, as everybody did in the early 1990s. We do a magazine for Lincoln Center Theatre, for example. In the last couple of years we've done a lot of work for the Gap and Nickelodeon. We just did their Nick at Night sales kit and their TV Land sales kit. We've also done a lot of broadcast and multimedia for Nickelodeon.

How did you get that job?
Nickelodeon was actually a cold call we made a couple of years ago and they've been a wonderful client for us. Likewise, we're doing a monthly promotional poster for VH1. We do small stationery and identity systems for smaller firms, some record packaging for Nick at Night Records and book covers for HarperCollins, Basic Books, Broadway Books. We've done tons of book covers. Our work is multidisciplinary and that's really how we like to keep it.

Did you decide early on that you would not specialize in one area of design, that you would be multidisciplinary?
I think initially it wasn't a conscious decision, but now we believe that this is the best way it could have happened for us.

Are you learning as you are earning?
Yes. With Nickelodeon, the thing that made it such an incredible chance for us was that our first job for them was an on-air job. We had never done this before; we had no real experience in this area. The person there just looked at our work and said, "I think you guys can do it," and gave us a chance. I think people in our business are not often given a chance to do something new.

Title: Zoetrope Magazine interior spreads **Designers/Creative Directors:** Tamar Cohen, David Slatoff **Company:** Slatoff + Cohen Partners Inc. **Client:** AZX Publications/Francis Ford Coppola **Illustrator:** David Plunkert **Photographer:** Geoff Spear **Typefaces:** Interstate, Minion, Franklin Gothic, Prestige Elite **Year:** 1997

Title: TV Land Programming Booklet **Designers:** Tamar Cohen, David Slatoff, Todd Barthelman **Creative Directors:** Tamar Cohen, David Slatoff **Company:** Slatoff + Cohen Partners Inc. **Client:** Nick at Nite's TV land **Photographers:** Geoff Spear, Slatoff + Cohen Partners Inc. **Typeface:** Meta **Year:** 1997

Do you think that the field of graphic design is becoming less specialized?
I think with small firms like us, that is true. Certain firms are geared to specialties like music or publishing. Specialization is a trend in other firms that I'm familiar with.

Would you say that you have a personal style in your design, either alone or you and your partner?
That's a tough question. I don't think that we have a style. We look at every design problem or project as a different and new thing to solve and we really try to adapt our talents to each specific client. I don't really feel like we have a specific style and I don't think it's necessary to being a successful designer. I think sometimes actually having too specific a style ends up being kind of redundant.

Title: Nick at Nite Sales Kit **Designers/Creative Directors:** Tamar Cohen, David Slatoff **Company:** Slatoff + Cohen Partners Inc. **Client:** Nick at Nite **Illustrators:** Chip Wass, Ed Fotheringham **Typefaces:** Clarendon, Trade Gothic **Year:** 1997

Lean, Mean, and Intimate

Title: Zoetrope Magazine Cover
Designers/Creative Directors:
Tamar Cohen, David Slatoff
Company: Slatoff + Cohen
Partners Inc. **Client:** AZX
Publications/Francis Ford
Coppola **Photographer:** Nola
Lopez **Typefaces:** Interstate,
Minion, Prestige Elite, Franklin
Gothic **Year:** 1997

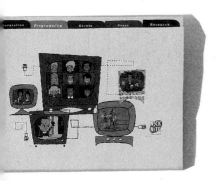

DAVID SLATOFF

Principal, Creative Director, Slatoff + Cohen
Partners Inc., New York City

You are a principal of a small, two-partner studio. What is the most fulfilling aspect of your job?
The most fulfilling moment is when my art vision and the client's vision come together at the same time. I think that the relationship between the designer and the client is really important. It's most fulfilling when I can get my personal vision into the work and still solve the client's needs, when I feel like I have a lot of creative freedom but can still work within all the limitations.

Do you think that you have a personal style?
No. What's important for me is to do what's important for the client. I'm the one who decides what's appropriate, but I don't feel like I have a bag of tricks and I pull out this one for this client and this one for that client.

How would you describe a good work environment?
Our work environment is very free and relaxed and it's open, not restrictive — it's a playful atmosphere. We play music. We're in a loft space, so there's a lot of interaction, there's no office politics, and everybody is treated with respect. It's important to keep the environment as creative as possible and I think these interactions lend themselves to that more than a really quiet office with cubicles does with everybody jammed in front of their computers. I've had experience in both so I know which I prefer.

Do you have a specific approach when you're hiring designers?
We find that word of mouth is the best way to find designers. The first thing I look for is a good sense of typography, and then I look at the bigger picture — what is the applicant's sensibility, what are her concepts like, what kind of images does she use, what is her personality like? Because we're small, we have to consider these things, and personality is really important.

Specialization = Death

Title: E-Pluribus **Designer/ Creative Director:** James Victore **Company:** James Victore, Inc. **Client:** De Paul University **Photographer/Illustrator:** James Victore **Typeface:** Hand-lettering **Year:** 1998

JAMES VICTORE

Principal, James Victore, Inc., Beacon, New York

How did you decide on your area of specialty in design?
I never decided, and I never will. Specialization equals Death.

You are the principal of your own one-person studio; do you run it?
I don't think I run my studio. At least I don't run it well. Maybe someday I will get good at that. Let me put that on my list.

How would you describe a good work environment?
A good work environ? For me? James Brown and ideas flying everywhere. Being tired at the end of the day and excited about getting back the next.

How have technological advancements affected your work?
I don't think about technological advances. They are something to learn to live with.

Do you have a specific approach to hiring designers?
I have a small shop. I need to hire good, interesting people who are nice to be around. I get a lot of very slick, polished, suited-up designers who come to us straight from schools with very fancy portfolios and huge egos. We give them directions to Pentagram. I need nice, eager intelligent folks who don't mind a good lashing occasionally.

Title: Shit Shinola **Designer:** James Victore **Creative Director:** Gimma Gatti **Company:** James Victore, Inc. **Client:** Portfolio Center **Photographer:** John Stormont **Typeface:** Sabon, Officina **Year:** 1996–7

Title: Aspen Design Conference
Designer/Creative Director:
James Victore Company: James
Victore, Inc. Client: IDCA
Illustrators: James Victore,
Rodrigo Honeywell Typeface:
Hand-lettering Photographer:
Stock Year: 1998

Title: Ignorance/Intolerance
Designer/Illustrator: James
Victore Company: James
Victore, Inc. Creative Director:
Roger Pfund Publication:
Aujourd'hui Pour Demain
Client: World AIDS Day Type-
face: Univers Year: 1998

Title: Use a Condom De-
signer/Illustrator: James
Victore Company: James
Victore, Inc. Creative
Director: Koichi Yano Publi-
cation: Dai Nippon Client:
DDD Gallery Photographer:
Bela Barsodi Typeface: Hand-
lettering Year: 1998

Out of State, Not of Mind

ALEXANDER ISLEY

Principal, Alexander Isley, Inc.,
Redding, Connecticut

Title: Annual Report **Designer:** Kim Okosky **Creative Director:** Alexander Isley **Company:** Alexander Isley, Inc. **Client:** Reebok International, Inc. **Photographers:** Various **Year:** 1995

Title: Architectural Graphics **Designer:** David Albertson **Creative Director:** Alexander Isley **Company:** Alexander Isley, Inc. **Client:** Rock and Roll Hall of Fame **Architect:** Pei Cobb Freed Partners **Photographer:** Barney Taxel **Year:** 1995

You relocated from a crowded studio in New York City to a commodious one in Connecticut. What prompted that decision?
For the first several years of my practice we were located in New York and the business had been steadily growing. We'd moved three times to successively larger quarters in the Lower Broadway area and we were up to around ten people. I'd been getting the feeling that I'd like a new challenge. While New York had been an exciting place to live and work, I had to admit that I had never really felt that it was my home.

Why outside of the media capital of the world?
We conducted a search throughout the Northeast for a place to relocate. I knew I wanted to stay in an area that was relatively close to New York, where a lot of my client base was, and I figured I'd still have to be there fairly often. We knew that we wanted to move our office as well to avoid a daily commute. At that time, I gave our employees a year's notice of our intentions to move and told them they would still have their jobs if they decided to move to the sticks with us. None took us up on the offer. During our search, we kept returning to the town of Ridgefield, Connecticut. It had a nice, friendly appeal and it was there that we decided to move. After a bit more searching, we found office space in the Georgetown section of Redding, the next town over from Ridgefield. Both are about one hour from New York by car, one and a half hours by train.

How is your Connecticut operation different from your former New York office?
We have more space and fewer staff members. Presently eight or nine people work at our firm. I find that this is just about the perfect size for me, as it's large enough to allow us to take on almost any type of project yet small enough so that I can be closely involved with every assignment. We still keep a small

office in New York. I usually go in one or two days a week to meet with clients; it has proved helpful to have a place there where I can make calls, receive faxes, have meetings, or have packages delivered. I think that it also helps to reassure potential clients that we still have a presence in Manhattan.

One significant change we've made in our business within the past year is that we now have a project director who works out of our New York office. This gives us the ability to offer immediate service to our New York clients who require it.

Do you still get the big jobs that you are used to?
We haven't seen a drop in business at all (in fact, we're busier than ever), and my initial concerns about clients being frustrated with our being out of the immediate area have proved unfounded. People still search us out, and most don't care where we are as long as our ideas are good.

Do you feel that your work is more integrated into your life because of this environment?
I can't say that the relationship between my work and life has changed a lot as a result of the move, which was made more for personal reasons rather than business ones. I'm certainly happier living where we are now. I spent the first several years of my career in New York, devoted primarily to my work and building my practice. My wife and I decided to embark on new adventures, which included moving to the country and starting a family. It's an old story, but the challenge for me has been to try to do all of this and keep working with a challenging mix of clients and assignments.

Was it necessary to begin your career in New York?
For me, it was important to start in New York. It is easy to get spoiled living and working there. Everything you need — from delis to dry cleaners to clients — is plentiful and usually within a five-minute walk. New York has design clients galore, job opportunities aplenty, and tough competition. Plus, after paying rent there, down the road everywhere else looks like a bargain.

Also, and importantly, a lot of attention is paid to design in New York. Design organizations are headquartered there. The publishing industry is centered there. The media in New York cover design frequently. I'd be dishonest if I didn't acknowledge that a certain amount of attention our work received when we were starting out helped my firm.

I like to think that we could have built a reputation regardless of where we started out, but I think that our progress might have taken longer if we hadn't been in New York.

Title: Interior Signage
Designers: Alexander Isley, Karen Healey **Creative Director:** Alexander Isley **Company:** Alexander Isley, Inc. **Client:** Shedd Aquarium **Year:** 1996

Title: TWX Issue 1 newsletter **Designers:** Colleen Sion **Creative Director:** Alexander Isley **Company:** Alexander Isley, Inc. **Client:** Time Warner **Illustrator:** David Sheldon **Year:** 1998

MEDIUM FIRM:
BIG COMMITMENT

HOW DO YOU KNOW when you are ready to graduate from small to medium? For some studios it just happens: After working on a number of comparatively low-budget jobs, you bid for the big one — and, to your surprise, you get it. Now don't get too nervous yet. Certain reality safeguards are in place. The really big corporation is not going to willy-nilly bestow a multimillion-dollar account on a small studio. But you just may find that the quality of your work is such — and your bid is competitive enough — that you are given the commission for a job or campaign that involves many more components over a longer time span and with a lot more responsibility than you are used to. Here are your options regarding growth.

1. *Stay small:* Use this opportunity to test whether expanding the size of your studio is viable. Hire freelancers to work on the big job while maintaining design control. Refrain from taking on too many other large jobs at this time.

2. *Seize the moment:* Use this opportunity to expand in a responsible way. Budget what it will cost to hire additional staff, buy or rent additional hardware, and otherwise take advantage of a good cash flow to increase the studio's potential.

Incidentally, sometimes small studios are asked to bid on a larger project, but the principal does not feel that the studio is adequate for the needs of this client. There is no shame in turning down an invitation to submit a proposal.

A medium-sized firm includes a principal (or partners) and an average of fifteen employees (including senior and junior designers, produc-tion personnel, receptionist, traffic manager, and probably a full-time accounts person or book-keeper). Obviously, how the size of a design studio or firm is measured is not necessarily comparable to other professions. In graphic design, however, maintaining a payroll of around fifteen full-time employees as well as a few freelancers suggests a respectable client base and a creditable cash flow.

Designers who run medium-sized firms are able to hire administrators and need not turn their attention exclusively to management; a good office manager (or managing art director) can efficiently run the day-to-day operation and allow the principal to continue to focus on designing. But client meetings are one of the key responsibilities for a principal or proprietor of any size design business. For the small studio principal, meetings can eat up considerable portions of the day, so multiply that for the medium-size firm, which by its nature must accept more clients to meet increased overhead. Clients who engage medium firms are usually not content to work directly with the senior or junior designer on substantive matters, which means the principal spends increasingly more time managing the overall commission than actually designing it. While this is not always the case, it is probable that the balance of time expended between business and design will tilt toward the former.

On the positive side, a medium-sized firm attracts clients that a small firm does not, which means higher budgets, more visible accounts, and, as a result, perhaps greater satisfaction. For the principal or proprietor who savors the art of business as much as the art of design, this structure is a good way to wed those interests. It may also serve as another stepping stone to a still larger business.

Title: Logo **Designers:** Tamar Cohen, David Slatoff, Alan Smith
Creative Directors: Tamar Cohen, David Slatoff **Company/Client:**
Slatoff + Cohen Partners, Inc. **Typeface:** Helvetica **Year:** 1997

Growth Spurts: The Story of Funny Garbage

Here is a case study of how one New York design firm grew by leaps and bounds.

1995: Peter Girardi, age 29, does production and design for Voyager, a pioneer new-media company specializing in CD-ROM and Internet.

1996: Girardi leaves Voyager, and with his friend Chris Capuzzo, age 29, and John Carlin (founder of the Red Hot Organization, a AIDS awareness music publisher), starts a partnership. Without financial backing, and with only one large project, Girardi and Capuzzo set up shop in a small room in the Red Hot Organization office in Soho, New York. They hire two employees and call the company Funny Garbage. That year Funny Garbage gets commissions from Compaq and Time Warner. They hire four more employees.

1997: With the addition of Nike, Warner Bros., and Sony, Funny Garbage must rent larger quarters to accommodate its ten employees. Owing to its increased visibility in the interactive field, additional clients are added to the roster, including the Cartoon Network. Funny Garbage hires eight more employees and four interns. Later that year, the volume of work demands more office space and a staff increase to twenty six.

1999: Founder Peter Girardi disappears, never to be heard from again. Many think he has taken a job crop dusting in Argentina. Funny Garbage thrives.

Title: Cartoon Network Main Page
Designers: Chris Capuzzo, Peter Girardi **Company:** Funny Garbage
Client: Cartoon Network Online

In Sickness and in Health

Are an inordinate number of designers married to other designers? It is not uncommon to be bound by both matrimony and a business plan.

Seymour Chwast and Paula Scher

Steven Heller and Louise Fili

David Slatoff and Tamar Cohen

Joseph Essex and Nancy Denny Essex

Michael Donovan and Nancye Green

... and Lella Vignelli

J. Abbott Miller and Ellen Lupton

Douglas Turshen and Rochelle Udell

Stephen Doyle and Gael Towey

Bill Drenttel and Jessica Helfand

Cathleen Neusham and John Korpics

Scott Makela and Laurie Haycock Makela

Pat and Greg Samata

James Victore and Leah Lacocco

Rudy VanderLans and Zuzana Licko

Equal Among Partners

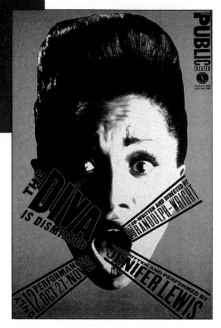

Title: The Diva Is Dismissed
Designers: Ron Louie, Lisa
Mazur, Jane Mella **Creative
Director:** Paula Scher **Company:**
Pentagram **Client:** The Public
Theater **Photographer:** Teresa
Lizette **Typefaces:** American
Wood Typefaces **Year:** 1994

Title: Le Parker Meridien
Designer: Anke Stohlmann
Creative Director: Paula Scher
Company: Pentagram **Client:** Le
Parker Meridien **Typeface:** Gill
Sans **Year:** 1998

PAULA SCHER

Partner, Pentagram Design, Inc., New York City

**You've worked in the music industry as a record jacket design-
er; now you are the partner in one of the largest international
design firms. What made you become a designer?**
I stunk at everything else.

What do you look for in a partner?
Somebody who brings things to the group or to the partnership
that I don't already have.

How do you work with your partners at Pentagram?
In two ways: formally and informally. We work together formally
if we're collaborating on a specific project and we work together
informally by the fact that we sit nose-to-nose together in a
kind of kibbutz, getting involved in each other's work whether
asked or not.

What is the most fulfilling aspect of your work?
I like doing things I've never done before.

What is the least fulfilling?
Doing billing.

**Do you think that the business of graphic design is a good
business? Is it an ethical business?**
If you mean a moral business, it depends how you feel about cap-
italism. If you believe that the profit motive is good, graphic
design is certainly as good as any other business. If you don't
believe in that, then no business is good. Graphic design gives
people a service that enables them to make themselves known in
some way, whether it's through selling a product or making information accessible, or getting somebody through a complicated
building, making somebody understand a film. Of course, I think
it's ethically and morally sound.

Can you describe your design style?
I design things to make an emotional impact. The emotions change all the time.

How much of your time is devoted to design and how much to business?
I used to think very little was devoted to design, because I saw myself always in meetings, but then I realized that I'm doing design and art direction in meetings. So I would say, with the exception of the time I spend gossiping, all the other time is really spent in design.

How do you know if you're a good designer?
You just work at it until you are.

What makes a good work environment?
I think a good work environment is little more than people being around people who are enthusiastic about their work. A bad work environment is being around people who are depressed about their work.

Is there anything that you'd still like to accomplish in your career?
I'd like to become much more involved in city planning. I'm starting to do that now. I'm very interested in how design marries into architecture to become environmental design. It's really more about design integrating into the cities and how large imagery and typography works within cityscapes — not in the traditional way in which we think of signage but in a more extravagant and dramatic way.

Title: Bring In 'Da Noise, Bring In 'Da Funk **Designer:** Lisa Mazur **Creative Director:** Paula Scher **Company:** Pentagram **Client:** The Public Theater **Photographer:** Richard Avedon **Typeface:** American Wood Typefaces **Year:** 1996

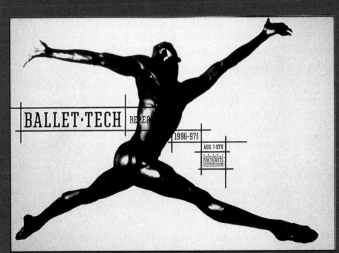

Title: Ballet Tech **Designers:** Lisa Mazur, Anke Stöhlmann **Creative Director:** Paula Scher **Company:** Pentagram **Client:** Ballet Tech **Photographer:** Lois Greenfield **Typeface:** Constructa **Year:** 1996–7

Title: Showcenter Haedo **Designers:** Ed Chiquitucto, Lisa Mazur, Anke Stöhlmann, Maria Wenzel **Creative Directors:** Paula Scher, Michael Gericke **Company:** Pentagram **Client:** Macodros Emprenditos **Photographer:** Documentation: Alejandro Leveratto **Year:** 1996

LARGE FIRM:
CAN'T GET ANY BIGGER

MOST DESIGNERS prefer designing to business and, therefore, choose to limit the size of their studios and firms. This type of business forms the bedrock of the graphic design profession. Nevertheless, in the current age of multi- and interdisciplinary design, many ambitious designers have either solely or with partners branched out into areas that demand large support staffs and teams. Few designers actually enter the profession with the goal of building a megafirm because too many variables are unknown. Nevertheless, circumstance and ambition do combine to make large firms happen. At times, before you know what is happening, a client base is in place and mergers with other disciplines are possible.

A large firm essentially comprises a principal or partners (two or more) with a staff of over fifteen and as many as several hundred. Some large firms are exclusively domestic; others are international (with offices in other cities). The infrastructure of a large firm is as hierarchical as any corporation, from the principals, who guide the design identity and philosophy, to the senior designers, art directors, and project managers, who work on specific projects, to the technical, production, and bullpen staff, who manufacture the work. Depending on whether or not a principal micro- or macromanages, a large firm has various levels of oversight. But it is the principal who is must represent the firm to existing and potential clients.

Large firms usually are not specialized. Some do focus their attention, especially on multimedia, but they may also include print, advertising, and other ancillary components to provide a fuller service. Others may be devoted to, say, retail product package design, but may also include a brand-

Title: Floating Billboard: Cancel/OK **Designer/Creative Director:** Robert Appleton **Company:** Appleton Design **Typeface:** Chicago **Illustrator:** Robert Appleton **Year:** 1996

ing division that involves multimedia. Still others may cater to Fortune 500 corporations, with emphasis on corporate identity, but include a division that handles, say, industrial or corporate films or Web sites. Most large firms are general in outlook. Some even go beyond today's fairly broad definition of graphic design and integrate architecture, interior design, or environmental design into what is offered to clients.

The division of labor, or how assignments are apportioned, in large firms varies as much as the firms themselves. When the firm is a sole proprietorship, the work may be assigned to individual project managers by the principal or the managing designer. In certain partnerships, each partner commands a subsection of the firm, responsible for its own clients and billing. In other partnerships, each partner dips into the common well. There are no standard rules that govern this.

For the average reader of this book, starting a large design firm is not going to happen now or ten years from now, but working in one is probable and advancing in one is possible. Rather than be concerned with how to reach the top rung on the business ladder, it is prudent to address how to join a large firm and learn what working in such an environment has to offer. It may be the best launch pad for opening a your own business.

Principally Conceptual

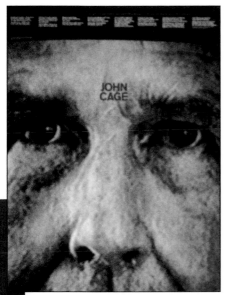

Title: Poster: John Cage
Designer/Creative Director: Robert Appleton **Company:** Appleton Design **Client:** Real Art Ways **Typeface:** Akzidenz Grotesk **Year:** 1982

Title: Bookcover: AIGA
Designer/Creative Director: Robert Appleton **Company:** Appleton Design **Typeface:** Univers **Client:** AIGA **Year:** 1990

ROBERT APPLETON
Principal, Appleton Design, New York City

How would you define your practice of graphic design?
I am a generalist. The work that has come to me over the past few years has also reflected my personal interests: art, music, and design. After fifteen years in Hartford, and now four years in New York, I've added some more strings. I teach, I work on the Web, and I play the piano instead of the drums.

How do you design? Are you concept-driven? Or does what you do depend on the project?
I think all work today is principally conceptual. Mine certainly is, whether it is created by hand or with computer technology.

Do you have to be as cognizant of the business side of design as the creative?
a. Unfortunately, yes. b. Fortunately, yes.

How do you interact with your staff — as art director, advisor, mentor, or iron fist?
I work with one or two assistants now. I enjoy collaborating with a very few people who share the same sensibilities. Whether I do most of the design work or not, I always focus on the concept.

How do you interact with your clients — as creator, consultant, or conciliator?
I want it to be equal, and I think it mostly is. Sometimes I listen. Sometimes I talk. But if there seems to be a problem of communication or understanding, I always talk first.

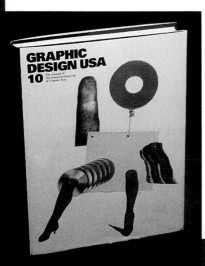

Title: Annual Report Cover **Designer/ Creative Director:** Robert Appleton **Company:** Appleton Design **Client:** Lydall Inc. **Photographer:** Tim Nighswander **Typeface:** Univers **Year:** 1983–4

Picky about Clients

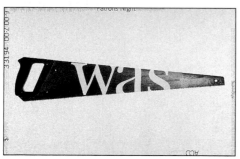

Title: The Book of Lamentations
Designers: Stephen Doyle, Gary
Tooth **Creative Director:**
Stephen Doyle **Company:** Doyle
Partners **Client:** Marsilio
Photographer: Stephen Doyle
Typeface: Sabon **Year:** 1996

Title: Was/Saw Poster
Creative Director: Stephen
Doyle **Company:** Doyle Partners
Client: American Center for
Design **Typefaces:** News Gothic,
New Baskerville **Year:** 1995

STEPHEN DOYLE
Partner, Doyle Partners, New York City

You worked at a number of staff design jobs. Why did you decide to open your own firm?
The reasons for starting Drenttel Doyle Partners with Bill Drenttel and Tom Kluepfel in 1985 was to get the inevitable failure of our own shop behind us. None of us actually expected to succeed but thought we had better get the notion out of our systems. That's the emotional base from which we were operating. Intellectually, we thought it was high time to blur some of the distinctions between design and advertising and marketing. We thought with our combined backgrounds of advertising (Bill), institutional design (Tom), and editorial (me), that some interesting fusion might result if we were to approach design and marketing for our clients as a cohesive force.

How did the partnership succeed?
One of the most gratifying things about running a company like ours is that we are constantly in a position to learn about new businesses (from the inside) as well as to meet new clients and friends in all categories, from art and publishing to filmmaking, retail, corporations, and other areas. It is wonderfully voyeuristic to be able to peer into so many industries and to participate in them as we do.

How have you structured your firm?
For the last dozen years we have employed between ten and thirteen people. This is intentional; we want to keep the firm sized so that it feels right to the partners and core design team. In order to strike that marvelous balance of managing projects and designing them, this small team is able to turn around a lot of work, handle large projects, is small enough to constantly be turning away work. We can be picky about which jobs we take on, and we can keep the partners designing as well as managing. We are careful to avoid the trap of trying to take care of all of the clients'

Title: XIX Amendment Installation Designers: Stephen Doyle, Lisa Yee
Art Directors: Stephen Doyle, William Drenttel, Miguel Oks Company: Doyle
Partners Client: New York State Division for Women Photographer: Scott
Francis Architectural Designer: James Hicks Project Manager: Cameron
Manning Year: 1995

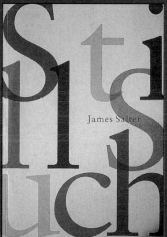

needs. This would have us mushrooming in size to meet this deadline or that, and we would be designing and managing things that
really don't merit our input. Often would-be clients actually come
back to us later with bigger or more strategic projects after we
turn them away the first time.

How do you operate creatively?

I have never, ever, told a designer not to work on something, not
to get carried away, or not to contribute to a project. I do say
things like, "I hate that color," or "Make the type bigger," or "Did
you just come from a David Carson lecture?" Remember, design is
not a solitary process; it is wholly collaborative, except for those
rare flashes of onanistic brilliance that we all hope pepper our
years. Clients come to us not for a certain look but a certain
approach, and we are careful to try to give enough attention to all
of our projects that our approach is considered and consistent. So
designers can't get carried away with some personal vision thing.
(Neither can the partners, for that matter, but for rare exceptions.)
On the other hand, no one is ever held down if he is able to contribute to a project. Our teams are variable, so you don't get stuck
with one particular client unless you want to. We work on wildly
diverse projects, all at the same time: books, packaging, signage,
identities, film titles, and exhibition graphics, so nobody has the
chance to get bored.

Do your designers have autonomy?

Certainly not. What would be the point of working at Doyle Partners if you wanted autonomy? I'm not interested in being a rep for
a bunch of designers — writing contracts, making phone calls, going
to meetings so some designer can sit in my office and design. A
designer who wants autonomy should do what we did: emotionally
and financially prepare herself for failure and open shop.

Title: Phaedra Poster
Designer: Katrin Schmit-Tegge
Creative Director: Stephen
Doyle Company: Doyle Partners
Client: Creative Productions
Typeface: Orator, Futura
Year: 1995

Title: Still Such Creative
Director: Stephen Doyle
Company: Doyle Partners
Client: William Drenttel New
York Photographer: Duane
Michaels (interior) Typeface:
Sabon Year: 1992

An Illustrator at Heart

Title: Peace Poster: 40 Years
Since Hiroshima **Designer/Creative Director:** Steff Geissbuhler
Company: Chermayeff &
Geismar, Inc. **Client:** The Soshin
Society, Washington, D.C.
Illustrator: Steff Geissbuhler
Year: 1985

Title: Centennial Logo
Designer/Creative Director:
Steff Geissbuhler **Company:**
Chermayeff & Geismar, Inc.
Client: The New York Public
Library **Year:** 1995

STEFF GEISSBUHLER

Partner, Chermayeff & Geismar Inc., New York City

You do a lot of identity work, but would you call yourself a generalist?
The focus of the studios I worked in and the projects I take on has a lot to do with identity design, but I'm still a bit of an illustrator at heart and like to believe that I'm a designer in the large sense, taking on each project as a challenge. To specialize was never my aim. If someone asked me to design a kitchen, a motorcycle, clothes, to paint a mural or do a sculptural piece, I would love to immerse myself in the subject.

Do you think having a personal style is important?
Chermayeff & Geismar Inc., prides itself not having a style, because each client and project calls for a distinct and appropriate solution. Of course, all the partners, myself included, have a personal way of expressing themselves visually. Upbringing, education, background, and experience shape the way we express ourselves. What we have in common is a certain attitude about design.

What is the most fulfilling aspect of your job? And the least?
The creative aspect is by far the most fulfilling aspect of my job — those few hours when I can think, draw, or work something out. Also, to present a successful solution to a client is a great high, testing my thinking, concept, visual solution, and all my communication skills. The least fulfilling aspects of my job are the administrative and organizational tasks and the basic bureaucratic paper-shuffling, weeding through fax and e-mail and snail mail.

Do you have a specific approach to hiring designers? How does it work? Where do you find people? Do you or have you hired interns? How does that work?

Our approach is to ask any interested designer to send a letter and a resume first. One can tell a lot from those two pieces: language, sincerity, clarity, attention to detail, typography and design. If the designer looks promising and we're in need of one, we interview the person and review the portfolio together. A recommendation from another designer also goes a long way. We often hire people with European education, which is often superior and broader in the development of skills, craft, and design experiences. We have always had interns off and on, but in recent years we've had at least one intern at all times in our studio. Interns are selected on the same basis as staff members and are often people from abroad who want the exposure to a U.S. studio, either as part of their education or immediately after graduating.

Title: Time Warner Logo
Designer/Creative Director: Steff Geissbuhler **Company:** Chermayeff & Geismar, Inc.
Client: Time Warner **Year:** 1990

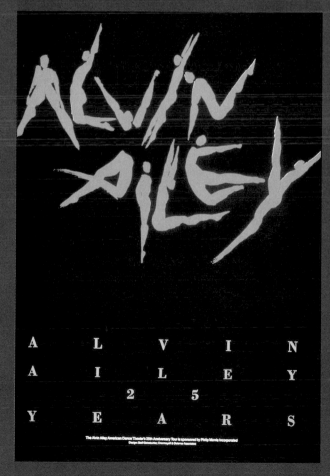

Title: Telemundo Logo
Designers: Robert Matza, Steff Geissbuhler **Creative Director:** Steff Geissbuhler **Company:** Chermayeff & Geismar, Inc. **Client:** Telemundo **Photographer:** Name Lastname **Year:** 1992

Title: Alvin Ailey - 25 Years
Designer/Creative Director: Steff Geissbuhler **Company:** Chermayeff & Geismar, Inc. **Client:** A. A. American Dance Theater **Illustrator:** Steff Geissbuhler **Year:** 1984

Words and Ideas

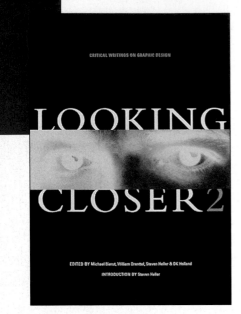

CRITICAL WRITINGS ON GRAPHIC DESIGN

LOOKING

CLOSER 2

EDITED BY Michael Bierut, William Drentel, Steven Heller & DK Holland

INTRODUCTION BY Steven Heller

Title: Looking Closer 2:
Critical Writings on Graphic
Design **Designer/Creative
Director:** Michael Bierut
Company: Pentagram Design
Inc. **Client:** Allworth
Press/American Institute of
Graphic Arts **Year:** 1997

Title: The Good Diner **Designers:**
Michael Bierut, Lisa Cerveny
Creative Director: Michael Bierut
Company: Pentagram Design Inc.
Client: Gotham Equities **Illustra-
tor:** Woody Pirtle **Year:** 1992

MICHAEL BIERUT

Partner, Pentagram Design Inc., New York City

What do you like best about being a graphic deisgner?
I like working with words and ideas. I'm not that interested any
more in finding out a new way to lay out the pages of a sixteen-
page brochure. Instead, I like to put the brief aside and sit down
with a client and talk about what we're trying to achieve. Who is
the audience? What is the message? This turns into my favorite
kind of process — one where the collaboration is open-ended and
the outcome is anyone's guess. That, more than anything, makes
me suspicious of specialization, which I think forces a designer to
frame every problem in terms of a predetermined solution.

What media are most creatively satisfying?
Because I like words and ideas, I suppose I am biased toward
books and magazines. But a pictorial logo, when it's done right,
can be more charged with more ideas than a 496-page book. Any
medium, potentially, can be satisfying.

**How do you design? Are you concept-driven? Or does what you
do depend on the project?**
Sometimes the project has a lot of constraints built into it; in
those cases, if I'm lucky, I define the problem and shake it hard
enough to make the solution fall out. Other times, the situation is
wide open, and it takes more intuition to get to the solution. In
either case, I usually try to get as far as I can by thinking it
through beforehand. Often, by the time I put pencil to paper, I've
gone a lot of the way toward the solution in my head.

Has working as a principal of a large firm increased or confined your creative output?

I work in a big firm, but my design team is similar to a small design office: me, an administrative assistant, four full-time designers and an intern or two. I work fast and I like to work on a lot of projects at once. At any one moment, chances are that I've got at least thirty projects going on. These range from an invitation to a benefit event at a museum to a book to a signage project for a public space to an international corporate identity project. Working as a partner of Pentagram has fed my hunger for more projects, and more varied projects.

Are clients more concerned with business than aesthetics?

I am always surprised by how few clients, in the end, have any ability to distinguish good design from bad design. Instead, most clients are primarily concerned with their own business success. Usually, I define my solutions to a problem not in aesthetic terms but in terms of my client's objectives. Successful designers figure out a way to align the client's business goals with their own personal goals.

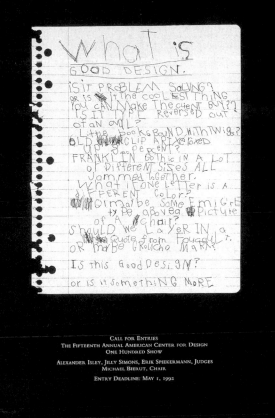

Title: What is Good Design **Designer/Creative Director:** Michael Bierut **Company:** Pentagram Design Inc. **Client:** American Center for Design **Typeface:** Handlettering-Elizabeth Ann Kresz Bierut **Year:** 1992

Title: Minnesota Children's Museum **Designer:** Tracey Cameron **Creative Director:** Michael Bierut **Company:** Pentagram Design Inc. **Client:** Ann Bitter and Jeanne Bergeron, Minnesota Children's Museum **Photographer:** July Olausen, Michael O'Neill (hands); Don F. Wong (documentation) **Year:** 1994–5

Primarily Print, but...

Title: Carnegie Hall Patrons Program **Designers:** Michael Aron, Adam Greiss **Creative Director:** Michael Aron **Company:** Calfo Aron LLC **Client:** Carnegie Hall **Illustrator:** Adam Greiss **Typeface:** hand-lettering **Year:** 1989

MICHAEL ARON
Owner, Calfo Aron LLC, New York City

How would you define your practice of graphic design?
I am primarily a print designer and I currently work for clients from every field except fashion and packaging, which are specialties that require strong experience in those industries, which I don't have. We do information design such as maps, timetables, financial services fact brochures and concert season listings. We also do marketing campaigns such as image-driven advertising, financial product sales brochures, and commercial real estate sales collateral. We do corporate annual reports for companies in a wide range of industries, including health sciences and aeronautics. Lately, our services have been broadened to include marketing strategy consulting, copywriting, video storyboarding and scripting, and new media consulting, including programming and database design.

How do you go about designing?
I usually start by establishing the context in which the design will be viewed. If a strong concept is the best way to form a dialog with the audience, then that's the direction I go. Information design, such as a timetable or concert listing, may not require a

Title: American Composers Orchestra 93-94 Season **Designer/Creative Director** Michael Aron **Company:** Calfo Aron LLC **Client:** ACO **Illustrator:** Neal Bantens **Typefaces:** Eagle Bold, hand-lettering **Year:** 1993

concept. Straightforward presentation of information
in a legible and orderly (but not boring) manner is
just as satisfying as creating a visual concept.

Does style play a role in your decisions?
I admit I am also a victim of style. I often visit a
museum or gallery and become inspired by a particular technique; then I try to find a way to incorporate
this style into a design. I recently saw an exhibit of
futurist painting and the following day designed a
cover for a real estate brochure using the futurist
method of painting.

**Do you have to be as cognizant of the business
side of design as the creative?**
Now that I am responsible for running a successful
business, I must be constantly aware of how to remain
successful. Doing great work is one of the most important components of remaining successful, so the creative side and the business side are sometimes intermingled.

How do you interact with your staff?
I show by doing. I sometimes take assignments away from a
designer if the work is not going smoothly in order to demonstrate
my vision of the solution in the most time-efficient way. I want
the young designers to show me new ideas; however, there is a
limit to what I can sell the client. It is very difficult to inspire
people to do great work that is unique yet still maintain the style
and professionalism that our studio is known for.

**Do you foresee that your business will change much — adapt-
ing, perhaps, to the shift in new media and entreprenuership?**
Yes. The primary catalyst for change is changing client relationships. As fewer clients appreciate the power and value of design, it
becomes each designer's responsibility to teach the client that
design is good business. Many clients are inexperienced and therefore don't fully appreciate how much skill it takes to design a
newsletter or a brochure with design integrity. Many of them are
falsely empowered by the design templates in Microsoft Word or
PowerPoint, which devalue professional design. In-house facilities
at many corporations are more technologically sophisticated than
many design studios. Often they are staffed by people with technology or production backgrounds. Manufacturing a newsletter is
not the same as designing a newsletter. Unfortunately, some clients
do not see the difference. We try to avoid those clients.

Title: International Center of
Photography 1992 Annual
Report **Designer:** Neal Bantens
Creative Directors: Michael
Aron, Jason Calfo **Company:**
Calfo Aron LLC **Client:** ICP
Photographer: Lois Greenfield
Typeface: Frutiger **Year:** 1992

Title: Biocircuits Annual Report
Designer/Creative Director:
Michael Aron **Company:** Calfo
Aron LLC **Client:** BioCircuits
Corp. **Photographers:** BioCir-
cuits Electromicrograph, stock
Year: 1992

Design, Writing, and More

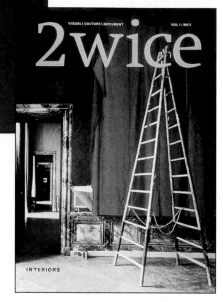

Title: 2wice Interiors Issue
Designers: Paul Carlos, Scott
Devendorf **Creative Director:**
J. Abbott Miller **Company:**
Design/Writing/Research
Client: 2wice Arts Foundation
Year: 1997

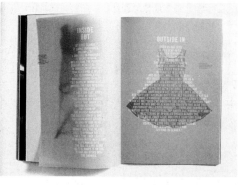

Title: 2wice Inside/Out
Designers: Paul Carlos, Scott
Devendorf **Creative Director:**
J. Abbott Miller **Company:**
Design/Writing/Research
Client: 2wice Arts Foundation
Photographer: Jay Zukerkorn
Year: 1997

J. ABBOTT MILLER

Partner, Pentagram Design, Inc.,
New York City and Design/Writing/Research,
Baltimore, MD

Has there been a major influence on your work?
The program I took at Cooper Union was extremely open-ended,
allowing me to take film and sculpture, and do a lot of reading in
theory and aesthetics. It was a fabulous education in the heart of
New York. Three teachers were highly influential: George Sadek, an
extremely typographically oriented Czech designer who was very
literate and witty; a political artist named Hans Haacke, who
worked with design in producing critical, issue-oriented work; and
P. Adams Sitney, an utterly brilliant scholar and theorist of film.

What kind of clients does your firm seek?
Cultural projects are really the only option for a company like
Design/Writing/Research, which approaches design like an artform.

What is the philosophy behind Design/Writing/Research?
The Design/Writing/Research model integrates visual and physical
form with editorial content in the process of development. The
idea is to reconnect the editorial shaping of content with the
visualization of that content. We present that model to clients
without much fanfare, as it is very logical and not so exotic.
Getting clients to pay for those services is often trickier, as
everything starts to look like an extension of the designer's original scope of work. The goal is to create work that builds on the
proximity of design and content development, to create work that
is more visually powerful because of that relationship and that is
more editorially engaged. In the end, the experience of the
designer/writer is meaningful because of this total immersion
in the project.

Do you have a specific approach to hiring designers?
I hire people who have an intellectual spark and a sense of
humor, and who are clearly obsessed with typography.

Title: Dance Ink **Designer:**
Paul Carlos **Creative Director:**
J. Abbott Miller **Company:**
Design/Writing/Research
Client: Dance Ink Foundation
Year: 1995

Title: 2wice Uniform Issue **Designers:**
Paul Carlos, Scott Devendorf **Creative
Director:** J. Abbott Miller **Company:**
Design/Writing/Research **Client:** 2wice
Arts Foundation **Year:** 1998

Title: Design Writing Research
Designers: Ellen Lupton, J.
Abbott Miller **Company:** Kiosk
Year: 1996

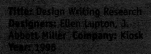

Title: Rolling Stone Covers Tour
Designers: Paul Carlos, Scott
Devendorf, James Hicks
Creative Director: J. Abbott
Miller **Company:** Design/Writ-
ing/Research **Client:** Rolling
Stone/At&T **Year:** 1997

A Business of Her Own

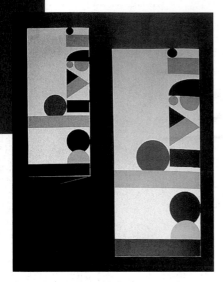

Title: Bolivar Restaurant Menus
Designers: Louise Fili, Mary Jane Callister **Creative Director:** Louise Fili **Company:** Louise Fili Ltd. **Client:** Bolivar **Typeface:** Hand-lettering **Year:** 1998

Title: "Pulse of the Planet" **Designer/Creative Director:** Louise Fili **Company:** Louise Fili Ltd. **Client:** Pulse of the Planet (Radio Program) **Illustrator:** Anthony Russo **Year:** 1990

LOUISE FILI
Principal, Louise Fili Ltd., New York City

What was your first "important" job, where you were able to exercise your own design sensibility?
Being art director of Pantheon Books gave me the opportunity to experiment daily with many periods of design history.

Why did you leave your staff job to start your own studio?
Although I loved designing book jackets, I wanted to diversify in order to pursue my other passion: food.

What was the major difference in being bossed and being your own boss?
Under a boss, I worked very hard. As my own boss, I work even harder.

You started small and have remained small? Why?
I am a hands-on designer. If I can't design, I have no reason for being in this business. Increasing my staff would mean spending more time in meetings—more revenue, perhaps, but much less satisfaction.

What do you look for in an assistant?
A great eye for type, a passion for design, and a working knowledge of design history. A pleasant demeanor also helps.

What has changed for you in terms of the kind of work you do over the years that you have had your own studio?
I am trying to focus on larger jobs primarily in the areas of food packaging and restaurant identity.

Do you think that small entrepreneurial studios are more effective and, for you, creatively satisfying than larger firms?
Yes!

Title: Grapeseed Oil Packaging **Designers:** Louise Fili, Mary Jane Callister **Creative Director:** Louise Fili **Company:** Louise Fili Ltd. **Client:** California Grapeseed Co. **Typeface:** Hand-lettering **Year:** 1998

Title: Monzù Restaurant Identity **Designers:** Louise Fili, Mary Jane Callister **Creative Director:** Louise Fili **Company:** Louise Fili Ltd. **Client:** Monzù **Typeface:** Hand-lettering **Year:** 1997

Title: Metro Grill Restaurant Identity **Designers:** Louise Fili, Mary Jane Callister **Creative Director:** Louise Fili **Company:** Louise Fili Ltd. **Client:** Metro Grill **Typeface:** Bernhard Tango **Year:** 1997

Title: El Paso Chile Co. Margarita Salt and Mix Packaging **Designer:** Louise Fili **Creative Director:** Louise Fili **Company:** Louise Fili Ltd. **Client:** El Paso Chile Co. **Illustrator:** James Grashow **Year:** 1997

The Swiss Direction

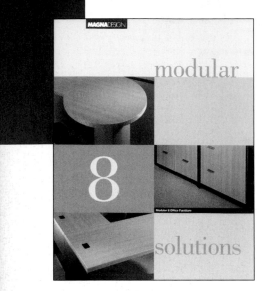

Title: Modular 8 Solutions
Designers: Pat Hansen, Paul Langland **Creative Director:** Pat Hansen **Company:** Hansen Design Company, Inc. **Client:** Magna Design **Photographer:** Patrick Barta **Typefaces:** Bodoni, Helvetica **Year:** 1998

PAT HANSEN
President, Hansen Design Company,
Seattle, Washington

How did you decide on your approach to design?
I think that the educational background that I had led me naturally to a design specialty of clean and simple interpretation and translation of visual images and an orderliness to information. One of the strongest areas of design success has been that of identities, which directly relates to simple visuals and typography.

Do you think a personal style is important?
I don't know that it is necessarily important, although I think it is somewhat natural. If I have a style it would be one that is clean, simple, and fresh. Those kind of qualities can be applied to any type of client and made specific to that client, so that it is our style — but their personality reflected.

How would you describe a good work environment?
One that has intelligent, imaginative, innovative, bright people with a passion for great ideas and design. Great clients. Great physical environment conducive to creativity — great lighting, good organization. Up-to-date technology and other good resources. An environment where there is hard work and hard play. Good attitudes and a lot of laughter.

Title: "30 days or less"
Designer/Creative Director: Pat Hansen **Company:** Hansen Design Company, Inc. **Client:** Advanced Development Center, Ernst & Young LLP, Microsoft **Photographer:** stock **Typefaces:** Garamond, Univers **Year:** 1998

What is the most fulfilling aspect of your job?
I feel most fulfilled when a client completely trusts us to design and produce a project as we see it. I love the great amount of knowledge we acquire from working with a diverse client base.

And the least?
When a client wants to design the job himself or thinks he is the expert, despite your most serious recommendations — or when a project goes haywire in the production/print/fabrication stage.

Title: Medicine Northwest, Winter 1998 Issue **Designers:** Pat Hansen, Carrie Adams **Creative Director:** Pat Hansen **Company:** Hansen Design Company, Inc. **Publication:** Medicine Northwest **Client:** University of Washington School of Medicine **Illustrator:** Peter Coates (cover) **Photographers:** Doug Plummer, William Stickney, Philip Amdal **Typefaces:** Times Roman, Helvetica **Year:** 1998

Title: Know about Microsoft Library **Designer/Creative Director:** Pat Hansen **Company:** Hansen Design Company, Inc. **Client:** Microsoft Library/Microsoft **Illustrators:** Pat Hansen, Dominic Dunbar **Typeface:** Franklin Gothic **Year:** 1997

Title: "Keeping People in Touch" Annual Community Report **Designer/Creative Director:** Pat Hansen **Company:** Hansen Design Company, Inc. **Client:** Nextel **Photographer:** stock **Typefaces:** Gill Sans, Cochin **Year:** 1998

Title: Product Guide and Pricing Catalog CD Package **Designer/Creative Director:** Pat Hansen **Company:** Hansen Design Company, Inc. **Client:** Magna Design **Typeface:** Bodoni **Year:** 1998

I Do Not Specialize

Title: The Mexican Museum 20th Anniversary poster **Designers:** Jennifer Morla, Craig Baily **Creative Director:** Jennifer Morla **Company:** Morla Design **Client:** Bacchus Press **Photographer:** Courtesy International Museum of Photography at George Eastman House **Typefaces:** Franklin Gothic Extra Condensed, various Mexican woodblock faces **Year:** 1996

JENNIFER MORLA
Principal, Morla Design, New York City

Why don't you have a design specialty?
I do not specialize because I enjoy the variety of opportunities that being a designer offers.

What was your first job?
My first formal job was working for the San Francisco PBS station, creating the identities for broadcast productions: designing the openings, creating and animating the logos, and designing the promotional posters and press kits. Three and a half years later I was hired as art director for Levi Strauss and Company.

How would you describe a good work environment?
An environment that allows information and ideas to be shared freely between designers, administrators, and principals.

How much of your time is devoted to design and how much to business matters?
It depends on how one defines business matters. I personally don't handle too much administrative paperwork (estimates, invoices, change orders, etc.), which would lead one to think that I spend all of my time designing. I spend a good portion of my time creating design briefs that keep the project visually on track by keeping the client informed and thereby giving us greater design flexibility.

What is the most fulfilling aspect of your job?
Being creative and getting paid for it.

And the least?
When a client does not recognize the potential for their product or service, thereby unnecessarily limiting their opportunities.

Title: Levi's Posters: Five Portraits **Designers:** Jennifer Morla, Angela Williams **Creative Director:** Jennifer Morla **Company:** Morla Design **Client:** Levi Strauss & Co. **Photographer:** Jock McDonald **Year:** 1998

Title: California College of Arts & Crafts New Building Poster **Designers:** Jennifer Morla, Petra Geiger **Creative Director:** Jennifer Morla **Company:** Morla Design **Client:** The New York Times **Photographer:** Morla Design **Typefaces:** Matrix Script, Trixie, Franklin Gothic, Adobe Garamond, Black Oak, Stymie, Univers **Year:** 1995

Title: Levi's Jeans for Women Shop **Designer:** Jennifer Morla **Creative Directors:** Brian Collins (FCB), Jennifer Morla **Company:** Morla Design **Client:** FCB and Levi Strauss & Co. **Photographers:** Sheila Metzner (instore murals), Cesar Rubio (documentation) **Typefaces:** Bodoni, custom calligraphy (rug) **Year:** 1997

Title: Discovery Channel Store Shopping Bags **Designers:** Jennifer Morla, Angela Williams, Yoram Woi Berger **Creative Director:** Jennifer Morla **Company:** Morla Design **Client:** The Discovery Channel **Typeface:** Helvetica Light **Year:** 1997

Creatively Restless

Title: HMV Store Prototype
Designer: Claire Taylor
Creative Director: Ken Carbone
Company: CSA — The Carbone
Smolan Associates **Client:** HMV
Records **Year:** 1995

Title: The White House
Millennium Council Identity
Designer: Justin Peters
Creative Director: Ken Carbone
Company: CSA — The Carbone
Smolan Associates **Client:** The
White House Millennium Council
Illustrator: Justin Peters
Typeface: Geometric **Year:** 1998

KEN CARBONE

Principal, CSA— The Carbone Smolan Agency,
New York City

Do you have a personal design style?
I have never focused on having a personal style because I am too
creatively restless. Also, we serve a diverse clientele demanding a
range of stylistic approaches; we pride ourselves on designing the
right solution for each client. I believe that our stylistic diversity
has contributed to our longevity as a company — now twenty
years old. A style is just that — a style. As in fashion, some
design styles can look dated in a very short time.

What is your greatest challenge as a designer?
Creating opportunities for my clients and seeing the power of
design help their business grow. The least fulfilling part of my job
is paying for constant computer upgrades.

How involved are you in the final production of your work?
My job is to hold the vision and allow those who are more skilled
in production to ensure that the vision is realized.

How would you describe a good work environment?
A lot of creative exchange, high enthusiasm about the work that
is being done, challenging assignments, and a diverse range of
projects.

Do you have a specific approach to hiring designers?
We constantly see portfolios, good portfolios. However, there is
often a big difference between portfolio and performance. Some
designers can't hold up in the line of fire even though they've
done some beautiful work. We usually insist on a trial period. At
CSA, we have a family-like environment and people stay for a long
time. Chemistry is almost as important as design talent because
there is a great deal of teamwork.

Title: Chicago Symphony
Identity **Designers:** Claire
Taylor, Justin Peters **Creative
Director:** Ken Carbone **Com-
pany:** CSA — The Carbone
Smolan Associates **Client:**
Chicago Symphony Orchestra
Illustrator: Justin Peters
Typeface: Gill Sans **Year:** 1997

Title: MacMillan's "Spotlight on
Literacy **Designers:** Jennifer
Domer, Lesley Feldman **Creative
Director:** Ken Carbone **Com-
pany:** CSA — The Carbone
Smolan Associates **Client:**
MacMillan **Year:** 1997

Title: Sotheby's Catalog Re-
design **Designer:** Carla Miller
Creative Director: Ken Carbone
Company: CSA — The Carbone
Smolan Associates **Client:**
Sotheby's **Year:** 1996

Designer With a Mission

MASSIMO VIGNELLI
President, Vignelli Associates, New York City

Title: Knoll Handerchief Chair
Designers: Massimo Vignelli,
Lella Vignelli, David Low
Company: Vignelli Associates
Client: Knoll International
Year: 1985

Do you have a specialty?
The whole field of design is my specialty. I always thought that specialization brings entropy and entropy brings death. I love cross-fertilization among disciplines, of which design is one. Design is an attitude, a process of solving problems for what they are, filtered through your interpretation.

Could you explain how a very large design firm works — the pros and cons?
This question requires a whole book to answer. In short, a firm becomes large not only when successful but when enough energy is spent in making it grow. Personally, I think that a design firm beyond fifty people per office becomes hard to control, from a character point of view. Inevitably, a larger firm is made of many teams who share a discipline but can hardly have a common handwriting. In a large firm, work comes because more people are involved in properly taking care of potential clients. There are many good designers, I usually say, but not many good clients. This is one of the problems with a large office. The moment that

Title: Guggenheim Museum, Bilbao **Designers:** Massimo Vignelli, Graham Hanson **Company:** Vignelli Associates **Client:** Soloman R. Guggenheim Museum **Photographer:** Graham Hanson **Year:** 1997

getting clients becomes more important than selecting them, the quality inevitably drops. I always preferred to have fewer good clients than many mediocre ones, but this attitude has a penalty: less profit.

How much of your time is devoted to design and to business matters?

Fifty-fifty. Design is a creative business and requires the attention that any business demands. I hate making proposals and presentations and I hate competing against designers that I respect. I consider that a tremendous loss of time and clients' money that could have been dedicated to the project more profitably, if the client had only done his homework more seriously. I hate political jobs done to please clients. I like to work with people at the top, the ones finally responsible for the project. I see the client as a partner in an effort to solve the problem.

Title: Great Northeastern Railway, UK Logo **Designers:** Massimo Vignelli, Peter Vetter, Dani Piderman **Company:** Vignelli Associates **Client:** Great Northeastern Railway **Year:** 1997

What is the most fulfilling aspect of your job?

The most fulfilling experience is to see my design working well, to see a proper implementation, and to see it grow successfully. The worst is to see my work wasted, improperly used, poorly implemented, out of control, out of awareness.

I see that as a betrayal of the original intention.

Do you have a specific approach to hiring designers? How does it work?

Quality, quality, quality. Not trendy portfolios, but a good sense of organization of the information, because that is what we are looking for. Every day we receive requests from people who would like to work with us. We keep their resume and call them when in need. We always have interns from all over the world, preferably from Switzerland, Germany, or great schools in the United States like Alfred, Cincinnati, and others. Interns are usually in the office for three months. They help and often, if they are good, we hire them after school.

Title: Fratelli Rossetti Packaging **Designer:** Massimo Vignelli **Company:** Vignelli Associates **Client:** Fratelli Rossetti **Photographer:** Luca Vignelli **Year:** 1986

I have been told that my style is to get attention. I have been also told I have a Southern California style — sometimes that is not said in a complimentary manner.

—**Mike Salisbury**

I couldn't really put my finger on my personal style. So I thought I'd ask a few people I've worked with. Lynda Bernard, a copywriter, said, "You use type as one of the graphic visual elements, so the words just don't sit there. They have a rhythm and a play to them. They are an intricate part of the design, making for a much more readable and good-looking piece of advertising. I've never seen you do something that wasn't pleasing to the eye."

—**Jean Govoni**

I try as much as possible to make our design solutions insightful, intelligent, and amusing. I listen to the problems as they're set before us and try to come up with an elegant and lively solution. For some, that may be a classical elegance that still feels modern in its approach and spare execution. For others, it can be composed of much more funky elements that still contain a unity and a central underlying idea. When you see the work together, you can see that it comes from the same place. But you can also see that we're working in or reinventing the client's world and taking the assignments to a new and adventurous place for them.

—**Don Morris**

Content is important, not style.

—**Greg Samata**

As my wife once said, and I quote, "Richard, you have no style." Being in both advertising and graphic design, most of my problems are solved from a conceptual point of view that dictates the style. Not having a personal style is my strength. At the same time, I realize a personal style can give a designer an identity that can help brand him accordingly. Although style works to one's advantage for a time, when it becomes less fashionable, it's time to reinvent oneself. The best designers find a way to do this.

—**Richard Wilde**

Personal style is important if you set out to become a design star. Then it definitely helps to have a style so that people can follow your work.

—**Rhonda Rubenstein**

There is definitely a feeling or style to my work that is more or less constant. On one hand, it's a hard-to-define feeling of casualness or play, even in serious projects. But there also are colors and typefaces that run repetitively through all my work that I am definitely known for.
—**Helene Silverman**

I think the question is: Is it important to make your own mark? And I think it's absolutely critical that you find yourself in everything you do and you commit to it.
—**Nancye Green**

I remember showing my work to some people and they'd say, "Wait, these things don't look alike." And I thought, Well, how could they? I worked with Paul Simon and his album is going to look completely different from a Warhol book I did. If my work all looks alike, then I think I'm imposing too much of my own ego, my own self, on the project.
—**Yolanda Cuomo**

My approach is contextual, free, tending toward boldness. I tend to thrive on large-scale programs, collaboration, and teamwork.
—**Deborah Sussman**

Illustrators and fine artists usually have (and need) a personal style; designers should be more concerned about identifying or creating a style for their clients. I was taught (and I teach) that the graphic designer's job is to facilitate and enhance communication between a sender and a receiver. Please note that, inevitably, many designers repeat certain forms or fall into a comfortable visual vocabulary. To me this is a forgivable tilt toward a style.
—**Wayne Hunt**

Personal style is inevitable. For years, all I wanted was to do layouts like Fred Woodward's at *Rolling Stone*. That was success to me. That's what real magazines looked like. At some point, it finally occurred to me that I wasn't Fred and I was never going to be Fred. I told myself that it was time to figure out what I've learned from trying to be Fred (and other designers) and do something of my own with it. My personal style came from paying closer attention to the magazines I was working on and letting their content dictate the design. It was very liberating.
—**Patrick Mitchell**

If you can identify a designer's work, he's an artist, not a designer. And as such, he doesn't serve his client well.
—**Joseph Essex**

I don't have much of a visual personal style that I'm aware of. On the other hand, one is always blind to one's own style.
—**Walter Bernard**

A personal style is lived and then it is expressed in what you do. I have, as a consequence of my education, a certain prejudice toward an international school of design that presents a clear, underlying grid, strong type structures, and such, but I don't aesthetically put myself in any particular school or camp of design.
—**David Peters**

Not to have a personal style would be like not having a recognizable voice. If I had to define elements of my style, it would be in sort of general terms: simple rather than complicated; clear rather than mysterious; integrated rather than diffuse; open to humor; friendly rather than formal; reliant on language as well as imagery.
—**Chris Pullman**

I may have a design signature, but that really is for others to judge. I believe that a personal style is a double-edged sword. It gives one a unique identity, but its novelty wears off in time and a designer often ends up ignored by a public always looking for the newest and latest. There's a lot to be said for a protean approach to design.

—**R.O. Blechman**

I've made it a point to design title sequences that serve the individual film that they become a part of. I feel that each film has a different personality and that, therefore, each title sequence should have a style that suits that particular film. I try not to repeat typefaces, nor do I use any visual trick or trademark that would identify me. I think that my work is a tool to create mood and content that complements the film — that it is not the place to create a signature or billboard about myself.

—**Randall Balsmeyer**

I can only process what I take in, so my own conventions are bound to creep into whatever I produce.

—**Ron Louie**

I like to think that when I'm developing a typeface, I'm creating something entirely unlike the rest of my body of work. One of my least favorite things is having one of my designs mistaken for another! Part of the reason to design more typefaces is that existing designs do not fulfill the same functions or exhibit the same characteristics. I'd argue that if I have a personal style, it's the residue of my own penchants and peccadillos.

—**Jonathan Hoefler**

Style is not at issue as much as the approach to content and the interpretation of the designer's role are. I would say that as a result of our perspective on design (historical, theoretical, interpretive), the work comes from a definite perspective and, as a result, that perspective brings some continuity to the way things look. We value a certain rigor, clarity, and directness in thought, and these values have a visual dimension.

—**J. Abbott Miller**

A personal style is like a handwriting — it happens as the byproduct of our way of seeing things, enriched by the experiences of everything around us.

—**Massimo Vignelli**

Yes, it's probably important for a designer to have a personal style, because those who don't have it are probably imitating other people's styles. It isn't that you develop a personal style, you usually just can't help yourself. It's involuntary. Style is something you develop by trying to imitate somebody else and failing.

—**Paula Scher**

Maybe, from a marketing point of view, style might make it easier, because somebody that's going for a designer can say I want him because he does this.

—**David Slatoff**

I hope my style comes out in the words I am writing now, or in how I teach class or in how I converse at my local pub. You can't avoid a style.

—**James Victore**

If I were to describe my personal style, it would be summed up in one word: appropriate. Each client and each project is unique.

—**Jennifer Morla**

Of contemporary type designers, many have a more discernible style than I think I do. There is a stronger consistency in the underlying models of their letterforms in the work of Hermann Zapf, Adrian Frutiger, and Gerard Unger, to take the most eminent examples, than in mine. I envy them this. On the other hand, if there was nothing of me in my types I would feel I had been wasting my time, as a fundamental driving force for any designer should be the desire to recognize some part of oneself in one's work. A kind critic once said I make letters with backbones. I like the sound of that. If it were true that letters with a sense of structure were characteristic of my style, then I would be happy.

—Matthew Carter

We have more of an approach rather than a style. I think style is too singular and limiting and doesn't address the breadth or diversity of our work, which is characterized by its strong visual impact mixed with equal parts of irony and humor.

—Charles Spencer Anderson

I don't think our job is to have a personal style. Our job is to interpret and create images for other people, for clients.

—Gael Towey

My designs have to have intellectual content. They have to have something that people can recognize. There has to be a human element, something that might involve humor or pathos or tenderness or silliness or lunacy or something. And if I can work those things, then I have a powerful piece.

—Michael Patrick Cronan

Personal style can easily be thought of as a personal cliche, or a personal stereotype. I don't like those things. I find that more with illustrators than with designers. I think it's important to try and cover new ground all the time, even if you don't succeed. I think if you're just going to do the same thing all the time, what's really the point? That just bores me.

—Chip Kidd

I think of personal style as not being imposed on work but rather as a visual quality and orientation that emerges.

—Sheila Levrant de Bretteville

I have a problem with designers and design firms who have one style and apply it to everything. I shouldn't actually say that because I firmly believe that there is room for everybody in this world to express themselves the way they see fit.

—Carlos Segura

This is the trickier one because personally I find it very difficult to define what my style actually is. Although, if you speak to somebody else, they'll be able to say, oh, well, I can always tell your work. The things that link my work would be the craft and the nuance. I think that stylistically there's a really broad range of work, and for me the vision isn't really apparent. But you know people say it's there. I don't think it's important to have a personal style. If there is anything about my style it is that I want to be true to the work. I'm going to have a preference for certain typefaces and certain effects, and compositional things and that comes through and that's really kind of the style that people are reacting to.

—Michael Ian Kaye

Options

Graphic design is a slippery term and not entirely applicable in the current design environment. Arguably, *commercial art* is more to the point but less sophisticated than other enigmatic nomenclature. The term *graphic design* is credited to W.A. Dwiggins, a letterer, calligrapher, and type, book, and advertising designer as well as a novelist, playwright, and marionette theater impresario, who in 1922 proposed the term as a definition of his own multifaceted professional activity. The coinage was matter-of-factly proposed in an article in which Dwiggins argued that new kinds of commercial advertising methods and techniques required a new kind of *graphic design-er* — a generalist proficient in wedding various media into

Title: Wool - MSL
Clotheskeeping
Special Issue
Designers: Gael
Towey, Michelle
Outland **Creative
Director:** Gael Towey
Publication: Martha
Stewart Living
Photographer:
Richard Phibbs
Typeface: Wello
Script **Year:** 1998

one inclusive practice rather than a specialist in an anonymous production line. As an alternative to more specific labels — including *layout-* or *board-person, comp artist, airbrush artist, illustrator,* and *letterer* — *graphic designer* was certainly a broad enough term to include all these jobs and more. But now, in an age of expanded media, it is an insufficient way to define the widening range of the design profession.

During the 1930s, graphic designers who were also involved in package and product design, as well as those who engaged in industrial design, called themselves "designers for industry." At that pivotal time of the Machine Age, a new breed of cross-disciplinary, independent design firm emerged that took responsibility for the conception and production of entire projects rather than specialized aspects of the whole. These identity, packaging, and signage projects were on a fairly grand scale for corporations as large as Ford Motor and DuPont Chemical Companies, among others. The staffs of these firms included graphic, interior, and architectural specialists working together in unified teams. While team members practiced their particular specialties, each contributed to the other's goals.

In the postwar period, as dedicated design departments and so-called design laboratories developed within progressive corporations, cross-disciplinary programs grew in both popularity and necessity. Moreover, the specialists had to know how their work fit into the larger context. It was not enough for a designer to practice typography alone, for example; knowledge of how it worked and interacted in the world was equally important. Therefore, previously standalone disciplines were integrated into overall practices and designers had to be fluent in much more than their own arcane specialties.

Starting in the 1950s, in an effort to expand and legitimize graphic design in the international business world, designers referred to themselves with more inclusive monikers: *visual communicator, visual designer, graphic communicator, communications specialist, communications consultant*, and so on. Although the majority of graphic designers continued to use conventional, though enigmatic, nomenclature, in the face of a growing shift from single- to multidisciplinary practice, the term *graphic design* lost some of its relevance as the focus of work gradually shifted from paper to three dimensions. *Graphic* suggests marks on paper (although it is really broader than that); *visual* implies images as well as graphics.

This section examines some of the options that graphic designers are offered today and analyzes the widening expectations of clients in relation to technological shifts that have allowed the graphic designer to branch away from traditional practice.

Title: Peaches
Designer/Creative Director: Gael Towey
Publication: Martha Stewart Living
Photographer: Christopher Baker
Typeface: Garamond, MSL Gothic
Year: 1995

CROSSING DISCIPLINES

MANY DESIGNERS ARE content to design beautiful lettering, splendid pages, or smart logos for the course of their entire careers. Developing such skills over time is both personally rewarding and professionally satisfying, to be sure. But others are not as sanguine about having only a single specialty. The reasons vary: Some do not have the talent or ability to master one thing brilliantly, while others lack the patience to do so. Some view specialization as offering too few challenges and therefore explore numerous options as a matter of personal pride and preference. Still others believe that specialization equals limitation, and limitation in this expanding field is professional suicide.

As a graphic designer, the secret to longevity is not a marketable style but rather keeping abreast of shifts in all media and incorporating as many of these as possible into your own repertoire. In recent years, the widespread access to so many kinds of media (as outlined in Section 1) has both opened the job market and stretched the boundaries of this field. Crossing disciplines is no longer an exception to the rule — it is the rule. If one is unable to solve problems in more than one discipline, a client will probably go to someone who can. Small clients may be content with a logo and stationery — and many designers can fill those simple needs — but medium and large clients prefer one-stop shopping for a variety of print (packaging, publishing, promotion, advertising) and multimedia needs (Internet, interactive kiosk, video). One of the clearest indications of this is the addition of Web site designers to most design studio, firm, and office staffs. Some design firms are now linked to architects and interior designers, too.

Crossing disciplines means that a graphic designer must be something of a chameleon. With the inclusion of graphic design as a component of screen-based media, understanding the kinetic properties of type and image, for example, is a given. While members of the older generation may have to grapple with such media, the younger generation, weaned on the computer, deal with this tool as a fact of professional life. In fact, this kind of discipline-crossing is now routinely taught in many art and design schools, and will become inextricably tied to whatever graphic design becomes in the future.

However, other crossover disciplines are not as naturally woven into the graphic designer's education or daily routine, and these must be sought out, learned, and practiced. The most common crossovers involve aspects of television, film, video, and exhibitions, requiring both interest and skill in complementary media, including music, lighting, and editing, for example. In addition, an increasing number of designers collaborate with architects on the graphics for building exteriors or interiors, which may include printed as well as three-dimensional executions. Architects who specialize in retail and restaurant interiors, for example, have become more aware of graphics and frequently collaborate with graphic designers on the look and feel of entire projects, not simply on the finishing touches.

Graphic designers have also become more proactive in the process of conception and management in a variety of areas. One example is city and community planning — developing visual identities, wayfinding systems, even determining the layout of streets and neighborhoods — and

Who You Callin' a Graphic Designer?

I hate the term *graphic designer* because it's extremely limiting and it has very little to do with our profession. The word *graphic* implies printed or offset matter. Because probably less than a third of the work we do has its end product as a printed product, it just seems kind of ludicrous.

I'm a designer. On my stationery it says "A Visual Communication Consultancy." That's probably a little long, but at the same time it's more important that I distinguish this from a graphic design office.

The Italians used to have a designation during the time of the Medici: *consiglieri*, people who advised on a variety of subjects, who were part of the organization but not *in* the organization. The consiglieri had an understanding of everything that was going on — of the people, of the products, of the businesses, of the culture, of the arts, of science. They had everything to do with the world and, in a sense, could bring a different voice or a point of view that may not have been considered.

That's how the design profession has evolved and will continue to evolve, because it's a personal service business. So the aesthetics are a mechanism for communication, not an end in and of themselves. I think that's part of where a good deal of the confusion about what a designer is comes from.

—Joseph Essex

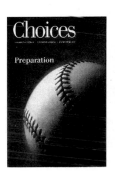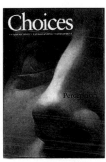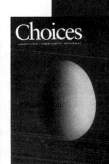

Title: Choices **Designer/Creative Director:** Joseph Essex **Company/Client:** SX2 **Photographer:** Mark Joseph **Year:** 1996

another example is the organization of retail and entertainment districts. Hence, the quintessential cross-disciplinary graphic designer is not merely a subcontractor serving the needs of so-called higher echelon designers but is an active participant in an overarching planning and design scheme, a valued member of a team that integrates several media into one entity.

A graphic designer can train to work in various disciplines through advanced study (continuing education courses are offered in virtually all complementary and supplementary professional spheres), but more likely a designer often backs into these other disciplines by chance. Necessity is the mother of most invention, and a client's need for interrelated disciplines is often just the impetus that a designer or design studio needs to branch into previously uncharted realms.

Designer as Curator

Title: Mixing Messages Sign
Designer: Ellen Lupton
Company: Cooper-Hewitt,
National Design Museum
Photographer: Bill Jacobson
Typeface: Interstate
Year: 1996

ELLEN LUPTON

Co-chair of Graphic Design, Maryland Institute,
College of Art, Baltimore, MD; and Partner,
Design/Writing/Research, Baltimore, MD

Why did you expand your practice to include curatorial and authorial work? Was this strategy or accident?
As someone who was always fascinated with the written word,
I felt design was an ideal forum in which to develop text and
image. I became a curator by accident. When I graduated from
The Cooper Union in 1985, I was invited to run the just-founded
Herb Lubalin Study Center for Design and Typography. It was a
shoestring operation occupying a few small rooms and hallways
of The Cooper Union. But it was a great opportunity to put
together exhibitions and publications about design history and
theory. I got hooked, and I was able to build a career as a critic
and curator.

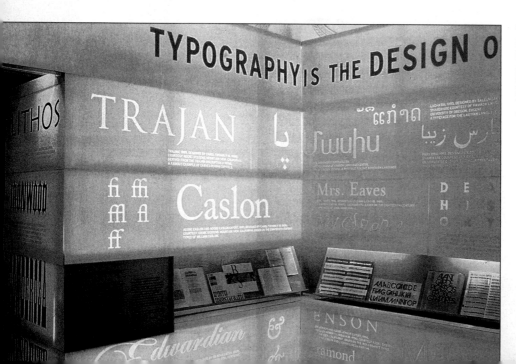

Title: Mixing Messages Font
Room **Designers:** Ellen Lupton,
Fred Gates, Kennedy & Violich
Architects **Company:** Cooper-
Hewitt, National Design Museum
Photographer: Bill Jacobson
Typeface: Interstate and various
Year: 1996

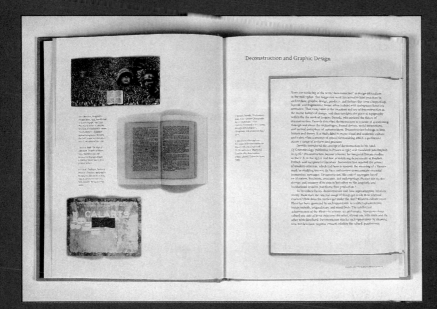

Deconstruction and Graphic Design

Title: Design Writing Research: Writing on Graphic Design **Designers:** Ellen Lupton, Abbott Miller **Company:** Design Writing Research/Kiosk **Typeface:** Scala **Year:** 1996

Is this cross-disciplinary activity viable in the market today or simply a fortuitous niche that you made for yourself?
My position as a museum curator is a rare one — there is only a handful of design curators around the country, at institutions including the Museum of Modern Art in New York and the San Francisco Museum of Modern Art. However, there are more and more opportunities for designers to develop and use their skills as writers/editors/publishers and for literary people to engage the processes of design. This is a broader cultural development with relevance beyond my particular experience.

Would you say that your interdisciplinary practice has given your firm, Design, Writing, Research, an advantage in the competitive design market? How do you account for your success?
As partners in Design, Writing, Research, Abbott Miller and I have done a series of key projects that exemplify the ideal of combining research and writing with visual work. These are not always the most lucrative projects, however, and the studio does many projects that are executed along a more traditional design services model. The studio is primarily Abbott's undertaking — I am primarily employed by Cooper-Hewitt National Design Museum and, more recently, the Maryland Institute College of Art. Abbott is doing a marvelous job at the studio, developing the ideal of a design-research continuum while still making a living for himself and his staff.

Title: Mechanical Brides (installation of typographic laundry in exhibition about women, work and technology) **Designer:** Ellen Lupton **Company:** Cooper-Hewitt, National Design Museum **Photographer:** Bill Jacobson **Typeface:** Scala **Year:** 1993

A Graphic Architect

Title: The Fashion Center
Information Kiosk **Architect:**
James Biber **Architect/Assistant:** Michael Zweck-Bronner
Graphics Creative Director:
Michael Bierut **Graphic Designer:** Esther Bridavsky
Company: Pentagram Architectural Services/Pentagram Design
Inc. **Client:** The Fashion Center
Photographer: James Shanks
Year: 1996

JAMES BIBER

Partner, Pentagram Architectural Services/
Pentagram Design Inc., New York City

Your interior design has always been very "graphic." Do you think in terms of architectonics or graphics?
I think entirely architecturally, but always with an image or a particular visual point of view to communicate, the operative word being *communicate*. I try not to get lost in the architectonics of the project but rather to use them as a language to make the design legible, accessible, and therefore, in my view, effective. This is probably not how most architects think. They prefer, in most cases, to solve the architectural problem at the expense of the accessibility of the ideas.

You often work with graphic designers. What is the dynamic of this relationship?
I love working with any creative individual. The possibility for real creative exchange, triggering of ideas, the back-and-forth of building an idea is increased when working with any visual artist, especially one whose work I respect and enjoy. It's a bit like teaching; you can tangle with ideas outside your normal realm and grow creatively.

Is being a partner in a graphic design firm with an architectural component different than working for an architectural firm?
To put it diplomatically, I have never felt the need to join a partnership of architects. This partnership, however, thrives on different ideas, different points of view, different talents. We

Title: The Globe **Architect:**
James Biber **Architect/Assistant:** Michael Zweck-Bronner
Company: Pentagram Architectural Services/Pentagram
Design Inc. **Client:** Jim
Heckler & Nick Polsky **Photographer:** Andrew Bordwin
Year: 1997

can work together on a project, or on different aspects of a single project, with less competition (of the destructive kind), more enjoyment of each other's ideas, and, I like to think, a better process and product as a result.

Is your position anomalous, or are there many openings for this kind of cross-disciplinary relationship?
This may be one of a very few situations where a series of disciplines (at the partner level) coexist in a single firm. We don't hire talent from other disciplines as staff members; we seek them out as partners. We are a firm of equals rather than a pyramid of management, and that is a big part of why it works.

What do you look for in an assistant — architectural *and* graphic design expertise?
I look for a keen architectural mind, good working habits, and a great attitude. Fortunately, our office is such a cauldron of design that the graphic parts just seem to rub off on my architectural staff. They all leave with an enhanced appreciation and eye for graphic design, and I like to think that the graphic design staff learns as much from us.

Do you envision architecture and graphic design becoming a more unified profession?
Any unification will probably always exist outside the mainstream of architectural practice. The professions are different in demeanor, working methodology, fee structures, and time scales. The biggest barrier, in my view, is that most architects don't consider graphic designers their professional equals. Collaboration only works among equals. Collaboration among unequals is called *employment*.

Title: "I Want To Take You Higher" Exhibition **Designer:** Nikki Richardson **Creative Directors:** James Biber, Michael Bierut **Company:** Pentagram Architectural Services/Pentagram Design Inc. **Client:** The Rock & Roll Hall Of Fame **Photographer:** Peter Mauss **Year:** 1997

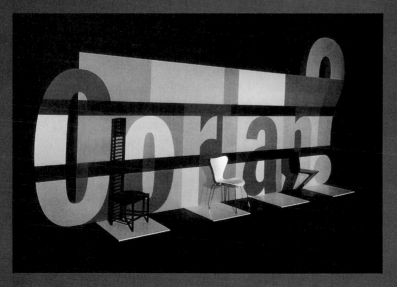

Title: DuPont Corian? Corian! Trade Show Exhibit **Architect:** James Biber **Architect/Assistant:** Michael Zweck-Bronner **Graphic Designer:** Nikki Richardson **Project Coordinator:** Leslie Wellott **Company:** Pentagram Architectural Services/Pentagram Design Inc. **Client:** DuPont **Photographer:** Peter Margonelli **Year:** 1996

Mixing Fields

Title: Sterling Executive Office Design & Fabrication Credits Plaque **Designer:** Katherine McCoy **Company:** McCoy & McCoy Associates **Client:** Formica Corporation **Typeface:** Helvetica **Year:** 1985

Title: Cranbrook Academy of Art Catalog **Designer:** Katherine McCoy **Design Assistance:** Lorraine Wild **Company:** McCoy & McCoy Associates **Client:** Cranbrook Academy of Art **Photographer:** Steven Milanowski **Typeface:** Helvetica **Year:** 1976

KATHERINE McCOY
Principal, McCoy & McCoy, Buena Vista, Colorado

In addition to being chair of the graphic design graduate program at Cranbrook for almost twenty-five years, you have worked in many design disciplines — graphic, interior, exhibition, product. Why did you combine these interests and how do you balance them?

I find it impossible to separate the design fields into tidy little compartments. Each has everything to do with the others. Graphic design has materiality and dimensionality, products and interior must communicate, and a large-scale exhibition combines communications, product, interiors, and even architecture. Mixing the fields comes especially naturally to me because my husband and design partner, Michael McCoy, is an industrial and furniture designer who also has a love of graphic design. Together we make an interdisciplinary design team. We also enjoy partnering with other designers, including architects and interior designers, on large projects.

What is the gratification in this?

One of the most gratifying of our interdisciplinary projects came a few years ago, when we were asked to design the office of the president of Formica Corporation using the company's products. We used Formica Colorcore to graphically mark work zones and traffic areas, combining our enthusiasm for both interiors and graphic design. The office's custom furniture integrated work surfaces and cabinetry into the walls, also with functionality markings embedded in the Formica surfaces. Before the office interior was installed, the company displayed it at the Pacific Design Center's West Week. As an exhibit, it needed a panel for fabrication and design credits. So I designed a plaque that translated the office's three-dimensional design language into a bas-relief of laminated Colorcore. The invitation for the exhibition's opening was another opportunity to translate the design vocabulary, this time into an offset printed paper piece. So what began as an exercise of bringing graphic design into an environment ended as a translation of an environment back into graphic design.

How is your graphic work enriched by other disciplinary work?
I find that other design fields are laden with fresh ideas that can
enrich graphic design. For instance, architecture is a much older
and more highly evolved field that has a whole body of history,
theory, and criticism that can be bent to apply to graphic design
as well. As postmodernism began to germinate in architecture, I
found architectural thinkers like Robert Venturi gave a useful context to our experiments in graphic design.

**Do you see cross-disciplinary activity as a future trend, or is
this something that is endemic to our practice?**
Design projects are becoming ever bigger and more complex, both
in content and technology, and require a range of expertise far
greater than one person can embody. This requires teamwork, and I
see three basic types of teams. One is composed of similar professionals; this has been common for years on large-scale communications projects like corporate identity systems and annual reports.
Second is an interdisciplinary team composed of a mix of design
professionals; for instance, the design of a large hospital requires
architects, interior designers, and graphic designers for the signage
and wayfinding. The design of a piece of electronic equipment
requires industrial designers for the major physical configuration;
they must develop an operational interface with software interaction designers, and both must work with communications designers
for the look and feel of the interface and the hard controls and
brand identity. The third type of team is an overlay of the first two
and positions design as a strategic component of business competi-
tiveness. Designers are becoming involved in product development
and communications planning on interdisciplinary teams that can
include specialists in finance, marketing, advertising, and engineering long before a project advances to the design brief. This type of
designer must know the theory and language of business and marketing, allowing equal participation on a high level in a business
organization. It is increasingly common for designers to pursue
MBAs in graduate schools of business management. In the undergraduate training of a designer, it is advisable to include as much
marketing and business management course work as possible.

FORMICA CORPORATION

Title: Sterling Executive Office
Exhibition Reception Invitation
Designer: Katherine McCoy
Company: McCoy & McCoy Asso-
ciates **Client:** Formica Corpora-
tion, Susan Lewin **Typeface:**
Helvetica **Year:** 1985

Title: Sterling Executive Office;
President's Office Interior, Formica
Corporation **Designers:** Katherine
McCoy, Michael McCoy **Company:**
McCoy & McCoy Associates **Client:**
Formica Corporation, Susan Lewin
Year: 1985

Title: Expo 2000 Hannover poster
Designer: Katherine McCoy
Creative Director: Egon Chemaitis
Company: McCoy & McCoy
Associates **Client:** Expo 2000
Committee, Hannover, Germany
Typefaces: Caslon Italic, Futura
Condensed **Year:** 1997

Making a Brand

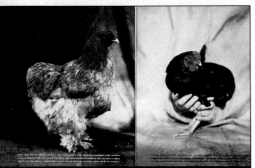

Title: Peaches **Designer/Creative Director:** Gael Towey **Publication:** Martha Stewart Living **Photographer:** Christopher Baker **Typeface:** Garamond, MSL Gothic **Year:** 1995

Title: Chickens **Designer/Creative Director:** Gael Towey **Publication:** Martha Stewart Living **Photographer:** Victor Schrager **Typeface:** MSL Gothic **Year:** 1994

GAEL TOWEY

Creative Director, Martha Stewart Living OmniMedia, New York City

You began as a book designer and now you are involved in all aspects of marketing. What is the most important lesson you've learned?

I've learned why product design has gotten to be where it is: Because the people who make design decisions are the financial people. They look at what was sold last year and base their decisions on what their sales were. This totally stymies any innovation or inspiration or ability to have impromptu ideas. Martha is able to cut through that because she is a believable personality. She's got great taste and style and she really is forcing manufacturers to think carefully about what they are doing. Just because something is discount, don't give people the bottom of the line. People who can't afford four-hundred-dollar bedsheets still deserve to have good design, even if they're only buying twenty-four-dollar sheets. It's a very populist idea.

How is the company organized?

We're trying to organize our businesses along the lines of our interests. So gardening, food, decorating, crafts, weddings, and holidays are the things that we are invested in across all media. We have experts here who work across media because they are the expert on gardening or cooking or whatever. Then each business has people who work solely on that business, but they have access to all the people in the core groups who are the experts. It's a complicated structure and what we are finding is that it's extremely difficult to maintain but we are at an incredible advantage because we have all of our experts here and they are trained by us, and Martha's very involved personally. We have K-Mart, Sherwin-Williams, who does our paint, and now we've just signed a deal with Kaufmann fabrics to do a line of fabrics, and we're also doing gardening with K-Mart.

You created a look for the magazine that many are now imitating. How do you feel about this?

I wish they'd get a life. Find their own damn photographer. Imitation is the best form of flattery.

How did the look develop?

The first thing I did was to think about Martha herself. She's very traditional, she's classic, but she's a very modern woman, and she's very visual. Photography has always been her love and her way of communicating, so we used photography in a way that is extremely respectful. Pictures are never ripped up or put on top of one another or anything like that; they're treated in a classical and delicate way. The typography tends to take a back seat; it's not very designed, it's quiet, and it's very readable because we want the person reading the magazine to have an intimate experience and not have to struggle.

What is the most fulfilling aspect of your job? And the least?

One of the greatest pleasures that I have is watching people grow, and I am lucky to be in a place where we've had incredible growth. The first assistant that I hired seven years ago is now running the *Wedding* magazine, and she's in her low thirties. Because of this phenomenal growth, people are amazed at what they've been able to do and how much they've grown — to be able to have gone from magazine design to product design and so on. It's very exciting. I feel enormous pride in the teaching aspect of being an art director and seeing people excel.

The hardest part of my job right now is managing the growth and the infrastructure, because we have grown so fast. I think we are over three hundred people now and two years ago we were eighty people. It's been horrifyingly fast and breathtaking. We are trying hard to build infrastructure right now, moving from one area of neediness to the next. I hate watching people struggle. But it's been a double-edged sword, because the people who are struggling are also the people who have grown so fast in their jobs.

You do a lot of hiring. What do you look for in a designer?

We use interns and, in fact, we've hired a number from Rhode Island School of Design. RISD students seem to acquire an understanding of texture. That's kind of a weird thing to say, but most schools don't teach photography and they don't teach storytelling. It's very hard to find people who have all of these talents. So we tend to hire people who are artists, who can go out and make stuff up, and who are interested in decorating and cooking and so on and know a lot about it, or are willing to really learn about it.

Title: Wash Day: MSL Clotheskeeping Special Issue **Designers:** Gael Towey, Michelle Outland **Creative Director:** Gael Towey **Publication:** Martha Stewart Living **Photographer:** Victoria Pearson **Typefaces:** Wello Script, Humanist **Year:** 1998

Title: Figs: Glossary **Designer/Creative Director:** Gael Towey **Publication:** Martha Stewart Living **Photographer:** Maria Robledo **Typefaces:** MSL Gothic **Year:** 1997

Title: Bouquets: MSL Weddings/ Spring Issue **Designer/Creative Director:** Gael Towey **Publication:** Martha Stewart Living **Photographer:** Victoria Pearson **Typeface:** Elzevir **Year:** 1998

ENTREPRENEURS

AN ENTREPRENEUR IS an independent creator, supplier, or distributor who establishes a business or develops a product, identifies a market, and sells the produced wares to the public. From its inception, the United States has been a country of small and large entrepreneurs, from Lisa the lemonade stand operator to Bill the Microsoft mogul. There is no shortage of viable business ideas in the air; furthermore, depending on the state of the national economy, there is easy access to start-up capital.

So what is a *graphic design* entrepreneur? Would not a designer who opens an independent studio, firm, or office be considered an entrepreneur?

In the strictest sense, the answer to the second question is *yes*. But to be more specific, graphic design studios and firms that offer only client services are not truly entrepreneurial because service businesses do not create, supply, or distribute their own products. Conversely, as an answer to the first question, a graphic designer who in addition to providing services also initiates products (or in the argot of today, "content") is indeed entrepreneurial. What's more, many designers who have the ability to skillfully package and promote other people's products have discovered that it is more satisfying and at times more lucrative to develop their own wares.

This concept is not new, however. Over the past decades, enterprising graphic designers have engaged in various forms of entrepreneurism, from small cottage industries to large retail establishments, from balsamic vinegar bottling to book packaging. A graphic designer is not locked into products related to graphic design alone but rather is free to develop any kind of merchandise (see sidebar) from candy to furniture — or whatever the imagination conjures. Entrepreneurial activity is either a supplement to an existing design business or a totally independent subsidiary of one, yet in both cases new products contribute to creative and business challenges that add value to a designer's personal and professional worth. All that is required is a good idea, some capital, a simple business plan, a means of manufacturing, a method of distribution, and a modicum of chutzpah.

Being an entrepreneur is not a viable direction for the designer who lacks the confidence to test the limits of creativity or the stamina to take business risks, but it is safe to say that almost everyone with creativity has at least one idea that

Title: Plastock CD Packaging
Designers: Jason Schulte, Todd Piper-Hauswirth **Creative Director:** Charles S. Anderson **Firm:** Charles S. Anderson Design Co. **Client:** Plastock

Title: Presentation Invite **Designer:/ Creative Director:** Charles S. Anderson **Firm:** Charles S. Anderson Design Co. **Client:** Charles S. Anderson Design Co.

is worth developing as product. For the faint of heart, as an alternative to starting an entrepreneurial business, many graphic designers develop products for other businesses and they either retain rights to or obtain royalties from the sale of their products. Although in this scenario the graphic designer is still working for a client, the result is not a framing of a client's product or idea with a brochure, package, or other service-oriented item but rather providing the client with an entity that adds value to the product line. Some of the most common products graphic designers have been commissioned to create are watches, clocks, bed sheets, towels, greeting cards, neckties, jewelry, even furniture.

Depending on the simplicity or ambition of the product, the learning curve varies greatly. While mistakes are invariably made, entrepreneurism offers the graphic designer insight into the nature of business as well as the satisfaction that simply toiling as a service provider will never generate. If the future of graphic design is greater involvement in the means and result of production, this cross-disciplinary activity is a large step in that direction.

Designers' Products

Many graphic designers and design studios have gone into entrepreneurial businesses either for the fun of it or to supplement their income. These are some of the firms and their products:

Sam Antupit: books
Dana Arnett: documentary films
CSA Archive: clip art books, watches
Doublespace: magazine
Doyle and Partners: watches
William Drenttel: books
Emigre: magazine, books, records
Nancye Green: chairs
Guarnaccia Studio: metal sculpture
Higashi Glaser Design: children's toys
Alex Isely: refrigerator magnets
Jerry Herring Design: books
Michael Ian Kaye: soft drinks
Louise Fili Ltd.: basil vinegar
M&Co: watches, stationery supplies
Richard McGuire: children's toys
Francois Mouly: regional map and guide
Pentagram: books, ephemera
Plazm: magazine, records
Push Pin Studio: gourmet candy
Supon Design: books
Michael Vanderbyl: furniture
Vignelli Associates: clothing
Walking Man: clothing

From Print to Pants

Title: California College of Arts and Crafts Catalog
Designer/Creative Director: Michael Cronan **Company:** Cronan Design **Client:** California College of Arts and Crafts **Illustrators:** Michael Cronan and various **Photographers:** Joel Rulliatti, Michael Cronan **Year:** 1993

MICHAEL PATRICK CRONAN

Creative Director, Cronan Design, San Francisco

How has your role changed, going from being a graphic designer to running a clothing business?

Someone recently said to me, "Getting old — you're really supposed to harvest your old age." I want to finally grow up and be able to offer things that are of value, to help other people do what a lot of people helped me do, which is to get a different perspective. The clothing company, Walking Man, is something that my wife, Karin Hibma, and I conceived of, and my wife runs it. She and I met in college and we had the same teacher, Kurt Von Meier. We built our creative lives around that experience. We had a chance to work a whole lot together, have kids, build businesses, try and fail at things together, and succeed at a few things. With Walking Man, we divvied it up such that I really work for her. This helped me get off of the hook of having to own it or think that I'm originating it. If you ask any designer, the hardest job they have is to design their own business cards. So now I can look at Walking Man as a client and I can address problems faster because I am not the progenitor or the leader. Karen has been nurturing the concept, getting it to make money, and getting it to be successful. It's a good example of where my limits are; I can't be responsible past a certain place, so she's taken over.

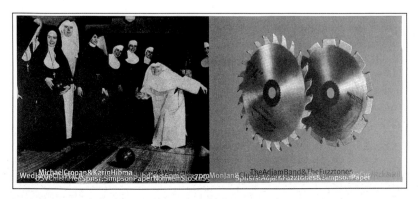

Title: Contrast **Designer/Creative Director:** Michael Cronan **Company:** Cronan Design **Client:** Dallas Society of Visual Communication **Typeface:** Officina **Year:** 1997

Did you have a strategy for how your business would grow and develop, or was it a natural evolution?

I had a focused strategy initially, which paid off. I rehearsed even what the forms would look like in my first office. Karin laughs about this because I literally sat around the house in my robe for about three weeks, panicked as heck, and just wrote notes about every single aspect of the office. I found a little teeny office and I just designed everything, including all the furniture. I designed everything in my brain and rehearsed it, so over the next couple of years it was like I was following a play, a prescribed plan. Then things just happened naturally, I knew exactly what to do. I believe that if you picture exactly what you want, life will give you that. In this last year, I have reentered the business. I've restructured it, made it a lot simpler. I think it's been a lot more fun for everybody involved, and it's become a lot more profitable than it was in the past. My ratio of pleasurable projects and clients has grown because I just try to love them and express my care, and I get bountiful returns for that.

Do you think the design field is moving toward specialization or more of an integration of various disciplines?

It's getting to be a cassoulet, a mixture. I see people becoming interested in what they do in particular, but by the same token, I think by working with other people and collaborating, they're having opportunities to do things they haven't done before and yet still stay within their parameters.

What knowledge do you possess now, as an entrepreneur, that perhaps you didn't have as a graphic designer?

It wasn't until I had a chance to start my own company with my own practice and manufacturing that I developed empathy for my clients. It's a very difficult job to buy creative services and to make something with other people's help on your mission. Most graphic designers don't think about making the clients money — they think about doing pretty design. When you get on the other side of the table, as an entrepreneur and a client, your decision-making becomes incredibly clear. I think designers should focus on how difficult it is to be a client and have respect for that. It would have aided me a great deal if I had learned that earlier.

Title: Radius Video Vision
Designers: Michael Cronan, Kevin Perrera **Creative Director:** Michael Cronan **Company:** Cronan Design/Radius In-House Team **Client:** Radius **Typeface:** Bodoni **Illustrator:** Kevin Perrera **Photographer:** Tony Russo and various **Year:** 1995

Title: Origami Coat **Designers/Creative Directors:** Michael Cronan, Karin Hibma **Company:** Cronan Design/Radius In-House Team **Client:** Walking Man.com **Photographer:** Terry Lorant **Year:** 1998

Design Is Business

Title: Frostone Brochure
Designers: Jason Schulte, Todd Piper-Hauswirth **Creative Director:** Charles Spencer Anderson **Company:** Charles Spencer Anderson Design Co. **Client:** French Paper Company

CHARLES SPENCER ANDERSON

Art Director, Charles S. Anderson Design Co. and CSA Archive Company, Minneapolis, Minnesota

Give us an idea of the range of entrepreneurial concerns you are involved in.

In 1995, we formed CSA Images as a separate company from Charles S. Anderson Design to concentrate on creating unique stock illustration and photography collections as well as on licensing images for use on retail products. The CSA Archive Stock CD and catalog contains over 8,000 line art illustrations. CSA Snapstock, a new collection of 7,000 illustrations, suggests the jazz/beatnik era. CSA Plastock is a new resource based on photographs of our synthetic friends: the plastic person, object, building, shot individually or in combination from our collection of 50,000 pieces of plastic to convey virtually any photo concept. After ten years of designing award-winning packaging and products for other companies, we decided to launch our own brand, Chuk A, a licensed young men's and women's apparel line. We are also currently in the process of upgrading our watch line with a Swiss manufacturer.

As the producer of a line of products, how much of your day is involved in business versus creative?

My time is split about in half. The eight employees of CSA Images spend all of their time on products.

Title: Albino Rudolph **Designer:** Todd Piper-Hauswirth **Creative Director:** Charles Spencer Anderson **Company:** Charles Spencer Anderson Design Co. **Client:** Chuk A Apparel **Photographer:** Plastock/CSA Images

Title: French Direct Packaging **Designer:** Jason Schulte **Creative Director:** Charles Spencer Anderson **Company:** Charles Spencer Anderson Design Co. **Client:** French Paper Company

Title: Seinfeld Poster **Designer/Creative Director:** Charles Spencer Anderson **Company:** Charles Spencer Anderson Design Co. **Client:** Entertainment Weekly

Title: French Revolution **Designers:** Jason Schulte, Todd Piper-Hauswirth **Creative Director:** Charles Spencer Anderson **Company:** Charles Spencer Anderson Design Co. **Client:** French Paper Company

What do you look for in the portfolio of a designer?

We look for image-makers, people with good ideas who can convey them with strong visual concepts using either photography or illustration. We also look for people with good typographic skills. What we don't look for is someone who is attempting to knock off what they think our style is, which usually turns out to look like a bad rendition of something we were doing five years ago that we have long since moved on from.

Many talented designers have moved through your firm. Is there room for advancement? To what level?

Nearly every designer started as an intern and advanced to a designer. Todd Piper-Hauswirth was made a partner last year and is still a designer. We don't have a lot of layers or titles. Good design is what we love to do and it's the goal of everyone here. In my opinion, the highest job position we have, and the most impressive title, is designer. With our launch into licensed products and images, the company has the potential for change and success that could hold a lot of promise for all of us.

Title: Portable Martini (annual report survival kit) **Designer:** Jason Schulte **Creative Director:** Charles Spencer Anderson **Company:** Charles Spencer Anderson Design Co. **Client:** French Paper Company

From Humble Beginnings

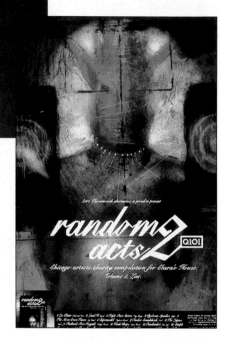

Title: Random Acts (Invitation and CD) **Designer:** Carlos Segura **Creative Director:** Carlos Segura **Company:** Segura, Inc. **Client:** Q101 Radio

Title: Universal Wax **Designer:** Carlos Segura **Creative Director:** Carlos Segura **Company:** Segura, Inc. **Client:** XXX Snowboards

CARLOS SEGURA

Designer, Segura Inc., T-26, and Owner,
Sick Face Records, Chicago

What motivated you to become a graphic designer?
Nothing. I actually didn't want to be a graphic designer. I wanted to be a drummer. And I actually was a drummer for twelve years. Our band, Clockwork, stumbled onto a number-one hit in Spain and we were on a pretty big label in the Florida circuit. We just got really big and famous and part of my duties of being in the band, beyond being the drummer, was to visually promote the band whenever we would do a concert. So, unknowingly, I was practicing graphic design. When I quit the band, someone recommended that I put all that stuff in a portfolio and go interview. That's how I got into the business. I didn't even know that there was a difference between design and advertising.

What was your first job?
My first job was working for Atlantic Envelope Company. For two years my sole responsibility was to design the return addresses on bank deposit envelopes. Of course, then I was moved up to designing the little patterns on the inside of the envelopes that you couldn't see. I learned so much at that job.

You now have a design firm, a digital type foundry, and a record company. How much of your business is entrepreneurial?
Segura, Inc., the design firm, is still the driving force. We're still the biggest of the three. T-26 is, however, big enough at this point to sustain itself. It's not something that is supported by Segura, Inc. And Sick Face Records is just in the beginning phase.

How has your role changed over the years?
Dramatically, by the fact that I have my own business. On many days I wish that I was working for somebody else and only had to worry about the assignment on my desk. I really miss that. I'm consumed by everyday stuff.

As your business developed over the years, was that due to natural evolution or did you have a plan?

No, I had no plan at all. I still don't have a plan.

Do you think the field of graphic design is moving toward specialization?

I think the field of design is moving to choppy waters and it is dictated by client behavior. I was reading an article recently by a famous older designer who observed that he was glad he grew up when he did because, although twenty years ago clients came to design firms for solutions, for their opinion, and for their vision, today clients come to design firms to execute their ideas. Basically, design firms have become risks to clients partly because there's an enormous amount of competition out there, but more importantly, I think, because the client's secretary can do what we do on her PC, or so they think. So they figure, "Well, if Joan can do it on her PC, why am I paying you all this money?" Somehow they believe that the computers being issued today come with some kind of special design button that you push and it spits all this stuff out. Just on the issue of copyright, I can't tell you how many times I have had trouble getting through to my clients' heads that you have to pay for an image and that you can't use this image if you bought it for this purpose and put it on the Web. They just don't understand that. That is so very, very, very hard.

Have changes in the business altered how you practice?

Of course, just like the computer has altered how I practice. I think we are all victims of our own creation and we try to make the best we can with what we have. I have relationships with clients that if I didn't have to eat I would just just as soon say, "Forget it, I don't want to deal with you," but I have to make the best of it.

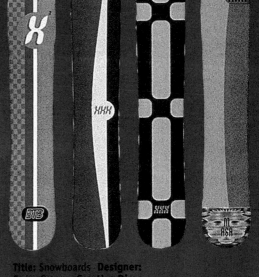

Title: Snowboards **Designer:** Carlos Segura **Creative Director:** Carlos Segura **Company:** Segura, Inc. **Client:** XXX Snowboards

Title: Q101 Radio Sticker **Designer:** Carlos Segura **Creative Director:** Carlos Segura **Company:** Segura, Inc. **Client:** Q101 Radio, Chicago

Title: Snowboard **Designer:** Carlos Segura **Creative Director:** Carlos Segura **Company:** Segura, Inc. **Client:** XXX Snowboards

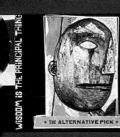

Title: The Alternative Pick Stickers **Designer:** Carlos Segura **Creative Director:** Carlos Segura **Company:** Segura, Inc. **Client:** The Alternative Pick **Illustrator:** Jordin Isip

AUTHORSHIP

AUTHORSHIP IS A CURRENT buzzword for graphic designers searching for new ways to broaden the scope and increase the relevance of their cultural contribution. The term references writing, but authorship is not exclusively about writing — rather, it is about producing entire projects. Now that graphic design is at the proverbial crossroads, where new media are forcing a reevaluation and redefinition of what graphic designers do, authorship distinguishes the old commercial art from the new visual communication. Unless authorship is clearly defined in the context of what graphic designers do (and will do in the future), this, like so many other self-proclaimed titles, will have as much significance as a mail-order Ph.D.

Nonetheless, authorship is a growing subspecialty of the broader field and must be acknowledged as a viable cross-disciplinary option.

There are two kinds of graphic designer: One is primarily production-oriented, the other primarily idea-oriented. Although the two are not mutually exclusive, a byproduct of the digital revolution is a clearer distinction between those with technical skill and those with imagination. Ever since prepress production was more or less taken out of the hands of craftspeople and placed in the laps (or laptops) of designers, for designers to grow in the creative realm they have to vigorously pursue all the options or get pigeonholed as production specialists. The computer has forced more responsibility onto designers to do work that was previously assigned to middlemen, yet it has also allowed for increased creative potential. The designer need not be a detached participant in an assembly line but can be the principal in a total production.

The most remarkable benefit of the computer is the potential it offers for those with vision to turn ideas into products. Of course, one does not need a computer to accomplish such feats — a human brain is good enough — but the machine houses a wellspring of possibility. As stated above, entrepreneurism is not new, yet never in the history of graphic design has there been such a huge potential for independent production.

Authorship is not a theoretical construct but rather a form of entrepreneurship where the designer takes responsibility for the quality and efficacy of a product, which can be anything from a book to an exhibition to a documentary film. What distinguishes authorship from other entrepreneurial pursuits is the marriage of word and image to whatever medium conveys it. It is closely linked to the French concept of the *auteur*, a filmmaker who is a writer, director, and sometimes producer.

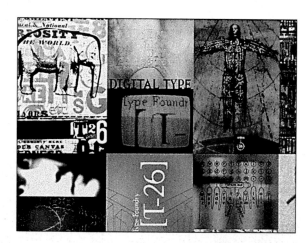

Title: Series of Stickers for T-26
Designer: Carlos Segura **Creative Director:** Carlos Segura **Company:** Segura, Inc. **Client:** T-26

The Whole Ball of Wax

In a typical publishing contract the author is the creator of the work or manuscript that will be designed, printed, and published by the publisher. However, not all book publishing is done this way. Today, the so-called author may be the packager or producer of a book who is responsible for hiring the writer, designer, photographer, copy editor, prepress production manager, and even for providing a publisher and distributor with the printed product. Graphic designers are well suited for this kind of authorship because they are already involved in all but the marketing and distribution processes. In fact, a number of graphic designers not only act as packagers but are themselves writers — some are even production managers. Ellen Lupton and J. Abbott Miller, who are partners in Design, Writing, Research, a multidisciplinary design firm, produce books and exhibition catalogs from start to finish. As the title of their firm indicates they control all of the creative — they design, write, and research books on the history, theory, and practice of graphic design — as well as prepress production. Knowing how to produce a entire book enables these authors to take full creative responsibility rather than be detached suppliers. Keeping control of the product allows them to control the costs and earn the most for their effort.

One may argue that authorship and entrepreneurship are distinct activities and, conventionally speaking, an author is a creator, not a manufacturer or distributor. Conversely, an entrepreneur may not be a creator but rather a facilitator of others' talents. Indeed, these distinctions are both valid and apt. But in the changing professional environment, combining these two trajectories into *authorpreneur* offers the designer increased freedom and flexibility. Authorprenuership can be accomplished solo or through an ensemble, by a few individuals or a collaborative team. There are no real bounds, but there is a defining tenet: An authorpreneur *provides* rather than merely *interprets* content.

Authorprenuership may be a tongue-twisting word to say, but it is not a convoluted notion. While there will always be those more proficient at editing than producing, or designing than writing, today's graphic designer should not be content only to design the book, magazine, or Web site. Either collaboratively or individually, the designer must be totally invested in a project and product. While there is no doubt that the graphic design field is mutating, perhaps the most meaningful shift will be when the concept of authorship (or authorprenuership) is not just a word that falsely bestows loftier status on designers but is an activity that all designers undertake.

A big early influence was a teacher I had at college named Hanno Ehses. He was pushing the study of semiotics at a time when nobody had applied it to graphic design and students were appalled to be studying rhetoric. But it was a really great course and a great way of thinking about design and understanding how to communicate using visual language, and that had a big influence on how I looked at design and the purposes of design as a communication tool.
—**Rhonda Rubenstein**

I would have to say that my husband, Etienne Delessert, has been a huge influence because of his connections to the European market. Through him I've been able to work with French publishers, Italian publishers — all sorts — so that now I can recognize and appreciate book design across cultures.
—**Rita Marshall**

I have to say it was having Walter Bernard as my first boss. He operates with such wisdom and skill and intelligence that he becomes a model for how you conduct yourself.
—**Tom Bentkowski**

I went to a theater school within my high school and we produced everything from the most outrageous New York happenings by Alan Caprow to *Macbeth*, from Ionesco to little-known Canadian playwrights. Having experienced the breadth of all of that, creating costumes and stage managing and producing and writing and directing and acting and having done all those roles, I come back again and again to the fundamental of theater, which is that communicating is a human endeavor.
—**David Peters**

Modernism, postmodernism, classicism, Bauhaus, and Thomas Jefferson.
—**Michael Vanderbyl**

Above all, the greatest influence on my work has been my working with my peers during the early years in Seattle. It was a collaborative, exciting period supplemented by an increasing knowledge of particular historical periods, specifically the publication and poster design of the 1930s–1950s.
—**Helene Silverman**

In many ways, designing typefaces has provided me an excuse to spend time looking at historical typefaces. Increasingly, I'm finding that I'm not influenced by the look of a historical typeface but wonder about the thinking behind it. It's usually a theoretical underpinning that precipitates a new design rather than merely the look of something old.
—**Jonathan Hoefler**

Posters, Beardsley, Wesselmann.
—**John Martinez**

Everything I touch, see, smell, hear, and experience is subject to use in my work. The same is true for everyone I encounter. I believe this to be true for everyone, whether we are conscious of it or not.

—Sharoz Makarechi

Some designers who I admired greatly haven't really worked in the same area. They're figures whom I'd heard about from my father, his heroes whom I adopted. I'm thinking of Cassandre, particularly, the famous French poster designer. And then later, other European designers, such as Massin, the French book designer. One of the better-known works of Massin is a version of Ionesco's play *The Bald Primadonna*, I think. He translated it into an absolutely amazing visual equivalent of the play itself.

—Richard Eckersley

I'd have to say Tom Ryan in Nashville. Certainly, he was the guy that taught me the ropes and enabled me to come to New York and have a portfolio that people would pay attention to. Other than that, a professor by the name of Charlie Marler who gave me the inspiration to become a designer and to go off and pursue this thing even after a liberal arts degree.

—Kent Hunter

When I first got involved with type (over forty years ago), it was still a mechanical industry in which the designing of type was separate from its manufacture. Since then, a succession of technical changes — photocomposition, digital type, desktop type — has progressively reunited the two things, designing and making, so it is now once again possible, as it was in type's early centuries, for one person to be both type designer and font maker. This development, the return of the punch-cutter as auteur, blessed by the coming of open font formats, has probably had the greatest influence on how I work and consequently on what I do.

—Matthew Carter

My graduate work at Yale clearly prepared me for the professional practice that I have undertaken since founding Two Twelve Associates in 1980. My two co-founding partners, Sylvia Harris and Juanita Dugdale, were great teachers and colleagues who helped nurture me through the trials of establishing a design practice in New York City.

—David B. Gibson

Everything influences my work.

—Abi Aron Spencer

Major influences are people who do what they do with a distinctive sensibility. Animator Richard Williams's dedication to resurrecting animation has been an influence. My father, Joe Sedelmaier, a live-action director and filmmaker who is involved in every aspect of the filmmaking process, has been an influence. Classic comedians like Keaton, Laurel and Hardy, and the Marx Brothers are also reflected in stuff I do.

—J.J. Sedelmaier

No specific influences other than the classic Swiss style practitioners of the 1960s and, ironically, the entertainment industry in the 1990s.

—Wayne Hunt

My earliest influences, aside from both my parents, were Ella Fitzgerald and Oscar Peterson, both of whom I heard around the house. At high school, I was lucky. I had one art teacher who was a fine artist and another who was a jazz musician. Willie Rodger introduced me and the half dozen other hopefuls in my class to something that wasn't easily found at home — art. Not as a series of watercolor exercises, guaranteeing the emulation of a particular style, but from the heart, as an exercise in seeing, thinking, and feeling.

—Bob Appleton

My dad always had subscriptions to *Graphis*, *Print*, and *The Push Pin Graphic*, so these books were always around. I grew up reading comic books and my Uncle Joe showed me underground comics — he showed me R. Crumb and EC comics from the 1950s. As for design, Peter Girardi opened up the 1940s and 1950s for me — Rand, Beall, Sutnar, Thompson, Burtin, Brodovitch. There was *Raw* magazine, Gary Panter, the fine art world, record jacket art, cartoons, graffiti art — the list goes on.

—Chris Capuozzo

In any creative endeavor, I think you learn to continually be inspired and influenced by people, and you keep that part of your heart open. I come from a mentor tradition that doesn't exist much today. I luckily stumbled onto people who are great. I also sought out people who are great and clung to them and hung out near them. My father said to me, many years ago, "Hang out with people who are brighter and smarter than you and they'll drag you up with them," and that has actually been the truth.

—Michael Patrick Cronan

Design history is an endless source of inspiration and learning, as is the work of contemporary designers. Because design is a cultural activity, all of the other creative practices, like art, music, literature, and film, also influence graphic designers' work. How could it not?

—Jeffery Keedy

My first love in typefaces was Palatino, which made me want to learn as much as I could about Hermann Zapf and his approach to design. This in turn led me to discover the work (and lives) of Eric Gill and Frederic Goudy. Roger Black's work in the *Rolling Stone* era had a tremendously liberating influence on me. The freedom to let things clash and the discovery of forgotten historical design treasures (typefaces and ornaments) was very liberating. Of course, I was aware of the early film work of Saul Bass, who showed how to strip an idea down to its essence.

—Randall Balsmeyer

The USC School of Architecture was an incredible influence. They taught me how to visualize and make presentations. They taught me to respect professionalism.

—Mike Salisbury

I studied with a graphic design guru, Armin Hofmann, and apprenticed with a master, Otl Aicher. Those two personalities, combined with the spirit of the 1960s youth movement, constitute the major influence on my work as a graphic designer and teacher.

—Robert Probst

The first thing to give my work context was the rave movement, which hit the southern United States around 1990 (we're always behind). After that, I took a cue from Chicago street artists (shortly after I moved here). Currently, I'm really into disposable consumer culture.

—Patric King

Teachers: Hugo Weber, Misch Kohn at the Institute of Design; Franz Kline, Merce Cunningham, and John Cage at Black Mountain College. Environment and students and interaction with avant-garde arts in Chicago. Modernism. Previously, my two years studying painting, literature, history, French, and symbolic logic at Bard College. Later influences: the Eames, Sandro Girard, international populist arts, and streetscapes.

—Deborah Sussman

Fine art has been a huge influence on my design, and I think that we're at a point at the end of the twentieth century where there is a huge criss-crossing of design and fine art. I go to museums all the time — I'm always looking at what fine artists do.

—**Janet Froelich**

My teacher, Armin Hofmann, had by far the most influence on me. Also my entire education, deeply rooted in drawing, taught me a discipline that has guided me throughout my career. Out of the up to 56 studio hours per week, perhaps more than half were drawing classes.

—**Steff Geisbuhler**

The strongest influence in my life was the modern movement as interpreted by LeCorbusier, Mies van der Rohe, the Bauhaus, the Swiss graphic designers like Müller Brockman, Max Bill, and Max Huber as well as designers like Nizzoli, Ray and Charles Eames, Dieter Rams, and many others, all people I was fortunate to know personally and from whom I learned to be what I am. It was not just their style but their commitments to design, society, and ethics that I admired.

—**Massimo Vignelli**

Back at the beginning, I was trying to be cool and do cool rock 'n' roll work. I was into the whole illegible layering thing. But then I realized that what I was really being asked to do was deliver information; the secondary aim was to elicit an emotional response like "That's cool." At a certain point I realized that while it is cool to be cool, it is not cool to be cool at the expense of communication. Above all, graphic design is about communication. When graphic design also stirs emotions in the brain of the beholder, then that is the postmodern bonus.

—**Chester**

My heroes are the big 1980s artists — Cindy Sherman, Barbara Kruger, Jenny Holtzer. The fine art works that I was doing at that time had a sensationalist quality that was commercial, in a sense, and very design-oriented. I was incorporating text but also using, for lack of a better word, gimmicks to capture the viewer.

—**Michael Ian Kaye**

I was fortunate enough to work for Paula Scher at Pentagram. A good college education is one thing, but seeing how it's done from start to finish, year after year, at a good design firm, is invaluable.

—**Ron Louie**

For as long as I can remember, I have looked up to Neville Brody and Rick Valicenti. Back then I thought they were doing great stuff, and I still do. But the influence was much, much bigger than a particular person. I was influenced by the Japanese market with regard to imagery and how they communicate.

—**Carlos Segura**

Everything influences me. Films, books, music from Bach to the Beatles, newspapers — there is nothing that somehow, in some way, doesn't enter my work. If you're alive, the world has to enter and influence you almost osmotically.

—**R.O. Blechman**

I really learned how to design from watching my mom cook. She was a great cook. She could walk into her kitchen and, in ten minutes, put together the most fantastic meal. I learned how to design that way. It was very spontaneous. That's how I work. I'm very intuitive. For me, the best designs always come out when I have my favorite ingredients around, and then I pick from that.

—**Yolanda Cuomo**

Design **Client:**
Exhibitor Magazine
Year: 1998

Design

Education

A generation ago, one could convincingly argue that art or design school was not necessary to a good graphic design education. On-the-job experience was a more than adequate means of acquiring necessary skills — and, after all, talent is inborn. Today, the self-taught graphic designer is unusual. Even with all the how-to books on the market, those who acquire their interest in graphic design through working on the personal computer or through other art fields definitely require intensive training, if only to be fluent in the computer. But in order to go beyond rote computer applications to make really smart graphic design, a formal education is strongly recommended. A fundamental graphic design education can begin as early as high school. Desktop publishing at this grade level provides an intro-duction to the rudimentary tools and basic forms of print and screen design. Teach-ing kids how to design editorial and advertising pages and Web sites is an excellent way to get them interested in visual communications and it also serves as a primer for what follows. The next step is to find a two- or, better yet, four-year undergradu-ate program at an art college or general university that offers a Bachelor of Fine Arts (BFA) or equivalent degree. This is not to imply that a liberal arts education is to be ignored; liberal arts is a prerequisite that must be pursued in tandem with design instruction. However, these days, two years is barely enough time to learn the tools, theory, history, and practice of graphic design as well as to develop a marketable port-folio. Of course, as four or more years in art or design school may be impossible for some and excessive for others, continuing education is also an option. For those with the desire and wherewithal, a graduate school education can be very beneficial.

A few people possess a natural gift for graphic design and, with only a modicum of training, might turn into significant designers. But they are exceptions to the rule. Untutored designers usually produce untutored design. Although good formal edu-cation does not make anyone more talented, it does provide a strong foundation upon which to grow into a professional. While taking the occasional design class is better than no schooling at all, matriculation in a dedicated course of study, where you are bombarded with design problems and forced to devise solutions, yields much better results.

What should you look for in a two-year, four-year, or continuing education design program? The following is a gen-eral guide to undergraduate, graduate, and part-time education programs.

Who's Going to School?

There are an estimated 2300 schools (two and four years) with dedicated and ancil-lary graphic design programs graduating about 50,000 students each year. Each year more schools are adopting some kind graphic design program that ranges from basic instruction of computer programs (Quark, Photoshop) to advanced typogra-phy and layout.

Undergraduate

NOT EVERY HIGH school graduate knows what graphic design is. Because design is considered something of an arcane profession, most guidance counselors do not vigorously promote it as a viable career option. Prospective design students should examine the programs of as many schools as possible. Those who go to design school are introduced to graphic design, among other arts and crafts, during the foundation year. This is a time when many design and art forms are sampled prior to the student's selection of a major. Those art college students who are transfers from liberal arts programs likely go through the foundation year with everyone else (unless they specify otherwise and show a specific interest in graphic design).

Whether you decide on a dedicated art school or a state or private university art department does not matter (financial and location concerns often dictate this decision). More important is knowing the strengths and weaknesses of the chosen program. The fundamental instruction in the second year sets the tone for those to follow. Here are the areas to examine.

COMPUTER. While some design courses offer instruction in computer programs after more basic conceptual and formal issues are addressed, others dive right into the tool as vital to design practice. It does not really matter at what point the computer is taught (although most agree that it is better to understand the theory of design before attempting its practice), but computer skills must be keenly supported through individual and laboratory instruction throughout the duration of the program. It is further recommended that students have home computers or laptops so that they can practice often.

THEORY. Understanding what design is and how it works in both a philosophical and practical context is more important than doing the work, at least at the outset. If a student does not know what design is used for, how it functions, and at whom it is aimed, then making marks on paper or screen is fruitless. Graphic design is not a self-motivated fine art, and although the lessons of art may be integrated, communications theory in its various forms (semiotics, semantics, deconstruction, and so on) are the essential components of a well-rounded design education.

CONCEPT. Design is not decoration but rather the intelligent solution of conceptual problems; it is the manipulation of type, image, and, most of all, an idea that conveys a message. A strong design program emphasizes conception — developing big ideas — as a key component of the curriculum. Concept courses should include two- and three-dimensional design in all the media covered in Section 1.

TYPE. This is one of the primary means by which civilization communicates. A type font is not just something that comes installed in a computer. Classes in type and typography should, therefore, begin with the history of letterforms from the fifteenth century to the present — the art and craft behind them and the reasons that type conventions exist. The application of type past and present, in various media, and the purposes for which types and type families have been used should be covered. Type instruction should include a range of endeavor from metal typefounding to digital fontography. Once type has been fully addressed, typography — the design of typefaces on the page or screen context — should be thoroughly examined as both a reading and a display vehicle. Any study of typography should include intense debate about its function — legibility versus illegibility.

IMAGE. Design is about image making, and a well-rounded program includes classes devoted to photography, typo-foto (the marriage of type and picture), and illustration. Certain courses emphasize computer programs such as Photoshop, and these are indeed necessary. But a good program puts computer-generated art into perspective and, therefore, devotes more class time to traditional forms.

ADVERTISING. Some design departments segregate advertising and graphic design; others integrate the two. It is, however, useful for the graphic designer — even if book jackets or record covers are the intended specialty — to learn the techniques that go into this very public medium.

HISTORY. Most design departments are not equipped to offer more than survey courses on aspects of design history. Nevertheless, this is an integral part of design education that should continue throughout the program (and not as an elective, either). It is essential to know that graphic design has a history, and to be familiar with the building blocks of the continuum.

MULTIMEDIA. The volume of cross-disciplinary endeavor that affects designers today is only going to grow in the future. While the better part of a four-year program is devoted to training a student to design in the print or Web environment, knowledge of other media — film, television, video — is not only useful but can also be inspiring.

PRINTING. How can you design without knowing the means of production? For a designer, being detached from the printing press is like being a doctor who never interned on a human being. Now that much prepress production is in the hands of the designer, knowledge of the final output process is more vital than ever.

BUSINESS. At the undergraduate level, few schools focus on the business of design in terms of starting a studio or firm, and all that it entails. Most design schools are concerned with developing the skills that lead to marketable portfolios, and energies are aimed at helping students get internships or jobs. Prudently, they do not encourage neophytes to start businesses immediately out of school. Nonetheless, business is an important aspect of the profession, so even if developing business plans and spreadsheets is inappropriate at this level, courses that address general business concerns are useful.

PORTFOLIO. The most important concrete result of a well-rounded education is the portfolio. Classes in how to develop portfolios usually begin in the senior year, when the student is given real-world problems in various media with the goal of creating a strong representation of talent and skill. A diploma is important, but the portfolio is evidence that a student earned it.

PLACEMENT. Schools with reputable internship programs are invaluable. Many programs have established relationships with studios, firms, and corporations throughout the United States and, often, the world. These schools place students and graduates in many working situations and monitor their development. Experience from these internships or temporary jobs (which may start in the sophomore year) is priceless and, on occasion, they lead to full-time positions. Good placement offices also keep job-bank notices and help the students prepare for these opportunities.

FACULTY. Let's not forget the teachers. A strong faculty is what makes all these programs work. Some schools maintain full-time faculty; others use professional faculty (part-time teachers who work full-time as designers, art directors, creative directors, etc.). Both situations are equally good. The value ultimately comes down to the individual. Inspiring teachers make the difference. Find out who they are.

Graduate School

A GENERATION AGO, only a few elite graduate schools offered programs devoted to graphic design. Today, quite a few two-year programs address aspects of the design profession. Graduate education is not for everybody, but it has become a viable means of developing areas of expertise that were ignored or deficient in most undergraduate schools. The Masters of Fine Arts (MFA), Master of Arts (MA), and Associate degree, which are the typical terminal degrees from graduate programs, are not necessary to obtain jobs or commissions (although if you want to teach at a university, the degree is usually mandatory), but they do indicate accomplishment: The designer has completed a rigorous course of study. For those interested in intensive instruction, the graduate school experience can be highly beneficial in creative and practical ways.

Graduate school is, however, a major investment in time and money. The average tuition is between $19,000 to 21,000. Some schools insist that students devote the majority of their time to school-related work; others are scheduled so that students can work at regular jobs or on commissions while attending evening classes.

Eligibility for graduate programs varies. All candidates must have bachelor or other degrees from undergraduate institutions (these need not always be design degrees). A few exceptions are made for work/time equivalency. Some programs accept all graduates immediately after graduating a four-year undergraduate art or design school; others seek out students who have been working professionally for a year or more prior to returning to school. Portfolios and interviews are usually required, and the portfolios must include school or professional work that shows distinct talent and aptitude. Some entry requirements are more lax than others, but if the portfolio is deficient — if the prospective student shows nothing, for example, but mediocre desktop publishing work — additional training and practice is recommended before reapplying. Graduate programs are open to applicants of all ages who meet the entry requirements. Graduate school is a viable means for those who want to switch careers or to achieve greater proficiency and credentials.

If a prospective student meets all the eligibility requirements, the next step is to explore programmatic options to determine which school is appropriate to the specific educational need. Possibilities are numerous. Some programs are fairly free-form, where teachers guide a student along a self-motivated course of study. Others are more rigidly structured, with a set of specific goals to attain by the end of each study period (which may be a semester or more). Some programs are geared toward specialties; others are more general in scope. Among the specialties are corporate design, advertising design, and Internet design. A number of programs have philosophical and stylistic preferences, while others avoid ideology of any kind. Some are concerned with social activism, while others are devoted to the commercial marketplace. Some programs are better endowed than others.

Most programs have a cap on how many students are accepted annually. It is recommended that prospective students request literature from programs and visit those that are of most interest (some have open houses, others grant tours). Applicants commonly apply to more than one program, although each may require different materials. The following are programmatic concerns that should be explored before applying:

SCOPE. A graduate program is advanced study, not simply an extension of undergraduate school. While a curriculum may include components that overlap an undergraduate or continuing education course, it must go way beyond what is provided at these lower levels. When looking at a prospectus or talking with a graduate school admissions officer, determine the scope and goals of the program and the expectations it has of its students.

PHILOSOPHY. This is related to scope but demands its own category. A graduate program may require that students adhere to a particular pedagogical concept. This can be anything from minimalist (modern) to complex (deconstruction) design, or classical, or avant garde, or any other approach. It could be based on a certain iconoclasm or eclecticism. Whatever the philosophy may be, decide by talking to former students and teachers about its compatibility with your own attitudes.

TRADITION. Contemporary graphic design is as much about understanding the past as it is about diving into the future. While undergraduates are wrapped up in technology and processes that will allow them to get jobs immediately upon graduation, graduate programs should allow for greater reflection. A well-balanced program encourages students to work with their hands as well as their machines. It has a strong historical component that can be, in some way, integrated into contemporary practice.

TECHNOLOGY. A graduate program should be state-of-the-art. The design world is becoming inextricably connected to the multimedia environment, and while tradition is an important component of design pedagogy, advanced knowledge of the tools of production and creation is becoming requisite. If you are interested in becoming a producer or director as well as a designer, select a program that addresses these needs. Most contemporary graduate programs spend at least 50 percent, if not more, of class time on technological concerns, and have the hardware and labs to support thorough study.

MULTIDISCIPLINES. Graphic design graduate programs cannot afford to be specialized to the point of isolation. The more relationships with other media and genres are explored the better, even if only in survey courses.

FACILITIES. Undergraduate education is a string of related classes in a supportive environment, but graduate schools should provide facilities that encourage students to work in a more focused environment, both separately and in tandem with others. Facilities may include small studios or networked workstations in an integrated studio setting. It is important to know how you work best and in what kind of context. Some programs encourage the open studio; others simulate a design firm environment. The location of the plant is also important — for example, its proximity to other institutions or businesses. Although the graduate experience means, for some, an escape from the rigors of the quotidian, for others, it is a way to be integrated into everyday life.

FACULTY. A program is only as good as its teachers. Some graduate programs pride themselves on employing the leading practitioners in the field; others rely on full-time professors. Balancing the two is usually a good solution. In most course descriptions, the faculty members are listed along with their credentials. These should be seriously studied.

EXHIBITION. Most graduate programs are concerned that student work be tested and, ultimately, published and exhibited. Although what a student learns is most important, the quality of the results is evidence of a program's effectiveness. It is useful to examine both the means of presenting student work and the work itself. Publications are available to applicants, as are schedules of student exhibitions.

RESPONSIBILITY. A graduate program may be considered a cloistered existence. Increasingly, however, this is an opportunity for students to do the kinds of socially responsible projects that may less frequently be options in the workaday world. It is important to explore how a program contributes to the broader community.

BUSINESS. Even in a cloister, the real world must have a place, and the graduate school is indeed a good place to examine the business world. Graduate students are more likely than undergraduates to open their own businesses once they have earned their degrees. Design management and property law are important areas of concern at this level.

THESIS. The primary degree requirement is the final thesis. It is important to know what each graduate program expects of its students and how it goes about developing student thesis projects. What is involved in this process? Are there thesis classes, faculty advisers, review committees? Must the thesis be published? Ultimately, the thesis can be a portfolio or a key to a new career.

Continuing Education

GRADUATE SCHOOL is not feasible for those who must work at full-time jobs or who choose to obtain specific skills as a means to widen their career path. Therefore, the most common method of developing additional skills (and receiving inspiration) is through continuing education, also called night school. Some general colleges and universities offer programs, but usually it is the province of the art and design schools and colleges to offer a wide range of professional courses, from introductory to advanced. In addition to a potpourri of nightschool professional courses, some institutions offer intensive weeklong workshops with master teachers. Some of these programs are designed exclusively for working professionals (and require a fairly accomplished portfolio as a condition of acceptance), while others are open to a broader public.

Enrollees in continuing education classes run the gamut from professionals who seek to better themselves (maybe to earn promotions in their current workplaces) to neophytes who want additional career options. Classes are available for any level of expertise and are useful in acquiring knowledge, experience, and, in some cases, job opportunities.

Obviously, reputable continuing education programs are best, and they are usually offered by art and design schools. Most computer tutorials are useful, particularly as insight into common layout, illustration, photography, and graphics programs (many older professionals use these sessions to learn or brush up on new skills). A current trend is weeklong regional seminars run by either professional organizations or independent educational groups. The only rule of thumb for a potential student is select a program that meets all needs based on the description or prospectus that is made available. Nevertheless, the financial investment is usually limited and, therefore, if a particular course does not offer enough useful or inspirational instruction, one can always try another. Still, the best continuing education programs are those that employ reputable professionals and offer a fair amount of hands-on work. Before you decide, carefully read and compare the catalogs.

Training for the Workplace

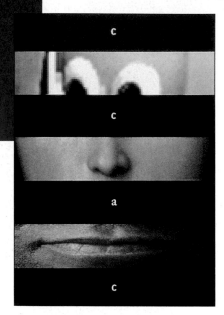

MICHAEL VANDERBYL

Principal, Vanderbyl Design, San Francisco;
Dean, Design Department, California College
of Arts and Crafts, San Francisco

Title: California College of Arts
and Crafts Catalog **Designer/
Creative Director:** Michael
Vanderbyl **Firm:** Vanderbyl
Design **Client:** California
College of Arts and Crafts
Photographers: David Peterson,
Todd Hido **Typefaces:** Agara-
mond, Officina **Year:** 1998

What is the purpose of your design program?
To train artists and designers who will contribute to and change
our culture.

How do you prepare students for the workforce?
We don't try to prepare them as a trade school might; training for
the workplace can be dangerous. Instead, we try to equip them
with the skills they need to reinvent themselves, to adapt to the
needs of commerce, and to preserve themselves as artists.

What do you expect them to learn from your program?
A respect for history and research, the ability to think on a broader
cultural plane, and an awareness of their work and influences. Also,
we hope that they will be able to find work that nurtures them as
human beings while solving someone else's problems. Furthermore,
they should be able to constantly reinvent their work themselves.

What makes a good student?
Passion and a broad base of education, especially in those seeking
a second degree.

**What is the single most important skill a designer needs to be
successful?**
Reinvention.

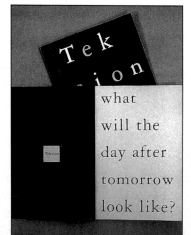

Title: Teknion Concept
Brochure **Designer/ Creative
Director:** Michael Vanderbyl
Firm: Vanderbyl Design
Client: Teknion **Photogra-
pher:** Geof Kern **Typefaces:**
Agaramond, ocrb **Year:** 1997

Title: Robert Talbott New York Retail Store **Designer/ Creative Director:** Michael Vanderbyl **Firm:** Vanderbyl Design **Client:** Robert Talbott **Year:** 1993

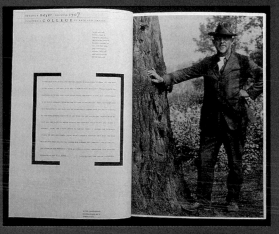

Title: California College of Arts and Crafts Catalog **Designer/ Creative Director:** Michael Vanderbyl **Firm:** Vanderbyl Design **Client:** California College of Arts and Crafts **Photographers:** David Peterson, Todd Hido **Typefaces:** Agaramond, Officina **Year:** 1998

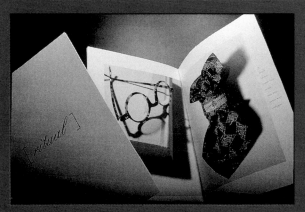

Title: Ritual (annual product brochure) **Designer/Creative Director:** Michael Vanderbyl **Firm:** Vanderbyl Design **Client:** Robert Talbott **Photographer:** David Peterson **Typeface:** Agaramond **Year:** 1998

Hard Work, Good Education

Title: CBS Cable Logo
Designer: Sheila Levrant
de Bretteville **Assistant:**
Jerry Kuyper **Client:** CBS
Photographer: Jerry
Kuyper **Year:** 1983

SHEILA LEVRANT DE BRETTEVILLE
Chair, Yale University Graduate Program in
Graphic Design, New Haven, Connecticut

What is the purpose of your program?
To provide students with the personal, intellectual, and technological support and challenges that will enable them to do the
work they want to do. The committed faculty, the quality of community in our studios, Yale University's libraries, lectures, and
courses, and citizenship in the city of New Haven all provide an
extraordinary banquet of experience for each student to draw
upon for his own unique body of work.

How do you prepare students for the workforce?
They come prepared for the workforce in that the workforce
expects only that you work hard. They go out with a body of work
that is their own, with all the skills any studio would be glad to
have and enough sense of their own worth to play a role in moving the profession forward.

How have technological advancements affected your work?
Each project I do involves different technologies and, for that
reason, I work with different folk for each technology I need.

Title: Path of (worker) Stars
Designer: Sheila Levrant de
Bretteville **Client:** McCor-
mack Baron/The Related
Companies **Photographer:**
Michael Morand **Typefaces:**
Nobel Condensed and
Regular **Year:** 1993

Title: Biddy Mason: Time & Place
Designer: Sheila Levrant de Bretteville
Client: Community Redevelopment Agency, Los Angeles, Power of Place
Photographer: Annette del Zoppo
Typeface: Goudy
Year: 1990

Title: Moving Introductions (film titles exhibition)
Exhibition Designer/Curator: Sheila Levrant de Bretteville **Catalog Authors:** Sheila Levrant de Bretteville, Barbara Bloom **Client:** Otis Institute of Art and Design Gallery **Photographer:** Alfonso Nodal **Typeface:** Univers **Year:** 1983

Title: Omoide no Shotokyo **Designer/Researcher/Author:** Sheila Levrant de Bretteville **Client:** Community Redevelopment Agency, Los Angeles **Photographer:** Annette del Zoppo **Typefaces:** Futura, Times Roman, Galliard **Year:** 1990–1997

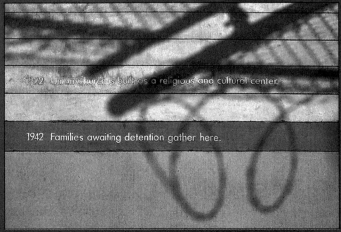

Experiencing Experience

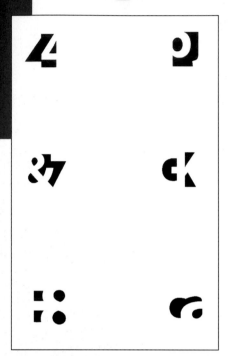

Title: Form and Counterform
Designer/Art Director/Illustrator: Yu-Wen Chen, Parsons Design & Technology MFA student **Client:** student work created for the Digital Typography course **Instructor:** Andrea Dezso **Year:** 2001

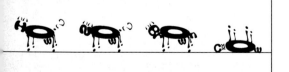

Title: Mad Cow Disease
Designer/Art Director/Illustrator: Rahul Siddharth, Parsons Design and Technology MFA student **Client:** student work created for the Digital Typography course **Instructor:** Andrea Dezso **Year:** 2001

ANDREA DEZSO
Digital Design Department, Parsons School of Design, New York

What is experience design?
Experience design is a complex design field for interactive media that integrates cognitive design, structural design (a.k.a. information architecture), visual design, editorial design, technical design (front-end coding), sound design, and motion design (a.k.a. multimedia). In the case of a Web site, cognitive and structural designers define what should be on the site and how the content areas should be divided. Visual designers create the visual communication, including the look and feel and information design. Editorial designers define the specific voice of the site and generate content. Sound designers create sonic identities and motion designers design animated components. Technical designers do all the front-end production, coding, and facilitate back-end (engineering, heavy programming, databases) integration. An experience designer can have one or several areas of expertise.

How do you teach experience design to design students?
I encourage my students to always thoroughly understand the media and its craft (whether the assignment is a book or an interactive digital interface) and the full context of their design. Who are they designing for? What purpose will the design serve? But especially because my design and technology students are less familiar with design and more familiar with technology, I also encourage them to play— and through playful exercises they quickly become familiar with the elements of design and typography.

What must a design student grasp to be a good experience designer?
First of all, the design student has to have all the skills that make a good designer in general. The student has to master the craft of design, including a solid grounding in visual communication, typography, color, composition, and style, and to be a proficient user of a range of design software. I believe that it's important for a student to have an understanding of art, design, and architec-

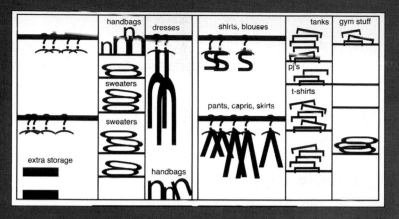

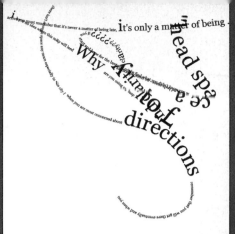

ture in the context of history and society and an awareness of the current discourse in design and culture.

What differentiates print from screen design?
Verba volant scripta manent. A printed page stays the way it was designed for eternity. A Web site, on the other hand, is a fluid construction. It allows the viewer to modify the design in many ways. Alter the default font or increase the size of the font on your browser and you will see the page completely differently than it was designed. Screen size and resolution, different types and generations of browsers, different color settings on monitors, T1 line versus 56K modem, all determine what the user experiences. Designers have to get used to working under a different set of limitations and possibilities than those for designing for print to create successful designs for an interactive environment.

That said, it is also important that the designer can work as part of an integrated team with designers from other backgrounds, engineers and businesspeople, in order to deliver the desired experience. Experience designers cannot be lonely creators. Because the work is so complex and there are usually many simultaneous workstreams that heavily depend on each other, there is a strong need for proximity.

Can a student be a viable graphic designer without knowledge of the new technologies?
I believe that for long-term viability, a graphic designer has to be familiar with the technologies relevant to her area, whatever area that might be.

As an experience designer, I believe in the same principle. The designer needs to know what is available, what is possible, and how things are set in motion. I don't need to be able to code or program myself, but I need to have an understanding of what technology is currently available and what its implications for design are. That these technologies are constantly evolving and changing makes keeping up more difficult than in other, more established design fields, but not less necessary.

ABOVE, left: Title: A Map of My Closet **Designer/Art Director/Illustrator:** Claudia Sondakh, Parsons Design and Technology MFA student **Client:** student work created for the Digital Typography course **Instructor:** Andrea Dezso **Year:** 2001

ABOVE, right: Title: Mood Map **Designer/Art Director/Illustrator:** Emily Shaw, Parsons Design and Technology MFA student **Client:** student work created for the Digital Typography course **Instructor:** Andrea Dezso **Year:** 2001

ABOVE: Title: Type Beasts **Designer/Art Director/Illustrator:** Michele Dubois, Parsons Design and Technology MFA student **Client:** student work created for the Digital Typography course **Instructor:** Andrea Dezso **Year:** 2001

Diverse Interests

Title: UMD Jazz Program poster/mailing cards **Designers:** Dan Baggenstoss, Amanda Groff **Photographers:** Dan Baggenstoss, Amanda Groff **School:** University of Minnesota, Duluth **Instructor:** Gunnar Swanson **Year:** 1996

Title: illustration for article about George magazine **Illustrator:** Timothy Gow **School:** University of Minnesota, Duluth **Instructor:** Gunnar Swanson **Year:** 1997

GUNNAR SWANSON
Teacher of graphic design, typography, graphic design history, and multimedia, Ventura, California

Is there a difference between digital design and traditional design? If so, what?
There are differences between design for screens and design for paper, but there are also differences between design for paper you walk past (like a poster), paper you glance at (like direct mail ads), and paper you study (like novels or science books.)

I don't know what's "traditional" in design anymore. Predigital? Today's college students were in kindergarten when I started using a computer for most of my design work. It's impossible to imagine today's world without computers, so I don't think I can compare.

As a veteran design teacher, how has the new technology altered how you teach?
Just as in the design business, students are now expected to produce finished work earlier in the process than they might have in the past—color prints rather than sketches, animations rather than storyboards. . . . We lose a lot because of this, but we gain a lot, too. There's also more to understand technically, so it's hard to resist dwelling on technical issues.

Is it mandatory for students to learn how to design for the Web? Can a student survive in today's industry without knowing and understanding Web-based technology?
There's no one thing that everyone should do. You could have a long graphic design career and never design a package or have a long career designing only packages. That said, you're at a competitive disadvantage if you don't have some Web and interactive experience, especially starting out.

How would you define a balanced education?
People with diverse interests are more likely to be interesting people and interesting people are more likely to be interesting designers, but there is no single balance.

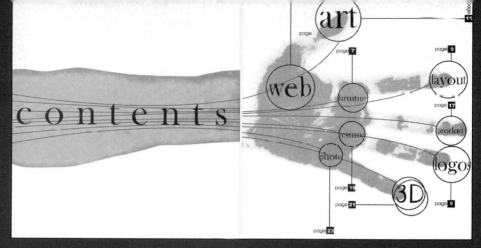

Title: portfolio booklet spreads **Designer:** Ian Brewer **School:** University of California, Davis **Instructor:** Gunnar Swanson **Year:** 1999

What qualities do you look for in students today?

I've never really chosen my students, so I look for the qualities they have and try to do something worthwhile with those. If the question is "what qualities allow me to help someone become a good designer?" then I'd have to say that I'd rather have a student who is smart than one who is more facile and visually talented; I'd rather have one who is hardworking than one who is smart. The best students— the ones with a good eye, an analytical tendency, a love of graphic design, and the drive to be good—are probably going to do well without us.

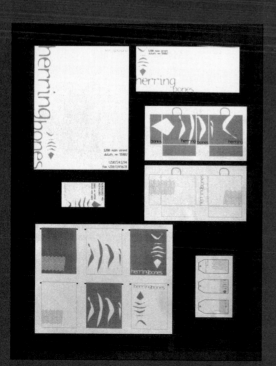

LEFT: Title: Herringbones (gift shop) ID program **Designer:** Kim Gaspard **School:** University of Minnesota, Duluth **Instructor:** Gunnar Swanson **Year:** 1997

Title: Boxer Rebellion (underwear) ID/packaging **Designer:** Amy Regis **School:** University of Minnesota, Duluth **Instructor:** Gunnar Swanson **Year:** 1997

Title: portfolio Web site **Designer:** Art Miller **School:** California Lutheran University **Instructor:** Gunnar Swanson **Year:** 2001

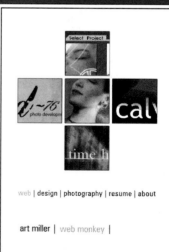

Designer as Entrepreneur

LITA TALARICO
Cochair, MFA/Design, School of Visual Arts,
New York City

What is your definition of designer as author?
The designer as author is someone who not only controls the design
— from beginning through end— but develops the content, either
alone or in tandem with a creative team. The reason the SVA/MFA
program is called "The Designer as Author" is because we believe
designers must be in a position to contribute more than aesthetics;
they should be creators, implementers, producers.

**Not all students want to be authors. How does this program
make them better designers?**
The program is an opportunity for students to explore their creativity and find different ways to express it. It is a two-year
exploration whereby the students work with a variety of media
with the goal of authoring in each one. This does not imply that
they will never work for someone else again, but they will definitely have more confidence in their ability as thinking designers.
Also, because they work in various media, the students gain
knowledge of how these processes work, which will allow them to
collaborate more closely with the engineer of a Web site or the
director of a TV show. They can choose to be sole creators or collaborators.

Title: Backflip **Designer:** Katy
Kennedy **School:** School of
Visual Arts - MFA/Design
Project: MFA Thesis, on-line
gallery devoted to artists' books
Year: 2001

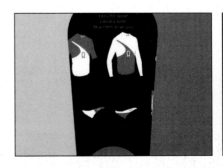

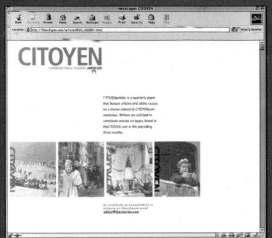

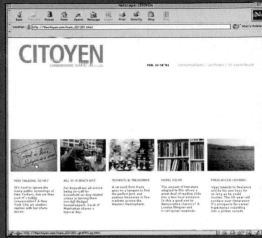

What skills and talents must MFA students have when they enter your program?

Generally, students must have either an undergraduate degree in graphic design or one to two years professional experience. However, because we are a multidisciplinary program, we encourage students from other disciplines, such as film and architecture to apply. In order for these students to be able to do the course work, we identify various courses they must take simultaneously, such as advanced typography. But we expect our students to give as much to the program as they take.

What experiences should they have when they graduate your program?

They should feel empowered to make things. Their thesis is a product that can (and sometimes should) go to market. Whatever they do after graduation, they will have this equity.

What do you look for in a student?

Understanding of the visual language and the desire to use this fluency in unique and individual ways. But what we really demand is that they are committed to contributing something of value to the culture.

Title: CITOYEN commentaries/ diaries/articles **Designer:** Tania Mailangkay **School:** School Of Visual Arts - MFA/Design **Project:** MFA Thesis devoted to worldwide forum **Year:** 2001

Title: Rayrider Web site **Designer:** Rire Nakpodia **School:** School of Visual Arts - MFA/Design **Project:** MFA Thesis devoted to Rayrider Boogie Boards **Year:** 2001

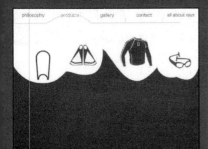

Ideas and Information

A THOUSAND PEOPLE IN THE STREET

Title: Sunset Strip **Designer/
Photographer/Director/
Illustrator:** Peter Bergeron, BFA
4 **School:** CalArts, Valencia, CA
Instructor: Anne Burdick
Year: 2000

Title: Typo Space **Designer:**
Joey Alviar, MFA 2 **School:**
CalArts, Valencia, CA **Instruc-
tors:** Tom Bland, Ed Fella, Jeff
Keedy, Lorraine Wild **Year:** 2001

LOUISE SANDHAUS
Codirector, Graphic Design Program,
CalArts, Valencia, California

**How has the integration of motion and sound changed the way
you teach design?**
Design is still about giving structure to ideas and information, so
in that sense, nothing has changed. However, motion and sound
add complexity as well as possibility to the structuring. Because
the sound often drives the timing and becomes the heartbeat of a
motion work, the structure often needs to have some sort of relationship driven by the sound. That means designers have to think
in aural structuring simultaneously with visual/information structuring while considering the connotative aspects of sound as well.
No small task, but again the important thing to stress is structure
and connotation, both nothing new for designers.

Is there any particular emphasis in teaching design today?
Words, the look of words, images, movement, behavior interaction,
sound: these are the elements with which communication takes
place today and, thus, the fundamentals of contemporary design
education. I've been thinking about the basics of visual literacy
and considering that perhaps these basics need to be updated for
dynamic environments (or maybe someone's already done this). Of
course, then one begins to wonder about the potential of education overload: How much can one designer can not only know, but
also develop enough proficiency in to be useful?

Is the Web about storytelling?
Storytelling, or I'd rather refer to it as *narrative*, is actually an
interesting example of an significant emphasis in design education today. There are two ways in which I feel this is important.

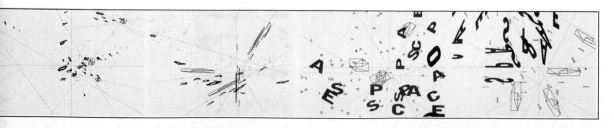

First, when I referred to design as structuring ideas and information, that structuring is a kind of narrative. The structure, or framework, considers the raw data and turns it into something meaningful, compelling, and useful. Second, the other part of sense-making/storytelling/narrative has to do with complex projects – for instance, Web sites. These are projects of a scale where you have to communicate such that an unfamiliar audience can grasp that the idea is viable and compelling before the idea is actually produced. The designer has to consider what to show, in what order, and with what sort of narrative so that the project can be imagined. But in going through this process, the designer is also forced into reasoning ideas in ways that develop the ideas themselves. So storytelling, as I'm describing here, isn't just about selling the idea but a process that allows the idea to be coherently developed.

How much of design is now technique rather than aesthetics?
The only graphic design I know is about aesthetics — but aesthetics that have everything to do with content. I once heard John Maeda speak, and while I don't think what Maeda does is design but, rather, art— an art form divorced from content— he was quite vocal about the need for those working in computer-related media to understand the nature of the material they're working with. In the case of the computer, he's referring to code. He stressed the importance of understanding that coding a computer is similar to creating a biologic form; it's distinct in its behavior, possibilities, and effects from any other tool or material. So technical understanding and skill is imperative to doing anything that truly might push communications into interesting new realms, but it should also be considered integral to messagemaking, the form of the information is the information.

What do you look for in a prospective student?
Grad students: Interest in culture in general, interest in design specifically. Formal skills, interest in inventive form. The understanding and appreciation of design as distinct from art. Strong points of view and the ability to express them. That's the ideal grad student. Undergrad students: Ideas of their own (not just life drawing or making pretty pictures— usually unicorns). The ability to draw. Understanding of graphic design. Enthusiasm. Good students.

Title: Fractured (stills from a video by Tuan Phan of a book by Jennifer McKnight) Designer/ Creative Director/Art Director/Photographer/Director/Illustrator: Jennifer McKnight, MFA. Videography: Tuan Phan School: CalArts, Valencia, CA Instructor: Michael Worthington Year: 2001

Title: Time Modeling Visual Research Designer/Creative Director/Art Director/Photographer/Director/Illustrator: Petra Michel, MFA 1 School: CalArts, Valencia, CA Instructors: Johanna Drucker, Louise Sandhaus Year: 2001

ART SCHOOLS AND COLLEGES: A SELECTION

The following institutions offer some of the best BFA, MFA, associate degree, and continuing education design programs in the United States. Before deciding on a course of study or institution, read and compare catalogs.

Academy of Art College
79 New Montgomery Street
San Francisco, CA 94105
415-274-2200 phone
800-544-ARTS toll-free phone
www.academyart.edu
degrees: BFA, MFA, Certificate
length of program: 4 years UG/2 years G

The Art Institutes
www.artinstitutes.edu
locations:
Arlington, VA
Atlanta, GA
Boston, MA
Charlotte, NC
Chicago, IL
Dallas, TX
Denver, CO
Fort Lauderdale, FL
Houston, TX
Las Vegas, NV
Los Angeles, CA
Los Angeles-Orange County, CA
Minneapolis, MN
New York, NY
Philadelphia,PA
Phoenix, AZ
Pittsburgh,PA
Portland, OR
San Diego, CA
San Francisco, CA
Schaumberg, IL
Seattle, WA
degrees: AA, AAA, AAS, AS, AOS, BA, BS, BFA, C, D
Head Office:
300 Sixth Avenue
Pittsburgh, PA 15222
412-562-0900

University of the Arts
320 South Broad Street
Philadelphia, PA 19102
215-875-4808 phone

800-616-2787 toll-free phone
215-875-5458 fax
www.uarts.edu
degree: BFA
length of program: 4 years

Art Center College of Design
1700 Lida Street
Pasadena, CA 91103
626-396-2200 phone
626-405-9104 fax
www.artcenter.edu
degrees: BFA, BS, MA, MFA, MS
length of program: 3–4 years UG/2–3 years G

University of Baltimore
1420 North Charles Street
Baltimore, MD 21201-5779
410-837-4777 phone
410-837-4793 fax
www.ubalt.edu
degrees: DCD, MA, Design Certificate
length of program: 4 years UG/2 years G

**Boston University
School for the Arts**
Visual Arts Division
855 Commonwealth Avenue
Boston, MA 02215
617-353-3371 phone
617-353-7217 fax
www.bu.edu/SFA/
degrees: BFA, MFA
length of program: 4 years UG/2 years G

**Brigham Young University
College of Fine Arts and
Communications**
Department of Visual Arts
C-502 Harris Fine Arts Center
P.O. Box 26402
Provo, UT 84602-6402

801-378-4266 phone
801-378-5964 fax
www.byu.edu/visualarts
degrees: BA, BFA, MA, MFA
length of program: 4 years UG/2 years G

**California College of Arts
and Crafts**
450 Irwin Street
San Francisco, CA 94107
415-703-9500 phone
415-703-9539 fax
www.ccac-art.edu
degrees: BFA, BArch, MFA
length of program: 4–5 years UG/2 years G

**California Institute
of the Arts
School of Art**
24700 McBean Parkway
Valencia, CA 91355
805-255-1050 phone
800-545-2787 toll-free phone
(outside CA)
800-292-2787 toll-free phone
(in CA)
805-254-8352 fax
www.calarts.edu
degrees: BFA, MFA
length of program: 4 years UG/2 years G

**The Corcoran School of
Art and Design**
500 17th Street NW
Washington, DC 20006
202-639-1800 phone
888-corcoran toll-free phone
www.corcoran.org/college
degrees: BFA, AFA
length of program: 4 years UG/ 2 years UG

**University of Cincinnati
College of Design, Architecture,
Art, and Planning**
P.O. Box 210016
Cincinnati, OH 45221-0016
513-556-6828 phone
513-556-0240 fax
www.design.uc.edu
degrees: BS, MDes
length of program: 5 years UG/2
years G

**Cooper Union for the
Advancement of Science
and Art**
30 Cooper Square
New York, NY 10003
212-353-4100 phone
212-353-4343 fax
www.cooper.edu
degree: BFA
length of program: 4 years

Cranbrook Academy of Art
1221 North Woodward Avenue
P.O. Box 801
Bloomfield Hills, MI 48303-0801
248-645-3300 phone
248-646-0046 fax
www.cranbrook.edu
degrees: MFA, MArch
length of program: 2 years

**Delaware College of Art and
Design**
600 North Market Street
Wilmington, Delaware 19801
302-622-8000 phone
www.dcad.edu
degrees: AFA
length of program: 2 years

IIT Institute of Design
350 North LaSalle Street
Chicago, Illinois 60610
312-595-4900 phone
312-595-4901 fax
www.id.iit.edu
degrees: MDes, MS
length of program: 2 years

Kent State University
Kent, Ohio 44242
330-672-2121 phone
www.kent.edu
degrees: MFA, MA, BA
length of program: 4 years G/2
years UG

**Maryland Institute
College of Art**
1300 Mount Royal Avenue
Baltimore, MD 21217
410-225-2222 phone
410-225-2337 fax
www.mica.edu
degrees: BFA, BFA/MAT, MA,
MAT, MFA
length of program: 4 years
UG/1–2 years G

**Minneapolis College of Art
and Design**
2501 Stevens Avenue South
Minneapolis, MN 55404
612-874-3760 phone
612-874-3704 fax
www.mcad.edu
degrees: BFA, MFA
length of program: 4 years UG/2
years G

Massachusetts College of Art
621 Huntington Avenue
Boston, MA 02115
617-879-7000 phone
www.massart.edu
degrees: BFA, Design Certificate,
MFA, MSAE
length of program: 2 years G/4
years UG

**Montana State University
Bozeman College of Arts
and Architecture**
P.O. Box 173700
Bozeman, MT 59717-3700
406-994-0211 phone
www.montana.edu
schoolofart@montana.edu
degrees: BA, MFA

length of program: 4 years UG/2
years G

**New York University
Tisch School of the Arts
Interactive Telecommunications
Program (ITP)**
721 Broadway
4th Floor
New York, NY 10003
212-998-1880 phone
212-998-1898 fax
www.itp.nyu.edu
degree: MPS
length of program: 2 years

Otis College of Art and Design
9045 Lincoln Boulevard
Los Angeles, CA 90045
310-665-6800 phone
800-527-6847 toll-free phone
310-665-6821 fax
www.otisart.edu
degrees: BFA, MFA
length of program: 4 years UG/2
years G

Parsons School of Design
66 Fifth Avenue
New York, NY 10011
212-229-8910 phone
800-252-0852 toll-free phone
212-229-8975 fax
www.parsons.edu
degrees: AAS, BA/BFA, BBA, BFA,
MA, MFA, MArch
length of program: 2–5 years
UG/1–3 years G

Pacific Northwest College of Art
1241 NW Johnson
Portland, Oregon 97209
800-818-7622 toll-free phone
503-226-3587 fax
www.pnca.edu
degrees: BFA
length of program: 4 years

**Penn State University
College of Art and
Architecture
School of Visual Arts**
210 Patterson Building
University Park, PA 16802
814-865-0444 phone
814-865-1158 fax
degrees: BA, BFA, BS, MFA
length of program: 4 years UG/2
years G

Portfolio Center
125 Bennett Street
Atlanta, GA 30309
404-351-5055 phone
404-355-8838 fax
www.portfoliocenter.com
degree: 2-year certificate

**Pratt Institute
School of Art and Design**
200 Willoughby Avenue
Brooklyn, NY 11205-3897
718-636-3600 phone
718-636-3670 fax
www.pratt.edu
degrees: BFA, MFA
length of program: 4 years UG/2
years G

**Rhode Island School of
Design (RISD)
Graphic Design Department**
2 College Street
Providence, RI 02903-2784
401-454-6171 phone
401-454-6117 fax
www.risd.edu
degrees: BFA, BGD, MFA
length of program: 4–5 years
UG/2 years G

**Ringling School of Art
and Design**
2700 North Tamiami Trail
Sarasota, FL 34234
941-351-5100 phone
941-359-7517 fax
www.rsad.edu
degree: BFA
length of program: 4 years

**Rochester Institute of
Technology (RIT)**
60 Lomb Memorial Drive
Rochester, NY 14623
716-475-2411 phone
716-475-7424 fax
www.rit.edu
degrees: AAS, BFA, MFA, MST
length of program: 2–4 years UG/
1–2 years G

**Savannah College of Art and
Design**
22 East Lathrop Avenue
Savannah, GA 31415
912-525-5000 phone
800-869-7223 Toll-free number
www.scad.edu
degrees: BFA, MA, MFA
length of program: 4 years UG/2
years G

**State University of New York
(SUNY) at Buffalo**
Art Department
202 Center for the Arts
Buffalo, NY 14260-6010
716-645-6878 phone
716-645-6970 fax
wings.buffalo.edu
degrees: BA, BFA, MA, MFA
length of program: 4 years UG/2
years G

School of Visual Arts (SVA)
209 East 23rd Street
New York, New York 10010
212-592-2000 phone
212-592-2116 fax
www.schoolofvisualarts.edu
http://design.schoolofvisualarts.e
du/
degrees: BFA, MFA
length of program: 4 years UG/2
years G

**Syracuse University
College of Visual and
Performing Arts**
Admissions and Recruiting
202 Crouse College
Syracuse, NY 13244-1010
315-443-2769 phone

315-443-1935 fax
vpa.syr.edu
degrees: BFA, BID, MA, MFA
length of program: 4–5 years
UG/2 years G

**Temple University
Tyler School of Art**
7725 Penrose Avenue
Elkins Park, PA 19027
215-782-ARTS phone
215-782-2799 fax
tylerart@vm.temple.edu
http://www.temple.edu/tyler
degrees: BA, BS, BFA, MFA
length of program: 4 years G/
2 years UG

**Virginia Commonwealth
University
School of the Arts**
325 North Harrison Street
Richmond, VA 23284
804-828-2787 phone
www.vcu.edu
degrees: MFA, MA, MAE
length of program: 4 years

**Yale University
School of Art**
P.O. Box 208339
New Haven, CT 06520-8339
203-432-2600 phone
www.yale.edu/art
degree: MFA
length of program: 2–3 years

ON-LINE SCHOOLS

The Art Institute Online
A division of the Art Institute
of Pittsburgh
www.aionline.edu

Sessions.edu/Online
School of Design and New Media
www.sessions.edu

r35
distance learning
www.r35.com

2-YEAR PROGRAMS

University of Advanced Computer Technology
2625 West Baseline Road
Tempe, Arizona 85283-1042
602-383-8228 phone
800-658-5744 Toll-free number
602-383-8222 fax
www.uact.edu
degree: MS, distance learning
length of program: 2 years

Brooks College
4825 E. Pacific Coast Highway
Long Beach, CA 90804
800-421-3775 Toll-free number
www.brookscollege.edu
degree: Associate
length of program: 2 years

Connecticut Institute of Art
581 Putnam Avenue
Greenwich, CT 06830
203-869-4430 phone
203-869-0521 fax
www.artinstitute.com
degree: Associate
length of program: 2 years

Spencerian College
2355 Harrodsburg Road
Lexington, Kentucky 40504
859-223-9608 phone
800-456-3253 Toll-free number
859-224-7744 fax
www.spencerian.edu
degree: Associate
length of program: 2 years

The New England Institute of Art & Communications
10 Brookline Place
West Brookline, MA 02445
800-903-4425 Toll-free number
www.aine.artinstitute.edu
degree: Associate
length of program: 2 years

TECH SCHOOLS

California Polytechnic State University (Cal Poly)
Art & Design Department
Dexter Building (34-170)
San Luis Obispo, CA 93407
805-756-1148 phone
805-756-6321 fax
www.calpoly.edu
degree: BS
length of program: 4 years

College of Eastern Utah
451 East 400 North
Price, UT 84501
435-637-2120 or
435-613-5618 phone
435-613-5814 fax
www.ceu.edu
degrees: C (certicate), Associate
also offered: distance learning
length of programs: 1 year (C), 2 years (A)

Community College of Denver Computer Graphics/Design Department
P.O. Box 173363
Denver, CO 80217-3363
303-556-2600 phone
www.ccd.cocoes.edu
degrees: C (certificate), AAS
length of programs: 1 year (C), 2 years (A)

Ferris State University
The Printing and Imaging Technology Management Department
915 Campus Drive, Swan 314
Big Rapids, Michigan 49307
231-591-2000 phone
231-591-2845 graphic arts
231-591-2082 fax
www.ferris.edu
degrees: BS, Associate, ptec, pmgt, nmpp
length of programs: 2 years G/4 years UG

North Carolina A&T State University
School of Technology
1601 East Market Street
Greensboro, NC 27411
336-334-7500 phone
336-334-7550 graphic communications
336-334-7577 fax
www.ncat.edu
degrees: BS, MS
also offered: distance learning
length of program: 4 years

Palomar College
Graphic Communications
1140 W. Mission Rd.
San Marcos, CA 92069-1487
760-744-1150, ext. 2452 phone
760-761-3517 fax
www.palomar.edu or
graphics@palomar.edu
degree: C (certificate), AA
length of programs: 2 years

Ryerson Polytechnic University
Graphic Communications
350 Victoria Street
Toronto, Ontario Canada M5B 2K3
416-979-5050 phone
416-979-5090 fax
www.ryerson.ca or
inquire@ryerson.ca
degrees: MA, BTech, PhD
also offered: distance learning
length of programs: 2 years G/4 years UG

University of Florida
School of Art and Art History
P.O Box 115801
Gainesville, FL 32611
352-392-0201 graphic arts
352-392-8453 fax
www.ufl.edu or
www.arts.ufl.edu
degrees: BFA, BA, MFA, MA
also offered: distance education
length of programs: 3 years G/4 years UG

For more schools, contact *sensebox*, a graphic design education source, at www.sensebox.com.

"What is the future of graphic design?"

The Web has changed everything. I think we're in a transitional time, and a very exciting time, because of the added dimensions of sound and movement on screen. We're designing an experience on the Web, and as that gets richer and richer with more memory and power, we'll be making movies and designing an experience rather than just a printed piece, which is more passive. We'll be taking people through a lot more dimensions.

—**Kent Hunter**

I think there will still be information on paper for somewhat longer, at least as long as I've got a working life left. And beyond that, I don't know. I don't feel as apocalyptic or as pessimistic about print as some people do.

—**Tom Bentkowski**

Graphic design will be needed more than ever to sell, communicate, and entertain.

—**Mike Salisbury**

There will always be print. Everyone is saying the book is going to disappear — it's going to turn into a screen. But I think books are going to hit a wall and bounce back. It always seems to happen. If you remember the 1960s and early 1970s, all food was becoming instant. Remember all that? They kept predicting that pretty soon our whole meal would be little pills. Well, you know, we hit a wall. Everyone said, I like food — I like real stuff. It all went way in the other direction. I imagine design, at some point, will do the same. I already know some people who are in multimedia and are getting tired of it and wanting to go back to print. And I'm just snickering to myself, yeah, you jumped into multimedia, and I've always been in print.

—**Martin Venezky**

Graphic design clearly has a phenomenal future because the computer and the visual awareness of people create a demand for more sophisticated solutions.

—**Janet Froelich**

Unfortunately, I don't have a lot of faith in the industry as a whole to elevate it beyond being a styling practice. In my opinion, that's the unfortunate downside of design as it exists now. The secret is that we really function as a strategic part of business. That's what we're doing. If you're doing a book cover, if you're doing a theme park, if you're doing an annual report, if you're doing an identity, it all fits into the business equation. People get nervous when you say design should be a strategic business tool, which shows you how paranoid our industry is. Well, it should be. It also should be a creative activity. It also should be fun. It should be a form of expression and, until we really grasp all those forces, which very few designers do, it will continue to be this rendering or decorative art. Business is moving faster than it's ever moved, and our ability to keep up with it and add value is, I believe, the key to the future of our industry.

—**Dana Arnett**

The questions to be asked about our role in the future come with the shift in our culture from the literal to the visual and the increasing power this brings to those who can shape and interpret things visually: designers. I hope we can use this power to enrich public awareness and discourse about our lives and communities — and expand our role beyond the one we are still currently best known for: seducing the public into buying things.

—**Kelly Doe**

Graphic design will become a much more comprehensive discipline that will include the ability to write, to design, to communicate, and to edit. It will become less specialized and more like philosophy, a greater discipline.

—**Veronique Vienne**

It's hard to say. I certainly don't think the book is going to disappear. I think somehow that physical relationship is necessary, that intimate relationship one has with a book as an object, so I think that will continue. But it seems to me graphic design is becoming more and more show business.

—**Richard Eckersley**

I think graphic design is going to be like computers. Ten years ago, when people worked with computers, it was a field. Now computers are ubiquitous; they're part of almost every job and everything you do. I think as more people have the tools of graphic design, have access to type and images, that there's going to be a much broader level of involvement in graphic design from everyone, and so people practicing graphic design as a profession are going to require a much higher level of skill. Graphic design is going to have to move into something beyond what it is now.

—**Rhonda Rubenstein**

As communication becomes global and increasingly visual, the demand for expert communicators grows. In both our shrinking physical environment and our new and expanding cyberspace, more effective systems regarding navigation, orientation, identification, information, and promotion are needed. This provides ample opportunity to apply the creativity and talent of our profession, graphic design.

—**Robert Probst**

The medium is always changing; if we are flexible, we can adapt. Graphic design is not a mature business. There will continue to be areas of opportunity that have not been fully exploited.

—**David B. Gibson**

There will be more small design firms, with two or three people, that will become more like the way a doctor's office is run, the kind of practice where there's the main doctor that you go and see.

—**David Slatoff**

My crystal ball is broken. I think the need for organizing information in creative and elegant ways will always remain. The appearance can change, but the essence remains.

—**Massimo Vignelli**

Certain characteristics of the graphic design profession will persist. I think it will always be about facilitating communications and making things understandable. It will be about finding connections between things and using language and images to make an idea accessible.

—**Chris Pullman**

The revolution that hit desktop publishing is hitting film making — graphic designers are much more in demand. Interests go in cycles; people have become more sophisticated, and right now they appreciate experimentation and irreverence. People may grow tired of the irreverence in graphic design. I see it going back toward things being simpler in many ways.

—**Kyle Cooper**

Graphic design is going to become part of a broader discipline of design. Graphic design will survive because people will always deal with print on paper, but graphic design isn't about print on paper. Graphic design is about communicating to other human beings through words and images. Not print on paper, or even electronic, or even interactive technology. Wherever there's a word and an image, a graphic designer has a role to play in terms of shaping the way in which communication happens.

—**Nancye Green**

The future of graphic design is unlimited.

—**Tommy Steele**

Graphic design in itself will (and has, to a degree) become a public activity — that is, many people consider themselves to be designing, no matter what their training level. So graphic designers, as we know them, will need to come up with better descriptions of what they do and continue to demonstrate the difference. The difference will be in the quality of the thinking, of the ideas, and in the quality of the execution. Graphic designers can become idea strategists, idea consultants.

—**Pat Hansen**

We have to watch out because more and more, with the computer, we're becoming service people instead of aesthetic people. I'm not interested in giving a service. I think that we have to watch out that we're not going to become cheap typesetters.

—**Yolanda Cuomo**

The future is bright because it seems that anything goes when it comes to the storytelling process. There undoubtedly will be a glut of formula-ridden crap to come, but unfortunately that is only natural when somebody wants to make a buck instead of a good product.

—**J.J. Sedelmaier**

Just when it seems impossible for anyone to come up with a new way to sell soap, someone comes along with an approach that hasn't been done. My clients' perpetual request is "Show me something I've never seen before." It's a rough challenge, but it's why design will always be in a state of flux. It's like when the Emigré people say (if I may paraphrase), "Legibility is not absolute; it depends on what you're used to." It's this attitude that keeps design alive, not just following formulas that worked in the past.

—**Randall Balsmeyer**

Graphic design is going through what the music industry is going through right now, which is a dearth of definable leadership. In the 1970s, there were the Led Zeppelins of the world; in the 1980s, there was the B-52s. There's really nothing special right now. There's a lot of good stuff, but nothing special. I don't mean a group that's leading the cause, I'm talking about just who's minding the home. When rap music first hit the music industry, whether you liked it or not wasn't the point. There was something new, there was something coming up from the street that was fresh and offered a new perspective.

—**Carlos Segura**

I think that the future of business is going to be profoundly influenced by graphic design and design in general because everyone else has had a shot at running business. The brass have all gone through military school and taken up roles as CEOs. The Harvard MBAs have taken up the businessman's role. It seems the lawyers have taken their shot at it. Each profession is going through a cycle of stewardship over business, and I think that design has an opportunity to play a much more powerful role in the future of business. I think we can really make a difference, and that's where I think a purely formal education in design is not enough. We can't be graphic designers without that, but to really be powerful in society we also need a richer and deeper background in disciplines like sociology and anthropology. From there, we can really be effective as the creators of human systems.

—David Peters

The future of graphic design rests in its ability to be absorbed into different sectors of public life, from entertainment and media to academia, to science, to political action.

—J. Abbott Miller

Graphic will no longer be the adjective to design. As designers, we design movement, sound, space, and objects, which are all forms of expression and problemsolving and not just limited to the traditional two-dimensional definition.

—Jennifer Morla

Frankly, I'm a little worried about the future because I see very few people going into graphic design and I don't know why. I'm making a lot more money than a lot of lawyers I know, so I don't get it. I know that it's a slow start, the money's not so great in the beginning, but if you're successful, it can be really great. The challenge is so huge to help people realize what's going on, whether it's finding the name of a store or being inspired in a magazine. We're supposed to be helping to organize the visual world for people, and there's so much visual world out there these days.

—Gael Towey

I think the future of graphic design is amazingly similar to the past. Lots of people will be doing all kinds of communicating through all kinds of media, and a few people will be very good at it and innovative, and a lot of people will be mediocre, and some people will be really terrible.

—Paula Scher

We're ready to face another one of those jolts that we got with desktop publishing. Everybody was really worried that graphic design would get washed out and go away, but the truth of the matter was that we became more valuable to our culture, and there were many more of us. There's been a real surge in people looking for the best work.

—Michael Patrick Cronan

I don't like being a Cassandra, but I find that the level of taste and craftsmanship in this country is in real decline. Just look at our redesigned fifty- and hundred-dollar bills. All sense of proportion and harmony have disappeared. The mortised portrait is outsized, its placement asymetrical, the sans-serif numeral (in itself inappropriate!) is mixed together with a serif numeral — what is the logic behind this jumble? If I dwell too much on this, it's only because it's symptomatic of all that's gone wrong with our sensibility. This does not bode well for the future of graphic design. And yet . . . taste does sell. There must be an audience out there. Please don't ask me to reconcile this apparent contradiction.

—R.O. Blechman

Title: PBS Kids **Designer:**
Richard McGuire **Creative
Director/Producer:** Lee Hunt
Associates **Client:** PBS
Year: 1999

Neophyte and veteran graphic desginers can benefit from participating in design organizations and reading the design periodicals. Both offer insight into the past and present of the profession and a showcase for exemplary work.

DESIGN ORGANIZATIONS

Alliance Graphique Internationale
contact: Ruedi Ruegg AG
Merkurstrasse 51
P.O. Box 8030
Zurich, Switzerland
011-41-1-261-0200 phone
011-41-1-262-0663 fax

American Illustration/American Photography
28 West 25th Street
11th floor
New York, NY 10010
212-243-5262 phone
212-243-5201 fax

American Institute of Graphic Arts (AIGA)
164 Fifth Avenue
New York, NY 10010
212-807-1990 phone
800-548-1634 toll-free phone
212-807-1799 fax
www.aiga.org
(also 35 chapters nationwide)

American Society of Magazine Editors (ASME)
919 Third Avenue
New York, NY 10022
212-872-3700 phone
888-567-3228 toll-free phone
212-888-4217 fax
www.magazine.org

Art Directors Club
106 West 29th. Street
New York, NY 10001
212-643-1440 phone
212-643-4266 fax
www.adcny.org or
messages@adcny.org

Broadcast Designers Association
2029 Century Park East #555
Los Angeles, CA 90067
310-712-0040 phone
310-712-0039 fax
www. bdaonline.org

Clio Awards
220 Fifth Avenue #1500
New York, NY 10001
212-683-4300 phone
800-946-2546 toll-free phone
212-683-4796 fax
www.clioawards.com

Cooper-Hewitt National Design Museum
Smithsonian Institution
2 East 91st Street
New York, NY 10128
212-849-8300 phone
212-849-8401 fax
www.si.edu/ndm

Graphic Artists Guild
90 John Street #403
New York, NY 10038
212-791-3400 phone
212-791-0333 fax
www.gag.org.

Graphic Communications Association
100 Daingerfield Road
Alexandria, VA 22314
703-519-8160 phone
703-548-2867 fax
www.gca.org
www.gracol.org

International Council of Graphic Design Associations (ICOGRADA)
P.O. Box 398
London W11 4UG
England
011-44-171-603-8494 phone
011-44-171-371-6040 fax
e-mail: 106065.2235@compuserve.com

Society of Illustrators
128 East 63rd Street
New York, NY 10021
212-838-2560 phone
212-838-2561 fax
www.societyillustrators.org

Society of Publication Designers (SPD)
60 East 42nd Street #721
New York, NY 10165
212-983-8585 phone
212-983-6043 fax
www.spd.org

Type Directors Club
60 East 42nd Street #721
New York, NY 10165
212-983-6042 phone
212-983-6043 fax
www.tdc.org

PUBLICATIONS

@Issue: The Journal of Business and Design
Corporate Design Foundation
20 Park Plaza #321
Boston, MA 02116
617-350-7097 phone
617-451-6355 fax
www.cdf.org

The AIGA Journal of Graphic Design
164 Fifth Avenue
New York, NY 10010
212-807-1990 phone
212-807-1799 fax
www.aiga.org

Communication Arts
410 Sherman Avenue
Palo Alto, CA 94306
650-326-6040 phone
650-326-1648 fax
800-258-9111 subscriptions
www.commarts.com

Corporate Annual Reports Newsletter
Ragan Communications
212 West Superior Street #200
Chicago, IL 60610
312-335-0037 phone
312-335-9583 fax
800-878-5331 subscriptions
www.ragan.com

Design Graphics
11 School Road
Ferny Creek
Victoria 3786
Australia
011-61-39-755-1149 phone
011-61-39-755-1155 fax
800-688-6247 U.S. subscriptions
www.designgraphics.com.au

Design Issues
The MIT Press
5 Cambridge Center
Cambridge, MA 02142
617-253-2864 phone
617-258-5028 fax
mitpress.mit.edu/DI

Emigre
4475 D Street
Sacramento, CA 95819
916-451-4344 phone
916-451-4351 fax
www.emigre.com

Eye
Quantum Publishing
Quantum House
19 Scarbrook Road
Croydon
Surrey CR9 1LX
England
011-44-181-565-4200 phone
011-44-181-565-4444 fax
800-633-4931 U.S. subscriptions

Graphic Artists Guild Handbook of Pricing and Ethical Guidelines
90 John Street #403
New York, NY 10038
212-791-0330 phone
212-791-0333 fax
www.gag.org

Graphic Design USA
Kaye Publishing Corporation
1556 Third Avenue #405
New York, NY 10128
212-534-5500 phone
212-534-4415 fax

Graphis
Graphis
307 Fifth Avenue, 10th floor
New York, NY 10016
212-532-9387 phone
212-213-3229 fax
800-209-4234 subscriptions
info@graphis.com
www. graphis.com
toll-free order-US
books 800-209-4234
magazine 866-648-2915
international orders
books 732-417-2112
magazine 973-627-5162

HOW
F&W Publications
1507 Dana Avenue
Cincinnati, OH 45207
513-531-2690 phone
513-531-2902 fax
800-888-6880 subscriptions
www.howdesign.com

I.D.
1507 Dana Avenue
Cincinnati, Ohio 45207
513-531-2690 phone
513-531-2902 fax
800-888-6880 subscriptions
www.idonline.com

Innovation
Industrial Designers Society of America
1142 Walker Road
Great Falls, VA 22066
703-759-0100 phone
703-759-7679 fax
www.idsa.org

Metropolis
61 West 23rd Street
4th floor
New York, NY 10010
212-627-9977 phone
212-627-9988 fax
800-344-3046 subscriptions
www.metropolismag.com

Print
Marty Fox
116 E. 27th. Street
New York, NY 10016
646-742-0800 or 9202 phone
646-742-9211 fax
800-222-2654 subscriptions
www.printmag.com

Step-By-Step Graphics
Dynamic Graphics, Inc.
6000 North Forest Park Drive
Peoria, IL 61614-3592
309-688-2300 phone
309-688-8515 fax
800-227-7048 subscriptions
www.dgusa.com

Visible Language
Rhode Island School of Design
2 College Street
Providence, RI 02903
401-454-6171 phone
401-454-6117 fax
www.id.iit.edu/visiblelanguage

Some books and websites that will increase your understanding and appreciation of graphic design.

BOOKS

Bierut, Michael, and others, editor. **Looking Closer: Critical Writings on Graphic Design.** New York: Allworth Press, 1994.

Blackwell, Lewis, contributor. **The End of Print: The Graphic Design of David Carson.** San Francisco: Chronicle Books, 1996.

Helfand, Jessica. **Screen: Essays on Graphic Design, New Media, and Visual Culture.** New York: Princeton Architectural Press, 2001

Heller, Steven and Seymour Chwast. **Graphic Style: From Victorian to Digital.** New York: Harry N. Abrams, 2001.

Heller, Steven and Julie Lasky. **Borrowed Design: Use and Abuse of Historical Form.** New York: Van Notrand Reinhold, 1993.

Heller, Steven and Karen Pomeroy. **Design Literacy : Understanding Graphic Design.** New York: Allworth Press, 1997.

Heller, Steven. **Design Literacy (continued) Understanding Graphic Design.** New York: Allworth Press, 1999.

Heller, Steven. **Paul Rand.** London: Phaidon Press Ltd., 1999.

Heller, Steven and Louise Fili. **Typology: Type Design from The Victorian Era to The Digital Age.** San Francisco: Chronicle Books, 1999.

Heller, Steven and Anne Fink. **Faces on the Edge: Type in the Digital Age.** New York: Van Rostrand Reinhold, 1997.

Heskett, John. **Industrial Design.** New York: Thames and Hudson, Inc., 1993

Hollis, Richard. **Graphic Design: A Concise History.** London: Thames and Hudson, Ltd., 1994.

Lupton, Ellen. **Mixing Messages: Graphic Design in Contemporary Culture.** New York: Cooper-Hewitt National Design Museum, Smithsonian Institution and Princeton Architectural Press, 1996.

Lupton, Ellen and Abbot Miller. **Design, Writing Research: Writing on Graphic Design.** London: Phaidon Press Limited, 1999.

McAlhone, Beryl, and others. **A Smile in the Mind: Witty Thinking in Graphic Design.** London: Phaidon Press Ltd., 1998.

Maeda, John. **Maeda @ Maeda.** New York: Rizzoli, 2000.

Mau, Bruce. **Life Style.** New York: Phaidon Press, 2000.

Meggs, Philip B. **A History of Graphic Design, Third Edition.** New York: John Wiley & Sons, 1998.

Meggs Philip B., **6 Chapters in Design: Bass, Chermayeff, Glaser, Rand, Tanaka, Tomaszewski.** San Francisco: Chronicle Books, 1997. Sagmeister, Stefan, and Hall, Peter, **Made You Look,** New York: Booth-Clibborn Editions, 2001

Thomson, Ellen M. **The Origins of Graphic Design in America.** New Haven & London: Yale University Press, 1997.

Thorgerson, Storm and Powell, Aubrey. **100 Best Album Covers.** London, New York, Sydney: DK Publishing, Inc. 1999. **American institute of Graphic Arts** www.aiga.org

WORLD WIDE WEB

Communication Arts. www.commarts.com

Cooper Hewitt National Design Museum. www.si.edu/ndm

Rochester Institute of Technology Design Archive. http://design.rit.edu/timeline.html

Emigre: www.emigre.com

Graphis. www.graphis.com

The Herb Lubalin Study Center for Design and Typography. www.cooper.edu/art/lubalin

Print magazine. www.printmag.com

Typereview. www.typereview.com

Typographic. www.TYPOgraphic.com

Designers